OPPOSITION IN EASTERN EUROPE

OPPOSITION IN EASTERN EUROPE

Edited by
RUDOLF L. TŐKÉS

The Johns Hopkins University Press
Baltimore and London

320.947
062

First published in the United States of America 1979 by
THE JOHNS HOPKINS UNIVERSITY PRESS
Baltimore, Maryland 21218

First published in Great Britain 1979 by
THE MACMILLAN PRESS LTD
London and Basingstoke

Printed in Great Britain

Library of Congress Cataloging in Publication Data

Main entry under title:

Opposition in Eastern Europe.

Includes index.
1. Europe, Eastern – Politics and government –
Addresses, essays, lectures. 2. Dissenters –
Europe, Eastern – Addresses, essays, lectures.   I.
Tőkés, Rudolf L., 1935–
DJK50.066 1979   320.9'47   78-32062
ISBN 0-8018-2214-9

Contents

Preface   vii

Notes on the Contributors   ix

Introduction   xiii

1 Human Rights and Political Change in Eastern Europe
   Rudolf L. Tőkés   1

2 Challenge to Normalcy: Political Opposition in
   Czechoslovakia, 1968–77
   Vladimir V. Kusin   26

3 Dissent in Poland, 1968–78: the end of Revisionism and
   the rebirth of the Civil Society
   Jacques Rupnik   60

4 East Germany: Dissenting Views during the Last Decade
   Werner Volkmer   113

5 Opposition and Para-Opposition: Critical Currents in
   Hungary, 1968–78
   George Schöpflin   142

6 Socialist Opposition in Eastern Europe: Dilemmas and
   Prospects
   Iván Szelényi   187

7 Industrial Workers: Patterns of Dissent, Opposition and
   Accommodation
   Alex Pravda   209

8 Potential Sources of Opposition in the East European
   Peasantry
   Paul G. Lewis   263

Index   292

Preface

This volume owes its origins to fortuitous circumstances and events that contributed to the decision to prepare a volume of original studies on the subject of political opposition in Eastern Europe in the 1970s. As the editor of another and, on the whole well-received, work, *Dissent in the USSR* (1975), and the recipient of much helpful advice from readers and reviewers, I became persuaded that the post-1968 record of dissident and open oppositionist politics of Eastern Europe warranted closer scrutiny and perhaps a book-length treatment as well. These initial thoughts became compelling concerns thanks to an intellectually rewarding six-month sojourn in 1976–7 as a Senior Associate Member of St Antony's College, Oxford, where I greatly benefited from stimulating discussions about communist politics with A. H. Brown, W. Brus, M. Kaser, R. Kindersley and other distinguished members of that University. While in England I also had the opportunity to read papers on questions of political dissidence and systemic stability at faculty seminars at Cambridge University, the London School of Economics, the University of Manchester and the Institute for Soviet and East European Studies, the University of Glasgow. I am indebted to friends and colleagues in those institutions for their searching critique and thoughtful advice about these matters. Aided by these preparations, I served as convenor of a panel on political opposition in Eastern Europe at the Ninth National Meeting of the American Association for the Advancement of Slavic and East Europe Studies in October, 1977 in Washington, D.C. Contributions from members of the panel (F. C. Barghoorn, V. V. Kusin, G. Schöpflin, H. G. Skilling and S. Staron) and offers of assistance from several colleagues, some of whom have subsequently contributed chapters for this volume, finally made it possible to develop a conceptual framework for a book of original studies on this subject.

Although indebted to many, my special thanks go to V. V. Kusin and G. Schöpflin for their encouragement and support; to the Editorial Board of the joint St Antony's–Macmillan publication programme for their agreement to publish this study under their auspices; to the Council of the University of Connecticut Research Foundation for its generous support of research and administration of the project, and to the staff of the Center for Slavic and East European Studies for many kinds of help and assistance.

As an expression of our support for the freedom of speech throughout the world, the authors and the editor dedicate this book to prisoners of conscience East and West and to Amnesty International, a steadfast defender of their cause.

Rudolf L. Tőkés
Storrs, Connecticut
July 1978

Notes on the Contributors

VLADIMIR KUSIN was born in 1929 in Czechoslovakia. He is Director of the International Information Centre for Soviet and East European Studies, University of Glasgow, the Executive Secretary for the International Committee for Soviet and East European Studies and editor of the *International Newsletter* of ICSEES. He earned a First Degree in Modern Czechoslovak History and Politics at the Prague School of Political and Economic Sciences in 1953 and a Ph.D. at Charles University, Prague in 1968. Since coming to Britain in 1968 he has been a member of the Institute of Soviet and East European Studies, University of Glasgow. He is the translator into Czech of three books, and is the author of *The Intellectual Origins of the Prague Spring* (1971), *Political Grouping in the Czechoslovak Reform Movement* (1972), and *From Dubček to Charter 77: A Study of 'Normalisation' in Czechoslovakia 1968–1978* (1978). He has co-authored, edited and compiled other publications and written many articles and reviews.

PAUL G. LEWIS, who was born in London in 1945, is Lecturer in Government at the Open University. He studied as an undergraduate and graduate student at the University of Birmingham (Centre for Russian and East European Studies) where he obtained his Ph.D. During the course of postgraduate study he also spent two years in Poland at the Universities of Poznan and Warsaw. The subject of his doctoral thesis was the politics of the Polish peasantry. He is the editor (with D. Potter and F. G. Castles) of *The Practice of Comparative Politics* (2nd ed., London, 1978). He has prepared a number of texts on comparative, Soviet and East European politics for publication by the Open University and has written several articles on East European themes.

ALEX PRAVDA was born in Prague in 1947, but was educated in England. After taking a degree in history as a scholar at Balliol College, Oxford in 1968, he completed a doctorate on the Czechoslovak Reform Movement at St Antony's College, Oxford, in 1972. He taught for a year in the Department of History and Politics at Huddersfield Polytechnic before taking up a lectureship in politics at the University of Reading in 1973. Alex Pravda is author of *Reform and Change in the Czechoslovak Political System: January–August, 1968*

(1975) and co-editor (with Andrew Oxley and Andrew Ritchie) of *Czechoslovakia: the Party and the People* (1973). He has published a number of articles on East European politics and is currently writing a comparative study of workers, trade unions and politics in Communist states.

JACQUES RUPNIK was born in Prague in 1950 and is a researcher on East European Affairs for the BBC External Services in London. He studied history and politics at the University of Paris (Diplome du Cycle Supérieur d'Etudes sur l'URSS et l'Europe Orientale, Institut d'Etudes Politiques de Paris, 1972). Following this he earned an M.A. degree (1974) at Harvard University and was a Research Associate at Harvard University Russian Research Center in 1974–5. The topic of his doctoral thesis at the Sorbonne was 'History of the Communist Movement in Czechoslovakia, 1918–1948', and it is scheduled for publication in Paris in 1979. He is the author of articles on the history of the international communist movement, and is co-editor of *The Working Class in Eastern Europe, 1945–1978* (Paris, 1978).

GEORGE SCHÖPFLIN was born in Budapest in 1939 and is Joint Lecturer in the Political Institutions of Eastern Europe at the London School of Economics and the School of Slavonic and East European Studies, University of London. From 1957 to 1962 he studied at Glasgow University, where he graduated with M.A. and LL.B. degrees. After pursuing his studies at the College of Europe in Bruges, he joined the Royal Institute of International Affairs in London, moving to work at the Central Research Unit of the BBC External Services in 1967. During 1973–4 he was Hayter Fellow at the School of Slavonic and East European Studies, University of London. He is the editor of *The Soviet Union and Eastern Europe: a Handbook* (London, 1970) and has contributed a number of articles to scholarly journals and symposia.

IVÁN SZELÉNYI was born in Budapest in 1938 and is Professor of Sociology and Head of the Sociology Department in the School of Social Sciences, the Flinders University of South Australia. He took an M.A. in Economics at the Karl Marx University for Economics in Budapest and a Ph.D. in philosophy and sociology under the auspices of the Hungarian Academy of Sciences. He was a Research Fellow at the Hungarian Central Statistical Office and at the Institute of Sociology, Hungarian Academy of Sciences; Scientific Secretary and later

Head of the Department for Regional Sociology at the Institute of Sociology, Hungarian Academy of Sciences. Prior to leaving Hungary to accept an invitation to be Visiting Research Professor at the University of Kent, he was editor of the quarterly journal *Szociológia*. He is the author of several books and scholarly monographs in Hungarian, English, French and German, including *Towards the Class Power of Intelligentsia* (1978), *The Socialist City* and other works currently being translated into Western languages.

RUDOLF L. TŐKÉS, who was born in 1935 in Budapest, is Professor of Political Science and Director, Center for Slavic and East European Studies at the University of Connecticut. After completing his doctoral work at the Russian Institute, Columbia University, he taught at Wesleyan University and has been visiting professor at Yale University. He was a Senior Fellow at the Research Institute on Communist Affairs, Columbia University (1969–71) and a Senior Associate Member of St Antony's College, Oxford, 1976–7. He is the author of *Béla Kun and the Hungarian Soviet Republic* (1967), the editor with H. W. Morton of *Soviet Society and Politics in the 1970s* (1974), editor of *Dissent in the USSR* (1975), and *Eurocommunism and Detente* (1978). Between 1972 and 1976 he served as Associate Editor of *Studies in Comparative Communism*. He is currently working on a book on the history of the Communist Party of Hungary.

WERNER VOLKMER was born in Berlin in 1943 and at the time of writing his chapter was a doctoral candidate in politics at University College, London and a staff member of the BBC German Service. He studied Politics and Economics at the Otto Suhr Institut, Free University of Berlin; Economics and Law at the University of Münster; Politics and Law at the University of Bonn; and earned a degree in Politics at the Free University in 1969. After moving to England he served with the BBC and was an editor at the *Los Angeles Times/Washington Post* News Service in London. He is the author of several articles on German affairs and European Politics, and the subject of his doctoral dissertation is 'Links between West European Socialists in the 70s'.

Introduction

by RUDOLF L. TŐKÉS

This book traces the revival of traditional and the birth of a new political consciousness among the peoples of the 'northern tier' (Czechoslovakia, Poland, the German Democratic Republic and Hungary) of Eastern Europe and analyses the sources of opposition and dissent among the socialist intellectuals, industrial workers and the rural population of all of Eastern Europe since the Soviet invasion of Czechoslovakia in August, 1968. The purpose of the following eight studies is to show national manifestations of regime–opposition interaction in four East European countries in the last decade by focusing on the socio-political forces, major turning points and the prominent actors of this process. The second half of the volume has a somewhat broader scope as it seeks to analyse in a comparative fashion the way in which socialist intellectuals, industrial workers and the rural population respond to regime efforts to mobilise, coordinate and control the system's political, economic and human resources in the 1970s.

By old and new political consciousness we understand the coalescence in the 1970s of historically evolved and contemporary libertarian and nonconformist values and beliefs of the peoples of Eastern Europe. These have found expression in demands for independence, national sovereignty and opposition to foreign rule; in striving for individual freedoms, especially in the realm of free choices in public affairs; and in aspirations for personal autonomy with respect to beliefs (prominently religion), cultural preferences and life styles. The question of human rights has been of paramount importance throughout Eastern Europe. Perhaps the most vigorously asserted of these rights has been a broad range of social rights. Of these, three specific aspects have been the foci of regime concern and popular discontent: the right to economic security, obstacles to social mobility, and delays in implementing regime promises of improved quality of life under socialism.

Leadership struggles in the communist party, sudden price rises, unexpected shortages of consumer goods, unprovoked acts of police repression and other manifestations of the regimes' underlying illegitimacy have complicated and postponed the orderly resolution of these policy dilemmas. Over the years, indecision and regime procrastination have generated adverse popular reactions in the form of opposition, dissent and nonconformist behaviour. When this happens, the circle is closed and the rulers respond in a variety of ways which differ from country to country, from year to year and range from conciliatory gestures to the unleashing of police terror against those held responsible for the disruption of the established order. These themes receive further elaboration in the following studies. However, a brief summary of each chapter seems appropriate at this point.

The first chapter discusses the issue of human rights and the way in which popular and elite demands, western pressures, internal and Soviet counter-pressures might generate political change in East Europe. The author's thesis is that western concepts, based as they are on indigenously evolved philosophies, patterns of property ownership and legal traditions are but marginally applicable to contemporary Eastern Europe. The burden of delayed modernisation, political authoritarianism and collectivist (rather than individual) definitions of human rights and the prominence accorded to economic rights have shaped a political culture which is not wholly susceptible to the appeals of western liberal democracy. From this it is concluded that political change might come when the regimes' potential opponents realise their common interests and agree on a joint programme of democracy and social justice. The chances of this happening are regarded as rather remote at this time.

Kusin's study of Czechoslovakia guides the reader through the four post-invasion phases of evolution of opposition to the Hušak regime. The author's purpose is to analyse the dynamics of the regime's 'legitimacy acquired through passage of time' from the viewpoint of its opponents and from that of an informed insider. The narrative offers a detailed discussion of the Charter 77 movement, its origins, leading personalities and the evolution of its ideological positions until early 1978. Kusin considers détente and Eurocommunism as important external components of the dissidents' struggle for democratic socialism under the shadow of Soviet bayonets, and believes that so long as these outside influences '. . . progress, or at least survive, so will the Charter-type form of Czechoslovak opposition'.

Rupnik's study seeks to trace the evolution and convergence of the three main components (intellectuals, the Catholic Church and industrial workers) of the Polish opposition from October, 1956 to the point of their convergence in the mid-1970s. The author's analysis provides a synthesis of the traditional (romantic nationalism and the ethos of

'organic work'), and new (modern nationalism and democratic socialism) beliefs and strategies of the regime's contemporary adversaries.
Rupnik also compares and contrasts the record of major confrontations (1956, 1968, 1970–1 and 1976–8) between the communist
party and the various groups that challenged its claims for the monopoly of political and economic leadership. The concluding part describes
the ideologies and programmes of the main dissident groups, including
the widespread unauthorised publishing (samizdat) activities of
Gierek's nationalist and socialist critics from all walks of life in Poland.

Volkmer's essay focuses on the internal evolution of the German
Democratic Republic since the early 1960s, with special emphasis on
the dissidents' record since the fall of 1968. The East German political
scene has been in the vortex of conflicting eastern and western
political, military and ideological pressures. The overwhelming presence of the prosperous and powerful Federal Republic as the alternative model of development for all Germans further exacerbated the
Ulbricht and later the Honecker regimes' difficulties in coping with
nonconformist politics in the GDR. Volkmer provides a description of
broad social and intellectual currents (some of these by showing results
of public opinion surveys conducted by the regime) and biographic
sketches of the prominent literary, philosophical and artistic critics of
the East German scene. The regime's policy of ideological and political
demarcation (*abgrenzung*) has been unsuccessful thus far in containing
the people's aspiration for political democracy and the good life under
socialism.

The 'deviant' case of Hungary is the subject of Schöpflin's chapter.
He suggests that standard western explanations of oppositionist behaviour under communism are not applicable to Hungary's conditions
under the leadership and political style of János Kádár. The adoption
of a 'live and let live' policy in the early 1960s by the regime and its
traditional adversaries, the politicised intellectuals, meant that only
two kinds of nay-sayers, the New Left and the 'para-opposition',
emerged. Adherents of the former included followers of the prominent
Marxist philosopher György Lukács and were critical of the social and
intellectual consequences of economic reforms, particularly of the rise
of a new socialist bureaucracy and its use of consumerism to manipulate public opinion. The 'para-opposition', on the other hand, cannot
be 'defined or understood by reference to any pro- or anti-regime
axis'. Rather, it should be seen as an amorphous entity which, while
united in its probing the boundaries of 'supported, tolerated and
prohibited' literary, scientific and artistic endeavours, parts ways and

forms cross-cutting alliances on either side of age-old intelligentsia
debates on populism, urbanism, nationalism, internationalism, ethnic
identity, religion and national destiny. The picture of Hungary in the
first decade of economic reforms that emerges from Schöpflin's
analysis is ambiguous: 'Its principal features include social inequality
exacerbated by an increasingly rigid stratification and low mobility;
aspirations which are in no way collectivist; weak institutionalisation,
the survival of authoritarian attitudes in human relations and a corresponding weakness of democracy.'

Szelényi's chapter represents a combination of elements of an
intellectual autobiography rooted in personal experiences in Hungary
in the early 1970s and of an overview of the East European critical
socialist thinkers' philosophical and ethical dilemmas in developing a
viable strategy against the entrenched alliance of technocrats and party
bureaucrats. Szelényi's purpose is to identify 'those theoretical issues
that critical intellectuals must address to develop relevant theories for
the emancipation of the working class [which] awaits its ideologies' and
a purposeful leadership that only critical intellectuals can provide.
Since the intellectuals, in comparison to members of less privileged
classes, have been virtually exempt from large-scale repression, they
find it extremely difficult to find a common ground with the workers.
According to Szelényi, 'When socialist intellectuals produce a critical
theory of state socialism that is directly related to the *praxis* of the
workers' opposition' (which revolves around questions of self-
management and political self-determination), the regimes will have
no choice but to come to terms with the demands of the united
opposition. However, the worker-intellectual nexus is not yet on the
horizon and, as Szelényi concludes, it is the task of the critical socialist
intellectuals to rethink their ideas and find new ways to link up with the
workers of Eastern Europe.

The industrial working class of Eastern Europe, its values and
attitudes, the form and content of workers' dissent, economic and
institutional factors and their relationship to political change are the
main concerns of Pravda's chapter. In it he draws on survey research
data from Yugoslavia, Hungary and Poland and seeks to outline the
country-specific and area-wide components of workers' opposition.
Pravda explains the causes of working class resistance to bureaucratic
controls from a combination of attitudinal (rising expectations),
economic (incomes policies) and specific situational factors which
represent overlapping dimension of a 'social compact' between the
workers and the regimes. According to Pravda, 'while workers support

socialism, and probably to a greater degree than their non-manual counterparts' this support is conditional on the authoritarian state's ability to satisfy expectations which are not confined to wages but extend to questions of authentic participation and decision-making prerogatives in factories and workshops. While strikes and other kinds of industrial action prompt immediate government response and often temporary remedial action, satisfactory political representation of working class interests still awaits the transformation of trade unions into influential pressure groups and the further maturing of industrial workers to embrace a new work ethic of settling for wages that are commensurate with their effort in the shop or the assembly line.

Lewis' chapter focuses on the peoples of the East European countryside, their attitudes toward collectivisation, rural transformation, the gradual disappearance of a traditional way of life and the emergence of modern industrial states around them. Resentment over collectivisation, once a focal point of anti-government sentiments, has faded into the background as the large-scale exodus of young people from the villages to the cities gradually eroded the mass base of opposition to the party and the state. Although traditional beliefs and values, mainly religion and nationalism, are still strong in the countryside, rural living standards have improved considerably and helped prevent the development of these traditional beliefs into platforms of resistance to the authorities. To be sure, the potential for opposition is still in evidence, though this tends to cluster around rural perceptions of relative deprivation of advantages and opportunities which are available to people in the cities and in other regions of the country. Sharp differences between living standards in Slovenia and Kossovo, between the Czech Lands and eastern Slovakia, between the quality of life (housing, cultural and health services) in cities and villages are the emerging problems which, depending on the regimes' ability to satisfy demands on these matters, might become core issues of rural opposition in the 1980s.

Perhaps the most important finding of these studies concerns the transformation of the relationship between the peoples and the regimes in the last twenty years. In the early 1950s popular resistance to Stalinist terror was kept in bounds by the all-powerful secret police in Eastern Europe. Following Stalin's death some of the pent-up frustrations surfaced, demonstrating, as the East Berlin uprising of June, 1953, the Polish October and the Hungarian Revolution of 1956 did, the limits beyond which East Europeans refused to abide by the dictatorship of petty tyrants and terroristic bureaucrats. Certain re-

gimes, especially the Polish and the Hungarian (though the former not
very long) seemed to have learned their lessons from these bitter
experiences. The Novotny-led Czechoslovak Communist Party chose
to delay liberalisation and internal reforms and thus postponed until
1968 the day of reckoning between the deeply alienated people and
the ruling clique. The East German regime, once it put up the wall and
an end to its opponents' ability to 'vote with their feet' by fleeing to the
west, began to experiment with piecemeal reforms and sought to foster
a new sense of national identity and pride among the people in the
state's achievements. The Romanian leadership, both to assure its
long-term survival and to free itself from Soviet tutelage in international affairs, made adroit use of nationalism as a substitute tool of
consensus-building and political consolidation. However, as the resurgence of open dissent in East Germany and the massive discontent
of the politically and economically disenfranchised ethnic minorities in
Transylvania have shown, neither consumerism nor militant nationalism are adequate substitutes for political democracy and respect for
human rights. Yugoslavia, being the only legitimately founded East
European communist state, has always been a special case with respect
to methods of internal conflict resolution. There the need for national
unity in face of Soviet threats to Yugoslavia's independence, bold
experimentation with economic reforms, opportunity for meaningful
participation through the workers' councils and the Socialist Alliance
have pre-empted much (though not all, as the examples of Djilas,
Mihajlov and the Belgrade Eight have shown) oppositionist potential
to the regime and its institutions.

The second main finding concerns the transformation of popular
perceptions of the legitimacy of the political system under which the
people of Eastern Europe have lived in the past third of a century.
Repeated failures by the regimes' opponents to bring about drastic
change through revolutions and armed uprising left all would-be
insurgents with no alternative to accepting gradual reforms as the only
realistic strategy of political change in the shadow of the USSR.
Successful implementation of reforms, however, involves emphasis on
economics rather than politics, scientific and technical expertise rather
than ideological orthodoxy, and persuasion and material incentives
rather than lawless coercion by the regime. The transition from
one-man despotism to bureaucratic pluralism, from a command
economy to decentralised management and a monolithic belief-system
to a (controlled) diversity of scientific, literary and artistic values calls
for significant leadership skills and a considerable amount of good luck

by all concerned. The central purpose is, of course, legitimacy-building and the non-coercive persuasion of the population of the 'rightness' of the regime's policies. This process also involves confidence-building measures by the government, the creation of an atmosphere of political stability and the delivery of economic, social and cultural benefits to the entire population. Policies of guaranteed employment, health, educational and welfare services and the availability of reasonably priced basic foodstuffs are proven techniques for preventing grassroots opposition from taking organised form. However, as Pravda's study demonstrates, long-term stability requires astute political leadership and a careful balancing of economic planning and incomes policies. In these areas the Polish leadership has failed and the Hungarian has succeeded in the last ten years. It is not that Gierek has been less willing to experiment and innovate than Kádár, but that the former came to power on the heels of a political and economic debacle of Gomułka's leadership of the second half of the 1960s; therefore, his good intentions notwithstanding, Gierek has not been able to undo the damage and restore popular confidence in the party and government. From this we might surmise that a combination of gradual political reforms and policies of consumerism, when consistently applied for an extended period of time, are fail-safe methods of legitimacy-building in Eastern Europe. This is not the case however. As Volkmer's study on the GDR, Schöpflin's analysis of the Hungarian scene and my discussion of regime dilemmas in satisfying East European expectations in the area of socio-economic rights indicate, 'full belly' strategies of legitimacy-building are inherently futile so long as the right of free expression of the people's political and personal beliefs are denied or severely curtailed by the monopoly wielders of power. Moreover, political systems which base the essential foundations of their legitimacy on their ability to satisfy ever-increasing popular demands for consumer goods and social services, yet are ideologically inhibited from making full use of economic and psychic incentives to maximalise the nation's productive potentials, are destined to fail in closing the gap between popular expectations and regime performance.

From the foregoing it does *not* follow that all forms of opposition and dissent should be equated with the rejection of communism as an ideology, the one-party state as a political system, central planning and the socialisation of private property (wherever and to the extent the latter is applicable) as ways of putting an end to 'exploitation of men by men'. Our evidence indicates that the sources of much discontent may be traced back to those elements of the 'social compact' between the people and the regimes which have little to do with wages and salaries. The root of the matter lies in the growing contradictions between the social realities (or, the *praxis* of countries of 'real socialism') and the regimes' founding myths, especially the egalitarian emancipatory ethos of Marxism-Leninism. It is no longer the simply dichotomy between a small undifferentiated 'New Class' and the rest of the underprivileged masses (if, indeed, this has ever been the case), but that of a far more insidious and, in its consequences profoundly destabilising, phenomenon of the rise of a carefully structured hierarchy of new notables along with the slow-down of social mobility and the hardening of class stratification which might describe the constraints on the non-elites' ability to receive their fair share from the benefits of the unwritten 'social compact' with the new ruling elite. Government-sponsored campaigns aiming at the 'cooling off' of ambitions to leave one's social class via the acquisition of higher or specialised education also help reinforce the existing social hierarchy. Decisions concerning the allocation of such scarce socio-economic resources as government-subsidised housing or low-interest loans for the construction of privately built housing and the commitment of funds for infrastructural improvements (paved roads, street lights, public transportation), and for community cultural and welfare facilities (libraries, cinemas, youth centres, hospital outpatient services, etc.) are all linked to the social status of the intended recipients. As readers of the East European press and that of published sociological studies on these matters can testify, it is invariably the high status, well-educated urban population rather than the semi-skilled long-distance commuter worker-peasant, the average factory worker, the old, the infirm and the less well-educated who benefit from the fruits of modernisation in Eastern Europe.

The paradox posed by the nonconformist and, at times, sharply oppositionist behaviour of the educated youth, particularly university students, represents another dimension of popular discontent with the quality of life under socialism. Although most students are beneficiaries of substantial state support and are conscious of their promising career prospects, many of them feel alienated from the system, its values and culture. Signs of disaffection manifest themselves not only in peer group fads such as infatuation with western pop culture, but in expressions of outright hostility to ideological indoctrination and in active search for alternative sources of intellectual enrichment. While most are grateful, or at any rate passive, recipients of state largesse and choose to conform to the ruling gerontarchies' expectations, the dissident (and often the most original and talented) minority find it extremely difficult to reach accommodation with the uninspiring realities. This is often the case with the offspring of the privileged party and government elites as well as with children of 'old Bolshevik'-type party intellectuals. Growing generational differences of beliefs and expectations between the ruling establishment and the university-educated youth with their untarnished idealism and critical attitudes toward the system's daily realities may lead to far-reaching consequences at the time when today's twenty-five-year-olds reach positions of power and influence in the ruling establishment.

Szelényi's and Volkmer's studies discuss the consequences of scientific-technical modernisation on the politics and beliefs of the intelligentsia. Those concerned with research, planning and management have formed a technocratic elite for whom Marxism-Leninism has lost its instrumental meaning and has been replaced by the pragmatic ethos of empirical reasoning and cost-effective problem solving. The communist party's unverifiable and, on the basis of its track record, unpersuasive claim for authority in non-ideological matters has contributed to technocratic resistance to party leadership. Although generally reliable supporters of the established socio-political order, the technocrats' growing influence in political matters helps broaden the spectrum of legitimate political participation and, with it, the further erosion of the party bureaucracy's hold on the society. Unlike in the GDR, where Rudolf Bahro's unorthodox treatise on the regime's performance earned him an eight-year prison sentence in June, 1978, no Hungarian 'para-oppositionist' intellectual, regardless how critical of the system, has been incarcerated for extended periods of time in the last ten years. Which is perhaps why there is scarcely any samizdat publishing activity in Hungary by comparison to Czechoslovakia, Poland and East Germany.

The regime–opposition interaction in Eastern Europe is susceptible to a wide range of external influences. Soviet concerns about the destabilising potentials of 'mismanaged' reform movements have been made explicit in the Brezhnev doctrine; and the East European parties have been acutely aware of the possible consequences of Soviet disapproval of their domestic policies. However, with the signing of the Final Act of the Helsinki conference of August, 1975, the USSR, in return for western guarantees of the security of its postwar territorial acquisitions and political hegemony over Eastern Europe was forced to concede, as a matter of international law, each regime's pro forma right to national sovereignty, including the right (exercised at the discretion of the native leadership with or without explicit Soviet approval) of cautious experimentation with the local implementation of Basket Three.

In certain respects the East European states' implementation of provisions concerning the free, or at any rate less restricted, movement of people and ideas and contacts with the west have only confirmed existing policies of the previous decade. Compared to the Soviet Union, Romania and Bulgaria, Hungarians and Poles enjoy considerable freedom of travel both in and out of the communist bloc; the annual influx of western tourists (and the ideological contraband of their very presence) now runs into the millions; and despite regime efforts at jamming western broadcasts, enough East Europeans rely on such uncensored news and cultural information to compel the regime media to provide a more objective and detailed coverage of local and international developments. Honecker's efforts notwithstanding, many East German TV viewers prefer West German programmes to the regime's own 'Moscow channel', and the people of Western Bohemia and Hungary show similar partiality to Austrian TV programmes. The Helsinki conference and the ratification of its provisions as the law of the land in East Europe have given legitimate footing to citizen efforts to monitor regime compliance with the letter, if not necessarily the spirit, of the Final Act. While there is little difference between the Soviets' brutal persecution of members of various Helsinki monitoring groups and Husák's treatment of the thousand-odd signatories of Charter 77, comparable activities in Poland are widespread and encounter less resistance than in Prague, Bucharest, Moscow, and the Baltic states. All of this, of course, further underlines the remarkable diversity of the East European scene and highlights the profound differences between the prospects of lawful opposition to regime policies in Eastern Europe and in the Soviet Union.

Next to Helsinki and the general atmosphere of East-West détente, both of which until early 1978 contributed to an atmosphere conducive to oppositionist activities, the appearance of Eurocommunism and the Italian, French, Spanish, British and Scandinavian communist parties' criticism of violations of human rights in communist countries, has introduced a new element into the regime–opposition dialogue in Eastern Europe. Although silent about the plight of low status (religious believer, peasant, etc.) dissidents and that of the internal opposition to the pro-Eurocommunist Yugoslav and Romanian parties, leading members of the Italian, Spanish and other western European communist parties have repeatedly and publicly castigated regime policies in the USSR, Czechoslovakia, Poland and the GDR. Interference of this kind with the presumably sovereign domain of internal policies is always resisted by the recipients of Eurocommunist criticism. On the other hand, most of the East European parties, excluding probably the Czechoslovak and Bulgarian, would welcome external political support, even from liberal heretics, on behalf of their autonomy vis-à-vis the Communist Party of the Soviet Union. For this reason, the East European regimes are on the defensive and are confronted with the necessity of coming to terms with conflicting pressures from the USSR, the Eurocommunists and their internal critics. It is at this juncture that other external pressures come into play and shape the outcome of internal disputes in Eastern Europe. These include the 'chill factor' of east–west (prominently US–Soviet) relations, Soviet perceptions of external threats to its security from Peking to Bonn, and the impact of global economic developments on the internal stability of the entire Soviet bloc. Therefore, the outcome of the regime–opposition dialogues is unpredictable, as is the balance of global forces which define the framework for the future evolution of East European politics.

Finally, a brief comment about the methodology and principles of conceptualisation utilised in this work. By editorial design, no attempt has been made to devise and adhere to a comprehensive definition of opposition and dissent which are the central themes of this volume. However valuable as road markers for the study of communist politics in the 1950s and in the 1960s, earlier efforts in this direction now appear contrived and inadequate when applied to the complex and contradictory realities of Eastern Europe in the 1970s. As the following studies will show, what may be a valid explanation for the dynamics of interaction between the regime and its opponents in Poland is not true for Czechoslovakia. The restrictions on nonconformist literati are substantially different in Hungary from those in East Germany. Strike action by industrial workers in Yugoslavia is dealt with in an altogether different fashion than was the work stoppage in the summer of 1977 of coal miners in neighbouring Romania. And the attitude of a 100 per cent collectivised state farm worker in Bulgaria toward government agricultural policies is bound to be different from that of the owner of a privately owned farm in Poland. Although the terms of the 'social compact' between the regime and the people might seem to be the same in Poland and Hungary, some of the underlying political, economic and religious factors are different; hence a government decision calling for price rises might trigger strikes in Poland, but generate only muted complaints in Hungary.

For similar reasons, no attempt has been made to develop

typologies, either by programmes or by social background of the groups and individuals whom we call dissidents and opponents of the East European regimes. Undertakings of this kind by western scholars have proved to be unenlightening and have failed to do justice to the rich complexity of anti-regime groups and individuals in the USSR; and the authors of this volume had no wish to duplicate the mistakes of their predecessors. Thus, instead of elaborate taxonomies and social science models of unorthodox political behaviour in Eastern Europe, all contributors sought to provide carefully researched country and case studies to inform the non-specialist reader rather than those with preference for abstract theorising from insufficient and still unfolding data. On a more positive note, we wish to call the readers' attention to the extensive utilisation in several chapters of public opinion and survey research data to document the authors' assertions about popular attitudes toward regime performance. It is hoped that empirical data of this kind will advance standards of inquiry and help promote a better understanding of the human drama of the East European peoples' struggle for human rights and political emancipation in the 1970s and 1980s.

1 Human Rights and Political Change in Eastern Europe

by RUDOLF L. TŐKÉS

Since the crushing of the Czechoslovak reform movement in 1968 and, with greater intensity and on a broader scale, since the signing of the Helsinki Final Act in 1975, a growing number of East Europeans have stood up for their right to individual self-determination and have demanded that the regimes honour constitutional guarantees of civil rights and to deliver on promises of a better life under socialism.[1]

The East European human rights struggles of the last ten years have involved two, internal and external, kinds of participants. The internal participants are the articulate representatives of the politically powerless: liberal and reformist Marxist intellectuals, industrial workers, the university youth, religious believers and average citizens on the one hand, and the regimes themselves, particularly the communist party, the police, the ideologues and the media, on the other. By virtue of its political-military hegemony over the area the most important external participant is the USSR. Dissident and human rights activism, wherever it might take place, represents a distinct threat to the political and social stability of Russia's client states, hence all cases of opposition and dissent are followed by Moscow with the closest attention.

The United States is another, albeit geographically quite removed and politically ambivalent, participant of the East European human rights scene. Although explicit in its emphasis on the primacy of détente over other, such as ideological, kinds of foreign policy objectives, the United States, mainly through international broadcasting (the Voice of America and Radio Free Europe) has nevertheless been a prominent provider of news and information that have helped keep up the momentum of the flow of nonconformist ideas among the East European regimes' internal opponents.

The Eurocommunist parties, mainly the Italian and the Spanish, are the third external participants of the politics of human rights in East Europe.[2] These parties, like the US and Western Europe and unlike the USSR, are on record as seeking to promote reform, liberalisation

1

and regime non-interference with the exercise of constitutionally guaranteed rights in Eastern Europe.[3] Over the years the multiplicity and the often clashing motivations of these internal and external participants have helped to blur the meaning of the human rights issue. For this reason, some substantive clarification seems to be in order.

'Human rights' has become, both in the east and in the west, a catch-all phrase denoting a wide range of grievances and regime violations of international declarations and covenants designed to protect the dignity of man. However, 'human rights' has a special meaning in the communist-controlled part of Europe.

In Eastern Europe the matter of human rights in the 1970s concerns the basic dimensions of citizenship under post-totalitarian communism and the way in which individuals may seek fulfilment of their aspirations without running afoul of legal and extra-legal restrictions of the same. In a different sense, the entire issue of human rights may be viewed as a major ideological manifestation of a contestation among all elements of the East European post-totalitarian societies for status, access, influence and security. Although this contestation has been in progress, partly behind the scenes, for some time, it was only in the 1970s that its participants included not only members of the political establishment but, at least potentially, the entire society as well.

The question of regime response to popular expectations in politics, economics, society and culture is posed rather differently in each East European state. However, certain core problems seem to be present in all of these countries. Conflicts between a nation's traditional political culture and the communist party's official doctrines, between individual and collective interests and between universal definitions of human rights and those norms of conduct that the political exigencies of a one-party state permit the ruling elite to observe are important sources of friction between the rulers and the ruled in Eastern Europe. Since the imposition of the communist hegemony thirty-three years ago these have produced latent and manifest tensions, occasional crises among the elites and open clashes between the peoples and their rulers.

To be sure, not all tensions and conflicts that have surfaced in East Europe in the last quarter century are attributable solely to Soviet dominance, totalitarian dictatorship and to other forms of authoritarian political control. Certain human rights problems such as adequate political representation, meaningful participation in public affairs, equal protection under the law, equal access to education, welfare and cultural benefits and fair sharing of the material comforts and psychic benefits of rapidly developing, or already highly developed, economies are just as much in evidence in non-communist as in communist countries. Regardless of the ideological orientation or institutional structure of the polity, processes of rapid economic modernisation, social transformation and cultural change leave scars and victims everywhere and no amount of human rights legislation can shelter people from the impact of such trans-national processes of socioeconomic change. Because of the East European regimes' chronic difficulties in gaining genuine popular support on ideological grounds these processes have compelled the communist party-states to shift the foundations of their legitimacy from political-ideological justification of domination to economic performance and satisfaction of popular expectations for increasing living standards, accelerated delivery of social services and other tangible material benefits. A corollary to such expectations is the demand for an expanded sphere of individual autonomy and improved quality of life under socialism. In the late 1970s the regimes seem to be caught in a trap and the slogan of human rights, should it find widespread support among both elites and non-elites, could become the lever with which to effect major changes in the communist world.

The thesis of this study is that all this might happen at some point in the future but not before the present, still fluid post-totalitarian socio-political equilibrium evolves into a more mature, a more firmly institutionalised and a more rigidly stratified level of political and social development. Therefore, the question, to paraphrase Amalrik, is not whether the regimes of Eastern Europe are going to survive until 1984 – because they will – but whether in the foreseeable future the people-regime dialogue about social, political and individual rights of the last and the next ten years will produce lasting changes in the ideologies, institutions and political behaviour of the rulers and the ruled of Eastern Europe.

Related to the main thesis is the proposition that the historical and philosophical foundations of western, particularly American, definitions of basic human rights are incompatible with the way East European perceptions of these rights have evolved in the last three hundred, and especially the last thirty years. Moreover, it will be argued that western perceptions of human rights, particularly those articulated by official foreign policy spokesmen, are based on erroneous notions with respect to the dynamics of post-totalitarian politics, society and economics of Eastern Europe and the way East Europeans view key political concepts such as rightful authority, good society and of what might be called their 'social contract' with the political regimes.

The following discussion will seek to develop the case in three steps: first to briefly reconstruct the components of a liberal democratic conception of human rights; second, to sketch the evolution and to identify the salient characteristics of traditional East European perceptions concerning human rights and fundamental liberties; and third, to offer guarded speculation about the potentials of the human rights issue to serve as a lever for political change in Eastern Europe.

THE COMPONENTS OF A LIBERAL DEMOCRATIC CONCEPTION OF HUMAN RIGHTS

In the broadest sense, western definitions of human rights stem from what Louis Hartz called 'fragments' of a once shared European philosophical, political, cultural and religious heritage.[4] Common to all basic documents of western liberal democracy is the belief in the a priori existence of natural rights that transcended the prerogatives of the state. The triad of 'freedom, security and property' or 'life, liberty and pursuit of happiness' have served to describe the 'inviolable', 'inalienable', and, by reason 'self-evident', boundaries of individual freedoms upon which no legitimately constituted authorities might encroach. The most important substantive underpinning of the liberal democratic definition of these basic rights has been the right to private property, the right to engage in profitable activity and the freedom of contract. It is these rights that were perceived by the framers of the American Constitution as the ultimate material guarantees of the exercise of individual and personal rights.

As Bernard Pfahlberg, in an excellent essay on the evolution of fundamental rights in the western world, points out, the early English (the Habeas Corpus Act of 1679), the American (the Virginia Bill of Rights and the Declaration of Independence of 1776) and the French (Declaration of the Rights of Man, 1789) maximalist definitions of human rights subsequently underwent significant changes in continental Europe.[5]

> In all those European countries, however, where the evolution of the constitution on the American or the West European model began only later ... the tension between (individual) freedom and (state) authority has always remained a *res gerenda*: here the individual all too often seems to be defined only by reference to the society and the state and by reference to himself.[6]

The reason, as Pfahlberg suggests, for the erosion of the core cluster of fundamental rights in continental European constitutional practice was due primarily to the historically delayed achievement of national unity and national integration. Whereas in England, the United States and France constitutional definitions of fundamental rights rested on the reality of a national unity and could serve as non-coercive legal tools of national integration, this was not the case in the continent. In Germany, Portugal, Spain, Italy and Greece new national constitutions sought, in an ascriptive fashion, to create by fiat both national unity and national integration. This inevitably introduced the element of compulsion and, with it, the relativisation of the meaning of individual rights. Thus, 'in countries in which the concepts of "people" and "nation" . . . have a dichotomous character' attempts by the state at administrative implementation and safeguarding of individual rights have been tempered by a corresponding emphasis on the citizens' duties and obligations.[7] In doing so, continental legal developments have, from the outset, undercut any attempt to assert the self-evidential nature of individual rights and made their enforcement contingent on the incumbents' political judgment.

The continental practice of extensive codification and the tendency to limit the scope of individual rights stood in sharp contrast to legal theories, especially those that evolved in the American 'fragment', which attached absolute value to individual rights and limited the state's claims for jurisdiction over the persons (*individual rights*), collective liberties (*political rights*) and economic privileges (*economic rights*) of the citizens.[8]

The classical laissez faire conceptions of these rights, both in the Anglo-American and in the continental European senses, did not, and indeed could not, survive the impact of political and economic modernisation and the rise of mass societies in industrialised nations. Modern party politics facilitated the expansion of the boundaries of public participation and electoral decision-making about shared concerns of economic stability, employment and helped introduce new issues such as health, education, welfare, housing into the public policy process. Voters' demands for the regulation of entrepreneurial activities of all kinds went hand in hand with the state's growing direct involvement and eventually dominant position in banking, transportation, communications, utilities and defence-related branches of the heavy industry. Liberal and socialist pressures and relevant legislative action aiming at the redistribution of wealth through progressive taxation and other special levies completed the process of dismantling of the once sovereign edifice of absolute property rights and, with them, the legitimacy of citizen claims for inalienable rights of any kind.

Thus, the state emerged as supreme arbiter over competing claims of those advocating absolute definitions of property rights and those who sought to mitigate their influence in the name of political democracy, social justice and emphasis on the individual's obligations to the welfare of the society.

From the erosion of unrestricted economic rights there developed a wide, and still growing, cluster of *social rights.* Post World War II western European constitutions, several United Nations declarations, conventions and other, communist, non-communist and non-aligned statements provide a fairly comprehensive catalogue of such rights.[9] Common to them is the expectation that the state would deploy its administrative, judicial and economic resources and actively assist its citizens to take full advantage of the fruits of income redistribution in their pursuit of social and economic rights.[10]

It is probably a moot question whether the expansion of social rights in liberal democracies in the last seventy years would have taken place without the benefit of continental precedents, the rise of social democracy, the trade union movement, the Russian Revolution, the Great Depression, World War II, the Cold War, the anti-colonial and national liberation movements and east-west détente, or all this was merely a natural consequence of birth of industrial and postindustrial societies.

For the purposes of this study the real question is whether the cancerous growth of the liberal democratic states' discretionary authority over the lives of individuals has sufficiently undermined the foundations of individual and political rights to render the classical democratic model of human rights irrelevant for those East Europeans seeking to expand the boundaries of currently tolerated individual freedoms into the realm of genuine, perhaps absolute, human rights of people under socialism.

TRADITIONAL EAST EUROPEAN PERCEPTIONS CONCERNING HUMAN RIGHTS

The development of human rights in Eastern Europe has been a protracted, contradictory and historically uneven process which, on the whole, has been inimical to the assertion of individual rights over those of the community, or that of the nation. National independence of all East European states was not achieved until the end of World War I and when independence was won, it proved to be extremely shortlived indeed. Long history of foreign oppression has conditioned East Europeans to rally around such collective unifying concepts as 'people' and 'nation' and fostered the habit to postpone the gratification of individual political, social and economic interests that always seemed too petty when contrasted to the community's need for survival.[11]

Foreign rule, colonial exploitation and the continued stubborn survival of feudalism contributed to overall economic retardation and delayed modernisation.[12] The native aristocratic elites, while in the forefront of seeking to overthrow foreign domination, were deeply attached to the values of the established social order. As the result, the emancipation of the serfs was not completed until the second half of the nineteenth century and a native entrepreneurial class whose search in the west for secure status and political influence made the liberal democratic definition of human rights possible, with the Czech Lands' exception, did not come about until the end of the nineteenth century.

In the course of the last two centuries the evolution of Eastern Europe was influenced by four external events each of which helped shape the people's fundamental political beliefs. The first was the French Revolution; the second the French revolution of 1848 (for the Balkans the Russo-Turkish war thirty years later); the third, the post World War I peace treaties of 1919–20; and the fourth, Soviet victory over Nazi Germany in 1944–5.

The introduction of liberty, equality and fraternity into the political vocabulary of the Polish gentry (*szlachta*), Bohemian intellectuals, Hungarian nationalist nobility, Romanian and Croat literati gave an historical impetus to the hitherto latent aspirations of these political and cultural elites to act on the spirit, if not necessarily the letter, of these revolutionary slogans. The Polish *szlachta*, more for the sake of self-preservation than to promote social emancipation, enacted the celebrated Constitution of the Third of May of 1791.[13] This document upheld the privileges of the ruling elite, promised limited freedoms to the towns and cities and defended the landlords' rights to keep their peasants in permanent servitude. The French Revolution prompted an entirely different kind of document in the form of an appeal 'Supplex Libellus Valachorum' by Romanian clergymen and literati to the Austrian Emperor in which they sought to obtain recognition of the existence of a Romanian nation.[14] At the same time, the Hungarian Jacobin conspirators' 'Catechism of the Secret Society of Reformers in

Hungary' argued for the overthrow of the foreign yoke and for the restoration of national independence and, with it, 'the freedoms of the nobility'.[15] In the absence of an East European 'third estate', individual rights remained reserved for the class of native aristocracy and were denied by native reformers to the common people of this part of Europe.

The Spring of Nations, or the independence movements of Central Europe of 1848–9 had been prompted by another French revolution. Two contemporary documents, the 'Declaration of Independence of the Hungarian Nation' of April 1849 and the Manifesto of the First Pan-Slavic Congress of 1848 attest to the continued primacy of national and collective ethnic-linguistic concerns over those of political and individual rights.[16] The opening sentence of the Hungarian declaration proclaims 'the inalienable natural right of Hungary, *with all its appurtenances and dependencies*, to occupy the position of an independent European state . . .'. The italics (not in the original) tell much of the story and go a long way explaining the animus behind the Panslav manifesto. Yet, despite the obvious differences between the objectives of Hungarian nationalist and Panslav cultural-philosophical positions, the following excerpts from the latter offer an accurate summary of traditional East European perceptions of individual and collective freedoms.

> We Slavs . . . reject and abhor every domination by mere force . . . we demand, without exception, equality before the law and equal rights and responsibilities for everyone. Wherever one person among millions is born into oppression, there true freedom is still unknown.
>
> . . . It is not only in behalf of the individual within the state that we raise our voices and make known our demands. The nation, with all its intellectual merit, is as sacred to us as are the rights of an individual under natural law. Even if history allows men to develop more fully in some nations than in other, it always shows that the capability of development of those other nations is in no way limited. Nature, which knows neither noble and ignoble nations, has not called upon any of them to dominate another . . . [17]

The establishment of independent nation-states in Eastern Europe after World War II offered an historic opportunity to develop from suitable combinations of indigenous traditions and foreign precedents a modern constitutional framework for regulation and protection of individual and collective rights. Processes of constitutional deliberations were influenced by native philosophical traditions, western legal-constitutional precedents, the principles of Woodrow Wilson's Fourteen Points and last but not least, by the example of the Russian Revolution and the Bolshevik blueprint for national self-determination.

However, what emerged from the constitutions of independent Eastern Europe may be characterised as a mixture of modest inventories of individual rights, liberal aspirations and very detailed descriptions of executive prerogatives. With the notable Czech exception, where native pragmatism, Masaryk's humane democratism and judicious borrowing from western traditions created a realistic framework for national progress and the protection of civil liberties, similar efforts elsewhere in East Europe proved to be less well suited for this purpose. Apart from the intrinsic inappropriateness of indiscriminately borrowed French, Belgian and German legal concepts to serve as safeguards of individual rights under the vastly different socioeconomic conditions of Eastern Europe, such constitutions left the actual implementation of procedural guarantees of civil rights to the administrative arms of the state. Without established traditions of an independent judiciary with a coequal standing vis à vis the legislative and, more importantly, the executive branch of the state, the protection of civil rights remained conditional on the political exigencies of state interests as interpreted by members of the state bureaucracy. However, what is of significance in this context is that most, if not all, alternative concepts of individual rights as advanced by nationalist, radical, Christian, Socialist, ethnic and, in Czechoslovakia alone in the interwar period, by communist party spokesmen, were formulated in collectivist, class, ethnic and linguistic terms. The most important exception to this were small groups of East European liberal democratic politicians who considered the rights of the individuals not only inalienable but attributed to them a *sui generis* status apart from and, if necessary, in opposition to that of the larger political, ethnic or religious entity to which, by birth, class and tradition, they belonged.

It is not my intention to suggest that the prospects for a democratic evolution of independent Eastern Europe were doomed at the outset. Instead, one might argue that the burden of the authoritarian and collectivist past made the ideals and daily political realities of liberal democracy vulnerable to right and left-wing criticism and the people open to the appeal of both the Fascist and Soviet models of economic modernisation and political development.

Corneliu Codreanu's 'Few Remarks on Democracy' seem useful to illustrate the burden of the native East European Fascist case against the theory and practice of liberal democracy in the 1930s.

... Let us ... concern ourselves with the reasons that would make us Rumanians ready to change the clothes of democracy.

(1) Democracy destroys the unity of the Rumanian nation, dividing it among political parties, making Rumanians hate one another, and thus exposing a divided people to the united congregation of Jewish power at a difficult time in the nation's history. This argument alone is so persuasive as to warrant the discarding of democracy in favour of anything that would ensure our unity – or life itself. For disunity means death.

(2) Democracy makes Rumanian citizens out of millions of Jews by making them the Rumanians' equals. By giving them the same legal rights. Equality? What for? We have been here for thousands of years ... Thus: no equality in labour, sacrifice and struggle for the creation of the state and no equal responsibility for its future. According to an old maxim: Equality is to treat unequally the unequal. ...

(3) Democracy is incapable of perseverance. ...

(4) Democracy prevents the politician's fulfilment of his obligations to the nation. Even the most well-meaning politician becomes, in a democracy, a slave of his supporters, because either he satisfies their personal interests or they destroy his organisation. ...

(5) Democracy cannot wield authority, because it cannot enforce its decisions.

(6) Democracy serves big business. Because of the expensive, competitive character of the multiparty system, democracy requires ample funds ... in this manner, the nation's fate is placed in the hands of a clique of bankers.[18]

With the exception of his anti-Semitic diatribes, Codreanu's critique of liberal democracy is wholly congruent with the Marxist-Leninist-Stalinist position concerning the necessity of centralisation, and the use of direct methods to obliterate the last vestiges of individual autonomy as a precondition of replacing bourgeois democracy with a new order in Eastern Europe. However, the essential question is whether these totalitarian views were at all congruent with the political culture of East Europe and whether these could serve to legitimate the newly imposed communist official political culture after the war.

Archie Brown in his introductory essay to the Brown–Jack Gray volume *Political Culture and Political Change in Communist States* offers an excellent theoretical framework for the analysis of political culture and political change.[19] According to Brown the relationship of the two might be explained by focusing on themes of previous political experience, values and fundamental beliefs, foci of identification and loyalty and political knowledge and expectations. Although these basic themes of inquiry are elaborated further by Brown, evidence introduced in the above historical sketch appears to be sufficient to comment on the non-communist legacy of human rights *qua* Brown's taxonomy of political culture.

To say that the East Europeans' previous political experiences provided but slender foundations for popular support of western definitions of human rights is to say the obvious. However, if we argue, as we might, that East European intellectuals have traditionally sought inspiration from western precedents of collective and individual human rights, we can point at the record of unceasing search for foreign political models with which to improve existing conditions and to effect political change through the expansion of traditional boundaries of liberties in an East European country. The national histories of efforts by liberal noblemen, radical literati and other traditional ideological spokesmen of Poles, Czechs, Slovaks, Hungarians, Romanians, Serbs, Croats, Slovenians, and other Balkan peoples to win, either through revolution or reform, the right to fundamental liberties are and have always been central to East European popular perceptions of their own history. For this reason, one must reject as historically inaccurate or at least qualify significantly, the hypothesis which postulates the existence of a perfect 'fit' between the traditional prewar and the official communist-imposed political culture of East Europe.

To the extent that such generalisations make any sense at all, East European values and fundamental beliefs display a fairly wide range of attitudes, to quote Brown, with respect to the 'degree of attachment of security, liberty, independence, egalitarianism, collectivism, or paternalism . . . (and) . . . beliefs concerning the *efficacy* of the individual in relation to the political process'.[20] As indicated above, East European political beliefs have tended to be dominated by questions of security (with a record of tradeoffs for liberty), collectivism (at the expense of satisfaction of individual rights and aspirations), and an historically conditioned sense of low regard for the political efficacy of the common man.

The foci of traditional East European political identification have been the nation (if and when ethnically homogeneous), national culture, social class and religion. The liberal democratic tendency of mythicising and endowing the common man with attributes of spiritual nobility, rectitude, sound judgment and ultimate political infallibility seems to be largely absent in Eastern Europe. For a member of the elite or for an intellectual the peasant was less of a 'noble' and more of a 'savage'. Thus, a sense of integrated national identity did not come about until the first part of the 20th century – much too late to produce a unified national outlook toward political symbols beyond that of a hazy consensus concerning the preferability of the political status quo and trepidation about the dangers of drastic change of *any* kind.

Prewar East European popular political knowledge and expectations are more difficult to discuss than the other attributes of each East European nation's political culture. Awareness of and receptivity to the institutions and ideas of other or alternative political systems has been confined mostly to restless intellectuals and to internationally sophisticated members of the ruling establishment. The 'people' had clear, and often extremely positive memories about the pre-World War I days, though on the eve of the *next* war few Central Europeans could escape the barrage of Nazi propaganda and its extolling the virtues of the Third Reich. The idea of communism was perceived by the Poles, Hungarians, Romanians and probably most Croats as a distinct national menace. Others, perhaps on grounds of ethnic-linguistic affinities or for historical reasons, tended to be more ambivalent about communism and Soviet Russia.

In sum, as the foregoing brief reconstruction of the main ingredients of East European traditional political culture indicates, historical experiences have conditioned the people and the elites to define fundamental rights more in collective, economic and political than in individual terms. Perceptions of legitimate authority varied from country to country. In Czechoslovakia it was personified by Thomas Masaryk, the benevolent father figure and the founder of the Republic, in Poland the romantic-nationalist symbol of military virtue Józef Pilsudszky, in Hungary that improbable throwback from the Austro-

Hungarian military, Admiral Miklós Horthy, in the Balkans several benign and not so benign royal despots were the authority figures whom their peoples admired, despised or tried to ignore. With Masaryk's exception none of them were teachers of their nations inculcating in them a sense of respect for individual rights and, in particular, the right to resist illegitimate authority.

Although this discussion appears to overlook the ideological legacy of the influence exercised by the liberal, socialist and other progressive political parties of interwar Eastern Europe, the fact is that none of them had been in existence long enough to remould widely shared popular scepticism toward the (admittedly rather flawed) game of liberal democratic party politics. As a consequence, the problems of human rights, especially the social and economic dimensions, remained in a limbo and awaited resolution by the dominant political forces of the postwar period.

THE HUMAN RIGHTS ISSUE: LEVER FOR POLITICAL CHANGE IN EASTERN EUROPE?

To speculate about possibilities for change under existing conditions in Eastern Europe we must understand the nature of the forces that keep the regimes afloat as well as the countervailing forces that threaten their stability and, at the same time, present opportunities for political change. It may be argued that from the viewpoint of human rights, the regimes' stability rests on the twin pillars of Soviet hegemony (hence, the regimes' staying power in the last thirty-three years) and on the Eastern Europe nations' traditional political culture which has produced popular dispositions that, under normal conditions, tend to be supportive of the status quo (and prepared to settle for the primacy of socioeconomic rights), and fearful of and inimical to the unknown exigencies of political change initiated by collective action on behalf of *individual* rights.

By Soviet hegemony one must understand not only the availability and deployment of that state's coercive resources to bail out the regimes in distress and the related domestic repressive facilities of each party-state, but the systemic political, economic and psychological consequences of the postwar record of development and change in Eastern Europe. One of the consequences of the postwar political and ideological division of the world has been Eastern Europe's involuntary alignment with one of the two superpowers. While this relationship has failed to produce national sovereignty and individual freedoms, it has thus far, and for the first time in the last one hundred years, enabled the peoples of East Europe to live in peace and to escape the ravages of a war for a third of a century. Though the silence of the guns should not be called 'peace', the absence of armed hostilities on this traditional battleground of Europe cannot but benefit political incumbents of *any* kind. Moreover, the regimes have succeeded in effecting significant breakthroughs in economic development, modernisation and the raising of living standards well above the prewar levels. Though all this might have happened without the benefit of forced industrialisation and collectivisation (and the trampling underfoot of the citizens' individual rights in the process), the results are undeniable and are often impressive.

The third source of stability has been the adroit manipulation by the regime of the population through political rewards, economic incentives and other less tangible, yet psychologically important benefits. This, as Vaclav Havel, in a profoundly moving letter to Gustav Husák, pointed out, amounts to the channelling away of private energies from politics to consumption, and the crippling of man's resolve to live in dignity as a citizen and not merely as a consumer.

In the interest of the smooth management of the society, then, society's attention is deliberately diverted from itself, that is, from social concerns. By nailing a man's whole attention to the floor of his mere consumer interests, it is hoped to render him incapable of appreciating the ever-increasing degree of his spiritual, political and moral degradation. Reducing him to a simple vessel for the ideals of a primitive consumer society is supposed to turn him into pliable material for complex manipulation. It is intended to nip in the bud the danger that he might conceive a longing for one of the innumerable, unforeseeable roles which his manhood fits him to play by imprisoning him within the wretched range of parts that he can perform as consumer, subject to the limitations of a centrally directed market.[22]

There are two main sources of political instability in Eastern Europe in the 1970s. These are the contingent nature of the political status quo and the unresolved policy dilemmas of post-totalitarian politics, economics and society. While the regimes' dependence on the USSR for security, international prestige and, until recently, supplies of raw material and energy can be viewed as a source of stability, the opposite is just as true. While the Helsinki Final Act guaranteed the national sovereignty of all signatories, the Brezhnev doctrine is a political fact, as is the growing demand by East Europeans for freedom to make choices in the national interest. Membership in Comecon and the Warsaw Treaty Organisation and the satellite status that a member nation's obligations to these Soviet-dominated bodies imply remains a focal point of nationalistic resentment from East Berlin to Bucharest – and perhaps in Sofia as well.

The question of political legitimacy, or regime ability to govern effectively and to evoke not merely compliant but positive supportive attitudes from the people represents a more complex dilemma than that posed by the naked subordination of a small nation's sovereignty to the interests of its giant neighbour. It is at this juncture that matters of traditional political attitudes (pro- or anti-Russian), traditions of democratic politics and of 'free choice, the legacy of historically evolved priorities of fundamental rights, and the role of religion and other core beliefs of the people tend to coalesce into national postures or public orientations toward the political incumbents, political institutions and processes of each East European regime. Judgments about regime legitimacy vary from year to year and from country to country. While there is no way of making valid generalisations about the popular attitudes toward regime legitimacy in East Europe, issues of free choice in political representation, participation and decision-making in matters of redistribution, welfare and public services, individual and group autonomy, social, educational and economic mobility, freedom of religion and of scientific inquiry appear to be shared (though far from widely articulated) concerns of the states' political legitimacy.

In Eastern Europe the transformation of *de facto* domination into legitimate governance hinges primarily on a regime's ability to satisfy popular expectations in economic terms. The strategy of massive depoliticisation of the population through consumerism was, of course, predicated on the increasing availability, both in terms of quality and quantity, of goods, services and other material benefits along with a growth of real income with which to acquire these coveted possessions. The success of this strategy depended on the vindication of the assumption that the state's available guidance and control mechanisms for the coordination of production and consumption were adequate to implement, to manage efficiently, and to effect the optimum utilisation of the available resources without compromising the primacy of the regimes' teleological objectives in the process. And when this expectation proved to be unrealistic and economic-political reforms, most often in the form of decentralisation and the enhancement of managerial autonomy, were introduced, the regimes assumed that economic reforms could be carried out without the introduction of corresponding measures in politics and public administration. And finally, these consumerist strategies, as originally conceived by the regimes' economic planners, did not reckon with the rising expectations of the intended beneficiaries of these policies.

Knowing what we (and the East European regimes) know in the late 1970s about the global energy crisis, spiraling inflation and the Soviets' reluctance to deplete their finite raw material and energy resources and sell them below world market price for the benefit of their East European clients, it becomes apparent how desperate and, in the final analysis, how futile it had been to embark on the consumerist path to political stability and legitimacy. Apart from the intrinsic folly of choosing this method to ameliorate deeply felt hostilities and persisting doubts about the regimes' political legitimacy, regime efforts to redirect citizen interests to private concerns has led, as an unintended consequence, to the rediscovery of the importance of individual autonomy and the need to make *free choices* first as a consumer and, as an inevitable consequence, as a citizen as well.

Thus, the 'point of entry' for human rights as a factor capable of producing political changes is causally linked with the post-totalitarian regimes' inability to deliver on the fullness of these rights. At the time when the communist parties have virtually conceded their inability to legitimate their rule on abstract doctrinal grounds and increasingly define themselves as problem-solving agencies, the threatened erosion of economic legitimacy poses the dilemma of political survival and necessitates a search for accommodation with this new reality.

Groups and individuals whom we call dissidents, for the want of a better term, have attempted to come to grips with the root causes and the manifestations of the malaise of political, economic and social legitimacy in Eastern Europe. Because of the diverse views they represent, the range of issues they address and the circumstances of their national dialogues with the regimes and potential sympathisers, and because the following chapters will address these concerns, no attempt will be made to provide a comprehensive summary of such views. Instead, I will attempt to offer a brief critical assessment of the relevance of selected dissident writings to the problems of human rights with special reference to the question of *democratisation* (rather than reform) of the existing East European political systems.

For most East European dissidents the original point of entry for criticism and the advocacy of alternative plans of development has been the crisis of social, rather than political rights in the 1970s. It is well to remember that it was the economic bankruptcy and social stagnation of the early 1960s that served as the point of departure for Czech and Slovak liberal intellectuals. Without their searching critique of *these* aspects of the Novotný regime's legitimacy there could not have been a political groundswell in the winter of 1967–8. In Hungary, it had been the policy debates preceding the inauguration of the New Economic Mechanism in 1968 and the record of the first four years of that reform that prompted much of the critical philosophical and sociological writings of the Budapest School. In Poland the Gdańsk strikes (precipitated by mismanagement of the national economy and ill-timed price rises of consumer goods) prompted Gomulka's fall, and this gave rise to a new round of oppositionist activity that is still in progress seven years later.

However, once having established the reasons for the most tangible and most widely understood economic shortcomings of a regime, various schools of East European dissent part company both with respect to their diagnoses of the visible economic malady and to judgments about the underlying political causes of the problem. The League for Polish Independence (one of the few non-Marxist dissident groups in East Europe) places the blame squarely on the regime, on its doctrinaire policies and on the loss of Poland's independence.[22] The League's manifesto does not advocate the establishment of a multi-party system or Gierek's overthrow but calls for a thorough reform of everything else, beginning with the country's Soviet-type constitution. The authors of the document argue for national unity as a sole means of collective self-preservation in the midst of the 'continuing, although concealed' crisis of 'countries subordinated to Moscow'. This manifesto is the only one among the documents under the purview of this discussion that explicitly endorsed the liberal democratic priority of human rights by placing individual rights and the inviolability of the person to the top of its human rights platform.

The Charter 77 group (see Chapter 2) has issued a veritable flood of documents on all conceivable human rights issues ranging from regime violations of constitutional guarantees of basic human rights, to instances of unjustified dismissal from work of suspected rights activists and cases of bureaucratic discrimination and police brutality.[23] Although several prominent leaders of the Group are former high communist party officials who still appear to believe in socialism, the tone of the Group's main documents is singularly devoid of the kind of party jargon that characterised the writings of various Czech socialist dissidents in the early 1970s. The act of juxtaposing selected passages from the Universal Declaration of Human Rights and from the Preamble of the Helsinki Final Act with the Czechoslovak constitution and the daily *praxis* of the state-party bureaucracy in the unemotional language of the law appears to be an earnest attempt to engage the wielders of power in a dialogue concerning the groundrules of permissible political behaviour in today's Czechoslovakia.

Unlike the Charter 77 dissidents whose messages to world public opinion, to Eurocommunist parties, to participants of the Belgrade conference, and to UNESCO clearly seek to mobilise external pressures on behalf of the internal human rights struggle, earlier efforts (1970–72) by the scattered forces of the Prague Spring sought to address internal audiences. Central to the Short Action Programme of the Socialist Opposition[24] is the realisation that the 'post-January' (1968) reform alliance could not withstand conservative pressures of the post-invasion period and that a new kind of organisation has to be created to carry on the legacy, to use Gordon Skilling's phrase, of 'Czechoslovakia's interrupted revolution'. The recommended solution was the creation of a 'democratic mass movement . . . led by a socialist vanguard'. The task of this vanguard is to present a 'democratic socialist alternative' should the population be at a loss for directions and guidance when confronted with a major crisis.

Jiří Pelikan's essay on the development of the Czechoslovak socialist opposition offers the following justification for the socialist claim for leadership of a popular movement to reform the present system:

> . . . we may be accused of limiting the possible alternatives for development in East European countries to the framework of a socialist society, and to exclude every other course, in particular the establishment of a Western-style liberal democracy. We are not unaware that such endeavours exist among a section of the population, particularly in reaction to the authoritarian model of socialism, to the monopoly of the Communist Party, to repression and errors in the economy. But we do not rule out this possibility simply because we are socialists. Indeed it rules itself out because of the reality which has come about in these countries since the second world war. It is true that the foundations for a socialist system were not always laid out by the will of the majority of the population but enforced at times by a minority supported from outside. Yet the transformations which have taken place are so profound and concern such broad

sectors that a return of the means of production, factories, mines, banks, and collectivised land to capitalist private ownership is out of the question. Neither does the majority want this. It has become accustomed to collective ownership, to a certain social equality, to a significant advance in the education and health services and to a greater democratisation of culture, even though a high price has to be paid for this, even though new kinds of discrimination arise, and even though the privileges of the leading group cannot be reconciled with all this.[25]

What seems puzzling about this apology for a 'democratic socialist' denial of opportunity for a free choice for the pro-liberal democratic 'section' of the population and for the imposition of minority rule with 'outside' support, is that the Czechoslovak socialist oppositionists seek to legitimate *their* leadership precisely by the same means (social and economic rights) which (plus the Soviet occupation forces) have made the Husák regime and indeed the vast majority of the people largely immune to the appeals of the opposition.

Perhaps Adam Michnik's remarkable essay 'The New Evolutionism' might best advance this line of inquiry by way of some hard-headed propositions about oppositionist strategy and tactics:

One must choose between the point of view of the oppressor and that of the oppressed. When the crunch comes, both revisionism and neopositivism, applied consistently, must inevitably lead to taking up the point of view of the regime. In effect, any solidarity with workers on strike, with demonstrating students or dissident intellectuals, puts into question the revisionists' tactic of seeking *entente* with the Party. When the conflict becomes open, both of these groups find themselves swiftly deprived of one essential factor: influence on power.

In my opinion the only policy for dissidents in Eastern Europe is an unceasing struggle for reforms, in favour of evolution which will extend civil liberties and guarantee a respect for human rights.[26]

By contrast to the theoretical writings of the Czechoslovak and, to some extent, of Polish socialist dissidents who seem to be preoccupied with organisational, tactical and strategic questions of the movement, members of the Budapest School – perhaps inspired by the *old* Lukács' belated interest in the existential problems of individuals in the age of goulash communism and economic reforms – are concerned with the *social* dilemmas of Kádár's Hungary. Much of the written output of Ágnes Heller, Mihály Vajda, Mária Márkus, Ferenc Fehér and András Hegedüs was actually published in Hungary prior to their expulsion from the party in the early seventies, and for this reason, it may be regarded as having had a possible impact on the party elites.[27] In one way or another all of them consider alienation under socialism the central issue of East European societies. Works by Márkus on the limits on womens' emancipation under socialism, Márkus and Hegedüs on the use of leisure time and the division of labour, Heller on alternative forms of community, and Hegedüs on bureaucracy are seeking to reconcile the teachings of classical Marxism with the often drab and unyielding realities of life in the age of bureaucrats and technocrats. Perhaps the most subtle and theoretically most original is Heller's analysis of human needs.[28] From what appears to be an extremely esoteric exegesis of Marx's economic theories, she develops a brilliant and subtle critique of the petty bourgeoisification and moral degradation of man from a 'creator' to a 'consumer' at a certain stage (read Hungary in the 1960s) of socialist development. She advocates the formation of communities 'in which quantitative needs are not dominant' and, in doing so, impugns the legitimacy of a social order that is based on essentially capitalistic incentives and organisational devices or, as she might have put it, Hungary in the age of economic reforms.

From the foregoing it appears that the East European dissidents' main, and thus far unresolved, difficulty is to find ways to communicate effectively their critical concerns to those segments of the population and the ruling elites that share their views and are prepared to act on them. This, in turn, depends on the accuracy of the dissidents' perceptions of the issues which have the potential to mobilise the policy-relevant elements of the society to take political action. From a careful perusal of much of the East European dissident literature it seems that with the exception of some Polish (KOR or ROPCO) and Czechoslovak oppositionist workers' groups, virtually all writings of this kind are forms of inter-elite communication rather than effective dialogues with the common man. This proposition is brilliantly articulated in a major study by György Konrád and Iván Szelényi on the sociology of the East European critical intelligentsia.[29]

Konrád and Szelényi trace the evolution of the East European intellectuals from their historic eighteenth and nineteenth-century origins and submit that they, as possessors of communication, technical and cultural skills, were rapidly coopted into the traditional ruling establishment. This pattern has continued uninterrupted well into the communist period. Because of the communist regimes' unconditional commitment to modernisation, social transformation and cultural change, the intellectuals' active participation is indispensable to successful implementation of these tasks. In return for guarantees of limited personal autonomy, privileged social status and financial security the intellectuals not only contribute their skills but acquire a vested interest in the stability of the political status quo. The major exceptions to this process of collective cooptation of highly skilled technical, cultural and scientific specialists are individuals whom Konrád and Szelényi call 'marginal intellectuals'.

Although Konrád and Szelényi define the marginal intellectuals as internal regime dropouts, this classification should probably include those who were driven out of the ruling establishment over their own protests. To the latter category belong the victims of the 1968 anti-Semitic witchhunt in Poland, the thousands of expelled, incarcerated and persecuted intellectual supporters of the Czechoslovak reform movement and of other party purges of the last several years. Both kinds of 'marginals' are looking for allies among those who are similarly deprived of political influence and those with activist dispositions who actually attempt to forge an organisation-ideological alliance with the industrial working class. While one need not inquire into the motivations behind the Saul-to-Paul transformation of many formerly privileged ideological, technical and cultural *apparatchiki* of Czechoslovakia, Poland, Hungary and East Germany, the nature of *their* commitment to human rights may be scrutinised without casting doubts on the sincerity of individuals falling into this category.

To the extent that all socialist dissidents are committed to bringing about a further transformation and a more humane, more democratic, and non-alienated development of the existing system, they are, by definition, addressing questions of power, leadership, management and, in the final analysis, that of ways of manipulating masses of non-elites for the realisation of the dissident intellectuals' alternative blueprints for change. Thus, the logic of the situation demands that proponents of change offer incentives (such as individual human rights) to their supporters, even though the objective interests of this group as putative members of an alternative leadership require the *continued deferral* of the granting of liberal democratic freedoms to all non-elites.

According to Konrád's and Szelényi's taxonomy, the *coopted* majority of intellectuals consists of empirical revisionist writers and social scientists and technocrats. The former, as sociologists, muckraking journalists and representatives of minority interests, though having limited access to actual policy-making, can nevertheless perform important services by calling attention to isolated incidents of regime failures and recommending specific remedies. In doing so, they act as within-system critics and at the same time objectively aid technocrats' search for a new kind of stability.

> . . . empirical revisionist writers or social scientists . . . are unaware of the ideological consequences of their activities. By articulating partial interests they bring to the surface all kinds of hitherto disguised or still repressed interests. . . . They bring to light specific individual grievances, thus the revisionist values become relativised and press for the toleration of inquiries into all dimensions of reality. . . . Thus, they are interested in a certain kind of pluralism, in the democratisation of public life, in constitutional liberties that guarantee partial interests, therefore are inclined to perceive themselves as spokesmen of interests of the entire society. They would feel slighted if they were regarded as ideologues of the class rule of the intelligentsia, let alone, in a narrower sense, that of the technocracy.[30]

As senior partners of the revisionist-intellectual alliance, the technocrats play a pivotal and, from the viewpoint of those working for the peaceful transformation and eventual democratisation of the system, an historically indispensable role. The technocrats are not starry-eyed reformers and probably are not democrats in the classical sense of the word. Rather, they are skilful problem-solvers driven by the rational, perhaps 'value-free', ethos of their professional standards as well as by their enlightened sense of collective self-interest. They respond to the regime's needs for continued scientific-economic development with solutions that are bound to transform the form and substance of post-totalitarian politics.

In the performance of their duties technocrats transform decisional alternatives into value-free directives and proposals and unwittingly contribute to the development of parallel hierarchies in economics and politics. The technocrat makes no distinction between industry and agriculture. Both are components of a resource-allocation-production model. Contrary to the ideological traditions of the regime's pro-industry resource-allocation policies, the technocrats might become an agricultural or service industry lobby. Once this happens the ideological anti-peasant and anti-consumer bias weakens and there will be a need for political mechanisms to give institutional expression to pluralistic interests in the economy and in politics.[31]

The eventual outcome of this optimistic scenario depends, of course, on the willingness on the alliance of the technocrats and enlightened party bureaucrats to expand the scope of legitimate political participation and to admit a growing number of non-elites into the privileges of first-class citizenship and the enjoyment of social, political and individual rights. All this might happen sometime in the future, though everything we know about East Europe's traditional political culture which has again become dominant in Poland, Hungary and perhaps in the GDR, the likelihood of politically well-entrenched elites suddenly opening the floodgates to admit masses of common people into the privilege of autonomous decision-making in politics and economics seems quite remote indeed.

A more realistic line of reasoning concerning the potentials of the current human rights movement to achieve its stated objectives must rest on historic, political and social realities rather than on an uncritical attribution of liberal democratic motives to all opponents of the East European status quo. What we know and can assert with confidence is that present regime policies, particularly the way in which the incumbents are seeking to legitimate their domination, are bound to founder on the rocks of economic realities and continued popular resistance to authoritarian rule. We also know from experience that regime reactions to political crises are more likely to be coercive than receptive to demands for reform and democratisation. The postwar record of elite behaviour under stressful conditions has been that of passivity rather than of vigorous activism on behalf of drastic reforms. And finally we also know that average East Europeans – as people everywhere – if given the choice, would rather come to terms with a difficult situation and settle for the satisfaction of their, admittedly growing, but nevertheless modest economic demands, than to man the barricades for a hopeless battle with the regime and its Soviet masters. Human rights, therefore, are likely to remain on the permanent agenda of the people of East Europe. Though the preferred hierarchy of rights will differ from liberal democratic definitions, it is the East Europeans' historic right to choose the time and method of their collective and

24   *Opposition in Eastern Europe*

individual emancipation from the oppressive regimes under which they live.

NOTES

1. The participants of the Helsinki Conference agreed to see to the widest dissemination of the text of the Final Act. In the United States it appeared as 'Conference on Security and Co-operation in Europe. Final Act', Department of State Publication 8826, General Foreign Policy Series 298, August 1975.
2. Cf R. L. Tőkés, 'Eastern Europe in the 1970s: Detente, Dissent and Eurocommunism' in R. L. Tőkés, ed., *Eurocommunism and Detente* (New York: New York University Press, 1978; London: Matin Robertson, 1979).
3. On this see Archie Brown and George Schöpflin, 'The Challenge to Soviet leadership: effects in Eastern Europe' in Paul Filo del la Torre, Jonathan Story and Edward Mortimer, eds., *Eurocommunism: Myth or Reality?* (forthcoming).
4. Louis Hartz, *The Founding of New Societies* (New York: Harcourt, Brace & World, 1964) pp. 3–24.
5. Bernard Pfahlberg 'Fundamental Rights in the Non-Communist Sphere' in *Marxism, Communism and Western Society*, Vol. 4, (New York: Herder and Herder, 1972) pp. 55–6.
6. Ibid.
7. Ibid.
8. Hartz, pp. 71, 72, 103–10.
9. Cf Z. Chafee, *Documents on Fundamental Human Rights* (Cambridge, Mass.: Harvard University Press, 1951).
10. W. Gellhorn, *Ombudsmen and Others: Citizens' Protectors in Nine Countries* (Cambridge, Mass.: Harvard University Press, 1966).
11. Cf Peter F. Sugar and Ivo J. Lederer, *Nationalism in Eastern Europe* (Seattle, Washington, and London: University of Washington Press, 1969).
12. On this see I. T. Berend and Gy. Ranki, *Economic Development in East Central Europe in the 19th and 20th Century* (New York: Columbia University Press, 1973).
13. The text of this and subsequently cited East European landmark documents may be found in Stephen Fischer-Galati, ed., *Man, State and Society in East European History* (New York: Praeger, 1970) pp. 169–72.
14. Ibid., pp. 141–3.
15. Ibid., pp. 147–55.
16. Ibid., pp. 160–8, 156–9.
17. Ibid., p. 157.
18. Ibid., pp. 228–9.
19. Archie Brown and Jack Gray, eds., *Political Culture and Political Change in Communist States* (London: Macmillan, 1977) pp. 1–24.
20. Ibid., p. 17.

21. Vaclav Havel, 'Letter to Dr. Gustav Hušak, General Secretary of the Czechoslovak Communist Party', *Survey*, Vol. 21, No. 3 (Summer, 1975) p. 173.
22. 'The Polish League for Independence – A Programme for Poland', *Survey*, Vol. 22, No. 2 (Spring, 1976) pp. 182–93.
23. *White Paper on Czechoslovakia* (Paris: International Committee for the Support of Charter 77 in Czechoslovakia, 1977).
24. Text in Jiří Pelikan, *Socialist Opposition in Eastern Europe. The Czechoslovak example* (London: Allison & Busby, 1976) pp. 135–56.
25. Ibid., p. 102.
26. Adam Michnik, 'The New Evolutionism', *Survey*, Vol. 22, No. 3/4 (Summer/Autumn, 1976) pp. 272–3.
27. András Hegedüs, *Socialism and Bureaucracy* (London: Allison & Busby, 1977); András Hegedüs, Ágnes Heller, Mária Márkus, Mihály Vajda, *The Humanisation of Socialism. Writings of the Budapest School* (London: Allison & Busby, 1976).
28. Ágnes Heller, *The Theory of Need in Marx* (New York: St. Martin's Press, 1976).
29. György Konrád and Iván Szelényi, *Az értelmiseg utja az osztályhatalomhoz* (Toward the Class Power of the Intelligentsia), unpublished manuscript, 1974. This study is scheduled for publication by Harcourt, Brace Jovanovich, in 1979 and by Suhrkamp (Frankfurt am Main, 1978), under the title *Die Intelligenz auf dem Wege zur Klassenmacht*. All citations are from the Hungarian original.
30. Ibid., Part V, 2.
31. Ibid., Part V.

2 Challenge to Normalcy: Political Opposition in Czechoslovakia, 1968–77

by VLADIMIR V. KUSIN

THE BACKDROP

The most recent period of opposition to the Czechoslovak regime began with the onset of what has become known as 'normalisation' after the invasion by Warsaw Pact troops in August 1968. 'Normalisation' is here understood as an attempt to promote an ideologically motivated and consumer-orientated legitimation of an unpopular regime under the close supervision of the USSR which retains the prerogative of supreme arbitration and interpretation but prefers to work through domestic agents.

This policy has had several contradictory objectives. The population had to be simultaneously mollified and intimidated in the wake of the invasion shock. The forces of reform, so strong during the Prague Spring, had to be broken up. The most radical elements had to be isolated and deprived of every influence both on the centre of power and on the population at large. The middle-range supporters of the reformist orientation had to undergo a re-education cure with decidedly more stick than carrot.

In order to achieve these goals, the leadership of the Czechoslovak Communist Party and Moscow had to sacrifice some of the modernisation requirements which are indispensable for the attainment of technical rationality and economic efficiency. Political constraints were once again imposed on scientific research, communication, economic planning, selection and training of cadres, consultation between political leadership and experts, and even elite security under the rule of law. While not tantamount to collapse, 'normalisation' has set the clock back in a country which was among the best suited in the communist orbit to meet the challenges of modernisation.

In the non-technical and non-economic fields the impact of 'normalisation' has been even greater and for a precariously long time the country has been tottering on the brink of a cultural disaster. The combined effect of restituted ideological coercion and enforced consumerism with the attendant practices of selfishness, career-seeking, economic larceny and corruption has all but wiped out participation, political awareness, cultural creativity, research in social sciences and morality, including human rights.

The Warsaw Pact invasion did not, however, eliminate the duality of Czech tradition and of Czech communism. The former still contains the syndromes of survival through accommodation as well as of aspiration for intellectual progress and freedom, while the latter crystallised into an organisational break between Stalinism and revisionism which had been coexisting in one party for so long.

Dogmatism and hard-line orthodoxy are almost the only distinguishing feature of a leadership which is now free of reform-minded and liberal innovators, as Zapotocký's inner circle was when it held Moscow's line in 1956 and as Novotný's was not in the run-up to the Prague Spring in the 1960s.

Passivity, escapism and even servility mark the attitudes of the population at large, which however no longer harbours any illusions about the blissful effects of communism, as it did prior to the takeover in 1948 and was still willing to tolerate in 1968.

A combination of beliefs in democracy and non-communist socialism now comprises the outlook of the constituency of active dissenters, no longer divided into democrats and socialists as many of them have been since 1945.

Czechoslovak opponents of the regime do not want to be called 'dissenters' or 'dissidents'. They contend that, while the majority of the Czechoslovak population may also be inactive and withdrawn into their private cocoons as their Russian counterparts are, they are no friends of the political philosophy and practice of their rulers. Ten years ago they were given a chance to say so openly, and they did it unmistakably. It seems highly probable that, should the opportunity repeat itself, they would do it again, even if perhaps more cautiously. Unlike in Russia, the Czech oppositionists say, the ideological confluence is between the critics and the masses, not between the leaders and the masses. This fact invalidates a sufficient part of the content of the term 'dissenter' to make it unusable in a country where the overwhelming part of the nation at least passively dissentiates from its government. Or, as one opponent of normalisation put it, it is the Czechoslovak leadership who are the dissenters.

The Czechoslovak population may dissent, but they do not actively

oppose. This is done on their behalf by the people about whom this
paper has been written.[1]

STAGES

For the purpose of tracing the chronology of opposition, the period
from August 1968 to the summer of 1978 can be subdivided into four
stages.

The first stage lasted from the Warsaw Pact invasion through the
replacement of Husák for Dubček in April 1969 to the Party Central
Committee meeting in September 1969 at which the bulk of the
reformers were purged from the party leadership. During this period
many Prague Spring protagonists still remained members of the Establishment holding positions of power. They had to share them, however,
with the revitalised conservative forces and their authority, influence
and control were gradually eroded. The basic reform programmes of
the Prague Spring were being stopped, shelved, dismantled or slowly
run to ground. This was the formative year of the anti-normalisation
opposition with a certain amount of surviving belief that a conduct
contrary to the die-hard course would still be possible inside the party,
even if on a considerably narrowed scale.

The second stage lasted from the September 1969 meeting of the
Central Committee to the political trials of the summer of 1972, and it
included the 1970 wholesale purge of the party. The post-Dubček
leadership, by now firmly and fully in control, launched a frontal
assault on the rank-and-file and lesser ranked reformers and drove
them out into the cold. A number of them responded by an attempt to
constitute themselves as an opposition force outside the party. This is
the period in which most opposition programmes were formulated and
a semi-organisational form of activity was developed, only to be
smashed in the first half of 1972.

The third stage, over four years long, lasted from the trials of 1972 to
the end of 1976. In this period the oppositionists were publishing
(unofficially) a stream of protest materials in order to keep an alternative public opinion alive, with the aim of establishing an awareness of
the kinship and even identity between Czechoslovak reformism and
Eurocommunism. Abuses of power by the Czechoslovak authorities
were systematically exposed in oppositional statements, appeals and
unofficially published (samizdat) material, both internationally and at
home.

The fourth stage began at the end of 1976 and is still in progress. Its main document is the Charter 77 (see p. 51) and its main content the human rights issue.

BETWEEN POWER AND OPPOSITION
(August 1968–September 1969)

Two or three days after they invaded Czechoslovakia, the Soviet leadership had to abandon at least one aspect of the plan which they had worked out for a speedy settlement of an awkward and embarrassing problem. Largely due to the active stand of the Czechoslovak population and the small strength (and possibly cold feet) of the pro-Moscow faction, the reformist leadership of the Czechoslovak Communist Party could not be fully and swiftly replaced by trusted agents. Hence the dual nature of the leadership to which Moscow grudgingly returned their reformist prisoners, of course with a strongly formulated brief that the country must be led along a counter-reformatory path.

Dubček's suspension was put off on condition that the reformers would themselves dismantle their own achievements and plans. Personnel changes at the top were at first relatively few. They were of two kinds: some of the more radical reformists, compromised in the Kremlin's eyes beyond repair, had to be discarded (e.g. František Kriegel, Ota Šik, Jiří Hájek, Jiří Pelikán, Zdeněk Hejzlar, Josef Pavel and others), and a number of the so-called conservatives who had been on the way out before the invasion were retained in leading posts (Vasil Bilak, Josef Kapek, Alois Indra, Drahomír Kolder, Miloš Jakeš, Viliam Šalgovič and others).

The mixed team was first of all expected to put an end to the activity of the radical reformers and anti-Soviet critics, to re-impose censorship, and to suppress independent organisations, such as the association of former political prisoners K-231, the society of non-party activists KAN, the Human Rights Society, and the embryonic Social Democratic Party. It was also assumed, and decreed, that further progress towards a reform of the party itself would be curbed and other reform plans curtailed. Obedience to Moscow would of course be strengthened.

One should note that, with the exception of the Czech–Slovak federal arrangement, the plank which the post-reformist government was supposed to walk was utterly negative. Dismiss, disband, cut back, stop!

The Dubček team, or what remained of it, thought they were buying time which eventually would work in their favour, once Mr Brezhnev's wrath passed and his most pressing demands were met. Not all reformers were of the same opinion. František Kriegel, a member of the party Praesidium, opposed the signing of the Moscow Protocol and communiqué right from the start. Together with three other members of parliament he also voted against the treaty legalising the stay of Soviet troops in Czechoslovakia when it was debated in the Assembly on 18 October. (There were also ten abstentions and 58 absences.) Jaroslav Šabata, a Party secretary from Brno, argued that on returning from Moscow the leaders ought to have submitted the coerced agreement for ratification to the full Central Committee which could have rejected it as signed under duress. At the same time the European communist parties ought to have been invited to act as mediators. Such an attitude, he suggested, would create a difficult situation for the Soviets who might be compelled to accept a solution more to the liking of the Czechoslovaks.[2]

Two things militated against this course of action. Eurocommunism was not a going concern in 1968 and the readiness of western communist leaders to put themselves in Moscow's way more than in words must be doubted. Secondly, the Moscow Protocol had been also signed by pro-Russian Czechoslovaks, Husák among them, who had already decided to place their money on collaboration. They would hardly be willing to turn coats again.

The 'Šabata alternative' seems to have had the quality of a half-way solution between reluctant collaboration for the sake of salvaging some reforms and the course which a number of radicals were advocating, i.e. determined and persistent popular action against the occupiers and their agents.

The 'radical' constituency consisted basically of intellectuals, writers, some social scientists and students, as well as a few party officials who had overcommitted themselves to reformism and were now being pushed out of office by the coalition of cautious reformers and diehards. They included some trade union and other officials, mainly at the lower end of the power-holding spectrum, but on the evidence available it would not seem possible to include among them workers as a class, or even large groups of them. The workers certainly rendered assistance to the clandestine 14th Party Congress on 22 August and to the three-day student strike in November (by sending delegates and food to the colleges), but no organised workers' opposition to the policies of the first post-invasion period is on record.

Popular opposition manifested itself above all in defiance in the media and some organisations of the infra-structure, such as cultural and academic societies, trade unions and 'mass organisations', as well as in various statements and acts demonstrating disapproval of the course the events were taking, and in ostentatious support given to the Men of the Prague Spring during their public appearances and in opinion polls.

The entire period from August 1968 to April 1969 was of course fraught with conflicts and clashes not only between the Russians (and their agents) and the Czechoslovaks, but also within the Czech camp. Many people outside the power structure – communists and non-communists alike – were calling for a tougher stand by the Dubčekites. 'No more retreats' was one of the messages that kept on being repeated. The students, themselves divided into a radical and a reformist faction, staged a three-day strike calling for continuation of the Prague Spring course, and concluded a series of action agreements with various trade unions. A massive majority of organised labour demanded (to no avail) that Josef Smrkovský be retained as National Assembly speaker after the Czech–Slovak federation came into being on 1 January 1969. 'Enterprise councils' were being formed despite the government's appeal that the 'experiment' should be discontinued. Jan Palach, a student, burned himself to death in January, carrying a note which called for the abolition of censorship and discontinuation of a Soviet propaganda newspaper in the Czech language. And the trade unions adopted a reformist Charter and statutes in March in which, among other things, the right to strike was embodied. In retrospect, these were acts of defiance and resistance, not reform. The odds were much too uneven for a meaningful continuation of the Prague Spring reformist course.

The Dubček wing of the party, while still largely in office, found itself exposed to two opposite pressures by the Russians and their domestic agents and by the population at large, organised and unorganised. The notion that opposition to a counter-reformatory policy could be conducted from within the government was slowly but irrevocably crumbling under these pressures.

An attempt to act radically and on left-wing lines was made by a group of students who called themselves the Movement of Revolutionary Youth and later the Revolutionary Socialist Party. This group of 19 people (18 of them under the age of 29, and 14 born after the end of the War) stood trial early in 1971 and were indicted and sentenced for being 'in opposition to the leading role and policy of the Czechoslovak Communist Party' and for producing 'various written matter and leaflets, the content of which could evoke disagreement with, and resistance to, the socialist order and impair the Party's endeavour to consolidate political and economic conditions in the Republic'. All this they had perpetrated 'from November 1968 to December 1969 in Prague . . . and elsewhere', thereby 'committing the criminal offence of Subversion of the Republic according to Section 98, para. 1 of the Criminal Law'.[3]

Most of them were sent to jail for periods from one to four years. The group also became known by the name of its leader, Petr Uhl. It included Miss Sibylle Plogstedt, a left-wing socialist from West Berlin. Next to the so-called 'Students-Workers Coordinating Committee' which sought to foster anti-normalisation cooperation between factories and universities, the Uhl group begun operating without any illusion about legality shortly after the invasion. At first they devoted themselves mainly to bringing the New Left message from the west to post-invasion Czechoslovakia. In late summer of 1969 they began outlining the prospects of a decentralised, self-managed, socialist Czechoslovakia which could materialise only after the 'normalising' system had been swept away by popular revolutionary action. The odds were against them, and the group was infiltrated and betrayed by December 1969.

In the meantime the counter-reformers and their allies gained a decisive majority in the party Praesidium in April 1969 with Dubček's replacement by Husák under direct Soviet pressure including military threats. Positions of authority were from then on being staffed with trusted people at increased speed, further reforms were terminated, more newspapers were closed down, and more organisations brought into line, including the trade unions, or suspended. The regional party level came under dogmatic control as well as a number of important district committees. The ranks of the ruling group grew daily as the 'sound core' of the party came out of hiding, while the active reformers decreased in numbers.

And yet some of the 'insiders', who believed in the continuation of a moderate reformist course within the party, clung to their hope beyond hope. Husák, they were saying, is admittedly not a Dubček, but he will do more or less the same things, only differently. After all, he had been in jail under the dogmatists, he is no lover of Novotný's methods and the henchmen of Moscow.

Then, in August 1969 the authorities provoked a series of clashes in the streets of Prague, resulting in deaths and injuries, on the occasion of the first anniversary of the invasion. The war of words came definitely to an end, and a state of repression by coercive means began.

With the potential popular support successfully intimidated by harsh police action, the road was cleared for a removal from the top echelons of the remaining reformers, by now reduced into helpless dissenters through the logic of their own attitudes no less than that of circumstances long beyond their control. The scale of expulsions, 'releases' and co-optations effected at the party Central Committee meeting on 25–26 September 1969 amounted to a major and decisive shift of power. The Central Committee sweep was accompanied by similar acts in the government and the parliament, as well as in regional party bodies and in Slovakia.

Neither the 'radicals' nor the public at large could offer a helping hand to their cautious 'insider' colleagues and former idols, simply because there was no way of doing it. Thus died the notion that 'normalisation' could be effectively resisted from inside the Establishment, including the ruling group.

The question remains whether the involvement of reformers in the top party caucuses for over a year after the reforms had been defeated did not, after all, bring worthwhile results, such as cushioning off the impact of a military regime which the Soviets had threatened to introduce in the absence of cooperation from Dubček and company. It will never be possible to answer this question satisfactorily and any possible future repetition of this experience, under different circumstances and perhaps in another country, will certainly have to be judged on its own merit. In Czechoslovakia the Prague Spring, as it gradually emerged, so it gradually died. Gradualism has the great advantage of providing more time for the reform to be more deeply implanted in the people's minds. It makes apparent the weak spots and constraints of the 'normalisers', while conversely exposing the limitations of the reformers. Other lessons can be learned than those which transpire from a short, perhaps violent, clash between a superior aggressor and a determined resister. Human lives are probably spared and more people can emigrate. The overall result in Czechoslovakia, however, was much the same, only delayed.

The final phase of this stage in the development of Czechoslovak opposition saw the emergence of an unofficial document, originating among the 'radical' ex-reformers who had not taken part in the lopsided coalition with the 'normalisers'. Known as the Ten Points Manifesto, it was dated 21 August 1969 and circulated widely afterwards. The authors gave it the form of a petition to the highest party and state organs. It rejected the invasion, the policy of continual retreat in face of threats, censorship and the role of the communist party as an organ of power superior to elected bodies. It further demanded that international covenants on human rights (signed in October 1968 by the Czechoslovak government) be ratified and implemented. This was to happen six years later when it became a part of the prelude to Charter 77. The Ten Points Manifesto also complained about the 'crippling' of the workers' councils, the suppression of economic stimuli, and the inflation of administrative and coercive apparatuses which the workers were said to be unwilling to pay for by their labour. Local government and general elections should be held on the basis of a law 'which will strengthen socialist democracy', i.e. in which 'the right for citizens' nomination committees to run their own candidates' will be embodied. 'We reject any elections conducted on the old lines and we shall not take part in them.' (In this respect the Manifesto anticipated the opposition's attitude to the election of 1971.) The Manifesto further 'accepted with satisfaction' that Czech–Slovak relations were rearranged on federal lines. Its authors 'reserved for themselves the right of dissent' which they promised to exercise 'by legal means'. They stated: 'Even when unfree politically, a mature nation can defend itself by asserting its lifestyle, its philosophy of life and its character by means of practical deeds of an unpolitical nature.' In conclusion they disclaimed anti-state, anti-party and anti-socialist intentions and stated: 'We have no reason to adopt an anti-Soviet stance insofar as the affairs of the Soviet Union are concerned; we are merely against the gross interference in the sovereignty of other states. We wish success to the Soviet people.'[4]

The Ten Points were a respectable programme of survival under adverse circumstances, and the authors touched on several points which were to develop into permanent features of the opposition's activity over the next years. Among them, the most important were the presaging of the importance of human rights as the main contentious issue between government and opposition, and the suggestion that struggle will be conducted on legal grounds.

The prospects of pursuing an effective opposition course even inside the party did not seem to have been irretrievably lost at this stage. The reformist top had been eliminated, but a mass of rank-and-file members could be reasonably expected to lend an ear to officially disavowed and cast-out politicians and intellectual leaders whom they had so enthusiastically followed just over a year ago. The trouble was that Mr Husák knew that much as well.

ORGANISATION ATTEMPTED
(September 1969-August 1972)

After September 1969 the uneasy three-cornered coalition of cautious ex-reformers, 'moderate' conservatives and intransigents (symbolised somewhat inaccurately by the names Dubček-Husák-Bilak) was reduced to an alliance pact between the last two. Judging by their declarations of intent, and the ensuing events, their aims were to complete the rout of real and potential opponents by depriving their leaders of a possible operational base in the lower ranks of the party and state machinery; to repair the country's economic performance; and to restore the ideological dimension of legitimacy which was badly lacking in the general atmosphere of disillusionment and disgust. They set about their tasks with great vigour.

After a few months of preparations, the greater part of the year 1970 was marked by a series of purges. Trusted party activists screened the entire membership, dismissing either by expulsion or by 'striking off the roster' all those who were found wanting when compared to the 'normalisation' criteria. The total loss of membership, including those who simply left of their own will without waiting for the purge, was around 500,000 out of nearly 1.7 million.

The party leadership itself seemed unable to put together a single set of figures, and all statistics must consequently remain suspect. At the Central Committee meeting on 10 December 1970, Husák gave the total number of those who had to leave the party as 326,817 (21.67 per cent), of which 67,147 were expelled and 259,670 struck off the party register. He also said that with those departing voluntarily the party had lost 473,731 members (28 per cent) as against 1 January 1968.[5]

Vasil Bilak, in an interview for the American *Daily World* in September 1975, said that the expellees numbered 70,934 and the 'struck-off' 390,817.[6]

Husák also reported in December 1970 that the purge had been conducted by 70,217 screening groups comprising a total of 235,270 activists. This works out roughly at 21.3 interviewed persons per group and 6.3 per hard-core screener, considering that 'over 1.5 million' members were vetted.

Purges notwithstanding, the Czechoslovak Communist Party still remained a large body, almost 1,200,000 strong. Some observers have estimated the real strength of the so-called 'sound core' of neo-Stalinist members at between 300,000 and 400,000, although of course such an estimate is notoriously difficult to make and impossible to verify. Certainly the 235,000 members of the screening commissions qualified easily, but probably not many more. One conclusion therefore would be that the 1970 purge did not weed out the inactive element, the hangers-on and the career-seekers.

Nevertheless, however large or small the hard-core element was, it could thenceforth be expected to hold sway over the passive majority with greater ease, if only because there would be no competition, or very little of it, for the souls of the 'soft core'.

The constituency of the expelled or otherwise discarded members included practically all of the reform-orientated element in the party. From then on there were no ex-believers looking for the exculpation of their guilt or sense of guilt, no enthusiastic idealists, no determined seekers of efficiency at the expense of ideology, and no pragmatic eager-beavers dedicated to furrowing towards a systemic change from within.

From this it did not, however, follow that all of the ex-members would automatically join a clandestine oppositional organisation or an actively dissentiating movement. The 'party of the expelled' carried some dead wood as well. But of course the general picture *was* simplified: from then on no intra-party opposition, other than that which manifests itself by lukewarm performance of duties, could be expected to play an important role in the search for systemic change, at least until a new generation of members, admitted after the purge, could find their bearings.

Officials of other, non-party, organisations were also purged, including a large number of trade unionists. The fact of a person being purged on political grounds almost automatically meant a loss of job or at least demotion. For many a virtual ban on work in their particular profession was pronounced and blacklists became numerous.

By the end of 1970, lean and hardened by the ordeal, with a fair sprinkling of comrades felled by heart attacks as a result of exhaustion, the 'healthy core' of a new, or one-third new, Communist Party of Czechoslovakia braced itself to start reaping the benefits of a crisis which it had won. The main features of an ideologically sound interpretation of events since the 13th Party Congress in 1966 were presented to the public in the form of 'Lessons from the Crisis Developments in the Party and Society'. A sad chapter in the nation's history could have been closed then, and 'normalcy' achieved, had it not been for the refusal of the ex-reformers and their allies to clear the field as they were told.

People who were willing to go on opposing the policy of 'normalisation' even beyond the September 1969 Central Committee plenum and the 1970 purge may be described as belonging to one of the following three categories.

The 'total' or 'integral' opponents of communism who had opposed the system before the Prague Spring and accepted the 1968 developments in good faith but with some reservations as to the 'family' nature of what could be just a quarrel between different factions of communists. (Non-party people who were not prepared to oppose 'normalisation' actively and publicly gained a curious advantage over the ex-communists as a result of the wrath which the new leadership and Moscow turned against revisionists in the party's own ranks. They were generally less victimised and, if they showed circumspection in 1968, could even hope to gain promotion to fill the jobs forcibly vacated by the removal of communists.)

The group of active non-party oppositionists comprised almost exclusively liberal-minded people, ranging from progressive Christians (mainly of Protestant denominations) to social democrats. No public act of opposition by truly right-wing, reactionary groups or individuals is on record. The Russian incidence of 'Slavophile', 'nationalist', 'orthodox' dissenters has no equivalent in Czechoslovakia. There are no pro-Hapsburg monarchists. Nationalism in the Czech context is distinctly liberal. The first, pre-War, Republic is a democratic term of reference. And the individual Catholics who joined the opposition community are almost invariably the product of the Second Vatican Council. A Black Hundred *non datur*.

The liberal non-communist intelligentsia accepted readily, immediately and without demur that the predicament which faced the nation called for a unity of basic strivings, if not of beliefs, goals and methods which under different circumstances would set people politically apart. In criticising the regime, they placed emphasis on the lawlessness and inhumanity of the persecution mania, the enforced retreat from the modest democratic achievements of 1968, and the fact that national sovereignty had been once again sold out for a bowl of political potage.

Reformist ex-party members constituted by far the largest segment of the active opposition front. Both wings were now out of power and out of the party: the radicals who had opposed post-invasion participation in government, and the newly expelled 'moderates'. The purges and demotions which they all suffered did a great deal to surmount the moderate-radical division. The slow and gradual disappearance of differences within the ex-communist camp was an interesting process. As time went by, the radicals became more and more adapted to non-radical alternatives, seeing as they must have done that popular action – a *sine qua non* of any truly radical anti-regime sortie – became less and less possible. On the other hand, the former 'insiders' came to recognise that their post-invasion precepts of cooperation with the 'hard core' had foundered and that at least they themselves were unlikely to carry them through, although the next generation might. Thus there occurred a certain meeting of minds, a mental adjustment, painful to some, to the fact that communism would have to be opposed from the outside and, by the same token, that its criticism could and should be further reaching than an inside operation permitted.

The emphasis of this oppositional category was on criticising the violence which the 'normalisation' policy was doing to the cause of true socialism, and even true communism, on objecting against the damage which was being inflicted on the international communist movement, on the irreparable harm caused to Czechoslovak feelings of goodwill towards the Soviet Union, and generally on the re-assertion of the programmes of the Prague Spring.

The third group, not a large one but growing, comprised *young people who had reached the age of political consciousness during the Prague Spring or shortly before or after it.* Most of the members of the Socialist Revolutionary Party belonged to this category. These were the 'radical radicals', socialists of a leftist but non-communist variety, akin to the New Left in the west. They had individual allies among ex-communists, and were willing to cooperate with the reformers. They were bristling with ideas and daring to the point of recklessness. They were mainly students, but as 'normalisation' progressed their ranks included more and more young workers and employees, if only for the simple reason that universities barred nonconformists and they themselves were unwilling to put on a protective mimicry to gain admission. They stressed radical systemic alternatives (particularly of a self-managed variety) and clandestine methods of organisation.

Not one single social group, or 'class', represented a natural ally of the opposition from which support could come in the form of a massive outburst of discontent. The ties between the opposition, mainly intellectuals, and the workers, while again and again emphatically proclaimed as a desideratum by the critics of 'normalisation', never came to fruition. Neither was there in Czechoslovakia a force comparable to the Polish Catholic Church. The farmers had no grievance of the magnitude which would induce them to act politically. And even within the white-collar sector, the embryonic stratum of independently thinking managers had its life cut short by the discontinuation of the economic reform, and the technical and research workers were cowed into submission.

In October 1970 the largest community in the opposition, the ex-reformers, produced a leaflet of some 3,300 words, widely circulating throughout the country, which became known as the 28th October Manifesto. (28 October 1918 was the day when independent Czechoslovakia came into being.) Like the 'Ten Points of August 1969', and possibly even more so, this was a restatement of beliefs rather than a programme of oppositional action. Its authors appealed to the nation to go on discussing Prague Spring ideas and the public was also asked not to shut themselves off from their fellow citizens, not to become cynical, and to help the victims of oppression. Perhaps the most important feature was the fact that the Manifesto was signed on behalf of a purported resistance movement, the Socialist Movement of Czechoslovak Citizens.

Some years later Jiří Pelikán outlined the discussions which the oppositionists had conducted among themselves about the form their organisation ought to take.[7] The options, each of them apparently advocated by some ex-communists, were as follows: (1) No opposition is possible either in or outside the party because international and national conditions are simply not ripe for it. (2) No effective action is possible outside the party and one must wait for reformist tendencies to re-assert themselves once again in the ranks of the purged party. (3) A new Communist Party of Czechoslovakia, opposed to the purged one, ought to be illegally organised and seek to integrate itself into the international communist movement. This alternative was given serious consideration and the disadvantages were eventually seen to outweigh the possible advantages. Opponents of the idea of a clandestine party objected that the very word 'communist' had been discredited, that the leaders would be well within police reach because they were so well known, and that the international context of the day made the new party's recognition in the communist movement unlikely. (4) Instead of doing nothing, or striving for a closely-knit clandestine organisation, whatever its name, the ex-communists decided to set in motion a broadly based *movement* of which they hoped to become an *intellectual leading centre*. To this movement they decided to give a programme both in the sense of a profession of faith and as a guideline to immediate action vis-à-vis the 'normalisation regime'.

The Socialist Movement of Czechoslovak Citizens (SMCC) was most active from October 1970 to January 1972, during which time it issued several proclamations and statements. It even survived, in drastically reduced form and size, the arrests and trials of 1972 and some materials were issued in its name later, but one has the feeling that the embryonic organisation had been effectively smashed. The most important of the proclamations was the 'Short Action Programme of the Socialist Opposition', about 8,000 words, issued in January–February 1971.

In its political aims, the Short Action Programme (SAP) remained committed to the combination of democratisation and socialism along the fashion of the Prague Spring. Unlike the Ten Points of August 1969 and the 28th October Manifesto of 1970, it devoted only comparatively little space to the general statement of principles. Not only did the authors take them for granted, but they also felt that post-1968 experience must be taken into account and a simple repetition of the Prague Spring tenets was not enough.

The SAP notes the existence of the SMCC which it aspires to develop into a 'new political vanguard of socialism'.[8] The Movement was said to consist of three layers: 'initiative groups' (i.e. those already active), comprising several thousand people; a 'potential leading political stratum' of several tens of thousands; and a 'membership base' of several hundred thousands.

The approach evidently owes much to Leninism with its categorisation of political actors into masses, party and leadership. The Leninist ring came through particularly loud and clear when organisational guidance was given. The first step, according to SAP, should be the setting up of 'a focal point of activity concerned with coordinating the forces' or, in other words, 'a vanguard of the vanguard'.

The programme itself comprised seven points (not numbered consecutively in the original which is somewhat rambling):

(1) Advocacy of specific interests of the various groups of the working people.

(2) Taking advantage of legal organisations, including the communist party, to promote genuine working people interests against the bureaucrats.

(3) Forging a bond between workers and the technical intelligentsia.

(4) Advocating the farmers' right to be treated in the same way as the rest of the population is.

(5) Striving for an alliance of all social groups among the younger generation.

(6) Opposing government influence on white-collar workers. (This section of the programme is hazy and jargonised beyond comprehension, but it appears that the SAP had no special provision concerning 'the intelligentsia'.)

(7) Developing ideological activity in opposition to the official one, mainly through samizdat of domestic and foreign materials. It is noteworthy that the 'vanguard of the vanguard' of the SMCC, i.e. presumably a small circle of leading oppositionists, reserved for itself the right to supervise the clandestine publication of 'longer documents of all kinds' expressing the movement's policy. In the words of the programme compilers, the content of such statements ought to be 'regularly assessed and checked to ensure that all programmatic, theoretical, analytical and polemical activity is closely linked to the needs of the movement'.

Finally, after an invitation to all and sundry to discuss the Action Programme, the authors stipulated four principles affecting the international aspects of oppositional activity in Czechoslovakia. As not all Czechoslovak émigrés are socialists, cooperation with them should be 'differentiated' which, however, need not mean 'mutual isolation'. Particular effort should go towards establishing ties with the European Left. 'Careful consideration needs to be given to the complex of Chinese and Sino-Soviet questions' and the non-European dimension of opposition ought to be examined. The communist opposition in Czechoslovakia should strive 'to win recognition from West European communists'.

The Short Action Programme highlighted the last-ditch effort of reform-minded ex-communists to oppose their former fellow party members, now in full power, by traditional communist means. It seems that the counsel of the 'insiders' prevailed during its compilation yet again, even though they were no longer 'inside'. Its appeal to non-communist oppositionists was of course much less, but even many ex-communists had by then parted ways with traditional party tenets.

Another proclamation which circulated in Prague in January 1972 was addressed to 'comrade workers' and signed 'workers, legally elected functionaries of the Czechoslovak Communist Party'. It also used some traditional concepts and terminology but generally had a more down-to-earth and pungent character. For one thing, it was much shorter and largely devoid of ideological meditation. Its seven points were as follows:

(1) Do not elect extreme dogmatists to party posts and demand observation of party statutes in your branch.

(2) Nominate good comrades to trade union posts and insist on a secret ballot.

(3) Stand up for adequate working conditions and safety-at-work regulations.

(4) Demand full observance of the Labour Code.

(5) Defend your wage packets and other benefits when collective contracts are drafted.

(6) Criticise incompetence of newly appointed managers who got the job for political reasons, but refuse to go along with party-inspired attacks on technicians.

(7) Do not take part in mass parades.

Some formulations presaged the insistence on the observation of existing, even though 'normalised', rules and statutes, a trait which was to become important in the opposition's programmes of the future.

The SMCC issued several other statements. When the government felt strong enough to master the holding of an election, scheduled for the end of November 1971, the SMCC organised its largest publicity campaign in the form of an 'Election Appeal to the Citizens'. Husák allegedly put the number of copies of the SMCC leaflet prepared for circulation at 100,000,[9] but some were seized by the police. The Appeal reached the public between mid-September and election day.

The Appeal warned that elections would not be genuine as the results had already been decided by the party leadership and percentages of affirmative votes had been allocated to electoral commissions. Nonetheless, these commissions had been told to report in confidence directly to the party praesidium the real results, including abstentions and deletions of candidates' names. While the SMCC would not presume to force the voters either way, it wished to point out that those who wanted to register their disapproval of 'normalisation' could abstain because voting was not a legally enforceable duty. They should also insist on secrecy of the ballot and they might replace the official list of candidates with one of their own or with a slip of paper bearing some such slogan as 'January, not August!'[10]

While the effect of the leaflets on the voters cannot be measured (Pelikán says that in large towns some 10 per cent of the public did not vote, and 10–25 per cent of those who did crossed out official names), it tolled a bell for the SMCC. In December 1971 and January 1972 some 200 persons were arrested and then, during the summer holiday period, from 17 July to 11 August 1972, ten political trials were held which resulted in 47 persons being sentenced to a total of 118 years in prison. The 'vanguard of the vanguard' of the Socialist Movement of Czechoslovak Citizens was effectively mowed down.

These were not the first political trials of the 'normalisation' period. Czechoslovak statistical yearbooks recorded the following numbers as tried and sentenced under Chapter One of the Criminal Code, entitled 'Crimes against the Republic': 942 in 1969, 1,576 in 1970, 861 in 1971 and 582 in 1972. (These figures do not include those additionally sentenced under Article 109 for 'leaving the Republic', i.e. unauthorised emigration.) Neither were the trials of the summer of 1972, during Husák's absence in the Crimea and when political responsibility for 'security' was in the Stalinist Vasil Bilak's hands, the first of well-known figures. Václav Prchlík, Petr Uhl, Vladimír Škutina, Jiří Lederer, Pavol Ličko, Luděk Pachman, Jiří Hochman and others had been sent to jail previously. The importance of the 1972 trials lay in the blow which they dealt to the more-or-less conventionally conducted oppositional activity of ex-communists. (There were several non-communists among the victims.) Almost at a stroke the government cut off the leading layer of a movement which threatened the progress of 'normalisation' by keeping the ideas of the Prague Spring alive and by doing something about it. Milan Hübl, Jaroslav Šabata, Jan Tesař, Jaromír Litera, Jiří Müller, Rudolf Battěk, Milan Šilhan and many others were in jail.

It seems that some of the most eager 'normalisers' sought to enlarge the scope of prosecution by implicating in the 'conspiracy' Jiří Pelikán, former head of Prague Television and now an émigré journalist in Rome, and through him the Italian Communist Party. At one stage during the interrogation period the police were preparing just one large show trial of all the arrested leaders of the SMCC to whom they would add émigrés and Italian communist sympathisers. The Italian connection would be provided through Pelikán's friendship with Enrico Berlinguer's brother Giovanni, and through the person of an Italian communist courier purportedly liaising between Pelikán in Rome and Hübl in Prague. Eventually, possibly on Moscow's advice, this scenario was not followed and the detained group was for the purpose of the trial split into nine smaller ones, with the tenth trial, of a Slovak dissident, held in Bratislava. The tug-of-war with Italian communists has then continued in a less obstreperous fashion until the present day. Pelikán also notes that Milan Hübl, one of the main defendants, had been 'an old friend of Husák's who under the rule of Novotný and with Husák's approval had maintained contact with a number of communist parties in the west, notably the Italian Communist Party'.[11]

The trials met with protests in the west, including some communist circles, but inside Czechoslovakia no one seemed to move a finger, although there is reason not to doubt popular disapproval. The 'vanguard' of the opposition was unable to mobilise its constituency of 'several thousands', let alone 'the membership base of several hundred thousands'. The estimates of potential willingness to act had obviously been inflated in the first place. The economic fruits of 'normalisation' had begun to show. Drastic curtailment of investment programmes and a certain amount of concentration on the production of food and consumer goods (the harvests were good) led to an improved situation on the market from mid-1971. At the same time, the various shows of strength by the regime made the public realise that a confrontation would be futile. The purges had scared people away from involvement in public matters, let alone such delicate ones. Also, cleverly, it was the second line of Prague Spring personalities that went on trial, not the men in the limelight, like Dubček, Smrkovský or Císař. Only the initiated knew who Hübl, Šabata and Tesař were, while quite a few of the victims had been entirely unknown outside the circle of their immediate friends. The distance between the generals and the troops had already widened.

SEARCH FOR EUROCOMMUNIST LINKAGE
(Summer 1972–Autumn 1976)

The government continued to consolidate its hold on the country mainly through the provision of material benefits (steady supply of essential goods, a price freeze and some social improvements, such as loans to newlyweds, salary and wage increases, higher family and maternity allowances and improved pensions); legal codification of its enhanced power (amendments of the Criminal and Labour Codes, a Police Law, tightening of rules on penal servitude, etc.); and a surfeit of ideology combined with further occasional purges. The population responded by continuing to retreat into private preoccupations, while showing appreciation of the results of consumerism.

The opposition was as a result pushed towards less direct forms of individual protest against oppressive behaviour by the authorities. It endeavoured, and succeeded, to keep alive the question of political prisoners by issuing petitions and appeals at home and abroad, and even by conducting a successful solidarity campaign with the families of the jailed comrades which were often left in dire material conditions.

As against the ex-politicians in the previous two stages, now it was mainly the writers and artists who took up the cause of free speech and protest. Interviews to foreign press became more frequent and a number of feuilletons and causeries began to circulate in samizdat form. Somewhat later, as the Eurocommunist cause grew stronger in western Europe, some of the Czechoslovak harbingers of the idea of a democratised communism took up the cudgel again.

A somewhat hazy contact appears to have been established between the Czech dissident community and the Kremlin towards the end of 1972 and in the first half of 1973, possibly over the heads of the Prague leadership of the day, at least at first. An unnamed Soviet official sought contact with Josef Smrkovský, ostensibly in order to communicate to Brezhnev his view of the situation which Moscow was said to have critical doubts about. After several meetings Smrkovský was invited to write a letter to the Soviet leader outlining his alternative solution to the policy of Husák and his die-hard allies. The text of the letter, dated in July 1973, is now available.[12]

In this letter, Smrkovský welcomed international détente and suggested that the harshness of 'normalisation' in Czechoslovakia cast a shadow over it. The Czechoslovak solution of 1968–9, he said, in fact belonged to the pre-détente era and became anachronistic in new conditions. Had not the time come when the 'Czechoslovak Question' ought to be changed from an obstacle to a stimulus of international relaxation? A part of the Czechoslovak leadership of the day, Smrkovský politely suggested, might be aware of this need, but the initiative would have to come from the Soviet side. This would be very well received by the communist population in Czechoslovakia, including the majority of the expellees. Was it impossible for the Soviet representatives to enter into negotiations with all the interested parties, including the exorcised communists? Smrkovský assured Brezhnev that he personally would be prepared to devote himself to working towards a settlement. Would Brezhnev let him know what he thought of all this?

In the event things remained as they had been and the episode, real enough to be taken note of, can be regarded as little more than one of the last (if not *the* last) attempts by the opposition to resolve their predicament within the confines of socialism of the Soviet type, while representing at the same time one of the first endeavours to link Soviet conduct towards East European dissent and opposition with détente.

Smrkovský never received an answer, except a cryptic message in October 1973, delivered verbally, to the effect that the letter had been positively received in the Kremlin and that important steps would be taken within a few months. Smrkovský died in January 1974, perhaps mercifully not knowing that nothing of the sort would happen.

The opposition had in the meantime been shedding communist

tenets and precepts from its political thought and language. The leadership-party-masses hierarchy of the oppositional front was dropped, and the use of 'communist' as a designation of a person's world view was replaced by 'socialist'.

Less communism in theory meant easier cooperation with social-democratic and liberal oppositionists. In fact, the difference in outlook between revisionists and liberals became soon so blurred as to be practically non-existent. It was the ex-communists who made most of the ideological concessions, while the liberals were quite happy to endorse the 'socialist' reference in public statements by the opposition, seeing as they did that the term now denoted something else than just a slightly adjusted communism of Soviet provenance. With a measure of oversimplification, one can suggest that opposition in Czechoslovakia became social-democratic in the period from 1973–6,

A perspicacious comment on this process was written at the turn of 1974–5 by a pseudonymous ex-communist in Prague, from which it is helpful to quote at some length:

> We have stopped worrying about the attachment of labels. . . . It is not, and has not been, easy to divest oneself of verbal symbols into which so much chiliastic faith, pragmatic effort, hate and anger had been invested. . . . A communist, a non-party man, an anti-communist, a no-more-than-a-socialist, an advocate of socialist democracy or democratic socialism, a Social Democrat, a Masaryk man . . . These and similar words were, and for some still are, overloaded to a point well below the draught line which permits secure navigation in the waters of political life. . . . Confessional disputations, let alone preoccupations with political trademarks of the future, are of interest to no-one, and by the same token divide no-one among those who have not grown indifferent and have not given up, regardless of their present or past party membership and outlook.[13]

As a direct corollary to the blunting of ideological edges, no more action programmes were being formulated. The opposition became pragmatic. The many unofficial communications which the opposition produced during these four years do of course contain advice and demands, but comprehensive platforms were no longer thought necessary. The one demand that kept cropping up was the release of political prisoners.

A Prague dissenter said that there was not enough desire to manufacture programmes and associate or close ranks around them. . . . The aspiration to address oneself to fundamental issues, . . . to identify what true socialism is and what it is not, to make decisions about a final taking of sides with and against people, to compile platforms and hoist political banners, however honest they may be – all this is in the Czechoslovakia of 1975 an increasingly foolish stance, even less commensurate with reality. . . . Ideological charades appear less and less fascinating. . . . All ready-made prescriptions and unequivocal answers are worth nothing; they melt as a handful of snow thrown on a hot stove.[14]

Since 1974 Czechoslovak opposition activity has been characterised by growing internationalisation. Western media were being increasingly used as channels of public communication and a growing number of 'open letters' was being despatched to prominent persons in the west, especially men of culture, such as Jean-Paul Sartre, Heinrich Böll, Günther Grass and Arthur Miller. The stepping up of détente became a major point of reference for domestic developments.

The mainstream of Czechoslovak opposition has always professed a positive belief in the benefits of international détente. This was consistent with the policies which a number of the oppositionists advocated in 1968 when they had been in power or near it. Zdeněk Mlynář and Jiří Hájek, in their interview for Swedish television in September 1975, stressed this aspect specifically:

The idea of European security and cooperation was one of the fundamental principles of Czechoslovak foreign policy embodied in the Communist Party's Action Programme of 1968. . . . The results of Helsinki must be considered as basically positive, and one ought to dissociate oneself from attempts to minimise and devalue them.[15]

An anti-détente trend of any significance would be hard to find, although there has been and still is a certain amount of caution and scepticism. The popular view, insofar as it can be judged, was less united and included a majority of sceptics next to a fairly large number of credulous people who expected immediate progressive changes.

A sociologist conducted a clandestine public opinion poll in February–March 1975 to find out what people expected of the Helsinki conference. The sample comprised 209 persons, of whom 25 per cent were below the age of 30, 50 per cent from 30–50, and 25 per cent over 50. 151 were men and 58 women, 198 Czechs, 9 Slovaks and 1 Hungarian. 138 said they expected nothing (66 per cent), 33 hoped for withdrawal of Soviet troops and restoration of sovereignty (15.8 per cent), one expected the west simply to reconfirm the immutability of East–West borders (0.5 per cent), and 37 gave no answer (17.7 per cent).[16]

When there was no sign of Soviet troops leaving or other relaxations affecting the internal political life, an attitude of almost cynical disappointment seems to have set in. An anonymous writer from Prague said: '. . . at best the Czech man in the street will dismiss European security as not worth a comment or, in a deeply sceptical mood, will sigh, "another little Munich at our expense"'.[17]

On balance, the Czechoslovaks prefer détente to cold war, but are worried lest the west comports itself as it did in the appeasement years of the 1930s. The ex-reformers' pro-détente stance derives from the conviction that notwithstanding the danger of appeasement, the prospects of democratisation are better under détente than they would be in conditions of a cold war. In particular, they have been stressing two dimensions of détente: it will compel the USSR and its client states to show greater concern for the material wellbeing of their populations, and it will enable the west and the dissenters to take the communist governments to task in regard to the pledges which they will have to undertake.

On the latter count the opposition began to advocate a clear-cut line immediately after the signing of the Final Act. (Smrkovský's letter to Brezhnev, quoted above, presaged this line of argument much earlier.) Mlynář stated in his interview for Swedish television in September 1975:

> The Helsinki principles, signed both by the representatives of the present regime in Czechoslovakia and the representatives of countries who had carried out a military intervention in Czechoslovakia in 1968, should not apply only for the present and the future, but should obligate the signatories, at least morally, to undo such events in the past which evidently contravene these principles.

And Hájek added that the signing of the Helsinki principles could be understood as self-criticism for all their violations in the past, such as the intervention in Czechoslovakia.[18]

Mlynář countered the argument about 'meddling in internal affairs of other countries':

We are not in favour of external meddling either, we only want the holders of power to abide by what they themselves have solemnly promised and signed. . . . Helsinki represents a recognition of what is common to Europe, a recognition of European civilisation and cultural values, European tradition of humanism, and European legal conscience. Coexistence of differing social and political systems can only be implemented on this basis. . . . It is contrary to the script and spirit of the Helsinki conference if certain European nations and states keep alive practices conflicting with the European civilisation and cultural background.[19]

Simultaneously, the opposition enhanced its emphasis on the Eurocommunist dimension against the background of the protracted preparations for an all-European meeting of communist parties. Expectations may even have been running too high, and at least some oppositionists overestimated the willingness of the three major Eurocommunist parties to make Czechoslovakia a pivotal issue in Berlin. Mlynář predicted that the Berlin summit 'can hardly pass in silence the fact that the evolution of socialism in Czechoslovakia was deeply disturbed after August 1968 and that a way out of the blind alley must be sought there'.[20] In the end the Czechoslovak issue found expression in a bracketed mention in Berlinguer's speech, and even that referred to the Italian communists' disapproval of the invasion, not the normalisation. Mlynář admitted two years later that his expectations had not been met.[21]

Zdeněk Mlynář was the most active proponent of the Eurocommunist link which offered itself quite obviously to people who had advocated very similar policies in 1968, albeit approached from within the Soviet orbit. Mlynář wrote a book-length manuscript in 1975, *Československý pokus o reformu 1968* (The Czechoslovak Reform Attempt of 1968),[22] which went into great detail to counter Soviet accusations and to explain the reformist policy and plans of 1968, including the mistakes. Its fifty-page last chapter concerns 'the international context of the Czechoslovak reform in relation to the European socialist states and the international communist movement' and its tenor is as follows: While recognising that the fate of socialism is the legitimate concern of every element in the communist movement (and that consequently the communist countries of the Soviet bloc had a right to be interested in Czechoslovak developments in 1968, though not to intervene), the so-called 'normalisation' course ought also to be subjected to an international communist examination by those parties which have had a stake in policies similar to those of the Prague Spring.

Mlynář also addressed an open letter to 'the communists and socialists of Europe' in February 1976, in which he further endeavoured to identify the cause of Czechoslovak reformers with the new trend in West European communism:

> In the Czechoslovakia of today the problem is not only that of the so-called dissidents; not only individuals who express critical views and discontent . . . are being silenced. Suppression and persecution affects hundreds of thousands of people who for many years advocated, and still do, a certain tendency in the European communist, socialist and democratic movement. This tendency is very similar and sometimes completely identical with the tendencies that are increasingly and positively asserting themselves in the European working class movement, especially in the recent political evolution of the communist parties in Italy, France, Spain, Great Britain, Sweden, Belgium and elsewhere. It is also very close to the tendency represented for many years by the Yugoslav communists and in some questions it comes near to the political attitudes of Romanian communists. . . . I am convinced that if the European socialist movement is genuinely concerned in safeguarding the aims expressed in the political platform of the Helsinki conference, it cannot evade giving help to the restoration of political democracy in Czechoslovakia.[23]

In short, Prague Spring *was* Eurocommunism, measured not only by the tenets of Berlinguer and Carrillo, but even those of Marx. You can easily be a Eurocommunist in the name of Marx, but not Lenin. The undoing of the concept in Czechoslovakia came about because it emerged on the wrong, Leninist, side of the artificial power-political divide in Europe.

The Eurocommunist dimension gave a fillip once again to at least some of the communist features which the Czechoslovak opposition had begun to lose after the defeat of its organised platforms in 1972. If they wished to speak to their West European comrades, the ex-reformers had to re-adopt some concepts and language of the movement, albeit of the Carrillo-Berlinguer rather than the Brezhnev variety. They were also knowledgeable and realistic enough to recognise that a possible re-opening of the Czechoslovak chapter in communist history would not be brought about by a confrontation between Eurocommunism and the USSR, but much rather from a compromise. A rift between Moscow and Eurocommunism, comparable to the

Yugoslav or Chinese ruptures of the past, would not be conducive to a settlement. Only as long as Messrs Berlinguer, Carrillo and Marchais can exert influence on the Kremlin from within the movement, can Czechoslovak 'Eurocommunist' opposition hope, faintly, for a change in the 'normalisation' course.

Gradually, during the period from 1972 to 1976, the human rights issue emerged as a common denominator of all oppositional striving. Political prisoners were maltreated, and their relatives produced and published documented evidence of it. People were dismissed from jobs for the views they held, and they took their employers to court, even if without avail, on grounds of infringement of the Labour Code. Others were subjected to police harassment and complained in open letters to the constitutional authorities. Books and films were banned, and the proscribed lists appeared in samizdat circulation. Manuscripts were confiscated from writers and scholars and they wrote to their western friends about it. People were prohibited from practising their professions, and they informed international agencies and societies of which Czechoslovakia was a member. Children of blacklisted persons were not admitted to higher and even secondary education in spite of excellent school records, and the world learned about it. It cannot be overemphasised that for the Czechoslovak opposition the human rights issue was not an instrument with which they decided to hook themselves on to super-power politics in 1977 in order to take sides with the Carter administration, but rather a very much alive experience of the entire 'normalisation' period to which they gradually gave priority over the elaboration of ideological and political programmes. This process represented a build-up to the next stage of oppositional developments, marked by the issuance of Charter 77.

CHARTER 77

In 1975 the Czechoslovak government decided to ratify and promulgate as part of the law of the land two international covenants on human rights signed on behalf of Czechoslovakia in October 1968 by representatives of a reformist government then still nominally in power. These were the International Covenant on Civil and Political Rights and the International Covenant on Economic, Social and Cultural Rights. Both came into force in Czechoslovakia on 23 March 1976, were published in the Collection of Laws dated 13 October and reached the stalls on 11 November 1976.[24]

Less than two months later the opposition responded by issuing a historic statement, 'Charter 77'.[25] This Charter was thus born out of a confluence of domestic and international developments and as a result of evident disparity between the repressive policy of the government towards a large group of people and its international legal commitments. It is not a political programme as it deliberately refrains from offering alternative societal arrangements to the existing ones. It does, however, contain a programmatic element in stating that not only the government but all citizens bear 'a share of responsibility for the conditions that prevail and accordingly also for the observance of legally enshrined agreements, binding upon all individuals as well as upon governments'. The Charter also submits that all signatories will strive 'to conduct a constructive dialogue with the political and state authorities by way of drawing attention to individual violations of human and civic rights, documenting grievances and suggesting remedies, and making proposals of a more general character'. The signatories offered themselves as intermediaries in situations of conflict which may lead to violations of rights. While disclaiming an organisational status and styling themselves 'a loose, informal and open association', the Charter's authors appointed three spokesmen to represent them vis-à-vis state and other bodies, and the public at home and abroad.

Most of the original 242 signatories of the Charter were intellectuals, either by training or at the time of signing. As their number grew to an estimated 900 by the end of 1977, the percentage of workers steadily increased to about one-third of the total. Reports from the country indicated that the Manifesto had become widely popular. Jaromír Obzina, the Minister of the Interior, said that 90 per cent of the public would not have realised wherein lay the danger if the Charter was published openly, and some two million might have signed it, had they not been afraid.[26]

Not all the signatories are well-known figures who had been prominent in political or public life prior to the purges. There is a high percentage of young people among them. The Charter reflects the alliance of all political groups and social sections with the one notable exception of present members of the party and the establishment. Also unrepresented among the signatories are the Slovaks, with a few exceptions.

In an informative interview given to a Swedish newsman at the end of October 1977, Jiří Hájek, the former Foreign Minister and a spokesman for the Charter, identified three large groups among the signatories: men of culture (literature, art, scholarship), expelled 'reform communists' and Christians. About Slovakia he had the following to say:

> In Slovakia the 'normalised' repression has been substantially more moderate than in the Czech Lands. Slovaks are the smaller of the two nations, people are closer to one another there, and their bonds of solidarity are stronger. Moreover, the Bratislava political leaders are evidently cleverer than their colleagues in Prague. They have no desire to destroy their creative intelligentsia. After the defeat of the Prague Spring, repression in Slovakia was almost exclusively directed against active 'reform communists', and not against large groups of people outside the party. Communists have never been as numerous in Slovakia as they were in the Czech Lands. Furthermore, federalisation of the country has been preserved as the only large-scale reform of the Prague Spring. It marked a big step forward on the national plane for Slovakia, and it has survived 'normalisation'. The Slovaks have no national reason to add to the general disappointment as the Czechs have. These may be among the reasons which have made fewer people in Slovakia feel that they should sign the Charter.[27]

Between 1 January and 30 June 1977 the Charter group issued twelve 'documents' on a variety of subjects, including the legal status of the Charter and the persecution of its signatories, labour, education and religious discrimination, the state of literature and victimisation of writers, and others.[28] A number of other statements connected to the Charter movement and appeals to the west about harsh repression of its followers were also made public.

The government's reaction was angry from the start. One spokesman of the Charter (V. Havel) was immediately arrested and kept in jail until May. In October he received a suspended sentence for contacts with émigrés after having been forced to resign as the Charter spokesman. Another of the three spokesmen, the philosopher J. Patočka, was interrogated for so long and in such a manner that he died of a stroke. The last one (J. Hájek) was subjected to an almost intolerable amount of physical and mental chicanery. Scores of the signatories were dismissed from jobs and otherwise victimised and harassed. Several were forced to emigrate. A furious media campaign was directed so as to put the signatories beyond the pale as renegades, morally corrupt people and agents of imperialism. Some 1,500 members of the intelligentsia, mainly in arts and literature, were coerced into signing an 'Anti-Charter' which, however, significantly had the form of a long proclamation of humanitarian intentions into which a paragraph was inserted castigating in general terms those who purportedly do not hold them true, without the Charter being mentioned at all.[29] Simultaneously, extensive space has been given over in the media to infringements of human rights under capitalism. It proved not so easy to compel workers to denounce the Charter, and many condemnatory letters from factories were signed by party and trade union functionaries rather than individual workers.

Despite the oppression, Charter 77 has become a resilient rallying point. The publicity campaign unleashed against it took the message to wide circles of the population such as the oppositionists themselves would be able to reach only with difficulty. The Charter has also become an internationally known document, with repercussions in other communist countries from which messages of sympathy and identification with the Charter's aims were sent. A number of western communist parties seeking independence of Moscow have once again affirmed their support for East European dissidents in connection with the Charter and its aftermath.

The Charter is the product of a combined democratic and socialist tendency which has evolved as the strongest element in the Czechoslovak oppositional spectrum. This is only natural in view of the country's political culture. At the very heart of this coalescence of democratic and socialist attitudes is an exchange of concessions both on the part of the socialist and the non-socialist dissenters. The reformists have given up the concept of the leading role of the party and the democrats have acknowledged a social-democratic framework for the oppositional programmes. In its explicit refusal to draw a distinction between communists (or ex-communists) and non-communists, the Charter went beyond the Action Programme of the Communist Party of April 1968 and the Short Action Programme formulated in opposition in 1971.

The Charter is however a programme only in the restricted sense of the word, namely in proclaiming the signatories' intent to stand up for lawful and moral relationship between the authorities and the citizens. It says nothing about desirable structural changes in the regime although one cannot doubt that the authors would like to see changes to occur. By not advocating systemic transformation in the Charter, they simply recognise that conditions are not apposite for such an advocacy, and that a *programma minimum*, based on the observance of existing laws and accepted moral standards, is the right step in the right direction at the right moment.

To be sure, the human rights issue is not without reform orientation. Not all human rights are the same. Some are unacceptable to an authoritarian regime because their application would negate its substance, such as rights that involve political contestation, full freedom of promoting political and ideological alternatives, uncontrolled contact with foreign countries, freedom to solicit, receive and impart all unauthorised information and freedom to engage in private enterprise.

The insistence of Czechoslovak and other oppositionists in the Soviet Union and Eastern Europe on the observation of laws by the authorities who created them in the first place, is significant. Leonard Schapiro, while noting the ease with which new laws or amendments can be effected in communist states (this has certainly happened in Czechoslovakia under 'normalisation'), says:

> But while individual laws as such are no obstacle, the legal *order* can well become one – in other words, the persistence of an established system of rules, habits and institutions operating within a fixed framework of limits, each single component part of which has to be overcome or set aside by a special enactment. And even if the old enactments can easily be replaced by new enactments, so long as the 'legal order' ensures that all existing enactments are complied with until repealed or amended, they necessarily present some barrier to free, unconstrained, arbitrary action by the Leader, if only by creating delay.[30]

This may well be, or become, the main target area of the 'legalists' among the dissenters and oppositionists: resistance to the fusion of the constitutional framework and the party-orientated legitimacy, and the holding together of a 'legal order', however inadequate. They will of course at the same time continue exposing individual 'bad' laws and relate their legalistic efforts to the international context which was brought about by growing Soviet involvement in world trade and détente.

Finally, the Charter movement has a strong moral charge, as of course had the Prague Spring with its emphasis on 'the human face' of socialism and the implied tendency towards national reconciliation. For the revisionists, this dimension originated, as Frederick Barghoorn aptly remarked, from 'the failure of Khrushchev, and to a greater degree of his successors, to complete the process of moral regeneration symbolised by the term "de-Stalinisation"'.[31] 'Normalisation' has a distinctly inhuman face and can be viewed as an attempt to introduce into governance a high measure of what is normally associated with immorality, such as double-face, trading of material benefit for political compliance, revenge, blackmail of parents over their children, inducement of fear, emergence of corrupt practices, etc.[32]

Every society and every body politic is in need of criticism on moral grounds, and I would submit that the role of a moral critic, assumed by oppositionists in various East European countries, including Russia, befits the opposition no less than that of a formulator of alternative programmes or an advocate of legality.

THE FUTURE

The externalities which influence the relationship between government and opposition in Czechoslovakia comprise a three-cornered knot of problems which are as much Soviet-related, as they pertain to Czechoslovakia herself. The first is the future of détente. In brief, and with simplification, it can be said that as long as détente prospers, or at least survives, so will the Charter-type form of Czechoslovak opposition. Secondly, much will depend on the degree to which the Soviet Union considers a badly normalised Czechoslovakia a liability. Mr Brezhnev may yet come to the conclusion that the replacement of the incumbents with a moderate leadership (with the potential to win genuine public support as Kádár had in Hungary), no matter how belated its start may be, would bring greater benefit to the USSR in the international arena and the world communist movement than the present embarrassing regime. But then, he may also regard the loosening of reins over Czechoslovakia as much too dangerous, remembering the 1960s. Thirdly, and least promisingly, the post-Brezhnev succession process may produce a leadership amenable to Kádárisation in Czechoslovakia, if only to make more palatable its dissociation from other parts of the Brezhnev legacy.

Domestically, I can see two important potential influences, an economic one and a repeat of the reformist one. There may prevail in the present leadership a tendency which will justify in Moscow's eyes above all the giving of full emphasis to improvement of economic competence. Towards this end, the advocates of modernisation may try to change the policy of ideological confrontation, which they must see as an obstacle, into one of bureaucratic enlightenment. A *modus vivendi* may be sought with the oppositionists, the aim being the establishment of the party as a rational tutor over the largest possible section of society. To paraphrase Richard Lowenthal, a regime created by foreign military intervention and consolidated through repression of a large part of the nation, can hope to acquire effective legitimacy both for its own subjects and the outside world, simply through passage of time. People grow up with such a regime and come to regard it as normal. But there is one condition: 'revolutionary violence' must stop. 'A regime that conducts recurrent war against important social groups cannot expect to benefit from it.'[33]

Finally, I would emphasise the regenerative force of reformism in Czechoslovakia. The party has even today in its ranks a sizeable percentage of people who joined it after the purge of 1970 and may yet refuse total identification with the other segment of the membership which was directly responsible for the purge. Admittedly, the new ones are a different breed from the zealots of the 1940s but they may clash with orthodoxy in the future for largely the same reasons. This is human nature. The Czechoslovak émigré journalist Pavel Tigrid has frequently referred to reformist 'insiders' as people whose aim is as impossible as the squaring of a circle. Jan Stárek, already quoted, responded by admitting that the aim may indeed be impossible to attain. Nevertheless, there will again be people who will try to do precisely that.

> One thing is important above others: these perennial repeaters know how to handle the machinery of the regime and its component parts, they know its weak spots and they understand its secrets. They show perception of the mechanism of the apparatuses, they know which secret passages lead to the decisive command posts, they know the paths of retreat, they know how to find safe bearings in the ideological mist. They know the psychology and psycho-pathology of the apparatchiki.... They will indeed not set out to alter the structure of the system ... because they will be less concerned with principles and more with tangible results. It will be they who in the end will create enclaves and elbow-room, set things in motion, induce changes and facilitate a more genuine differentiation in views and actions, even though the avenues leading to it all will be very, very tortuous. They will not aspire to solve logical or geometrical problems: while not succeeding in squaring the circle, they may well manage to shape a rectangle out of it.[34]

58   *Opposition in Eastern Europe*

Reformism practised inside the Czechoslovak Communist Party is a time-honoured profession now. On account of its existence alone some doubt must remain as to whether the party can be as thoroughly 'normalised' as its Soviet counterpart has been over the six decades. The propensity of the Czechs to lick them by joining them may flourish once again. I would not be surprised if it did. Czechoslovak reformism is an evergreen.

NOTES

1. This paper is concerned with political opposition proper and its focus excludes consideration of 'corporate dissent' and power struggle within the ruling structure. Slovakia is not treated adequately, essentially because of lack of information. Constraints of space have also eliminated consideration of post-1968 emigration. These lacunae are being made good in a larger study of 'normalisation' of which the present chapter forms a preliminary part. Financial assistance from the British Social Science Research Council is gratefully acknowledged; in this day of cuts and squeezes it has been indeed instrumental. Much gratitude goes to Rudolf Tokés for friendly but firm editing of the first version, and to numerous discussants among my Western and Czechoslovak colleagues.
2. Jiří Pelikán, *Socialist Opposition in Eastern Europe. The Czechoslovak Example*. (London, Allison & Busby, 1976) pp. 26–7.
3. *Listy* (Rome) 2/1971, p. 9.
4. All quotations from the full text in Pelikán, op. cit., pp. 118–24.
5. *Rudé právo*, 15 December 1970, p. 3.
6. *Rudé právo*, 13 September 1975, p. 2.
7. Pelikán, op. cit., pp. 41–3.
8. All quotations from full text in Pelikán, op. cit., pp. 136–56.
9. Ibid., p. 157.
10. Ibid., pp. 158–9.
11. Ibid., pp. 66–7.
12. *Listy* (Rome), 2/1975, pp. 26–8.
13. Jan Stárek, pseud., 'Emigrace a opozice', *Svědectví* (Paris) 50/1975, pp. 211–2.
14. Ibid., pp. 215 and 217.
15. 'Hovoří Z. Mlynář a J. Hájek', *Listy* (Rome) 7/1975, p. 15. This interview and many other documents relating to the internationalisation of Czechoslovak opposition were handily reprinted in *Hlasy z domova 1975* (Cologne, Index, 1976).
16. Věra Nováková, pseud., 'Výzkum na aktuální téma', *Listy* (Rome) 6/1975, pp. 11–13.
17. Anon., 'Helsinki a my doma', *Listy* (Rome) 7/1975, p. 15.
18. *Listy* (Rome) 7/1975, p. 15.
19. Ibid., p. 16. Of the documents which supported this approach to détente in general and Helsinki in particular, several were reprinted in *Hlasy z domova 1975* (op. cit.), e.g. a letter from Jiří Hájek to the Prime

Minister, dated 1 October 1975; Karel Kaplan's letter to the Party Praesidium, the Federal Assembly and the government, dated 20 October 1975; and a letter by František Kriegel, Gertruda Sekaninová and František Vodsloň to the Federal Assembly, dated 8 November 1975.
20. *Listy* (Rome) 7/1975, p. 17.
21. Interview in *Espresso* (Rome) 30 July 1977. In Czech in *Listy* (Rome) 5/1977, pp. 17–19.
22. Published in Czech by Index, Cologne, 1975. 275 pp.
23. *Listy* (Rome) 3/1976, pp. 41–5.
24. *Sbírka zákonů ČSSR*, Part 23, 13 October 1976, pp. 570–83.
25. Full text for example in *White Paper on Czechoslovakia* (Paris, 1977. This collection of many documents relating to the Charter is available in English or in French from Mme France de Nicolay, 3 rue des Lions, 75004 Paris).
26. Anonymous report from Prague quoted in *Listy* (Rome) 3–4/1977, p. 4.
27. *Svenska Dagbladed*, 13 November 1977.
28. Full texts or substantial extracts of Documents Nos. 1–10 in *White Paper on Czechoslovakia* (op. cit.) Documents Nos. 11 and 12 in *Listy* (Rome) 5/1977, pp. 42–5.
29. 'Za nové tvůrčí činy ve jménu socialismu a míru', *Rudé právo*, 29 January 1977, p. 1.
30. Leonard Schapiro, *Totalitarianism* (London, Macmillan, 1972) p. 31.
31. Frederick C. Barghoorn, *Detente and the Democratic Movement in the USSR* (New York, The Free Press, 1976) p. 11.
32. See for example Václav Havel's open letter to Husák, dated 8 April 1975, in *Hlasy z domova*, op. cit., pp. 9–36. In English in *Voices of Czechoslovak Socialists* (London, Merlin Press, 1977) pp. 90–125, and elsewhere.
33. Richard Lowenthal, 'The Ruling Party in a Mature Society' in Mark G. Field, ed., *Social Consequences of Modernization in Communist Societies* (Baltimore, The Johns Hopkins University Press, 1976) pp. 81–118.
34. Stárek, op. cit., p. 221.

3 Dissent in Poland, 1968–78: the end of Revisionism and the rebirth of the Civil Society

by JACQUES RUPNIK

Over the last decade manifestations of dissent have been more wide-spread in Poland than in any other country in Eastern Europe. These involved three main forces: the intellectuals and students, the workers, and the powerful Roman Catholic Church. The common origin of their renewed independent activity goes back to 1956, but all three have followed separate itineraries until 1968. The period 1968–78 has been marked by the evolution of these three main components of the Polish opposition from isolation to a degree of convergence in their challenge of the party's grip over the society. In 1968 students and creative intellectuals, who demanded greater freedom of expression, were suppressed and were in complete isolation from the workers. In 1970–1 workers went on strike for essentially economic demands and confronted police repression without gaining the support of the intellectuals. Both in 1968 and in 1970 the Catholic Church protested against the repression, but without actually endorsing the intellectuals' or the workers' demands. The most significant change in the develop-ment of the Polish opposition in the 1970s has been the broadening of its social base, fostered by the creation of new ties between the three main forces of the opposition. This mutual interaction and synchron-isation of their respective activities without the loss of their specific interests, brought with it sometimes a convergence of goals and often unity of action.

The centre of gravity of the social base of the opposition has shifted from rather limited circles of intellectuals to broader social strain, which, in turn, has affected the formulation of opposition strategies. The protest is no longer expressed just by isolated intellectuals and groups and addressed to the authorities, but now involves thousands who are prepared to make public their protest addressed to the society as a whole. The convergence of different social groups involved in the opposition to some extent accounts for the evolution of the opposition movement from a strategy designed to reform the system by exerting pressure from within the party, to a concept of social pressure from outside which aims at the progressive transformation of the relations between state and society in a one-party system.

It would, however, be erroneous to see this convergence, which undoubtedly is a source of strength and vitality for the Polish opposition, as proof of its unity and homogeneity. In fact, each of the three main components has its specific place in the society and a different relationship with the state and therefore has different aims and limitations in expressing protest. Similarly, the type of issues raised by each reflects this diversity: the workers' actions question a model of economic development and a system of industrial relations inherited from the Stalinist era; intellectual protest has tended to focus on the absence of democratic freedoms, while the Catholic Church provides a unique example of institutionalised opposition. More importantly, development of the opposition since 1976 has been characterised by an impressive variety of independent grass root social initiatives, with no claims to 'political' change or a particular political programme. Both point to the revival of pluralism in Polish society and to the resurfacing of traditional Polish political culture both of which challenge the established mechanisms of social control. Thus, in the Polish context the separation between the 'social' and the 'political' dimensions of oppositional activity has been made almost irrelevant by the introduction of external social pressures as the new political strategy of the opposition.

Opposition in today's Poland has come to mean independent social activity which virtually ignores official institutions and has no ambition to produce a new party leader. For this reason by opposition we understand articulate expression of disagreement with official policies by an organised body whether permanent or not, whether legal or not.[1] By dissent we understand spontaneous, sporadic or continuous manifestations of dissatisfaction or disagreement with official policies in all spheres of social life. Expressions of non-conformity or resistance can often spill over into dissent. The criterion here is not merely a concept of 'alienation'. The posture of simply holding values and beliefs contrary to the official ideology is called 'internal emigration' in Eastern Europe. Dissent begins with the public expression of this alienation.

MARCH '68: THE INTELLECTUALS AND THE LIMITS OF REVISIONISM

Historically, the role of the Polish intelligentsia has been marked by a paradox. The intelligentsia has played a leading role in preserving Poland's national and cultural identity against external domination, and this partly accounts today for its prestige and status in the population. The product of an impoverished aristocracy, in a country where the bourgeoisie developed late, remained weak and was largely of non-Polish origin, the intelligentsia's status vis-à-vis the establishment has always been marginal and no organic ties with the predominantly rural population were ever developed. Rejecting bourgeois values of modernisation, it jealously preserved an elitist ethos, playing no role in the country's economic development and remaining socially in a 'ghetto'. Thus, the creative intelligentsia's mission as spokesmen for the nation was quite compatible with their alienation from the state power.[2]

After World War II the new political situation brought significant changes in the composition of the intelligentsia. Some emigrated, some were eliminated; others accepted collaboration with the regime (whether on the extreme right like Piasecki or extreme left socialists like Cyrankiewicz). Most chose the so called 'organic work' of limited cooperation but not of collaboration with the new regime which tried to create a new socialist intellectual elite of working class origin. This accounts for the numerical growth of the intelligentsia if not for its augmented social status, which nevertheless remains high. The development had more the effect of assimilating the new intellectuals into the old intelligentsia, rather than the bridging the gap between the intellectuals and the masses. Despite these changes the creative intelligentsia has retained its essential pre-war characteristics of professional independence and solidarity, but remained divided about the best way to voice national aspirations through serving the state or the civil society.

Postwar developments have reinforced these characteristics. The communist regime is perceived by the intelligentsia as anti-national and imposed from outside. Because of the political dimension of culture, in a system where no other means of expression of dissatisfaction are available, intellectuals retain their traditional role as the spokesmen for national aspirations. After total suppression and subservience to the regime in the early 1950s, it was their role as spokesmen for the 'pays reel' that the Polish intellectuals recovered during the Polish October of 1956.

The character of the 1968 intellectuals' confrontation with the regime has been shaped by the intellectuals' support for Gomułka in October 1956 and by the ensuing resistance to Gomułka's 'retreat from October'.[3] The October '56 movement produced some lasting consequences which distinguish Poland from any other Soviet bloc state whose common denominator is the re-emergence of pluralism and the limit put on the party's grip over the society. Agriculture was decollectivised, a far-reaching decision ideologically and socially in a predominantly rural country; autonomy was both acquired and consolidated by the Catholic Church, which represents an alternative ideology and institutional framework, and has the support of an estimated four-fifths of the population. And the existence of more than one party ceased to be a mere formality by the communists' acceptance by the formation in the Sejm, the Polish Parliament, of at least one genuine opposition group, the Catholic club Znak.

The de facto recognition by the regime of social and cultural pluralism, as well as the retreat from 1956 reforms, provided the background to the emergence of intellectual opposition. The system's ability in 1955–6 to absorb pressure from below on one hand and the Soviet suppression of the Hungarian revolt on the other, found its corollary in the two mainstreams of thought of the oppositional intelligentsia: the Marxist 'revisionists' and the Catholic 'neopositivists'. Both sought gradual transformation of the system by exerting pressure on it from within (in the party or other institutions) but without directly challenging the party's leading role in the society, and its adhesion to the Soviet bloc.

The aim of the revisionist intellectuals in the 1956–68 period was to improve or 'humanise' the communist system from within, through the communist party or more precisely through the liberal wing in the party leadership. They participated in the system by proxy, as a pressure group, criticising party policies on specific issues, but sharing with the party the same ideology and a common language. The initial impetus was derived from the disillusionment with Stalinist practices of the 1950s and from the gulf between the regime's socialist ideals and political practice. The motivation was thus ideological with the aim to revitalise Marxism-Leninism, in ideology and practice, so as to restore to it some of Marxism's earlier qualities of idealism, notably its emphasis on humanist values.[4] Philosophers Leszek Kołakowski[5] and Adam Schaff, were the best-known exponents of this humanist Marxism, while economists such as Oscar Lange and Włodzimierz Brus were the leading advocates of economic reforms combining planning with market mechanisms and workers participation in management. The viability of such an opposition depended on two conditions: the support of a faction in the party leadership and access to the media i.e. limited degree of tolerance by the system. The gradual disappearance of both conditions in the late 1950s and early 1960s, were the main reasons of the decline of revisionism. Bienkowski, the liberal Minister of Education, was removed from the government in 1959, and has since become one of the most articulate spokesmen of the revisionist trend. So have members of the 'Pulawy group'[6] composed mainly of wartime Muscovites, communists of Jewish origin, who after 1956 tried to keep a middle course between the 'revisionists' and the 'dogmatics' and basically supported Gomułka. However with the hardening of Gomułka's policies and the rise of the so called 'Partisan' faction led by Mieczyslaw Moczar, they became tacitly associated with the 'revisionists' which, in the era of restoration, could only lead to their eviction from power. By 1963 most leaders of the liberal faction led by Jerzy Morawski and Zambrowski had been removed from the leadership.[7]

At the same time the revisionist intellectuals, increasingly disillusioned with Gomułka's retreat from ideals of October were losing their means of expression as their journals were suppressed. (*Po Prostu* in 1957; *Nowa Kultura* and *Przegląd Kulturalny* in 1963.) By the end of 1963 the October intellectuals were confined to discussion clubs (the most famous of these clubs had been Krzywe Kolo ('Crooked Circle') in Warsaw), with the University as the main reservoir of support for their increasingly sharp criticism of Gomułka and of their own illusions of 1956. On the eve of the 1968 confrontation between the party and the writers most of the most prominent of the latter had already left the party. This in part explains their outspokenness and the inability of the party in a crisis situation to appeal to any sense of loyalty – only repression was left.[8]

October 1956 has also produced, besides revisionist writers and academics, a more left wing Marxist critique of the Gomułka regime, and of the reformist hopes of 1956. In 1964 Jacek Kuroń and Karol Modzelewski, both instructors in history at Warsaw University, circulated their 'Open Letter to the party'.[9] Though formally the Letter was addressed to the party, its contents represented a radical rupture with the strategy of pressure on the liberal wing in the party. Only the working class, according to the authors, could, with an independent organisation and a political programme, overthrow the ruling 'central political bureaucracy' and start building a genuinely socialist society. The two authors were expelled from the party and sentenced in 1965 to three years in jail. Kuroń's and Modzelewski's work as political activists however, helped bridge the gap between the 1956 generation and the young generation of student activists of the 1960s. Both were active in the communist youth movement which would eventually produce the so called third generation of Polish dissidents, also known in 1968 as the 'commando', the most prominent of whom is Adam Michnik.[10]

By the mid 1960s the writers felt nothing was left of the freedoms that had been won in 1956. Tension was also rising at the universities, where young lecturers were formulating a theoretical analysis of their society which sought to provide explanations for the failure of the reformist hopes, while a group of young students (the 'Commandos'), predominantly children of communist parents, were becoming increasingly politicised. The March 1968 events were the culmination of these two trends of dissident activity of the 'commandos' and the writers. All these tensions were brought into the open in the student-intellectual rebellion at the beginning of 1968. The catalyst for the upheaval was the banning, at the end of January, of 'Dziady' ('The Forefathers' Eve'), a play written by Adam Mickiewicz after the suppression of the 1831 uprising against the Tsar.[11] Since 1955 the play had been performed in Poland in seventeen different productions and the Dejmek's new production prepared for the fiftieth anniversary of the Russian October Revolution, seemed initially to satisfy everybody, including the Politburo ideological expert, Zenon Kliszko. The fact that the predominantly youthful public enthusiastically applauded, especially the anti-Tsarist and anti-authoritarian passages, reveals as much about the level of their frustration as the authorities' banning of the play reveals about their paranoid fear of expressions of popular national feeling. This move by the authorities resulted in the most massive tide of unrest in Eastern Europe since 1956.

What was at stake clearly went beyond a protest against a banned play. The philosopher Leszek Kołakowski saw the incident as only the tip of the iceberg of a broader issue and went on to attack the party's monopoly of power over culture:

> The monopoly is a means to sterilise all intellectual life, to prevent all confrontation, to reduce all cultural expression to a caricature. The monopoly brings the rot to those who practice it. The monopoly

only answers the criticism by threats. All criticism is an attempt to restore capitalism. This has a name – blackmail. . . . What we have in our country now is not socialism, it has nothing in common with Marxism.[12]

Other writers spoke along similar lines. Stefan Kisielewski, the Catholic writer, attacked censorship as illegal and denounced 'the dictatorship of ignoramuses'. Antoni Słonimski, the well-known poet, concludes his speech with a phrase which reflects well the situation of the writers: 'To defend myself I have no administrative means at my disposal, just as I have no guns, no militia, no battalions; all I have is words. To defend the highest values of the national culture we only have words'.[13] The students however believed there were other means as well.

On March 8 1968, some five thousand students assembled (peacefully) at Warsaw University to protest against the expulsion of two student leaders, Adam Michnik and Henryk Szlajfer, from the University. The violent attempt by the police to disperse the crowd, provoked angry student resistance and two weeks of student protest (demonstrations, petitions, sit-ins) in several Polish cities, the most active centres of the movement being Warsaw, Wroclaw and Kraców.[14] A detailed account of the March events is clearly beyond the scope of this study, however the following points deserve to be made here. The March movement was undoubtedly the largest mass protest movement to appear in Eastern Europe since 1956; on March 11 over 10,000 students were in the streets battling with the police.

The 'commando' group of student activists or the 'third' generation of dissidents had been in the forefront of agitation at the universities throughout the sixties. However, on March 8 1968, the day when the movement acquired a mass dimension in its confrontation with the state apparatus, its leaders were already arrested, and their role became artificially magnified by the official media for propaganda purposes. The chief characteristics of the student movement were spontaneity, massiveness and little emphasis on ideology. Most resolutions adopted by the students in March focused on specific demands concerning intellectual freedom and the organisational autonomy of the representative student bodies. The declaration of Warsaw University students, on 28 March combined statements presenting the March crisis as reflection of political tensions in the society, with specific demands concerning the student and intellectual body, such as the need for the 'reactivation of a journal for students and young intelligentsia which will assure a large social echo to the political preoccupation of the youth'.[15] The reference to ideology was minimal. Sentences such as 'We believe that the awareness of the possibility of discussion of all problems will be a step forward on that road which brings socialism closer to the community'[16] can hardly be seen as a proof of the influence of the ideologically motivated 'commando' group; it is rather an indication of the general framework within which the students saw their action. In trying to break their isolation and communicate with the rest of the society, the students saw no other alternative than to address the authorities in the name of commonly shared values. The use of 'official nationalism' by the authorities served two purposes: it helped exploit social dissent to obtain desired outcomes in intra-party power struggles and won popular support for the regime's repressive anti-intellectual policies.

To discredit the student movement the official media resorted to an anti-Semitic campaign, which has had no equivalent in Eastern Europe since the Nazi era. The crypto-communist daily of the Catholic group, Pax, *Slowo Powszechne* in its issue of March 11 led by the pre-war antisemitic campaigner Piasecki, gave the most comprehensive version of the plot. It was picked up immediately by the party press and went something like this: The March events were only part of a larger Zionist plot.[17] The 'commandos' were, under the cover of democratic demands, promoting Zionist interests. Where could the proof of their Zionists demands be found? In their names: Szlajfer, Zambrowski, Werfel, Blumsztajn, Dacjgewand, Michnik . . . The dissidents were presented as the privileged children of high party officials who had been 'responsible for the illegalities of the Stalinist era'. Unable to preserve the Stalinist system they had reverted openly to Jewish nationalism. After the 'Six Day War' the alleged plotters began working 'directly or indirectly in the service of the anti-Polish policy of the FRG'. Indeed the campaign contained in a concentrated form the necessary ingredients to discredit the student movement and its 'Zionist' or 'revisionist' sponsors, and this partly accounts for the authorities' successful containment of the movement within intellectual circles. The exploitation of the anti-Jewish and anti-German issues can be summed up under the term 'official nationalism'. It did not represent a resurgence of nationalistic feelings within the society, but rather an attempt to revive and manipulate latent nationalistic and anti-Semitic feelings by the so-called Partisan faction in the party for the purpose of its factional struggle.[18]

The March events also brought into the open the challenge to Gomułka from the 'Partisan' nationalistic faction led by the Minister of the Interior, General Moczar, who not only tried to present himself as a law and order man, but also used the campaign against 'Zionism' and 'revisionism' to purge all the opponents of the Partisans from the party and from public life in general.

Whether or not one adopts the 'provocation' theory as the key to the March 1968 'explosion' in Poland, an essential characteristic of the latter is that it brought into the open and exacerbated simmering group conflicts in the party apparatus. The intellectual unrest of 1968 indicated the limits of Gomułka's 'little stabilisation' which led to stagnation in the party and state apparatus. The open crisis of the society expressed by the movement introduced a transitional stage in the rise of a certain modernistic current in the party leadership which would only be completed with Gierek's accession to power in December 1970. Here also lies the link between the otherwise isolated explosions of unrest in 1968 and 1970-1. It was pressure from below, however manipulated and suppressed, which revealed conflicts and catalysed changes in the political structure.

The final blow to the 'revisionist' concept of opposition came with the Warsaw Pact invasion of Czechoslovakia in August 1968. The Prague Spring undoubtedly fostered a growing pressure for the democratisation of the socialist system. During the March demonstration the students shouted, 'Poland is waiting for her Dubček'.[19] Indeed the risk of contagion in Poland was high and Gomułka proved to be one of the most vehement advocates of the Soviet-led invasion. For the opposition the political conclusions to be drawn from the 1968 invasion were the opposite from those drawn after the invasion of Hungary. In 1956 the Soviet armed intervention in Budapest was seen as demonstrating the risks involved in a movement outside the control of the communist party, and thus seemed to confirm the soundness of the revisionist approach. The invasion of Czechoslovakia, on the contrary, seemed to prove that any in-depth reform from above and within the system was eventually doomed in the Soviet bloc as a whole, because, in the final analysis, Moscow feared revisionism within the party as much as spontaneous national outbursts from below.

In the same way that the Prague Spring gave a new lease of life to the revisionist hopes, so the invasion of Czechoslovakia shattered the belief that Stalinist repression had been the product of a specific phase in Soviet history and aberration which would be removed through the gradual regeneration of the socialist system.[20] The invasion also put an end to the opposition's belief that the party liberals shared with it the same values and that protest should therefore be directed to the party authorities and formulated in a language acceptable to them. The reformist attempts of the Khrushchevian de-Stalinisation era had failed, and the revisionists were totally eliminated from the party and other institutions, and the crushing of the Czechoslovak experiment, for a time also reduced the Polish opposition's capacity to act. But in the long run these events started a new process: the opposition had to rethink the premises of its activity and gradually formulate a new concept of opposition, no longer based on an attempt to regenerate the party but rather the whole Polish society.

THE POLISH WORKERS' STRIKE 1970–71

If the workers remained passive during the intellectuals' confrontation with the authorities in March 1968 it was hardly because they had no motives for discontent. In fact, during the late 1950s and 1960s the manual workers had lost gradually their two main postwar gains. The first was the relative improvement in economic status, which they owed to Stalinist egalitarianism and levelling concept of socio-economic development. The second, the workers' councils as institutions of workers' self-management, was introduced at the time of the breakdown of the Stalinist system during the Polish October of 1956.[21] The contradictory nature of the workers' 'gains' in the 1950s illustrates their ambivalent relationship to the regime and, at least partly, explains their complex and difficult relationship with the intelligentsia.

After 1958 the workers' councils had become subordinated to the party through so-called conferences of workers' autonomy[22] while the trade unions and the party recovered their 'leading role' in the factory. The survival of the workers' councils was merely formal. A study published in 1967 shows that the leadership of workers' councils became totally dominated by managers and engineering and technical personnel.[23] The workers had lost all genuine channels to voice dissatisfaction. This explains in part the suddenness and radicality of their action in December 1970.

The second major reason for workers' dissatisfaction was the relative deterioration of their economic situation. Between 1956–60 the monthly income of the industrial worker grew at an average rate of 9 per cent p.a.[24] According to a Politburo report published after the December–January strikes the average annual rise in the 1960s dropped to less than 2 per cent. Some groups even actually witnessed a drop in real wages. As the report puts it: 'Since the proportion of the cost of food in the cost of living rose relatively rapidly, its negative consequences were felt particularly by the families with the lowest incomes . . .'[25] Parallel and certainly no less important was the decline since the late 1950s on the social mobility and the growth of income differentials between the workers and technical intelligentsia.[26] These differentials were strongly resented by the manual workers. A survey conducted by Nowak in 1961 clearly shows that egalitarian tendencies were stronger among workers than among the intelligentsia.[27] Although this may account to some extent for the lack of unity of action between intellectuals and workers in 1968 and 1970 it is also interesting to note the resentment against this situation is primarily directed against the state, in its capacity as the chief economic and social regulator. This resentment is stronger among unskilled workers than in any other social group since they not only feel most strongly about inequality, but also they are the most pessimistic about the likelihood of its reduction.[28]

The social origin of university students is another factor that might help shed some light on the worker-student relationship. After a period of drastic 'affirmative action' in favour of the workers in the early 1950s, when almost one third of students were of working class origin, the figure had dropped to a quarter by 1967–8 while the percentage of students of intelligentsia backgrounds had steadily grown.[29] Although this figure is still high by western standards, this decline of working class educational mobility might explain why, in 1968, the authorities' attempt to present the students to the workers as a privileged minority held some appeal.

It is against this background of the relative decline of the workers' economic position, the stagnation of living standards and neglect of consumer needs, that we can examine the workers' response to the sudden food price increase of December 12 1970. A strike developed in three phases revealing different aspects of the working class crises in Poland.[30] The first strike occurred immediately after the announcement of the food price rise. It started on Monday, December 14 1970 at the Lenin shipyard in Gdańsk. While union officials were reluctant to take any action, the workers demonstrated in the streets, shouting 'Bread' and 'The press lies'. They went to the local Polytechnic to ask the students to join them but were unsuccessful.[31] The party buildings were set on fire and clashes with the police continued throughout the evening.

The disturbances spread to practically all the industrial cities of the Baltic coast, and the massacre of December 17[32] only served to deepen the gulf between workers and the authorities. By then it was the

Szczecin Adolf Warski shipyard strike committee which appeared as the leading and coordinating force of the movement and which also formulated the workers' demands. Firstly, they demanded the 'resignation of the Central Trade Union Council which fails to defend the interests of the working class' and asked for the formation of an independent trade union. Other demands included a return to the price levels in force before December 12, and salary rises of 30 per cent. The incapacity of the Gomułka-Cyrankiewicz leadership to deal with the workers' crisis by means other than repression provoked (as with the students in 1968) open divisions in the party leadership, and created the conditions for the emergence of an alternate leadership. On December 18, following seven hours of discussion in the Politbureau, Gomułka was asked to resign, and the next day Edward Gierek became First Secretary. He immediately blamed previous leadership for the mistakes and promised change. The strikes were called off one by one. This first phase could be characterised as spontaneous workers' strikes and riots sparked by essentially economic causes though their political dimension becomes obvious because it is a strike against the state – the only employer – and the main targets of workers' demonstrations were the party headquarters.

The second phase of the strike movement, again started at Gdańsk this time on January 7, and by the 20th had spread to Gdynia and Szczecin, the two cities which became its centre. This time the workers struck against Gierek and the inability of the new leadership to heal the wounds of December. The January strike was more openly political. The workers still demanded the return to the pre-December prices, but the emphasis was mainly on democratically elected organs of the party, trade unions, and factory workers councils (a leftover from 1956); and insisted on the dissemination of factual information about the repression of their movement. The workers wanted to make sure their voice would be heard and decided, on the suggestion of the strike leader, on an unlimited strike until the state authorities would come to negotiate with them. And indeed Gierek and new Premier Jaroszewicz, on January 24 in Szczecin had an unprecedented dialogue with the workers. Gierek presented himself as a former worker, and a competent, successful administrator of his constituency, Silesia. He put all the blame on Gomułka; then proceeded to raise the alleged manifestations of anti-Sovietism (an indirect allusion to the risks involved) and concluded with an analysis of the economic difficulties which prevented him from satisfying their demands. He conceded to most of the workers' demands, especially those supposed to provide

better workers' participation of their representative organs, but he did
not concede to the two most important ones, which had provoked the
first and also the second wave of strikes: the price increases and the
demand to publish in the press the truth about the repression and the
list of workers' demands.[33] The workers asserted to Gierek that the
motives for their strike had been purely economic and openly denounced the official arguments for the price changes which held that
the rise of food prices was balanced by the decrease in the price of
certain consumer goods. They denounced the social repression of the
economic reform. In the words of delegate W3: '2600 and even 3000
złotys represents nothing at the current prices, especially if there are
three or four people to support. . . . What will it bring to us if there are
goods (on the market) and if we don't have any money? We'll remain
hungry. Because "when a Pole is hungry, he becomes angry". Hence
the origin of all the present conflicts. It stems directly from our
dissatisfaction'.[34]

Despite the violence of the repression the workers were unclear
about the nature of their relationship with the party and government.
They saw these ties, even after the bloodbath, in both class and
national terms. Delegate K1 said: 'What is really difficult to take is that
it is our hard earned money which paid for these very bullets which
were shot against us . . . How is it possible for workers to shoot against
workers (us)? After all, aren't we brothers, part of one people? And
what would have happened if . . . as in 1939 somebody tried to take
advantage of the situation.'[35] What they expressed most forcefully
both in their demands and in the dialogue with Gierek was the need to
institutionalise new channels of communication between rulers and
ruled. Delegate W2: 'I would like a clear and frank answer from the
First Secretary of the PUWP. Is it necessary to shed blood in order to
change the Central Committee and the government? Is it not possible
to consider a fixed term of office in order to avoid a repetition of 1956
and 1970?'[36] It was on this question of establishing genuine channels
of communication that the authorities were prepared to meet, at least
partially, the strike committee's demands. Indeed Gierek surprised the
workers when approving the idea of free elections in the trade union
and workers 'council'. He even approved that the strike committee
should become a 'workers' commission' in charge of supervising these
elections. The strike committee remained the only real authority in the
shipyard from the end of the strike on January 25 until the election.
However, due primarily to the strike leaders' inexperience, they did
not preserve that role.[37]

Soon the party's 'loyal' opposition within the strike committee took over the functions which they had previously performed. So the elections brought back into office the party member shop steward and progressive 'normalisation' of the shipyard workers was on the way. The general conclusion that can be drawn from the Szczecin experiment in direct democracy is that organs of direct democracy represent a radical challenge to the authority of the state and that they emerge in situations when, as a consequence of a spontaneous movement from below, there is a temporary crisis or collapse of the state authority. However, as soon as the state authority is established, as gradually happened in Poland between January and February 1971, the mobilisation declines and the organs of direct democracy either collapse or are absorbed into the system.

The third phase of the winter 1970–71 strike movement in Poland presented yet another type of worker-strike conflict. At the beginning of February the Gierek leadership thought it had successfully survived an unprecedented strike wave without giving in on the question of food prices which lay at the root of the movement. However, on February 11 over 10,000 predominantly women workers in the textile industry in Łódź went on strike over new work norms and food prices.[38] Premier Jaroszewicz was dispatched to Łódź hoping, as in Szczecin, to solve the crisis through direct dialogue with the workers, but this time the response was different. Demands were simply shouted from the floor and the Prime Minister hardly got a chance to speak. Finally when, according to reports, he managed to ask the strikers, 'Are you going to help us?' the workers answered, 'No! It's your turn to help us first.'[39] Confronted with a movement with which no communication seemed possible, on February 15 the government announced that it had decided to cancel the December food price rises.

Two different types of the workers' population produced two different types of industrial action. The Szczecin workers, with their own representative bodies and demands for the official recognition of their right to strike, no doubt presented a more serious political challenge to the party and union authority in the factories. But it was the Łódź workers, with their uncompromising economic stance though without representation, who forced the regime to back down.

The lasting result of the workers' 1970–1 strike lies in the de facto veto power gained by the workers over government economic policies. A power that was to be remembered and reasserted in 1976. The workers had showed remarkable capacity for resistance in defence of their economic interest. But in their challenge to the authorities they did not openly formulate an alternative to the existing economic power structure, and a positive programme for the society as a whole. The specific nature of workers' demands, as well as the suppression and demoralisation of the intellectual opposition between 1968–70, partly accounts for the lack of worker-intellectual communication or cooperation during the crisis. On the other hand, the strike recreated, after more than 14 or even 30 years, a strong sense of solidarity and confidence among the workers. This strike was the first successful strike movement in postwar Eastern Europe. As such, it represented a major turning point in working class cohesion and in the relations between the different social groups and the state power. Here lie the origins of the new worker-intellectual relationship that was to emerge between 1976 and 1977.

MERITOCRACY AND 'CONSULTATION': THE PARTY AND THE SOCIETY UNDER GIEREK

The December 1970 revolt on the Baltic coast revealed the gulf separating the workers from the party and thus shook the very foundations of the latter's political legitimacy. Beyond the official explanations of Gomulka's 'isolation'[40] the revolt revealed the explosive social dimension of the economic crisis and the inadequacy of the trade unions, and other mass organisations, as instruments of social control. Thus Gierek's programme of modernisation, combining the 'rationalisation' of the economy with greater flexibility of state and party institutions, was designed to remedy this situation and prevent another similar explosion, without at the same time reviving the 'revisionist temptation'. March 1968 in Warsaw and August 1968 in Prague were still on everybody's minds.

This double concern guided Gierek's reforms and explains not only their pragmatic thrust but also – and this is of greater significance for future developments – their limits.

On the political level the replacement of Gomulka by Gierek represented the last episode in the transition from the old time ideologists to a more pragmatic and technocratically minded party elite. The new elite's claim to rule, as A. Bromke pointed out, is not based – as was that of the Gomulka group – on long participation in the revolutionary struggle, but rather on educational achievement and administrative experience.[41] Moczar and his supporters from the Partisan faction, had been promptly demoted. Each tide of unrest in Poland brought in its wake the elimination of a party faction. In 1956, it was the Stalinists, in 1968 the so-called 'Zionist-revisionists', in 1970, it was both the Gomułka group and the authoritarian nationalist faction led by General Moczar. So, paradoxically, the first successful strike against a communist party in power in Eastern Europe also helped to bring about a homogenisation of the party elite, a greater unity in the leadership.

Following his revitalisation of the party elite, Gierek strived to reshape the party apparatus, in order to consolidate changes at the top and also to try to make it more responsive to pressures from below. The operation began with a massive screening of the party membership and resulted in a purge of some 100,000 party members.[42] During the riots on the Baltic coast workers attacked primarily provincial party officers, thus particular attention was devoted, by the central party authorities, to re-establishing a relationship between factory party organisations and the provincial (Wojewodstwo) committees. The proportion of manual workers in the provincial executive committees rose from 25 per cent in 1969 to 37 per cent in 1974.[43] This effect, however significant from the institutional point of view, could not remedy the basic problem: that of disaffection of workers from the party. While their proportion was steadily increasing in the society (50 per cent in 1970) it was at the same time declining in the party membership: from 64.7 per cent in 1946 to 39.6 per cent in 1973.[44] The erosion of the working class base of the Polish United Workers' Party (PUWP) continued after the December events up until 1975. Despite efforts to promote workers to strategic posts in the provincial party committees, the main feature of the social composition under Gierek has been a closer correlation between education, qualification and party membership. To the extent that levels of party membership are indicators for any given social group of a degree of political participation, one can say that the main beneficiaries of the reshaping of the party under Gierek were certainly not manual workers but primarily the scientific and technical intelligentsia.[45]

The limits to workers' participation appeared even more clearly in the trade unions. On January 27 1971, Gierek told the striking workers he 'totally' supported the second point of their demands for 'immediate and legal elections to the trade unions and the works councils . . .'[46] But in spite of rather minor changes, trade unions, after a congress held in November 1972, soon resumed their role as 'transmission belts' of the party line.

A similar tendency can be found in the new leadership's attempt to reinforce the authority of the state. The most significant attempt to improve the communication between the state and its citizens was a far-reaching administrative reform introduced by stages since 1972. The structure and size of the provincial administration (both state and party), traditionally conservative strongholds, was altered: forty-nine new provincial authorities were introduced instead of seventeen.[47] To sum up, one can say that besides the economic concessions granted to the workers, the regime carried out important changes in both the party organisation and the state institutions, in order to make them more flexible, more responsive to pressure from below, and essentially more efficient, but without creating genuine channels of participation in economic management or in the political system: rationalisation and decentralisation rather than actual democratisation of decision-making. This was in line with the technocratic spirit of the institutional reforms of the Gierek leadership. In order to avoid a repetition of the December crisis Gierek was anxious not to lose touch with public opinion. Decision-making was to take into account the voice of the press, the findings of the Centre for Public Opinion Research attached to the Radio, 'readers' mail' in various papers, and complaints made to the administrations.[48] Investigation of public opinion was seen as a substitute for democratisation.

But behind Gierek's attempt to make the state and party ostensibly more responsive to the society there was an attempt to win a new type of consensus among the Polish people. This was to be achieved by launching Poland into an exciting drive to modernise the economy and raise living standards. This change reflected the new stage of the country's economic development. The Polish economy had been shifting, since the 1960s, from the 'extensive' model of development based on heavy industry and high capital investment, to an 'intensive' concept of a more diversified economy with stress put on new technology and increased productivity of labour. During the 1950s (in the period of 'extensive' development) the regime relied on coercion and ideological mobilisation. The officially promoted egalitarianism, an essential component of the ideological legitimation of the regime, corresponded with the scarcity of available consumer goods. However, the intensive phase with its more diversified methods of production and thus also of the labour force, as well as a greater volume and variety of consumer goods available, eroded the rigid egalitarian ideology of the 1950s and was replaced progressively by a 'meritocratic' model reintroducing unequal income distribution according to the nature of work accomplished and individual skills required.[49] The meritocratic model of society is central to understanding the limits of Gierek's political reforms and his focus on economic modernisation.[50]

The chief beneficiary of the new meritocratic mobilisations under Gierek was the scientific and technical intelligentsia who were the most directly involved in the rationalisation of economic management. This had two main consequences with regard to the subsequent development of oppositional activity among intellectuals and workers. Firstly, it accentuated the differentiation between the scientific and the creative intelligentsia. In the 1960s both participated in the 'revisionist' attempt to rid Polish society of the Stalinist heritage even though in their rejection of the centralised bureaucracy, philosophers or writers, placed more emphasis on democratic freedoms while the scientists saw 'incompetence' as the main obstacle to modernisation. Under Gierek the scientific intelligentsia found new scope for its aspiration,[51] while the creative intelligentsia's quiescence depended, at least in a first phase, on the tolerated degree of freedom of expression.

Secondly, a parallel differentiation which the reforms were designed to bring to manual workers (skilled/non-skilled) has not developed, at least not on a sufficient scale to win a significant proportion of manual workers for the anti-levelling, meritocratic logic of the economic reforms. Thus the workers' tacit support remained merely based upon the food-price concessions won in the strike of 1970–1. For a time it seemed that the regime had recovered from the traumas of 1968 and 1970 and achieved a greater degree of stability: real incomes of workers were going up, generous economic incentives (higher procurement prices) and security (free health care) were offered to the peasants; Church–state relations had improved; travel abroad eased, the press was made slightly freer and intellectuals allowed greater freedom of expression.

However, by 1974 difficulties began to build up on all fronts; the international recession was a blow to Gierek's economic strategy, the full impact of which would be felt in June 1976. The return to ideological orthodoxy brought with it new curbs on intellectual freedom and the first signs of tension between Church and state. The tone of the ideological offensive was set by Jan Szydlak, a Politburo member, who at a conference of ideological activity in March 1974 developed a theme dear to Soviet ideologists, linking détente to the intensification of the ideological struggle: '. . . Under the conditions of peaceful coexistence the significance of ideological struggle increases considerably.'[52] This was promptly translated into cultural policy guidelines by party secretary Jerzy Lukaszewicz: The content of cultural creation 'must be consistent with socialist ideology' and had as a task to prove the necessity of close ties with the Soviet Union. The party would support only those artists who understood their role as a 'social service to the nation'.[53] As the limited freedoms enjoyed by intellectuals, after Edward Gierek came to power, slowly vanished, the relations between the intellectuals and the party deteriorated bringing a revival of oppositional activity. It is against this background that one has to understand the expression of dissent among intellectuals and workers in 1975–76.

THE HUMAN RIGHTS MOVEMENT

The question of the Polish minority living in the Soviet Union since the war and a petition also known as the 'Letter of the 15'[54] addressed to the liberal Minister of Culture, Józef Tejchma, was perhaps the first public manifestation of concern with human rights in Poland in the 1970s. The petition asked that the authorities devote the same attention to their fate as they do to that of Poles living in the west. This expression of discontent was the prelude to the emergence, at the turn of 1975–6, of a widespread human rights movement among Polish intellectuals which had the support of the powerful Catholic Church. And it was the opposition to constitutional amendments in late 1975-early 1976 that crystallised the emergence of human rights movement in Poland and laid the foundations for cooperation between lay intellectuals and the Catholic Church.

In December 1975 the substance of amendments to the 1952 Constitution was revealed at the VIIth party congress. The two most controversial amendments concerned the stipulation of the 'leading role of the Polish United Workers' Party' in the Polish state which was to be renamed Polish Socialist Republic, and a second proposal to include in the constitution a reference to the 'unshakeable and fraternal bonds with the Soviet Union'.[55] Both became the targets of the opposition campaign. The commitment to perpetual alliance with the Soviet Union, as a legalised updated version of the Brezhnev doctrine, was seen as an unacceptable limitation of national sovereignty especially in an era of colonial emancipation and recognition of state sovereignty by international documents such as the Helsinki agreement (Letter of the 14).[56] Second, the recognition in the constitution of the 'leading role of the party' in the state, and the tying of civil rights to the performance of duties, made other human rights provisions meaningless leaving the party the possibility of depriving non-conformist citizens of their rights (Letter of the 101).[57]

But possibly the most significant among the numerous protest letters was signed by 59 prominent intellectuals and sent to the Speaker of the Sejm (the Polish Parliament).[58] It did not explicitly discuss any particular amendment, but demanded that the Polish constitution be brought into harmony with international human rights conventions signed by the Polish government. Refering explicitly to the Helsinki conference and to the Universal Declaration of Human Rights the signatories called for guarantees of the following rights: Freedom of conscience and religious practice ('All citizens irrespective of their religion, ideology or party-political affiliation, must be assured of equal rights to take up government posts'); Freedom of work (free trade unions, the right to strike); Freedom of speech and exchange of information (abolition of censorship); Freedom of education (autonomy for Universities). By January 1976 some two hundred prominent political cultural or religious figures had signed the manifesto. Within a few weeks the government was submerged by a flood of collective petitions and individual protest letters.

Although the official press ignored the campaign the authorities were clearly taken aback by its strength and ended up meeting the opposition half-way: the controversial formulation of the 'unshakeable' bonds with the Soviet Union became in the final version: 'Poland strengthens its friendship and cooperation with the USSR and other socialist countries'. Similarly, the PUWP was presented as the 'leading force in the construction of socialism' and not in the 'state' as initially envisaged. The linkage between the rights and the duties was dropped as well. The text was finally voted with one abstention – that of Professor Stomma of the Znak group.[59]

Because of the reference of the Manifesto of the 59 to the Helsinki agreement, its focus on the discrepancy between constitutionally guaranteed civil rights and the practice of the regime and because it sparked off public protest by several hundred people, the Manifesto of the 59 can be considered as the antecedent of the Charter 77 human rights movement launched in Czechoslovakia a year later.[60]

The Polish constitutional campaign marked the beginning of a new type of oppositional movement no longer challenging the legitimacy of the communist regime in the name of the official ideology, but merely asking the regime to observe the laws it had itself introduced. Another entirely new aspect of oppositional activity was the skilful exploitation of east–west détente and of the moral support received from western governments or public opinion.

A central feature of the Polish human rights movement was the interplay between the defence of national sovereignty and of individual civil rights. Both are deeply rooted in the profoundly pluralistic ethos of the Polish political culture.[61] Clearly the constitution was perceived as a bridge between the two as witnessed by the fact that during the constitutional controversy the human rights campaigners explicitly referred to that historic document of Polish national liberty, the Constitution of May 3, 1791.[62]

It had been argued that for historical reasons, the foci of traditional political identification in Poland have been the nation, national culture and religion; this accounts for the primacy of the collective national concern over the issue of individual civil rights.[63] In 1975–6 constitutional movement of the defence of national sovereignty and of individual civil rights seems to have coalesced.

The irony in this case was that the Polish opposition defended a constitution inherited from the Stalinist era (1952) against that promoted under a more pragmatic and tolerant regime. The explanation lies in the fact that the Polish 1952 Constitution (like the famous Soviet 1936 Constitution) was essentially a propaganda statement, not a legal code actually regulating relationship between the state and the citizens. In contrast the Gierek 1976 Constitution (as well as the 1977 Brezhnev Constitution) was designed to narrow the gulf between the constitution and reality,[64] and thus provide a new source of ideological and legal legitimacy. Instead, the human rights campaigners argued that the best way to bridge the gulf between the old constitution and reality was to start applying the former.

THE 'SOCIAL CONTRACT' AND WORKERS' STRIKES OF JUNE 1976

History does repeat itself. Indeed, on the surface, the events of June 1976 appear to be a replay of those of December 1970. On June 24 Premier Jaroszewicz presented to the Sejm a proposal providing for a dramatic increase in basic food prices by an average of 70 per cent (butter 50 per cent, meat and fish 69 per cent, sugar 100 per cent). The next morning workers in several factories throughout the country went on strike and in some cases demonstrated in the streets.[65] In the Ursus tractor factory, near Warsaw, workers broke up the main railroad line. In Radom the workers from the Walter weapon factory, joined by women from the Radoskor shoe factory, marched to the party headquarters and demanded that senior party officials come from Warsaw to discuss the price increases. When they realised that no such delegation would be sent, demonstrators set fire to the party headquarters and violent confrontation with the police continued through the night. That night (June 25) Premier Jaroszewicz reappeared on television and stated that in view of the 'valuable amendments and contributions' put forward by the workers the government withdrew its price increase proposal and would, after further consultation, re-examine the matter. The protest stopped immediately and workers resumed work the next morning.[66]

The June 1976 scenario (price increases – spontaneous workers' action – cancellation of the increase and immediate end of the movement) bears some resemblance to that of December 1970, with the difference that the crisis lasted merely two days instead of two months. If one can say that Gierek had not really learnt from December 1970 what it is that sparks working class unrest, he *had* learnt when to back down and how to handle the crisis once it had broken out. Despite the similarities between the two crises there are important differences in their causes and context. First, the economic situation and the social condition of the working class had changed considerably. The 1970 explosion came after a decade of quasi stagnation in the growth rate of the economy and a relative deterioration in workers' living standards. In contrast, the Gierek period can be considered as one of economic boom with rapid growth of the GNP (estimated between 10–12 per cent a year from 1970 to 1975), and of investment (91.5 per cent increase in comparison with the 1966–70 period). Real wages went up by over 40 per cent (7 per cent a year, while food prices remained at their 1966 level.[67] Traditional patterns of East European economic development have seen periods with heavy emphasis on investment in heavy industry alternating with periods of increased consumption.[68] Gierek's economic strategy was an attempt to pursue fast growth on both fronts: investment and consumption. This meant basically a faster growth of national income distributed over income produced, and was achieved only by a big increase in international debt, which reached $10 billion in 1976. By 1974 the oil crisis and recessions in the west had shown that the East European economies were not insulated from the troubles of the capitalist west. Prices of imported western technology and of Soviet oil went up; wages continued to grow while food prices remained stagnant. The price increases had become a necessity. Clearly, the country was living beyond its means and needed to be told so. The question was how. In contrast to the 1970–1 situation, the 1976 food price riots followed a period of substantial improvement in workers' living standards and thus do not sustain a strictly economic explanation. In the Polish post-December 1970 context the question of price stability had clearly a political dimension. It was used by Gierek to win popular support when he took over from Gomułka and this became a central factor in preserving his political legitimacy. As we have seen earlier Gierek's response to the 1970 riots failed to provide channels of communication or coordination among workers, who did however share a common perception of the price issue as central to their relationship with the government. The price rise announcement acted in a sense as a unifying signal for industrial action.

In more general terms, relations between the authorities and the workers in Poland, as in the rest of the Soviet bloc, are based on a tacit social contract (inherited from the Stalinist era).[69] The regime provides job security and slow but regular increases in the standards of living. In exchange, workers forfeit their traditional union, political and civil rights. But if one side decided unilaterally to break this tacit contract – through price increases for instance – the other side is also likely to do so and either ask for a return to the previous state of things or claim back the forfeited rights. The 1970–1 strikes started with the first alternative (the abolition of price increases) and later saw the development of the second alternative (free workers' representation). In June 1976 it was the brevity of the explosions which accounts for the fact that the movement did not formulate its own alternative independent representations to articulate workers' demands. This is precisely what the regime wanted to avoid and thus it preferred to return to the old terms of the social contract. However, now not only stable prices but also significant growth of real wages were part of what workers expected from the social contract.

After the 1970–1 events the key word was 'consultation' with the workers in order to avoid another explosion. Gierek regularly visited factories and his personal popularity undoubtedly benefited from this. However, neither occasional contact with leaders, nor the most sophisticated opinion polls and sociological surveys of the working class proved to be a sufficient substitute for genuine institutionalised channels of communication.[70] The result was that workers achieved a power of *veto* over certain government policies, but not that of positive participation in the making of these policies.[71]

The June 1976 events failed to remedy the fundamental inability of the existing structures to absorb popular discontent. The Gierek regime was caught in an insoluble dilemma: it has inherited from the Stalinist era of 'extensive' economic development a pattern of industrial relations which is now understood by the authorities as being harmful to the present ('intensive') stage of development of the Polish economy. On the other hand, any attempt to alter profoundly the system of industrial relations, and by extension the 'social contract' on which the very foundation of the regime's stability rests, involves risks neither Gierek nor anybody else in the leadership seems prepared to take.

INTELLECTUALS' AND WORKERS' OPPOSITION

The June 1976 events open an entirely new phase in the development of the Polish opposition, based on the collaboration of two of its essential components, the intellectuals and the workers. The relationship between the two is central to the understanding of the development of the Polish opposition. Since the death of Stalin the sequence of regime–opposition confrontations included periods of intellectual unrest (1955–6; 1968; 1975–6) followed by worker action (Poznań, June 1956, the Baltic coast strikes of December–January 1970–1, June 1976). Between 1956 and 1976 new patterns of workers' and intellectuals' opposition developed. In March 1968 intellectuals and students demanded greater freedom of expression but remained isolated from the workers; in December 1970 the intellectuals stood by as police fired into the workers' demonstration. However, the repression which followed the June 1976 food price riots gave birth to a worker-intellectual alliance of a new type. Clearly, the timing, or 'synchronisation' of the two movements, was essential to their convergence: the June 1976 worker action followed immediately after the intellectual protest against constitutional amendments in the first months of 1976. The workers' action itself was too brief (one day) to establish any contacts. It was the antiworker repression which lasted throughout the summer of 1976, which provided the conditions for the human rights movement to link up with the workers' opposition.

The authorities' response to the June 25 events was both conciliatory and coercive. At first, they staged mass meetings in factories designed to show working class support for the Gierek leadership. However immediately thereafter repressive measures (arrests, dismissals and trials) were introduced against workers involved in the June strikes. According to estimates, some 2000 people were originally detained by the police at Radom and 500 at Ursus.[72] By November there was evidence of 261 persons sentenced either by a court or a special tribunal in Radom and 112 in Ursus.[73] The prison sentences ranged from a month to ten years. Dismissals from work were also reported from Nowy Targ, Łódź, Gdańsk, Pruszcz, Elblag, Szczecin, Starachawice and Warsaw – an indirect confirmation of the widespread character of the June 25th strike.

Both as a formidable force, with the capacity to topple the government and as a social group particularly deprived of democratic rights, the industrial workers became important to the opposition intellectuals' vision of the society's problems. The letter of the 59 said under the chapter 'Freedom of work':

> There is no such freedom while the State is the sole employer, and while the Trade Unions are forced to conform to the administration of the party which actually wields the power in the State. In conditions such as these – as events of 1956 and 1970 testify – any attempts to protect the workers' interests are threatened by bloodshed and can lead to serious outbreaks of violence. For this reason employees must be assured that their own trade representation is independent of both the State and the Party. The right to strike must also be guaranteed.[74]

And indeed since the end of June the main focus of activity of the human rights movement has been the defence of workers' right to strike. A few days after the strikes opposition intellectuals came out in support of the workers with a series of declarations protesting police brutality. Statements of this kind were not addressed to the authorities but to the workers or to public opinion.[75] It was this idea of expressing solidarity and establishing direct contacts with the protesting workers that lay at the roots of the Workers' Defence Committee (KOR) created in September 1976. The 14 member Committee included some of the most well known names of Polish cultural life: the writer Jerzy Andrzejewski, the economist Edward Lipinski, the actress Halina Mikolajska, Jacek Kuroń, a leading figure in the opposition movement since the early 1960s. The 'Appeal to the People and the Government of Poland' launched on 23 September asked for an investigation into police brutality against the workers and set itself to provide financial and legal assistance for victimised workers and their families.[76]

The Committee organised collections for the workers and within a

year distributed over 3,000,000 złoty to workers in need. In line with
its first appeal, which stated its conviction that 'public exposure of the
conduct of the authorities can provide an effective means of defence',
the Committee distributed through samizdat channels 'The Information Bulletin' (26 issues) and communiques publicising all known cases
of anti-worker repression.[77] In doing so the Committee performed a
double role: it provided immediate aid to the workers and mobilised
public opinion in order to put pressure on the government. In the
initial phase the first aspect had priority and the Workers' Defence
Committee attempted to play the role of a substitute trade union. As
communique no. 3 stated: 'Since the trade unions, the social welfare
agencies and official bodies whose duties should include the defence of
workers' interests are unable or unwilling to do so, a voluntary group
had to take over their responsibilities.'[78]

From this relief action there developed a second wave of workers'
protests. Conscious of the support they enjoyed among the people and
resorting to what was until then considered to be a traditional
'intellectual-dissident' method, 889 workers from Ursus sent on 9
November a protest letter to the Polish government asking that all
those who had been dismissed from work as a result of the strike and
demonstrations of 25th June be reinstated.[79] Two days later the
Workers' Defence Committee fully endorsed the Ursus workers'
letter, called this action an 'example for all working people subject to
repression', and expressed the hope that it would be the embryo of a
'spontaneously growing self-defence organisation as a first step towards a full and authentic representation of workers' interests'.[80]

Later (March 1st) Jacek Kuroń explained in an interview that the
implementation of such an organisation would only be possible with
the aid of intellectuals, who could help to spread the solidarity movement throughout the country and provide specialised expertise in
order to challenge government and official trade union economic
policies.[81]

The project of an independent workers organisation did not
materialise despite the KOR efforts. The workers' collective petition
did not produce immediate concrete results; the disappointment that
followed increased police pressure on the signatories put an end to this
unique attempt to organise a collective protest. On the other hand,
intellectual opposition took a new lease on life with a KOR-initiated
campaign of petitions to the Sejm demanding the creation of a
Commission to inquire into the behaviour of the police in the June
1976 events.[82]

From February 3 1977, when Gierek first announced at Ursus that he planned an amnesty for imprisoned workers who regretted their part in the June food price riots, to 22nd July, when amnesty was actually granted, protest activity among workers gradually subsided while still broader sectors of the creative intelligentsia and students became involved with the opposition. Similarly, oppositional activity was gradually shifting from the specific defence of workers' rights to the defence of democratic freedoms in other areas of social life.

The KOR experiment is of interest in gaining an understanding of the worker-intellectual relationship for the following reasons. It can claim some credit for the amnesty, and thus helped created a precedent, showing that collaboration of this kind can force the regime to make concessions. The Committee represents an entirely new attempt to establish ties, based on solidarity, between two social groups independent of official institutions. However, the initiative for the creation of the Committee came from the intellectuals, and solidarity with workers proved a powerful mobiliser, for intellectuals and students, who from there moved on to other areas of dissident activity. But workers' protest and cooperation with intellectuals subsided once the issue that caused it had disappeared. The cooperation thus proved difficult to sustain although small groups of workers became involved in dissident activity initiated by KOR on a regular basis.[83]

THE CHURCH AND THE OPPOSITION

The context in which the Polish opposition has developed over the last ten years has been profoundly influenced by the increasingly active role of the Roman Catholic Church in the social and political life of the country. The position of the Catholic Church in Poland has no equivalent in any other East European country. First because it is 'hegemonic' as it represents over 80 per cent of the population. The Church has been the only institution which has remained entirely independent of the regime, and its official ideology, and thus has provided an alternative focus of identification. Because of its historical legitimacy derived from a close identification with Polish nationalism and because it rejects the atheistic basis of the regime and must defend the freedom of religious practice, its role has been since the war that of the only opposition recognised by the regime. A loyal opposition, since some form of modus vivendi with the communist authorities is a necessity.[84] Hence the mixture of principled stance and of *Realpolitik* in the

Church's involvement in the country's social life. In theory the precondition for the Church-state relationship was that the Church would limit its activities to religious matters while the government would refrain from interfering with religious practice. In 1968 Cardinal Wyszyński defined the role of the Church as follows: 'The Episcopate takes a public stand only in the indispensable defence of religious life, Catholic education, Catholic culture, and the right of the Catholic institutions to develop to meet the demands of the believers.'[85] The full meaning of this apparently restrictive formulation can best be seen in crisis situations, such as those of 1968 and 1970 (or even, at least in the initial phase, in 1976). In all cases the Church protested against repression and police brutality while at the same time using its authority to preserve domestic peace – demanding understanding and dialogue and asking for greater freedoms for the Catholic Church.[86]

Relations between Poland's Catholics and the communist authorities are maintained on several levels. Besides the Church hierarchy the most important is the Znak movement which has essentially two components. First, the clubs of Catholic intellectuals (KIK), which control a number of publications and act as a voice for Catholic public opinion. The Znak parliamentary circle, which since 1956 has been the only genuine institutionalised opposition tolerated in the Soviet bloc. The group's political significance was out of proportion with its numerical strength (5 deputies in the Sejm out of 458) and lay in its ability to articulate and channel the feelings of Polish Catholics to the authorities. The Znak group was influenced by the tradition of political realism and 19th century positivism at least in its rejection of any idea of revolutionary struggle for Poland's independence. Instead, the Znak group adopted a programme resembling that of the 19th century 'organic work', a tacit compromise with the regime combined with non-acceptance of its ideology. The ideology of 'neo-positivism' was developed in the aftermath of the Polish October of 1956 and shared with the Marxist revisionists the belief that change could be brought about gradually from inside the institutions. When the revisionists' hopes collapsed in 1968 Stanislaw Stomma and the Znak group thought that 'neo-positivism' could accommodate itself to the modernistic pragmatic course inaugurated by Gierek in 1971.

In the wake of the riots on the Baltic coast the regime offered concessions to the Church in return for support. In his inaugural statement to the Sejm Premier Jaroszewicz said: 'We shall try to ensure full normalisation of state and Church relations, expecting at the same time that the government's efforts will be adequately understood.' The Church hierarchy responded with a call for forgiveness[87] on Christmas Day and on New Year's Day presented a far-reaching list of demands clearly asking for a greater margin of manoeuvre for the Catholic Church.[88] After the Wyszyński-Jaroszewicz meeting on March 3, 1971 the Church indeed obtained important concessions, such as permission to build new churches, and the recovery of Church property from the western territories. However, signs of tension appeared in 1973, when the regime introduced an educational reform which was seen by the Episcopate as further restricting religious education. By 1974 the regime considered the Church to be the main threat. At the ideological conference in March 1974 Jan Szydlak asserted:

> The main organised antisocialist power in our country – a veritable centre consolidating all the currents that are hostile to our system . . . – is the reactionary core of the Episcopate, acting on the strength of the institutional structure of the Roman Catholic Church.[89]

The decisive test of the Church's role came with the debate over constitutional changes. The Church hierarchy expressed clearly its hostility to the amendments in strongly worded sermons by Cardinals Wyszyński (November 25, 1975) and Wojtyla (January 6, 1976). On January 9 the Polish Bishops addressed a memorandum to the government opposing the three controversial proposals and issued another statement on January 25.[90] In all these documents the Church authorities were defending not only the rights of the Church and believers, but also human rights in general. As the Church and Catholic intellectuals became increasingly involved in the opposition to constitutional changes, a deep crisis appeared in the Znak movement.[91] On January 17 a meeting of presidents of clubs of Catholic intellectuals and editors of the main Catholic journals failed to produce a unified position on the constitutional question. J. Zablodski, editor of ODISS (the Catholic publishing house), and J. Ozdowski, head of the Poznań Catholic Club, rejected a statement signed by Stomma even after Cardinal Wyszyński, who received them, apparently gave it his approval and urged them to remain united.[92] But the movement had been split and on February 10 out of 458 only one, Stomma, abstained. Stomma's name was then dropped from the list of candidates accepted by the National Front for the May election. Instead Lubienski was promoted to the highest post.[93]

The isolation, and finally the elimination, of Stomma from the parliamentary group and the cooperation of new members affiliated with ODISS marked the end of an era, the end of an independent Catholic 'neo-positivist' opposition within the Parliament. This had two consequences: first, coming after the demise of 'revisionist' opposition within the party, the end of Stomma's neo-positivism contributed to the shift from oppositional activity from inside the existing institution to pressure from outside. Second, the silencing of the only genuine Catholic political opposition left the Polish Catholics without any political outlet and thus compelled the Church to speak out on a range of social and political issues and the human rights movement in particular. In this process, as the constitutional debate demonstrated, the Church's efforts converged with those of the lay Left intellectuals, now emancipated from revisionism, and it was the Catholic intellectuals and Catholic publications who provided a bridge between the two. This convergence between the intellectuals and the Church began in the winter of 1975–6 was to acquire a new dimension after the June 1976 workers' protest and the appearance of an organised opposition, the Workers' Defence Committee.

As in previous crisis situations, the attitude of the Catholic Church after the June 1976 food price riots oscillated between appeasement and a call for concessions from the authorities in the handling of the crisis as well as in religious affairs. In July Cardinal Wyszyński sent Premier Jaroszewicz a private memorandum about the June events, urging clemency for workers involved in the riots.[94] As he had done after December 1970, Gierek tried to stabilise the unsettled situation of the summer 1976 through greater cooperation with the Church. He made this clear at a speech in Mielec (September 3, 1976) saying: 'Patriotism calls for unity of feelings. There is no conflict between Church and State in Poland . . . This is the feeling of the party Politburo and the highest authorities of the country.'[95]

The initial Church response was positive. The Episcopate met at Częstochowa (September 8–10, 1976) and appealed to the authorities to observe civil rights and to the people to 'preserve domestic peace and order'.[96] The rapprochement between oppositional intellectuals and the Church that emerged during the constitutional debate was being revived and acquired a new dimension only with the formation of an organised opposition. The creation on September 23 of the Workers' Defence Committee as an organised pole of opposition altered the situation. Only three days later Cardinal Wyszyński stated in a sermon that it was 'painful when workers must struggle for their rights from a workers' government' – a move that was interpreted as giving tacit support to the Committee.[97] The next day the Committee publicly announced its existence, and among its members was a Catholic priest, Jan Zieja.

On November 18, two days after a KOR petition to the Sejm for amnesty and the investigation of police brutality, an even clearer endorsement of the Committee's activities by the Church was given in the communique by the Episcopal conference. The Episcopate considers that assistance given to people and families deprived of work and of means of existence is a duty for all people of good will and particularly for all believers.[98] On Sunday November 28 all Church collections were dedicated to helping arrested or sacked workers, and the money was handed to the families.[99] Thus, with the growth of the oppositional ·movement the Church hierarchy decided to throw its great authority and influence behind the protest movement while at the same time always putting forward the specific demands of the Catholic Church. Cardinal Wyszyński frequently stressed the Church's need for more church building permits and greater facilities for religious instruction. In a particularly strongly worded sermon delivered at Częstochowa on May 3, 1977 the Cardinal said that the church was no longer prepared to see its demands ignored: 'We have not only the right to request . . . we have also the duty to demand'.[100] An example of the convergence between the specific church demands and criticism of the system parallel to that of the opposition was the Bishops' attack on the communist media that came in the form of a pastoral letter, read from the pulpits of churches. On the one hand, the media were denounced in general terms as being used 'to consolidate total dictatorship, to employ cultural coercion, to spread lies and justify violations of human rights' but also as being particularly hostile to the mission of the Catholic Church:

> The media are in the hands of people guided by principles of militant atheism and an ideology hostile to all religion. They are used to carry on persistent propaganda of godless ideology and the cult of the robot man, to spread secular moral attitudes as a human model, to justify political violence, class hatred and struggle . . .[101]

The growing involvement of the Church with the human rights movement also helped stimulate dissent and shaped the ideological framework within which the opposition saw its role. It helped revive the 'politically dormant' sections of the more traditionalistic Catholic public opinion. The formation on March 25 1977, of a new oppositional group, the Movement for the Defence of Human and Civil Rights (ROPCIO) is the best illustration of this phenomenon.[102] One of the Movement's first initiatives was a protest letter to the Sejm saying that the government's attempts to repress religion were in violation of its commitments under the United Nations human rights covenants. The support provided by the Catholic Church to the opposition also led the formerly Marxist oppositional intellectuals to reappraise the role of the Church in Polish society. This evolution is best expressed by a leading member of the Workers' Defence Committee, the historian Adam Michnik, in a new book entitled *The Left, the Church, the Dialogue*, revising some of the views traditionally held by the left:

> For many years now, the Catholic Church in Poland has not been on the side of the powers that be, but has stood out in defence of the oppressed. The authentic enemy of the left is not the Church, but totalitarian power, and the Church plays in this battle a role which it is impossible to overestimate.[103]

On the ideological level the rapprochement of the lay intellectuals with the Catholic Church centred on a new concept of politics based on ethical values rather than a social or economic doctrine. In all the efforts of the opposition one constantly finds an insistence on the primacy of ethics, the moralisation of politics, the search for 'truth and dignity', the rejection of the utilitarian ethics and of the Orwellian double-think. This evolution in the thinking of the lay Left is central to an understanding of its drift away from Marxism. It can be traced back to the late 1950s and the moral dilemmas raised by the discussion of Stalinist crimes, and particularly to the introduction by Kołakowski of neo-Kantian ethical categories into 'revisionist' Marxist writing.[104] The rediscovery by the opposition of the absolute primacy of ethical values in social and political life was, according to Michnik, only possible thanks to the Catholic Church, which had managed to preserve them in the society through its courageous, principled stance vis-à-vis the communist regime. Today, following years of mutual mistrust, the Church also provides, according to Michnik, a new basis for cooperation:

> For us the lay left, the meeting with Christianity around such values as freedom, tolerance, justice, dignity of the human being and the longing for truth, has not been achieved for tactical purposes. It suggests the possibility of working together with important ideas

which will help formulate a way to struggle for democratic socialism.[105]

At a time when the Christian-Marxist dialogue of the 1960s has vanished and when there is no meeting of minds (merely a compromise) between the Church hierarchy and the communist authorities in Poland and in the rest of Eastern Europe, a new sort of dialogue between Christians and (ex)-Marxists centred around the human rights movement has been developing.

This capacity of the Catholic Church to 'integrate' the intellectual opposition, in the midst of great tensions between the regime and the society, has contributed to the strengthening of its authority (and status) vis-à-vis the state. It puts pressure on the regime to reformulate the terms of its *modus vivendi* with the Church. The more the Church appears as a spokesman for society and the greater its ability to 'integrate' opposition, the greater is also the necessity on the part of the state to 'integrate' the Church in its concept of the relations between state and society. This was the meaning of the Gierek-Wyszyński meeting on October 29 1977[106] as well as Gierek's audience with the Pope in the Vatican on December 1 1977.[107] As an institution seeking to extend the freedom of religious practice, the Catholic Church has thus far been the winner of the confrontation between the human rights movement and the state. However, if the Church is seen as a spokesman for the society, then the strengthening of its position vis-à-vis the state amounts to a de facto recognition by the state of a greater autonomy for the society as a whole.

THE 'SELF-ORGANISATION' OF SOCIETY *vs* THE PARTY-STATE: A NEW STRATEGY FOR THE POLISH OPPOSITION

One of the chief obstacles to KOR's attempt to play the role or to initiate the formation of an alternative trade union was the rapidly declining level of workers' mobilisation since the fall of 1976. In contrast, the remarkable success of the student movement in a similar venture, creating an alternative student mass organisation, was precisely due to the sustained and possibly even growing level of mobilisation over a long period of time (in fact also since the fall of 1976). In May 1977 the explosion of the student movement after the tragic death of Stanislaw Pyjas and the arrests of Kuroń, Michnik and other KOR activists created the conditions for the first broadening of the scope of KDC activities.[108] An 'Intervention Bureau', designed to register and publicise violation of human rights, and a Social Self-Defence Fund, to provide financial help for the victims of repression, were created on May 10 1977. So that once its original demands (amnesty, reinstatement of all participants in the June 1976 riots)[109] were met the KOR, conceived as an *ad hoc* committee to defend the workers, transformed itself into a *permanent* body 'Social Self-Defence Committee – KOR' destined to oppose human rights violations in all walks of life. The KOR initials were added to show the continuity of the movement and to demonstrate that the new Committee was not only composed of the same people but it also retained the same concept, that of a human rights movement uniting people of various political persuasions to help establish new ties between different social groups independently of the state.

In its declaration on October 1, 1977 the Committee said it wanted 'institutional guarantees for the rights and liberties of citizens' and would 'support all social initiatives aimed at implementing human and civic rights'.[110] These 'social initiatives' represented a distinctly new phase in the development of the Polish opposition, which moved from a merely 'defensive' human rights campaign towards a 'positive' programme, providing its own independent alternative institutions when limitations were placed on freedom of thought and action by the existing institutions.

The development of the student movement is possibly the best illustration of this trend. Students provided since its inception the main base of 'logistic' support for KOR activities. They acted, first, as disseminators of KOR's 'Information Bulletin'. In December 1976 1,600 students signed a petition to the Sejm asking for an investigation of anti-worker police brutality. However, it was the Pyjas affair that transformed the student movement into a separate component of the opposition with its own goals and methods of action. On May 15 an estimated throng of 5,000 students marched through the City of Kraków to the Wawel Castle mourning Stanislaw Pyjas. That day a petition, stating that the regime-sponsored Socialist Student Union (SZSP) 'has lost the ultimate moral right of representing the academic community' was signed by hundreds. Therefore a Committee for Student Solidarity (SKS) was to be created as an 'authentic and independent student organisation'.[111]

Almost a year later the SKS had spread to most university cities in Poland. It has been acting as an organisation promoting specific student interests and activities – thus breaking the monopoly on student representation of the official organisation (SZSP). SKS has also succeeded in involving in its activities students otherwise working with one of the two politically rival oppositional groupings, the left leaning KSS-KOR and ROPCIO (see below) representing the more traditional Polish right of centre nationalism.

Since the fall of 1977 the Student Committee's activities have mainly tried to challenge the way existing academic institutions operate and to break the party monopoly on knowledge. The campaign was at first directed against the 'RES', a code for books about Poland or by Polish authors in exile removed from libraries or put 'on reserve' only for politically reliable scholars.[112] A more direct challenge of the party monopoly on education crystallised in October 1978 with the launching of the 'Flying University'.[113] A manifesto signed by 58 prominent intellectuals announced in February the creation of a 'Scientific Education Society'. The group designation is filled with moral and historic significance in Poland:

> If men fail to seek their own truth and that of the world, it said, they cannot conscientiously participate in the construction of the country and its future. . . . No official system of education and particularly no system subservient to politics as is the one in Poland can fulfil this need.[114]

The signatories included prominent members of the Polish Academy of Science such as Professor W. Gajewski, a biologist, J. Kielanowski, a physiologist, Edward Lipiński, the well-known economist; but also a number of writers and a former Minister of Education, Bieńkowski.

The 'Flying University' lectures take place in private flats. They cover a variety of subjects and disciplines. The first lecture interrupted by the police given by Adam Michnik, a historian and leading figure in the KSS-KOR movement, was about 'The political history of the Polish People's Republic'. The programme includes lectures by Catholic intellectuals like Bohdan Czywinski, editor of the magazine *Znak*, Marxists like the economist Tadeusz Kowalik, or socialists and members of the PUKP Jan Strzelecki.[115] The 'Flying University' is not a substitute for a political discussion group. Its lecturers merely refuse to honour the official taboos on politically sensitive topics. The University attempts to break the government's institutional monopoly on knowledge and substitute for the ideological monolithism of institutional scholarship the freedom and pluralism it considers necessary for development of the national culture. In other words the 'Flying University' no longer tries to press for University reform through existing institutions. Instead, it turns towards the society to reconstitute the national memory of Poland and to redirect the nation to its independent and democratic sources of culture. Hence, also its political dimension: in the words of Adam Michnik: 'An enlightened society is the most efficient weapon against the abuse of power.'[116]

Unofficial publishing is another area of social activity outside state control. Conceived initially merely as a means to disseminate protest against the antiworker repression of the summer of 1976, the Polish version of 'samizdat' evolved with the opposition and reflects the general ferment of independent initiatives in a variety of social circles. There are about 38 bulletins and journals appearing outside state censorship with circulation ranging from a few hundred to several thousand copies.[117] Perhaps the most significant example of the interaction between oppositional activity, official curb on free expression and independent publishing is provided by *Zapis*, a literary 'underground' review.[118]

The initial meaning of *Zapis* in Polish is 'written record', but the term is now popularly used in Poland to denote the censor's 'black list'. It is thus a particularly appropriate title for this volume which is meant both as a selection of banned writings and as a 'record' of 'unofficial' literary life in Poland.

A typewritten version of *Zapis* has already been circulating from hand to hand inside Poland over the last five months – a distribution reminiscent of the 'samizdat' in the Soviet Union.[119] The real originality of *Zapis*, and its major difference from samizdat publications in Czechoslovakia or in the Soviet Union, is that all these manuscripts were not written 'for the drawer', as East European writers like to say; originally they were written and submitted for publication to various government publishing houses – but rejected by the censor. The arbitrary nature of censorship is not new in Poland, and in his introduction to *Zapis (1)* Stanisław Baranczak, a leading poet and a critic of the younger, post-war generation, describes in detail the complex and subtle interaction among the three main elements involved in literary censorship.[120] These are the censor's office, which claims to interpret the Party line; the editor who claims to know what the censor will tolerate; and, last but not least, self-censorship by the writer himself who instinctively guesses how far he can go if he wants to be published. To be sure, there were always official taboos but not absolute criteria for censorship, and some of the works published in *Zapis* could have perhaps appeared in the early 1970s. However, by 1975 the limited freedoms enjoyed by Polish intellectuals after Gierek took over the party leadership from Gomułka seemed to have slowly vanished. Gierek's regime reverted to some of the censorship practices of his predecessor, using the same political criterion. In the course of the last eighteen months the currently blacklisted authors have signed various petitions expressing their opposition to the proposed amendments to the Polish Constitution, and have also been calling for a public inquiry into alleged police brutality against the workers during and after the June 1976 food price riots.

Censorship is thus used by the authorities as a form of punishment against dissident writers. It is also meant as a warning to others not to join the human rights campaign. Recent developments, however, suggest that this attempt to isolate the most outspoken of the writers has failed. Following the arrests in May 1977 of six members of the Worker's Defence Committee and three of its sympathisers, seventeen Polish writers (none of them members of the Committee) sent a letter to the authorities asking them to 'revoke this sort of action which harms innocent people and increases social tension in Poland'.[121] On May 30, 1977 the Polish P.E.N. Club and the leadership of the Polish Writers' Union appealed for the immediate release from prison of Jan Józef Lipski, a dissident literary critic. In other words, jailing the Committee members has only earned the authorities the ill-will of the vast majority of Polish writers.

This had two complementary effects: on the institutional level it has considerably strengthened the critical stand of the Writers' Union where non-conformist writers are now not only tolerated but even represented in the leadership.[122] At the same time the support given to the opposition by some of the best names of Polish literature has also fostered the writers' involvement in unofficial literary and publishing life. Besides *Zapis* and *Puls* there is also NOWA, an independent publishing house which has already published some twenty books.[123] Although alternative publications were initially an outlet for works rejected by the censor, today many writers write directly for them.[124] This represents not only an important change in the writers' attitude towards the official institutions, but also a change in their understanding of their own creative activity. The new opposition is also a new state of mind.

PROGRAMMES AND STRATEGIES OF THE POLISH OPPOSITION

As in other East European countries, the Polish opposition initially was reluctant to act as a political opposition and claimed to merely demand the observance of constitutionally guaranteed human rights. However, the unparalleled level of oppositional activity involving different social groups, different cultural and intellectual milieux, brought with it also an intense preoccupation with questions of political programmes, strategy and tactics which is reflected in a wide spectrum of oppositional writing on these subjects.

Quite characteristically all the programmatic statements of the Polish opposition take as a point of departure the geopolitical position of Poland and the constraints imposed by Soviet influence. This in itself is nothing new. In fact the foreign policy factor has been central in Polish politics throughout the last two centuries. Ever since the decline of Poland as an independent power the dilemma of Poland's politics has been the problem of what attitude to adopt towards the direct or implicit threats from Russia and Germany. The Polish-German Federal Republic treaty of December 1970, recognising the Polish western borders, not only weakened the credibility of the bogeyman of German 'revanchism' used by the government propaganda, it also weakened the underlying premises of the 'neo-positivist' programme. Indeed, after 1970 the attention of the Polish public switched from concern over the German threat to internal socioeconomic matters and to the nature of Soviet domination.

This focus on questions of national sovereignty and Soviet domination is as common to practically all political programmes of the Polish opposition as is the goal of recovering political independence. The programme of the Polish League for Independence (PLI) puts at the top of its lists the 'regaining of genuine national sovereignty'.[125] In his open letter to Gierek Professor Edward Lipiński states bluntly that the

> Soviet road [to socialism], conditioned as it is by the traditions of Russian state despotism . . . is not the road which should be followed by socialist practice in Poland . . . Only political independence would permit us to implement a consistent economic reform and to reconstruct the political and social system in such a way as to release the creative forces existing in the nation.[126]

For the PLI, and for Lipiński, the precondition for good relations with the USSR is the Soviet 'denunciation of crimes' committed against Poland. These include the attack against Poland in 1939 in collusion with Germany, the transportation of millions of Poles to Siberia, and the Katyn massacre.[127] Jacek Kuroń, leading figure in KOR, sees Poland's situation in the global context of change within the Soviet bloc.

> The fundamental factor which constrains the social action towards democratisation is consciousness of Soviet military power . . . Poles may win sovereignty only in combined efforts with other captive nations of the Soviet empire, Russians, Czechs, Hungarians, Lithuanians, etc., but this programme cannot be realised now.[128]

The prospect of Soviet military interventions is a shared concern of the.Polish opposition. The dissident historian Adam Michnik sees this matter as the main 'area of common interest' between the Soviet and Polish leaders and for the Polish opposition: 'for all three, Soviet military intervention in Poland . . . remains a disastrous prospect'.[129] Hence, paradoxically, the concept of 'Finlandisation' put forward as the only realistic and desirable prospect.[130] According to Michnik, change in the status quo should not come through unilateral revolutionary outbursts, but rather through gradual evolution which should take place simultaneously in the east and in the west. In this process the western left and particularly the Eurocommunists have a part to play because both they and the Polish dissidents oppose the big power status quo and the 'Sonnenfeldt doctrine'.[131] The Eurocommunists' commitment to independence from Moscow and democratic freedoms has no doubt strengthened the East Europeans' opposition challenge of Soviet bloc ideological monolithism and provided an additional source of legitimation.[132]

The broadening of the social base of the opposition and the decline of the revisionism and neo-positivism provided the conditions for the emergence of a broadly based human rights movement uniting the different components of the opposition around issues transcending ideological standpoints. However, the re-surfacing of the traditional political culture in this process, has in turn led to a new political crystallisation within the opposition. Although traditional political cleavages such as right/left are not always helpful for the understanding of East European politics, the formation of political groupings in the Polish opposition may be summed up as follows:

Revisionism, as a political strategy, collapsed after 1968 and the revisionists, with the exception of W. Bieńkowski,[133] the post-1956 Minister of Education, have vanished from the political scene. However at the beginning of 1978 fourteen prominent former party officials sent a letter to Gierek proposing alternative policies for the party. The signatories included Edward Ochab a former Secretary General of the party and Head of State in the 1960s, and three other former Central Committee secretariat and Politburo members of the post 1956 'liberal' faction: Albrecht, Matwin and Morawski. They see the roots of Poland's difficulties as lying in its 'undemocratic form of government'. According to their letter it is 'the lack of democratic exchange of opinions in the choosing of goals and the selection of means for solving socio-political problems' which explains the emergence of opposition movements such as KOR. The trade unions must acquire independence and 'become equal partners of the government departments' in matters of social and economic policy.[134] By addressing themselves only to the party leadership and expecting change only from above, the signatories remained faithful to the 'revisionist' concept and revealed the gulf that separates them from the rest of the opposition. The document is symptomatic of a type of discussion which the emergence of an opposition outside the party provoked inside the party, but its impact however remains rather limited since the authors are former prominent party veterans who have little influence on present-day policy making. The letter was made public without the consent of its authors in the January issue of the unofficial opposition journal *Opinia* (published by ROPCIO) exposing outside the party a document designed for intraparty discussion and thus rendering it impotent.

Democratic socialists. Although not claiming allegiance to any specific political strands it includes on the one hand former leaders of the student movement of the 1960s such as J. Kuroń, A. Michnik, A. Macierewicz, P. Maimski, and on the other, former members of the Polish Socialist Party (PPS), E. Lipiński, L. Cohn, A. Pajdak, A. Steinsbergowa. One of the original feature of this current of the Polish opposition is its remarkable sense of continuity and capacity for self-examination. In the same way that the discussion clubs of the 1960s provided a framework for a critique of the post 1956 reformist hopes, so also the post 1968 period, and especially the 1975–6 emergence of the human rights movement, brought a critique of the neo-positivist and revisionist strategies of the past and an elaboration of a new concept of opposition, the 'new evolutionism'.

For Michnik the underlying foreign policy assumptions

(Russia/Germany) as well as the domestic policy dilemmas inherited from the 19th century by both the 'revisionists' (reform/revolution) and the 'neo-positivists' (revolt/collaboration) are obsolete and lead to disastrous dead ends as soon as the opposition has to take part in an open conflict between the state and the society.

One must choose between the point of view of the oppressor and that of the oppressed. When the crunch comes, both the revisionism or neo-positivism, applied consistently, must inevitably lead to taking up the point of view of the regime. In effect, any solidarity with workers on strike, with demonstrating students or dissident intellectuals, puts into question the revisionists' strategies of seeking entente from within the party. When the conflict becomes open, both these groups find themselves swiftly deprived of one essential factor: influence on power.[135]

Given that the 19th century categories are obsolete, and the possibility of structural change limited as long as the Soviet system remains what it is the strategy proposed is 'unceasing struggle for reforms, in favour of evolution which will extend civil liberties and respect for human rights'.[136] What then distinguished the 'new evolutionist' concept from the 'revisionist' or the 'neo-positivist' one, is that the programme 'should be addressed to independent public opinion and not just the authorities. Instead of telling the government how to improve itself, the programme should tell the society how to act. As far as the government is concerned, it can have no clearer counsel than that provided by the social pressure from below.'[137]

Two social groups have a central role in this 'pressure from below': the workers, because they represent the only force that can, in the last instance, make the government back down, and the intellectuals who, in a country where no free means of expression and opposition are available, have an enormous 'moral and political responsibility' in preserving 'the values without which a nation cannot survive'. Step-by-step resistance by all the sections of the society and independent grassroot organisations are designed to weaken the state's grip on the society. In short, if 'Finlandisation' is the foreign policy framework towards which the democratic Left in Poland gears its activity, the 'Spanish model'[138] is clearly in the minds of those who in the Polish opposition strive for a gradual transition from a totalitarian regime towards a pluralist socialist democracy.

Nationalism: The centre right. The broadening of the social base of the opposition and the growing involvement of the Catholic Church has also activated certain sections with no available channels of political expression since the late 1940s. The Movement for the Defence of Human and Civil Rights (ROPCIO) created in March 1977 and led by L. Moczulski and A. Czuma has acquired support in these traditional nationalist, Catholic circles. The movement provides a rallying point for several recently revived political organisations whose origins go back to prewar Poland: The Christian Democrats, the Centralist 'Pilsudski Movement', the Peasant Party,[139] the Movement for National Independence.[140] Further to the right there is the conservative National Democratic Party (ND), which refused to be associated with ROPCIO and which is characterised by its strong attachment to Polish nationalism and conservative Catholicism.[141] After thirty years of Communist rule the emergence of the Polish opposition has brought with it the resurgence of the pre-war political spectrum. Clearly Polish political culture has more than 'survived' under communism and today it poses a serious challenge to the communist structure.

CONCLUSIONS

There are several domestic and international factors that help explain the growth and strength of opposition activity in Poland. While the regime expected from détente and the Helsinki conference merely international recognition and the consolidation of its power, the opposition demonstrated its ability for skilful exploitation of the opportunities provided by the third section on 'Cooperation in Humanitarian and other Fields' (better known as 'Basket Three') of the Final Act of the Helsinki conference and of support received from western, including the Eurocommunists', opinion. The international dimension of the oppositional activity concerns not only western pressure on the authorities, but also interaction with human rights movements in the rest of the Soviet bloc, mainly in Czechoslovakia and the Soviet Union. The insistence on the observance of constitutionally guaranteed civil rights and the decline of the ideological factor in oppositional activity help explain the relatively broad base of support the opposition has been able to gather.

Another new and unique feature of the Polish opposition was the worker-intellectual alliance. The timing of two measures (constitution, food price increases) helped the convergence of the two movements but has not caused it. Similar measures were implemented at approximately the same time in other Soviet bloc countries (Hungary for instance) and without causing unrest. The years 1975–8 saw the gradual erosion of the social base of the regime particularly among workers and intellectuals. Perhaps only the scientific intelligentsia, attracted by the 'meritocratic' model of society, and the peasantry, encouraged by significant concessions to the private sector, represent two ambiguous factors of stability and are perhaps the only two social groups whose quiescence could be won through economic concession without altering the fundamental premises of the 'social compact'. The rise of the opposition has also accelerated the decline of the role of ideology. The fact that intellectuals did not challenge the legitimacy of the regime in terms of the official state ideology but in terms of its (formal) legality illustrates the crisis of the official state ideology.

Paradoxically, the two social groups that most directly challenged the authority of the regime represent the new post-war Poland and can hardly be dismissed by the regime as mere 'survivals' of past times. When the communist regime was introduced in Eastern Europe, Poland was predominantly a rural country and the regime had to 'create' the proletariat in the name of which it claimed to rule. This was achieved through rapid industrialisation which, from the point of view of the organisation of labour or even social costs, reproduced most of the features present in capitalist industrialisation. Having to defend its economic interest without independent trade union organisations this new proletariat strikes, much like in Marx's days in the capitalist west, spontaneously, sometimes violently, for bread and the right to organise. Similarly the young generation of intellectuals which was the driving force of the opposition around the KSS-KOR was socialised within the post-war system and shared with the regime, at least until 1968, the same ideological framework. In this sense the intellectual and worker opposition has different social and political and cultural origins from the Catholic milieu or the groups within the ROPCIO which, to simplify, represent the traditional pre-communist Poland.[142]

This in turn accounts, at least partially, for the different, though not contradictory, ideological and political premises of these two main oppositional trends, the former having roots in the socialist tradition, the latter in nationalism. While the KSS-KOR concept of opposition was to foster the development of independent social movements, ROPCIO's strategy is formulated in more traditional political categories. When ROPCIO's spokesman L. Moczulski presented as a goal the 'reinstatement of political pluralism in Poland', he meant explicitly pluralism of political parties. Discussion clubs and samizdat journals were understood as a means to achieve this goal. The revival of traditional political culture is matched by a political vision inspired from a somewhat idealised version of pre-war Poland. In contrast, the KSS-KOR concept of promoting the self-organisation of the society vis-à-vis the state, goes beyond the traditional concept of politics centred on the question of state and political power. The 'new politics' of the Polish opposition are turned towards the society. The goal is not to replace one state power by another; the opposition sees its recent attempts to create areas of independent social activity as a means to extend the limits of tolerance, as the beginning of a long journey aimed at progressive transformation of relations between state and society in Poland.

Two trends, two concepts of oppositional strategies but also a series of shared features are characteristic of present day Polish opposition: a reliance on independent organisational structures, a new institutional pluralism, the recreation of new social ties based on solidarity and ethical values transcending ideologies and political programmes.

Politically, the unrest and oppositional activities revealed the pluralism in the society, but also the inability of the political system to 'absorb' it. In contrast to the 1970 workers' riots which brought to power a new leadership, June 1976 workers' unrest had practically no effect on the political structure and the composition of the ruling political organs. June 1976 considerably weakened Gierek's authority in the society but at the same time confirmed his position in the party as the only 'available' politician able to continue the programme of economic modernisation and prevent a possible comeback of hard-line Stalinist *apparatchiki* to the top.

Thus the emergence and growth of opposition has eroded the social base of the regime and its ideology while the political structure seemed unable to find new answers to the changed situation. While the stability of the regime has been shaken, its policy choices seemed limited. The scale of dissident activity in present day Poland rules out the possibility of eradicating opposition. So far, in dealing with dissent, the authorities oscillated between conciliatory moves (price increase cancellation, amnesty, improved relation with the Church) and selective repressive measures, but neither have proved able to defuse oppositional activity. Clearly, the risk of a Soviet intervention, should unrest go too far, acts as a moderator on both the government and the opposition. But neither of them today knows what the limits of tolerance are supposed to be in the post-totalitarian era. In this sense

Poland is today a laboratory for political change for the whole of Eastern Europe.

NOTES

1. Cf Leonard Schapiro, ed., *Political Opposition in One-Party States* (London: Macmillan, 1972) p. 3. Professor Schapiro sees the difference between opposition and dissent as a distinction between 'those who wish to replace a communist regime by some other regime, and those who merely wish to assert the right to criticise' the existing regime.
2. Cf George Gömöri, 'The cultural intelligentsia: the writers' in David Lane and George Kolankiewicz eds., *Social Groups in Polish Society* (London: Macmillan, 1973) pp. 153–62, and Alexander Matejko, *Social Change and Stratification in Eastern Europe* (New York: Praeger, 1974) pp. 140–54.
3. On the meaning of 1956 for future developments of the Polish opposition see Krzysztof Pomian and Pierre Kende eds., *Varsovie-Budapest 1956, la deuxième révolution d'Octobre* (Paris: Ed. du Seuil 1978).
4. See William E. Griffiths 'The decline and fall of revisionism in Eastern Europe' in Leopold Labedz ed., *Revisionism* (London: Allen and Unwin, 1962) p. 224.
5. For a selection of Kolakowski's writing from that period see Leszek Kolakowski, *Marxism and Beyond* (London: Pall Mall Press, 1969).
6. Group formed in 1956 and named after its meeting place of Pulawy, south of Warsaw; see A. Ross Johnson, 'Poland: end of an era?', *Problems of Communism*, Vol. XIX, no. 1 (Jan-Feb. 1970) pp. 28–39.
7. M. K. Dziewanowski, *The Communist Party of Poland* (Cambridge, Mass: Harvard University Press, 1976) p. 292.
8. On the intellectuals' relationship with the Party prior to 1968, see Georges Mond, 'La presse, les intellectuels et le pouvoir en Union Sovietique et dans les pays socialistes europeens', II. *La Pologne et la Tchecoslovaquie* (Paris: Notes et Etudes Documentaires) pp. 3729ff.
9. Jacek Kuroń and Karol Modzelewski, *Lettre ouverte au parti ouvrier polonais* (Paris: Maspero, 1966). A reformist evolutionary answer to the Kuroń-Modzelewski approach was formulated by another economist from Warsaw University, Antoni Zambrowski, the son of a former Politburo member. The text called for the democratisation of the socialist system and revival of Marxist thought along lines suggested by the experiences of the Italian and Yugoslav communists. Text in *Kultura* (Paris) 1968 no. 1–2, pp. 122–6.
10. On the influence of Kuroń on the young generation of 'red scouts' later renamed 'commandos' see Michnik's testimony in court in 1969, quoted in Christian Jelen, *La purge* (Paris: Fayard, 1972) pp. 46–51.
11. Since 1955 the play had been performed in Poland in 17 different productions and the Dejmek's new production prepared for the fiftieth

anniversary of the October revolution, seemed initially to satisfy everybody, including the Politburo ideological expert, Zenon Kliszko. Ch.
Jelen (op. cit.) provides the most detailed account of the March events.
A positive review of the production appeared in *Pravda* on 30.1.68.,
the very day of the banning of the play in Warsaw.

12. Jelen, op. cit., p. 15.
13. Ibid., p. 12.
14. A. Zara and J. Zygier, 'Mars en Pologne' in *Partisan* (Paris), No. 60,
1968, pp. 51–62.
15. Full text in *Wydarzenia marcowe-1968, Dokumenty* (Paris: Instytut
Literacki, 1969) pp. 99–103.
16. Ibid.
17. *Słowo Powszechne*, 11.3.68., *Trybuna Ludu*, 13.3.68., *Kurier Polski*,
12.3.68.
18. For an analysis of the function of the anti-Semitic campaign in the
intraparty rivalry see A. R. Johnson, 'Poland: End of an era',
pp. 28–39. The clearest formulation of the equation: Jews =
Zionism = revisionism was offered by Andrzej Werblan (member of
the Central Committee) in *Miesięcznik Literacki*, June 1968.
19. There were in Czechoslovakia during the Spring of 1968 numerous
manifestations of sympathy with the Polish March movement; a
mimeographed translation of Kuroń and Modzelewski's 'Open letter'
was put out by the Student Union in Prague; and dismissed Polish
academics were offered visiting lectureships.
20. The invasion did not cause widespread protest in Poland. Among the
exceptions were anonymous leaflets such as the one comparing the
Polish participation in the invasion to the Polish takeover of Zaolzie in
1939. Cf *Polskie Przedwiosnie: dokumenty marcowe* (Paris: Instytut
Literacky, 1969) II, p. 130.
21. On the workers' councils movement in 1956 see Jean-Jacques Marie
and Balázs Nagy, *Pologne – Hongrie 1956* (Paris: E.D.I., 1966)
pp. 3–149 and Pierre Kende and Krzysztof Pomian eds., op. cit.,
pp. 93–110.
22. Marie and Nagy eds., op. cit., pp. 136–44.
23. Quoted from a study by M. Hirszowicz and W. Morawski by George
Kolankiewicz, 'The working class', in David Lane and George Kolankiewicz, op. cit., p. 149. Another sociological survey published in
Poland in 1968 shows that relative to other social groups the working
class seems to display least interest in official state politics. Cf. George
Kolankiewicz and Ray Taras, 'Poland: Socialism for everyman', in
Archie H. Brown and Jack Gray eds., *Political Culture and Political
Change in Communist States* (London: Macmillan, 1977) p. 113.
24. Kolankiewicz, 'The working class' in Lane and Kolankiewicz op. cit.,
p. 130.
25. *Nowe Drogi* (Special Issue) May 1971, p. 67.
26. For a comparative analysis of the decline in social mobility, see chapter
7 by Alex Pravda in this volume. Growing differentials appear clearly in
comparisons of manual/non-manual household income per capita (the
average size of a workers' families is larger than non-manual). See

figures in Kolankiewicz in Lane and Kolankiewicz op. cit., p. 124. Similarly, differentials are marked when one compares the percentage of employees earning less than average monthly income. The figure in industry is 55 per cent for blue collar workers against 36 per cent among white collar workers, cf. Alexander Matejko, *Social Change and Stratification* . . .

27.   S. Nowak 'Changes in Social structure and social consciousness', in C. S. Heller, ed., *Structured social inequality* (New York: Praeger, 1969) p. 244.
28.   Ibid.
29.   Kolankiewicz in Lane and Kolankiewicz, op. cit., p. 129.
30.   For a detailed account see Paul Barton, *Misère et révolte de l'ouvrier polonais* (Paris: Edition Force Ouvrière, 1971) pp. 113–55.
31.   Here again the reality is not as black and white as often presented; some students did join the workers; among the student activists arrested in the Gdańsk demonstrations of 1970 were those who also became the organisers of the 1976 solidarity campaign with the workers in Gdańsk.
32.   The official toll was 45 dead and 1,165 injured. *Nowe Drogi*, op. cit.
33.   *Gierek face aux grévistes de Szczecin* (Paris: S.E.L.I.O., 1972) p. 49.
34.   Ibid., p. 106.
35.   Ibid., p. 78.
36.   Ibid., p. 97.
37.   Boleslaw Sulik, 'Les ouvriers', in Z. Erard and G. M. Zygier, eds., *La Pologne: une societé en dissidence* (Paris: Maspero, 1978) p. 61. This is the best analysis of the workers' revolt.
38.   Little is known about the Łódź strike; see Paul Barton, op. cit., pp. 147–50. Interestingly the strike spread to several industrial cities, including the Ursus factory near Warsaw.
39.   *The Times*, 27.4.71.
40.   For an interesting sample of variations on this theme, see the statements made at the 8th plenum of the Central Committee of the PUWP (6–7.2.1971) in Adam Bromke and J. W. Strong eds., *Gierek's Poland* (New York: Praeger, 1973) pp. 216–19.
41.   A. Bromke, 'Poland under Gierek', in *Problems of Communism*, Vol. XXI, no. 5 (Sept-Oct 1972) p. 6.
42.   Ibid., p. 7. This figure is by no means exceptional. The PUWP has generally speaking a very high turnover of membership: in a relatively 'quiet' year such as 1967 the expulsion reached almost 100,000. Cf. M. K. Dziewanowski, *The Communist Party of Poland* (Cambridge, Mass.: Harvard University Press, 1976) 2nd edition, p. 73.
43.   *VI Zjazd Polskiej Zjednoczonej Partii Robotniczej* (Warsaw: 1972) p. 73.
44.   Dziewanowski, op. cit., p. 325.
45.   For a more detailed analysis of the evolution of Party membership under Gierek see K. Pomian, 'Le Parti: vérités et mensonges', in *Les Temps Modernes* (Nov-Dec 1977) (Special Issue on Eastern Europe) pp. 588–607.
46.   *Gierek face aux grévistes*, op. cit., p. 49.
47.   Previous changes at the top of the Party leadership in 1956 or 1968 had

not altered the power of the regional bureaucracy. There was a continuity of the regional apparatus that went back to the Stalinist era.

48. *Polityka*, 15.5.71 and 4.12.71.
49. *Kultura* (Warsaw), 21.5.72., *Polityka* 4.10.75.
50. For an analysis of the emergence of the meritocratic concept between 1970–75, see G. Mink 'La Pologne: à la decouverte de la méritocratie' in *La Pologne de Gierek*, in 'Problemes politiques et sociaux' no. 290 (Paris: La Documentation Française, 1976) pp. 5–13.
51. G. Kolankiewicz 'The technical intelligentsia', in Lane and Kolankiewicz, op. cit., pp. 227–32.
52. *Nowe Drogi*, July 1974.
53. *Zycie Partii*, March 1974.
54. Text in Andre Martin, *La Pologne défend son âme* (Paris, 1977) p. 258.
55. *Zycie Warszawy*, 20–21.12.75.
56. Text in A. Ostoja-Ostaszewski, *et al*, eds., *Dissent in Poland*, Reports and documents Dec. 1975 – July 1977 (London: The Association of Polish Students and Graduates in Exile, 1977) pp. 15–17.
57. Ibid., pp. 17–18.
58. Ibid., pp. 12–15.
59. The full text of the amendments was published in *Dziennik Ustaw*, no. 5, 14.2.76. pp. 45–8.
60. On Charter 77 see *The White Paper of Czechoslovakia* (Paris: The International Committee for the support of Charter 77, 1977). See also Chapter 2 of this volume.
61. Cf. Kolankiewicz and Taras, op. cit., pp. 101–4.
62. Jacek Kuroń, 'Pour une plate-forme unique de l'opposition' in *Politique Aujourd'hui*, 1977, no. 3–4, p. 93; Cf. also Wyszyński's reference to the Constitution of 1791 at the ceremony of the renewal of the Vows of Jasnogora on 3 May 1977, text in *Dissent in Poland*, op. cit. pp. 163–4.
63. See Chapter 1 by Rudolf L. Tökés in this volume, pp. 1–25.
64. '. . . our Constitution is and should be an adequate reflection of the specific sociopolitical reality as well as a guide post for action in the fundamentally important areas of state affairs'; Professor M. Dobrosielski, Director of the Polish Institute of International Affairs – interview in *Trybuna Ludu* 6.2.76.
65. For a detailed account of the events see *Liberation* (Paris), 20.7.76, *Neue Zürcher Zeitung*, 24.6.76. and the *Information Bulletin*, no. 1, Sept. 1976 (Published by sympathisers of the Workers Defence Committee). Text in *Dissent in Poland* pp. 52–63.
66. The next morning, however, *Trybuna Ludu* 26.6.76. attributed the disturbances to hooligan elements.
67. Thomas Schreiber ed., *L'Europe de l'Est en 1976* (Paris: La Documentation Française, 1977) p. 50.
68. Wlodzimierz Brus, 'Ökonomie und Politik in Polen', *Wiener Tagebuch*, 1976 pp. 15–16.
69. Antonín J. Liehm, 'Intellectuals and the New Social Contract' *Telos*, no. 23, 1975.
70. For an illustration of the routine, formal and production-oriented practice of 'consultation' see the report on the conference on the role of

PUWP units in large industrial plants in *Nowe Drogi*, March 1976
pp. 211–12. After the June riots Marian Rakowski, the editor of the
influential party weekly *Polityka*, even explained that there was no
consultation with the workers about the price rises prior to the announcement on June 24 so that 'hostile elements' would not 'exploit'
the situation. *Polityka* 3.7.76.

71. A survey concerning 'Views of Szczecin working youth about the role of
social classes in Poland' in *Kultura i Społeczenstwo*, no. 2, 1976 (April-
June) pp. 125–42 shows this is perceived so by the workers: 'Most of
the young people questioned cite December 1970 as the date from
which we should consider the role of the working class in Poland to have
really begun to accelerate. In their opinion the December (1970)
events showed that the working class in Poland really does set the limits
beyond which the state does not go'.

72. According to the communique no. 4, of 22.11.76. of the Workers
Defence Committee, in *Dissent in Poland*, op. cit., p. 88.

73. Ibid. *Le Monde*, 21.7.76; Two of the accused at Radom were presented
as 'inveterate recidivists' (PAP, 17.7.76) and were sentenced to 9 years
in prison.

74. In *Dissent in Poland*, op. cit., p. 13. In his Open Letter to Gierek,
Professor E. Lipiński had 'predicted' the June explosion: 'It is impera-
tive to make fundamental changes or at least a clear start on them.
Otherwise we shall not avoid a tragedy which may take the shape of
violent revolt or a return to Stalinist methods of ruling', in *Survey*, Vol.
22, no. 2 (Spring 1976) p. 203; similarly Kuroń and Modzelewski had
in 1965 predicted a workers' explosion at the end of the 1966–70 plan.

75. A Declaration of Solidarity with the workers by 14 prominent intellectuals on 29.6.76. J. Kuroń's appeal to Berlinguer on 11.7.76.; Andrzejewski's open letter to the persecuted participants of the workers'
protest, in *Dissent in Poland*, op. cit., pp. 70–6. The committee was
later to include 24 members.

76. Ibid. pp. 81–2.

77. For a fairly comprehensive collection see *Documents du Comité de
Défense des Ouvriers de Pologne* (Paris: Comité International Contre la
Repression, 1977).

78. *Dissent in Poland*, op. cit., p. 95.

79. Ibid., pp. 112–14.

80. J. Kuroń, 'Pour une plate-forme unique de l'opposition', op. cit.,
p. 105.

81. Text in 'L'opposition ouvrière et intellectuelle en Europe de l'Est' in
Problèmes politiques et sociaux, n 311 (Paris: La Documentation Française, 1977) pp. 14–15.

82. 'Appeal to the Nation', 15.11.76., in *Dissent in Poland*, op. cit.,
pp. 124–9.

83. In November 1977 an independent 'cell' of the journal *Robotnik* (the
Worker) published by 'KSS-KOR' was formed at Radom, the place
where the June 1976 riots broke out. The cell pledges itself to defend
the workers' rights independently of the official trade unions which it

described as 'dead institutions'. The journal *Robotnik* represents the only institutionalised link between the workers and the intellectual opposition.

84. On the role of the Church in post-war Poland see F. Kaminski 'Religione e Chiesa in Polonia 1945–75' *Il Politico* (CESEO, Padova) 1977/1.
85. *Słowo Powszechne*, 11.1.68.
86. For the Declaration of the Polish Episcopate in March 1968 see *Polskie Przedwiosnie-dokumenty*, op. cit., pp. 65–66; for 1971 and 1976 see below.
87. After the bloody anti-worker repression on the Baltic coast Cardinal Wyszyński said in a Christmas sermon: 'We beg you do not accuse, show understanding, feel compassion . . . we feel co-responsible and we beg the families of those who were beaten to accept our confession and our plea for forgiveness.' In *Poznan 56-Grudzien 70*, op. cit., p. 135.
88. The New Year message of the Episcopate demanded 'freedom of conscience and of religious life and full normalisation of Church-state relations; the right to shape freely the national culture according to Christian principles, the right to social justice, right to truth in social life, to true information and free expression of one's views and demands'; text in *Poznan 56-Grudzien 70*, op. cit., pp. 146–7.
89. *Nowe Drogi*, May 1974.
90. Lucjan Blit 'The Polish Episcopate: Spokesman for Society', in *Religion in Communist lands*, Vol. 5, n 2 (1977) p. 81.
91. R. Slowacki 'Catholic Intellectuals and Constitutional change in Poland' in *Religion in Communist lands*, Vol. 4, n 3 (1976) pp. 12–15.
92. 'The Znak Affair' in *The Tablet*, 26.3.77, p. 300 (anonymous text from Poland).
93. Although Lubienski approved the amendments he also said he hoped the authorities will do everything to reassure the 'serious concern' about religious freedom voiced before the vote. His text published in *Za i Przeciw*, 7.3.76, was probably the only officially published statement acknowledging the lack of consensus on the constitutional question among Catholics.
94. *Le Monde* 17.8.76.
95. *International Herald Tribune*, 6.9.76. This was quite a change from the militant tone adopted in May 1976 by the Minister of Religious Affairs, Kakol. He concluded a lecture to Party activists by saying 'If we cannot destroy the Church, let us at least stop it from causing harm'. Full text in A. Martin, *La Pologne défend son âme*, op. cit., pp. 187–95.
96. In *Dissent in Poland*, op. cit., pp. 154–5.
97. Quoted in L. Blit, 'The Polish Episcopate spokesman for society', op. cit., p. 82.
98. Text in Zigier and Erard eds., *La Pologne: une societé en dissidence*, op. cit., p. 69.
99. L. Blit, op. cit., p. 83.
100. *Dissent in Poland*, op. cit., pp. 163–64.
101. *Le Monde*, 22.9.77.

110   *Opposition in Eastern Europe*

102. *Dissent in Poland,* op. cit. pp. 182–86.
103. Adam Michnik, *Kosçiol, Lewica, Dialog* (Paris: Instytut Literacki, 1977) p. 140.
104. Similar efforts in Czechoslovakia in the 1960s are associated with the name of the philosopher Karel Kosík, the author of the *Dialectic of the Concrete* (Prague, 1963 and Boston: D. Reidel Publishing Company, 1977).
105. A. Michnik, op. cit., p. 166; Similar opinions are expressed by J. Kuroń in 'Zasady ideowe', 'samizdat' manuscript, 1978).
106. *Le Monde,* 1.11.77.
107. *International Herald Tribune,* 1.12.77.; *Le Monde,* 3.12.77.
108. Pyjas was a Cracow University student and a known KOR sympathiser. On 7th May 1977 he was found dead under circumstances that the Committee for Student Solidarity and others familiar with the case found suspicious and probably attributable to the secret police. The latter were also alleged to have interfered with the mourning services for Pyjas. See also L. Unger 'Two weeks that shook Poland', *International Herald Tribune,* 30.5.77.
109. *Frankfurter Allgemeine Zeitung,* 26.7.77.
110. Full text in *Est et Ouest,* n 604 (1–15. Dec. 1977) pp. 410–12.
111. *Dissent in Poland,* op. cit., pp. 141–42. *International Herald Tribune* 30.5.77.
112. *Liberation,* 1.3.78.
113. This initiative follows similar attempts by the Czech opposition, the Jan Patočka University set up in Prague and Brno by academics expelled from their jobs after 1968 and attended by children of politically 'unreliable' parents who were not admitted to the University. The first lecture was given by Professor J. Machovec and was disrupted by the police (27.10.77). *Le Monde.* 1.11.77.
114. *International Herald Tribune,* 20.2.78.
115. *Le Monde,* 12.3.78.
116. *International Herald Tribune,* 20.2.78.
117. The 'Information Bulletin' published by KSS-KOR sympathisers is the oldest of these publications and has mainly publicised cases of repression. *Robotnik* addresses itself to workers' problems. *Bratniak* is a student publication confining itself deliberately to youth problems. *Opinia* is the journal of the Movement for the Defence of Human and Civil Rights (ROPCIO); *Spotkania* (Encounters) is a new journal put out by young Catholic intellectuals; *Puls,* like *Zapis,* is a literary journal (information provided by A. Smolar, editor of *Aneks,* a Polish political quarterly published in London).
118. *Zapis I.* and *II.* were published in Polish by *Index on Censorship,* London, 1977; Four volumes are circulating in Poland.
119. 'Samizdat', along with the emphasis on constitutionally guaranteed human rights, is another feature of oppositional activity that spread from the USSR to Eastern Europe.
120. *Zapis I,* op. cit., pp. 1–2.
121. *Sunday Times,* 29.5.77.
122. The Writers Union Congress of April 1978.

123. Niezalezna Oficyna Wydawnicza (NOWA); directed by M. Chojecki, a chemist and KOR activist, NOWA publishes on modern 'offset' equipment. Its publishing plan includes brochures about the March 68 events in Poland, the Prague Spring of 1968, the human rights movements in Eastern Europe. For a detailed account see M. Thiery, 'La stratégie de l'espoir de l'opposition polonaise' *Liberation*, 27.2.78.
124. A documentation relating to the functioning of censorship in Poland has been made available to the KSS-KOR and published in London, *'Czarna Księga Cenzury PRL 1'* (London: 1977). A detailed analysis of the document was presented by L. Labedz in *The Times* 26. and 27.9.1977; for English language excerpts see 'Official Censorship in the Polish People's Republic' (Ann Arbor, Michigan: The North American Study Center for Polish Affairs, 1978).
125. Text in *Survey*, Vol. 22, n 2 (99) (Spring 1976) p. 184.
126. E. Lipiński, 'Open letter to Comrade Edward Gierek' in *Survey*, ibid., p. 196.
127. Point 13 of PLI programme, op. cit., p. 188.
128. Interview in *Le Monde*, 1.3.77.
129. A. Michnik, 'The New Evolutionism', in *Survey*, Vol. 22, n 3/4 (Summer-Autumn, 1976) p. 273.
130. Kuroń in *Le Monde*, 29.1.77.
131. G. Herling-Grudzinski and A. Michnik 'Deux voix sur l'Eurocommunisme' in *Les Cahiers de l'Est* (Paris) 1977, n 11, p. 48; This text (pp. 39–51) contains the most detailed analysis by a Polish dissident of the impact of Eurocommunism in Eastern Europe and particularly in Poland. Michnik says in it 'It is not the Agnellis and the Pirellis of this world, but the metallurgists' Trade Union led by the communist Bruno Trentin who published a solidarity statement with the KOR and promised financial aid for the persecuted workers (in Poland)'. Ibid., p. 49.
132. In July Jacek Kuroń sent an appeal to the Italian Communist leader Enrico Berlinguer for support against the antiworker repression after June 1976. The text was published in *Unita* (20.7.76). The Italian communists gave a positive response to Kuroń's appeal and have since given regular and well informed coverage of the activities of the Polish opposition. The same cannot be said of their French comrades.
133. W. Bienkowski has written over the last ten years a series of open letters to the Polish leaders proposing sweeping reforms: Letter to Gomułka (11.3.70.) in *Politique Aujourd'hui*, 1971, n 11, pp. 105–12. 'Open letter to the authorities of the Polish People's Republic' in *Dissent in Poland*, op. cit., pp. 38–9.
134. Full text in *Labour Focus on Eastern Europe* (London), Vol. 2, n 1, (March-April, 1978) pp. 15–17; see also K. Unger, 'Ascent of Eurocommunism in Poland', *International Herald Tribune*, 1.2.78.
135. A. Michnik, 'The New Evolutionism', op. cit., p. 272.
136. Ibid., p. 263.
137. J. Kuroń, 'Pour une plate-forme unique de l'opposition' op. cit., p. 94.
138. A. Michnik explicitly refers to the Spanish model (the workers' commission, the collaboration of the Catholics with the Left etc.) in the

above mentioned debate of Eurocommunism 'Deux voix sur l'Eurocommunism' op. cit.

139. The Party edits *Gospodarz* (the Farmer), a samizdat journal for private farmers in order to revive the traditional PPP influence in the Polish countryside.

140. For an interesting survey of the ROPCIO milieu see M. Thiery, 'Le national patriotisme ou la nostalgie de la Pologne d'avant guerre' in *Liberation*, 28.2.78.

141. N.D. edits the 'Bulletin of the Association for the Protection of Life and Family' (*Biuletyn Towarżystwa ochrony życia i rodziny*), a traditionalist brand of Catholicism with special concern with promoting the Catholic position on demographic problems.

142. There are now indications that the Polish Government is facing a growing tide of protest from Polish farmers over the introduction of a compulsory new pension scheme. Several hundred thousand peasants withheld their payments of pension premiums in the summer of 1978. The Peasants' Self Defence Committees have established cooperation with both KSS-KOR and ROPCIO. See *Le Monde* 22.9.78; *The Times* 6.10.78.

4 East Germany: Dissenting Views during the Last Decade

by WERNER VOLKMER

East Germany's image as the hard core of Prussia, where soldiers still goosestep and where discipline and order are the cornerstones of everyday life,[1] makes it difficult for many people to picture that dissenters[2] exist there. However, opposition in the GDR exists, but it exists under conditions which are different from those in other East European countries.

A DIVIDED NATION

The most obvious way in which East Germany is different from other East European states is that the division of Germany makes the GDR a state within a nation. It is apparent that a country, where the western neighbours speak the same language, have the same history, the same cultural heritage and where there are strong cross border family ties, is in a special situation. The GDR is a country where watching western television is a common habit even among the most loyal party cadres.[3] Moreover, the treaty which it signed with its western neighbour in December 1972 was an expression of the special relationship between the two German states. Living in such a country creates a different type of national consciousness than that of the Poles, Czechs, Slovaks or Hungarians. The second feature particular to East Germany is the 12 year span during which the country lived with an open border between East and West Berlin. By the time the Wall was built in Berlin on August 13 1961, closing this loophole, more than two and a half million East Germans had left their country.[4] This was their way of expressing disagreement with the communist party in East Germany, the Socialist Unity Party, and with the system.[5] This tremendous outflow of critically minded people spared the party tensions which otherwise would almost certainly have developed. At the same time, however, this mass migration represented a serious brain-drain and

113

seriously depleted the GDR's labour force. The authorities, therefore, had to take into account that, if the pressures they exercised became too harsh, the exodus towards West Germany would gain in momentum. The party was thus to some extent forced to be moderate in its treatment of dissenters. For example, none of the critics of Walter Ulbricht, party leader until 1971, was executed or sentenced to life imprisonment.[6] By the same token the critical intelligentsia, who identified with socialism and did not want to leave the country, kept rather quiet during the period prior to the building of the Wall and often afterwards – out of solidarity with the party. A certain siege mentality prevailed. During the 1960s this mentality began to wither away. The worldwide diplomatic recognition of the GDR in 1973 in the wake of Willy Brandt's *Ostpolitik* furthered this process.

A third factor contributing to the special situation of East Germany has been the annual inflow of five to seven million visitors from the West since the Berlin agreement in 1972.[7] Discussions between hosts and visitors, adding to traditionally held values and the evidence supplied by western radio and television, encouraged the trend towards a consumer society more than in other East European countries. It is unheard of elsewhere in the eastern bloc that workers go on strike because they cannot buy their coffee, a luxury item, cheaply enough.

The party tried to counterbalance still existing all-German national feelings, the developing consumerism and the growing demand for the implementation of human rights by pursuing a policy of political and ideological demarcation from West Germany. When this policy was introduced at the end of 1970, however, it was already too late to maintain the loyalty of the critical intelligentsia. The shock of the Soviet-led invasion of Czechoslovakia on August 21 1968, had shattered the idealism and solidarity of many, particularly the young East Germans. It dawned on hitherto loyal party members that the teachings of classical Marxism and the existing system of socialism were entirely incompatible. In this sense critical thinkers in East Germany underwent a normalisation process in the 1960s and early 1970s,[8] marked by a shift from ideological orthodoxy towards a more critical attitude to socialist solidarity.

Opinion polls in West Germany have shown that thirty years after the end of the war, 70 per cent of the population is still convinced that the GDR and the Federal Republic are part of one nation.[9] The East German authorities found, in an opinion poll among young people which has not been published, that they also see themselves as Germans in the first place and as GDR citizens in the second.

The rapprochement between East and West Germany, imposed on the GDR by the Soviets in their pursuit of détente policy, and the following demarcation strategy have led to a reversal of previous positions on the national question. Official policy, even in the 1968 GDR constitution, had held that although there were two German states there was only one nation. Walter Ulbricht stated unmistakably in 1968: 'Yes, there is one German nation.'[10] However from 1971 onwards, it was claimed that East Germany had developed into a socialist German nation with stronger allegiances towards other east bloc countries than to West Germany, which represented the bourgeois German nation. Erich Honecker, Ulbricht's successor in 1971, declared in 1972 that West Germany was a foreign and imperialist country.[11]

The proponents of demarcation policy had been alarmed by the national emotions provoked by the futile negotiations between East German party officials and SPD leaders about an exchange of public speakers in 1966. Ulbricht had put the exchange into a national context. In his open letter to the SPD leadership in Bonn he said: 'The policy of a German party will be measured most of all by its position on the German question.'[12] Hopes were raised in East Germany of a closer relationship between the two working class parties, the communists and the socialists, starting with an open dialogue and 'leading one knows not where'.[13]

In 1970, when Willy Brandt, then Chancellor of West Germany, and Willi Stoph, the then Prime Minister of East Germany, met in Erfurt/GDR for discussions on the relationship between the two states, national feelings were riding high again. The scenes in the station forecourt and in front of Brandt's hotel in Erfurt must have made those of the party establishment, who cared about security, shudder. Thousands of people had gathered shouting for Willy Brandt to appear at his hotel room window. Police soon moved in, however, and *Betriebskampfgruppen* (factory based para-military organisations) were brought in demanding to see Willi Stoph.

A related event earlier on in that year had also shown how strong all-German feelings still are in East Germany. After Brandt had given his annual report on the state of the nation to the Federal Parliament in Bonn in January 1970, students in East Berlin distributed privately produced leaflets demanding that Brandt's suggestion about a rapprochement between the two German states should be discussed in East Germany as 'a national duty'.[14]

The policy of describing East Germans as socialist Germans, who no longer had anything in common with the bourgeois West German nation, led to utter confusion of the population and even among party cadres. Readers' letters to local papers and discussions in schools, universities and at factory gatherings showed that from the growing contentment with the material and welfare achievements during the 1960s and early 1970s it did not follow that an East German nation had developed.[15] Brandt's understanding that, apart from culture, language and history, nationhood comprises primarily the feeling of belonging,[16] still proved to be correct in the early 1970s.

The party, however, wanted to stop discussions about the national question and at the 13th Central Committee meeting in December 1974, Honecker clarified the situation somewhat by stating, for the benefit of those filling in forms, that the answers were: Citizenship GDR, nationality – German.[17] Since then the emphasis has changed. Although the party still distinguishes between a socialist and a bourgeois German nation, as is only consistent with Marxist thinking, there is no doubt any more that GDR citizens are German.

However, demarcation policy continues. Particularly outstanding since Honecker's takeover from Ulbricht is the emphasis on the country's close relationship with the USSR. The praise given to the Soviet Union at any possible, and many an impossible, opportunity is astonishing. In political and scientific writings reference to Soviet sources has increased noticeably.

The revival of anti-Soviet feelings is thus easier to understánd. On October 7 1977, the anniversary of the founding of the GDR, a clash took place between several hundred East German teenagers and the police which allegedly led to some deaths and many injured.[18] Hooliganism is not new to East Germany. For the first time in many years, though, anti-Soviet ('Russians out') and national ('Germany awake') slogans were shouted during these riots in East Berlin causing considerable high level embarrassment.[19]

PARTY IDEOLOGY AND 'REAL SOCIALISM'

Ideology has failed to provide a sufficient substitute for the desire for national self-identification. It has also failed so far in integrating young people smoothly into the existing system. The difference between Marxist theory, as it is taught in the GDR, and the actually existing system causes the party leadership some headaches. Ways and means were therefore sought to bridge this gap between theory and reality.

As an instrument of control but also of propaganda, sociology, established itself as a recognised discipline in the GDR in the 1960s. Dieter Voigt, a sociologist who came to the West in 1969, distinguished three purposes of sociological research in East Germany: (i) to provide empirical data for the highest political level, reflecting objectively the mood of the population and their opinion (such surveys are top secret and form the basis for decision-making on matters of principle); (ii) to provide empirical data objectively reflecting the situation in companies, in administration and research institutes (these surveys are sometimes published); and (iii) to provide biased propaganda surveys which are used for purposes of indoctrination.[20] Horst Taubert, a sociologist still in the GDR, described the tasks of his discipline as contributing to the development of society on the one hand, and as researching the progress of socialist consciousness on the other.[21] This blends in precisely with Voigt's three purposes of sociology in East Germany.

One of the few objectively conducted surveys which has been published in the GDR is Friedrich Walter's *Jugend heute* (Youth today), (Berlin, 1966).[22] In this survey, youngsters of between eleven and eighteen years of age rank their interests in order of priority. The ordering of these interests provides an idea of how successful the party has been in indoctrinating the young people with its ideology. A comparison between the results of this survey and data obtained in West Germany using the same method reveals that the majority of young people in East and West Germany are equally interested in pursuing pastime occupations. The GDR youths rated travelling and light music highest. Politics came seventh among school boys and twelfth among school girls. Economics and Marxist theory were rated very low indeed. They were mentioned in 16th and 17th place among school children and students.[23]

In contrast to their East German counterparts, West German youngsters are less interested in travelling. This follows from the fact that they can take the freedom to travel for granted. Young East Germans have been making full use of the increasing opportunities to travel in Eastern Europe, particularly since the early 1970s.[24] Talking to young people in East Germany, a western visitor gets the impression that most would like to travel without any of the restrictions at present imposed on them by the authorities. They would not necessarily want to stay in the west, as long as they knew the opportunity to travel there would always be open to them. The frequent mention, in many works of East German writers, of the desire to travel more widely indicates how serious a problem travel restrictions are in the GDR.

Sociological surveys in East Germany, as Voigt pointed out, are often short of interpretation for political reasons. Frank Graetz, another sociologist who fled the GDR, describes how K. Ducke concludes, in a survey of behaviour at work, that the stimulation of creative and disciplined working behaviour was necessary, without pointing out that discipline and creativeness often require contradicting stimuli.[25] Voigt, who conducted a survey among East German building site workers, constantly on the move with their company from one end of the country to another, found that among the five most often named factors which stimulate production, there was no mention of political motivation, only materialistic reasons.[26] Such an open indictment of party ideology could have damaging consequences for a sociologist who wanted to give an honest interpretation. However, as Voigt pointed out, company management often encouraged deviations from the official line in order to get to grips with the economic problems at hand. Voigt had to find out why the turnover of these construction workers was as high as it had been at the time of his research in 1966. To underline the rejection of ideological values by workers in East Germany, Graetz quotes what building site workers had to say to a western visitor about the ideological incentives for working harder: 'Money comes first. We are working overtime because we want to earn more. We are just as much materialists as everyone else.'[27]

The increasing standard of living in East Germany led to ever higher expectations among the population. Wages rose faster than the supply of consumer goods. This is also reflected in a significant increase in savings. During the years 1967–77 private savings increased from 35,000 million to 80,000 million Marks. In order to cream off part of the unused purchasing power, the Ulbricht regime, prior to 1967, had opened up new sales outlets, called *Exquisit* and *Delicatess* shops, which sell luxury goods for East Marks at prices of between twice and four times their value in western currency. The proverbial *vox populi* had it that these shops should be called Uwubus, which is short for Ulbricht's Wucherbude (Ulbricht's ripoff shops).

As the problem of unused purchasing power had remained unchanged, in 1977 Honecker decided to expand this chain of shops, and another kind of special sales outlet, the Intershops, which had existed for many years in East Germany.[28] The Intershops are for western customers paying in western currency and are situated in hotels, at railway stations, at border checkpoints and in city centres. They sell similar goods to those sold by the *Exquisit* and *Delicatess* shops: clothes, shoes, cosmetics, cigarettes, cameras, alcohol, and also electric equipment and western television sets.

As part of the expansion programme the requirement that customers of Intershops had to be westerners was dropped. At the same time it was made legal for East German citizens to receive gifts in the form of hard cash from their relatives and friends in the west. East Germans are now even allowed to open a special bank account for their western currency. In fact, they are obliged to deposit the proceeds of family or other friendly ties within three days of receipt, though they have free access to the account afterwards.

The expansion of the Intershop facilities was meant to provide further incentives for cash gifts from western visitors, and to generate more hard currency income. However, not all East Germans have generous relatives or friends in the west. Moreover, not all GDR citizens are in such a preferential position as the inhabitants of cities like Rostock, Leipzig and East Berlin, frequented by many western visitors, and hence with ample opportunities for 'friendly contacts'. The unofficial exchange rate at such unofficial transactions is three to four East Marks to one West Mark, while the official rate is one to one.

Thus a new strata of GDR citizens has started to develop – dressing in western clothes, sipping Scotch whisky and watching western television on Japanese colour tv-sets. Meanwhile their fellow countrymen have to make do with Adlershofer Vodka (a local brand) and are restricted to black and white television viewing. Workers in industrial centres such as Halle-Leuna, Eisenhuettenstadt and Berlin reject this consumer class system. In one district of East Berlin an Intershop had to be closed shortly after it had opened because of public protests.[29] In several big companies strikes were threatened should proposed Intershops be opened nearby. And in a big machine construction company to the north of Berlin, producing goods mainly for export to the west, the traditionally militant work force demanded that their wages be paid partly in hard currency so that they could join in with the new Intershop consumerism.

In one case, East German workers actually went on strike. The authorities had withdrawn one brand of coffee and virtually withdrawn another, so that only the most expensive brand was available. To add insult to injury, they then introduced a coffee and chicory mixture. The labour force in the Fritz-Heckert-Werke in Karl-Marx-Stadt walked out in protest.[30] Having been told by Ulbricht during the 1960s that

East Germany had beome a 'socialist community of men', East German workers found it difficult to accept new social divisions developing in such a society. All in all, fifty workers were taken into custody because of the strike. They were accused of agitating in favour of the class enemy. In the following weeks, the coffee mixture was quietly withdrawn from the market.

Despite the new affluence of the 1960s and 1970s, discontent with the East German government and with the party continued. The main complaint regarding the violation of human rights concerns the restricted freedom of movement. Immediately after the building of the Wall, escaping from the country became something of a challenge for many youngsters. Heavy sentences were given initially to frighten them off and also the more serious would-be-escapees. With the improvement of the border safeguards in the mid-1960s, the authorities were more interested in reintegrating people convicted of trying to escape than in imprisoning them for too long. However, Ostpolitik and demarcation policies saw another heavy clamp-down on those refugees who were caught. In 1977, a reform of the criminal code of the GDR led to more draconian prison sentences for political crimes.

Since the mid-1960s fleeing East Germany has become a profitable business for enterprising westerners who charge considerable amounts for risking long-term imprisonment while helping East Germans to leave their country illegally. Thus it is the well-to-do new middle class of East Germany who can afford to leave illegally, or those who have relatives in the west who are willing to pay up. A brain-drain, particularly amongst doctors, has been the result.

Less well-connected and less well-heeled East Germans have to choose cruder ways of leaving the GDR, either via the Baltic Sea in makeshift floats, rubber dinghies or rowing boats, or via the borders at home or in a third country. Most people intending to flee try to avoid the murderously sophisticated border installations in East Germany with their trip-wires, high electrified fences, barbed wire, mines and automatic shooting devices in addition to the normal border guards.

On average roughly 5,000 East Germans are successful in fleeing to West Germany every year. About 10 per cent of them actually cross the border.[31] The majority use false documents, hide in specially prepared cars on the transit routes between West Berlin and West Germany or choose a way out via a third country. Another method of getting out of the GDR developed in the early 1960s, when the East Germans persuaded the West German government to bail out political prisoners who wanted to leave the GDR. West Germany pays with goods and industrial equipment. Not all of the prisoners freed in this way have families in the west, and not all of them have really been imprisoned for political offences. However, these exchanges are still flourishing. The key figures are two lawyers: Wolfgang Vogel in East Berlin and Juergen Stange in West Berlin. The initial agreement was made with the Bonn Minister for all-German questions at the time, Erich Mende.[32]

In 1972, East and West Germany agreed to facilitate the reunification of families in an official treaty signed in the context of the Treaty on the Basic Relationship Between the Two German States. The price per person varies and is a matter of individual circumstances. Where the GDR can claim high costs for further education, Bonn has to pay more. However, often no money at all is paid.

The number of GDR citizens who want to leave the country permanently is far greater, though, than the number of refugees and those who are 'bought free' would suggest. Precise figures are obviously not available. Since the signing of the final document of the European Conference on Security and Cooperation in Helsinki in 1975, the number of people who have applied to leave legally is reported to have increased dramatically. Many of those who want to leave but are not prepared to risk being shot, or who tried and were caught, or have said right from the beginning they want to leave legally, are applying to be released from their East German citizenship and permitted to move to West Germany. Conservative estimates mention 100,000 applicants,[33] which means that roughly 1 per cent of the total population wants to leave and is willing to say so openly. In an interview with a West German paper, party leader Erich Honecker said that during 1975 and 1976, altogether 20,000 GDR citizens had left the country legally.[34]

The authorities have generally ignored these applications, using threats and sometimes even stronger pressure, ranging from dismissal to imprisonment, to dissuade applicants from pursuing their aim. Many of the applicants cite the freedom of movement guaranteed in the final document of the Helsinki agreement, which the GDR signed.[35] In answer to the West German media's comments on this subject, the East German press argues that: (a) human rights are foremost social rights, which are fully adhered to in the GDR, and (b) that the right to move to West Germany is not covered by the freedom of movement clause in the Helsinki document.[36] But East Germans are not so easily persuaded. One year after Helsinki, on July 10 1976, a doctor from Riesa, Karl-Heinz Nitschke, initiated a human rights petition demanding, in particular, freedom of movement. On the first day, he got the spontaneous support of thirty-three people, mainly workers. All in all, seventy-nine people signed the document.[37] Most of them demanded to be allowed to move to West Germany and had their plea rejected. The list of their names was published by the western media and their cases were fully discussed in the west. On August 31 1976, Nitschke was imprisoned and escaped a show trial only by making clear that he would use the occasion for a public protest against the violation of human rights in the GDR.[38]

Nitschke has now been released to West Germany with the help of the lawyers Vogel and Stange, but several others of the group are still held in custody. At least eight have been sentenced to several years imprisonment, one managed to flee the country, and one girl was allowed to leave in the same way as Nitschke. Most of the remaining members of the group have lost their faith in the pressure that western politicians and the media are willing to exercise to get them out. However, they have continued to press their demands.

The second International Sakharov Hearing in Rome in 1977 heard numerous eyewitness reports of the violation of human rights in Eastern Europe. Several East Germans put their case. The writer Siegmar Faust, who had left the party after the invasion of Czechoslovakia in August 1968 and been imprisoned for his political views, reported that political prisoners in East Germany were beaten with iron bars. A former East German policeman reported that, since the building of the Wall, 173,000 had fled the GDR and 171 had been shot dead while trying to escape. A linguist from East Berlin, Hellmuth Nitsche, told the hearing that he was sentenced to five years' imprisonment for an eight minute demonstration in which he demanded to be allowed to leave East Germany.[39]

Small wonder that the East German weekly *Junge Welt* accused Amnesty International, the organisation which took part in setting up the Sakharov Hearings, of being an 'instrument of imperialism'.[40] The paper, however, found it difficult to explain why Amnesty International concerns itself not only with Eastern bloc countries, but with fascist regimes and western democratic states, wherever complaints are made. The main ideological problem for the East German party is the contradiction between the policy of denying some basic human rights, but at the same time signing international documents which guarantee these very same freedoms.

The GDR's 1968 constitution guarantees the right to practice religious beliefs (Article 39). Of the population of 17 million, 11 million belong to a church: 9.86 million Protestants and 1.28 million Catholics. While the Catholic Church keeps relatively quiet and, in turn, is not subjected to much pressure, the Protestant leadership has on several occasions taken on the authorities. Only at the insistence of the Protestant Church, for example, does the 1968 constitution include the guarantee of equal treatment, regardless of religious confession.[41] The struggle of the Churches for freedom of manoeuvre, as this instance indicates, is conducted by insisting on adherence to the Universal Declaration of Human Rights of 1948 and the ECSC Helsinki document.[42]

The constitutional guarantee of equal treatment for Christians, however, is in practice ignored. In 1976 nearly 97 per cent of fourteen year olds took part in the *Jugendweihe*, the state-organised equivalent to confirmation. Those who do not want to participate are usually not allowed to enter grammar school or university. A note in the personal file of a young East German, which accompanies him throughout life, makes it difficult for him to find a job or to take further education. The choice is often put crudely: It is either the Church or us, the atheist state. In one of his books the author Reiner Kunze describes a young man, an atheist, who is treated as a politically doubtful character after a Bible is found among his books.[43]

The Church has become a symbol of freedom for many young people in the GDR, freedom from being patronised and from being forced to be hypocritical. Young people feel attracted to the open-minded atmosphere of the Church community, where no pressure is exercised and where they can be themselves, as Reiner Kunze put it. In protest at the discrimination towards young Christians in the GDR the Protestant pastor Bruesewitz from Zeitz burned himself to death on August 18 1976. This suicide led to passionate discussions in the whole of Germany and left the Protestant Church in the GDR in a state of newly gained self-confidence, not least because of the support it has since gained from young people in particular.

In many churches it is not unheard of for more than 1500 young people to attend to listen to the sermon and often also to a concert. Pastor Theo Lehmann in Karl-Marx-Stadt has a rock group playing pop songs, and the congregation sings Lehmann's Christian lyrics to the Beatles tune of 'Yellow Submarine'.[44] The state allows in churches only religious activities; for anything else permission must be sought beforehand.

Before his enforced exile, the East Berlin singer and poet Wolf

Biermann had made only two public appearances in East Germany after he was declared persona non grata and all his works were banned in 1965. Once, during the World Youth Congress in East Berlin in 1973, he took his guitar and sang in the city centre without asking the authorities whether he could do so, and then in the Protestant Nicolai Church in Prenziau in 1976.[45] The Nicolai Church was crowded for the performance.

A year after the suicide of pastor Bruesewitz, the Bishop of Magdeburg, Werne Krusche, wrote in a circular letter: 'The deed of our brother has affected life in our Church deeply and has caused wholesome disquiet and impassioned thought far beyond the boundaries of our Church.'[46] The churches have so far successfully withstood all attempts to make them instrumental in integrating Christians into the politicised spheres of atheist East Germany. The party rejects the idea that the Church can be politically neutral; the churches, however, maintain that fruitful cooperation need not mean that the churches adopt the party's ideology. At the same time the Church leaders stress that they are not in opposition to the state. They see the Church's task as working within socialist society.

MARXIST HERETICS

Dissident thinking in East Germany, as far as it is expressed in the written or spoken word, takes mainly the form of artistic works. There are, however, some critics of the Soviet system as applied to the GDR, who concentrate their intellectual efforts on ideological and political questions of principle. During the last ten years four outstanding critics of the Soviet system in East Germany have emerged who will be dealt with in the following pages.

Robert Havemann is a man who was sentenced to death by the Nazis and, by the end of 1977, had been in virtual solitary confinement in his house in Gruenheide near Berlin for over a year. The reason is that as a communist since 1932, and an active member of the resistance movement during the Third Reich, he holds that socialism and human rights belong together. In his view, freedom and social justice cannot be separated. The party believes that Havemann organised the protest against the expulsion of his friend, Wolf Biermann, from the GDR in November 1976.[47]

Havemann became the first prominent dissident after the building of the Wall when, in 1962, he started a series of lectures, first in Leipzig then in East Berlin, in which he denounced the ideology taught in the GDR as neither dialectic nor materialistic, as required by Marx.[48] At the Humboldt University in East Berlin thousands of students listened eagerly to the rebellious professor. In 1964 he was dismissed and finally relieved of all his functions. Since then, he has lived from a small pension which he receives as a result of the seven years he spent in prison under Hitler. Together with Wolf Biermann, he has been a centre of intellectual resistance in the GDR since the mid-1960s. Havemann fought with his weapons as a philosopher and scientist. In his prolific writings he takes issue with the theory, as taught, and the practice of socialism in the GDR.[49] In *Dialektik ohne Dogma* and *Fragen, Antworten, Fragen* he logically dismantles the claim of the party to be the source of all wisdom. *Rueckantworten an die Hauptverwaltung 'Ewige Wahrheiten'* and *Berliner Schriften* contain a collection of selected interviews, speeches and articles which deal with a variety of subjects ranging from physics to many political questions.

In his essay on 'Communism – Utopia and Reality' Havemann sums up what he had explained in painstaking detail in his lectures during 1962–4. He denounces the abolition for its own sake of irreplaceable achievements, particularly parliamentary democracy. However, he goes one step further and demands the understanding of the utopia of communism as an acceptable challenge to the existing societal forms, 'which we have created'.[50] Such a critique implies that the GDR system is not sacrosanct.

His enthusiasm for the Czechoslovak experiment in 1968 is expressed in two essays which appeared in 1968 and 1969 respectively.[51] In an interview on the occasion of the publishing of *Fragen, Antworten, Fragen* in 1970, Havemann summed up what, in his opinion, the GDR essentially lacks and why this is so. He thinks, while capitalism develops because of the profit motive, socialism needs the freedom of public dissent to develop – more so than the western system.[52]

His Marxist explanation is that the revolution of 1917 was only half a socialist revolution. While the political and economic order of the bourgeois class was destroyed, the democratic element was also destroyed instead of being developed fully. In East Germany, as in other East European countries, the petit bourgeois desire of accumulating private wealth and of achieving a higher material standard of living was as highly developed as in the west. In Czechoslovakia, in his view, the second part of the socialist revolution had been taking place in 1968, but was forcibly interrupted.

Havemann's most challenging essay for the East German authorities, though, deals with an essential Marxist dictum: Freedom is the recognition of necessity. This maxim, which goes back to Hegel, is practised by the party, according to Havemann, such that the freedom of the state necessitates the lack of freedom of the individual.[53] Havemann calls this pseudo-socialism. He holds that the economic purpose of socialist society should be fundamentally different from capitalism, and therefore rejects consumerism. Referring to western studies critical of the misuse of the limited resources of our planet, he indicts the party's decison to support the development of mass ownership of private cars. His conclusion is that freedom can only be preserved in a world of scarce resources by stopping the unwarranted waste of these resources. The alternative is a police state – 'dirigism'.

By the mid-1960s, Havemann had become something of an internal socialist opposition to the ruling party and a direct opponent of Ulbricht. Ulbricht was not very popular. His relationship to the people was summarised by Bertolt Brecht after June 17 1953, which Havemann quotes: 'The people have lost the trust of the government. The government has to choose a new people.'[54]

It may be somewhat surprising to call a former leader of the East German ruling party a Marxist heretic. However, bearing in mind that the prime source of power in East Germany is still the Politbureau of the CPSU, and that Honecker succeeded Ulbricht in 1971 with the backing of the Soviets,[55] Ulbricht's ousting can be seen as a result of his dissenting views on a variety of political and ideological questions. Urgent political issues, the pursuit of détente policy and a greater flexibility vis-à-vis West Germany, seem to have played a more important part in forming the Soviet view on who should be leading the East German party than ideological questions. Even so, Ulbricht's claim to a higher stage of societal development in East Germany compared to the USSR could not have pleased the Soviet leadership.

Walter Ulbricht, encouraged by economic and political success at home after the building of the Wall in Berlin, declared at the VIIth Party Congress in 1967 that a 'developed societal system of socialism' existed in the GDR.[56] In doing so, he dropped the traditional definition of socialism, which until then had been regarded as only a transitory stage to communism, not as a historic formation in its own right. In Ulbricht's view, socialism was not a short term development of society, but a relatively self-contained socioeconomic formation between capitalism and communism.[57] This rewriting of Marxist theory, and the rejection of Soviet leadership in ideological matters, was accompanied by two other new developments in East Germany: the economic reforms known as the NES, the New Economic System, and the increased importance accorded to the sciences, particularly cybernetics in the 1960s.

The NES was introduced in 1963 and was aimed at 'the exploitation of economic levers, especially price, profit, credit and interest, as well as wages and bonuses'.[58] The NES followed the general lines of the model developed in the USSR in 1962, based on the thoughts of Professors Liberman and Nemchinov. It was the economic success achieved with the reforms which provided Ulbricht with a solid base from which he could develop his ideas about the 'socialist society of men'.

The importance of the scientific community as an advisory arm of the party had grown gradually since the mid-1950s. In 1968, the GDR politbureau even decided to regard science as one of the major productive forces.[59] This was also in line with what Soviet leaders thought. Where Ulbricht, however, spoke about the 'self-steering of parts of the societal system',[60] he was outlining a model which would have been more advanced than the Soviet Union and implied a diminishing role for the communist party.

Neither Ulbricht's cybernetic socialism, nor the critique of the shortcomings of his implementation of the NES towards the end of the 1960s, alone led to his downfall. The USSR leadership could probably have lived with his view of the GDR as a self-steering society, as long as the role of the party was not affected. By 1970–1 Ulbricht had already withdrawn the most heretical parts of his concept. However, his resistance to Soviet pressure that he should take a more cooperative line towards West Germany for the sake of détente was still a bone of contention. Ulbricht feared that closer inner-German relations would automatically lead to decreased internal stability and endanger the party's position. He had to step down as party leader on May 3 1971. With the benefit of hindsight, one can say that Ulbricht's fears were not entirely unjustified. The question to be asked, though, is whether the outspoken criticism of the party and the system since the early 1970s would have been moderated if the party had been more intransigent. The opposite could easily be argued.

In 1956, Wolfgang Harich was the intellectual leader of an opposition group which was even prepared to seek the assistance of West Germany in order to push through reforms in the East German ruling party. After ten years' imprisonment, Harich has now become an orthodox Marxist who nevertheless seeks open intellectual discussion. In 1956, he was urging for a democratisation of the party, and a reunification of the two working class parties, the Socialist Unity Party in East Germany and the Social Democratic Party in West Germany, as a prelude to a reunited neutral Germany. In his writings in the 1970s, he has developed a different line of thought. In a booklet, published in Switzerland in 1971, he argues against the revolutionary impatience of the New Left in France.[61] He justifies the hardship and undemocratic rule imposed by the dictatorship of the proletariat and holds that the despotism of the Stalin period could not have been avoided, for historic reasons.

. These views are not acceptable to the present party leadership because Harich implies – not without logic – that under present circumstances East Germany can only be a dictatorship, with all that this implies. When one reads that Harich even accuses Marx of revolutionary impatience, of an over-optimistic projection of history, and of falling into the same trap of religious consciousness and wishful thinking which he was trying to refute, it is not difficult to understand why Harich's books can only appear in the west. In another book,[62] Harich proposes three theses which are anathema to official East German dogma. First, he holds that communism does not necessarily have to be achieved in the so-called socialist countries first. It is conceivable, in his view, that the west can reach this societal formation earlier. Second, he suggests that the theory of the withering away of the state, one of the basic Marxist assumptions, should be denounced as anarchistic utopia. And, third, he believes that only a rigid distributory state system can cope with the ecological and economic problems of the future.

Harich is representative of most of the critical East German intelligentsia insofar as he is a Marxist. He is also representative of a certain German tradition of intellectual rigidity. His vision of the future society is apparently that of a puritan police state. Not all East German dissident thinkers, however, have been led by the rigidity of Marxist logic to such an inhuman vision of the future.

The most surprising and perhaps the most skilled attack on the party and its system in the 1970s came from an entirely unknown man, a former trade union official, journalist and economist. Rudolf Bahro, born in 1935, applied to join the party in 1952 and had made a picture-book career until, in the mid-1960s, he fell foul of the party.

After studying philosophy in East Berlin, Bahro worked as a journalist and was then asked to join the Bureau of a trade union as an assistant. He returned to journalism in 1965 and became the deputy editor of the students' weekly *Forum*, but had to leave the paper after starting a literary discussion in the paper, and after printing the controversial play *Kipper Paul Bauch* by Volker Braun. With the help of friends he then went into industry and became a director responsible for labour organisation, rationalisation and fulfilment of norms in a Berlin rubber company.

On August 22 1977, *Der Spiegel*, the Hamburg news magazine, published an excerpt of a book which Bahro had written: *Die Alternative*.[63] As the subtitle suggests, it is a critique of the actually existing socialism. In it, Bahro analyses the development of the existing form of socialism in the Soviet Union from a historical/philosophical view, pointing out where and why it was different from what Marx had said. He then gives a devastating analysis of the system in the GDR, an analysis which is applicable, in his view, to the whole of the east bloc countries. The party apparatus and the state bureaucraƚy were the focus of much of the criticism. Bahro then describes what he regards as the possible way to a better society in the GDR. This involves an institutionalised extra-party opposition. Bahro calls this opposition a new federation of communists or, figuratively speaking, a collective intellectual.

The surprise effect of the book was considerable. Until August 1977 nobody knew who Bahro was and what he had to say. The publication of parts of his book in *Der Spiegel*, television interviews with both West German TV networks and with the representative of West German radio, the distribution of brief samizdat versions of his book and the publication of the book itself in West Germany (of which a few hundred undoubtedly will find their way into East Germany), ensured that Bahro's views were circulated in both Germanies. Whatever the party did to him, party functionaries cannot avoid being confronted with his criticisms. Bahro said: 'I have written a book against which the political police will be powerless because it hits the party apparatus in its heart.'[64] Bahro was taken into custody one day after the publication of parts of his book in *Der Spiegel*. The official news agency ADN announced that Bahro would be charged with espionage,[65] and on June 30 1978 he was sentenced to eight years' imprisonment on this charge.

Bahro believes that a thinking process has started in the GDR, particularly in the wake of eastern bloc troops marching into Czechoslovakia in August 1968. As so many of his fellow countrymen, Bahro thought initially of resigning from the party in protest. But he decided to do something more constructive and started writing his book.[66] Although the concept he develops is utopian, his sharp analysis and high level of thought in the first two parts of the book make *Die*

Alternative one of the best intellectual efforts ever from within the GDR, of critically assessing the existing system.

In contrast to the party, or Harich for that matter, Bahro rejects authoritarian rule and refers to Marx' analysis of the Paris Commune. He thinks, as Marx did, of the state as a societal parasite. Stalinism for him, as for Harich, was unavoidable under the specific circumstances in Soviet Russia at the time. However, he holds that the general emancipation of men has become more urgent. Bahro suggests the priority of freedom over necessity in future society. This, in his view, can be achieved by adhering to the federal principle of social organisation which is embodied in the idea of free association. Bahro advocates the free association of the individual instead of its subordination by the state.

The party took three and a half months, though still in rather general terms, to answer publicly to any of Bahro's arguments. In a speech to cultural functionaires in Schwerin/GDR, Professor Hans Koch of the Social Science Institute of the Central Committee called Bahro an anti-communist because his critique had shown impatience, weakness and defeatism. It was a nondialectic negation of the existing socialism.[67] Koch's reply made it clear that the party regards it as one thing to criticise the existing system, but to suggest that the system should be replaced by another one, was an entirely different thing.

The East German party hierarchy could not accept Bahro's ideas because they felt that he had called the party's authority into question. Bahro wants free discussion and an end to the principle of democratic centralism; in his words, an end to subordination. While Harich, after ten years' imprisonment, became a pessimistic thinker, admiring Arnold Gehlen and seeing no future for a society without authoritarian power structures, Bahro put himself into a position where he faces long term imprisonment, and physical and psychological hardship, in order to have his optimistic and utopian views discussed in East Germany.

The publication of a manifesto at the end of 1977,[68] drawn up, it is claimed, by the 'Federation of Democratic Communists of Germany', shows that Bahro's idea of an extra-party opposition in the GDR is taken seriously. The Federation, according to *Der Spiegel*, was formed by medium and high-ranking functionaries of the East German party, organised into small clandestine groups. The members do not want to come into the open as yet. This opposition demands an end to one party dictatorship and to democratic centralism and wants to see an independent parliament and judiciary established. The reunification of Germany is dealt with at some length. Although the manifesto may well be authentic, since it reflects mainly Havemann's, Bahro's and Eurocommunist ideas, an attack on the Soviet leadership as neo-Fascist casts some doubts on the genuine character of the publication. It seems improbable that high-ranking East German functionaries expect change in the GDR by antagonising Moscow. Repeating Chinese accusations of Soviet imperialism will certainly not make things easier.

ARTISTIC FREEDOM AND SOCIALIST SOLIDARITY

After the thaw period from 1962 to 1965 which ended with the 11th Plenary Session of the Central Committee,[69] artists were again expected to conform strictly with the party line. However, the seeds of independent critical thinking could not be rooted out by decree. While many writers simply proceeded more cautiously, but without renouncing what they had said previously, the young poet and singer Wolf Biermann chose not to compromise. He and his friend Robert Havemann became an intellectual focus of resistance to the party orthodoxy. These two men, by their very existence, encouraged many others not to toe the line. A circle of young writers gathered around them in the 1970s.[70]

After Erich Honecker declared at the IVth Plenary Session in December 1971 that 'there can be no taboos in the fields of art and literature provided the starting point is basically socialist',[71] a new thaw began. Biermann and like-minded people, however, were still kept in intellectual quarantine, although attempts were made by the authorities occasionally to reintegrate them. The dramatic clash between the critical intelligentsia and the party, after the expulsion of Biermann on November 16 1976, was the peak of this war of principles and put the more flexible approach of the party toward the arts into question again.

At the end of 1977, the reins were shortened considerably. The Politbureau decided to fight vigorously against attempts 'to spread hostile, revisionist and ultra-left ideologies dressed up as art and directed against the existing socialism and against the policy of our party'.[72] Literary and art critics were given the task of checking and examining the works of artists according to these principles.

The open letter by thirteen well-known East German artists,[73] in which they pleaded with the authorities to change their decision on Biermann's expulsion, was the beginning of an unprecedented public protest. At the same time, however, it meant that troublemakers could easily be earmarked for special treatment. The party took severe reprisals against the less established intellectuals, often imprisoning them. More famous artists were demoted from office in the Writers Union, expelled from the party and their works tacitly banned. The protest against Biermann's enforced expatriation was by no means confined to some of his artist colleagues.

After the initial signing of the protest letter by twelve writers and one sculptor, more than a hundred artists in the GDR declared their solidarity with Biermann. In Jena a young clergyman was imprisoned, together with three nurses, an electronics specialist, several engineering workers and a writer, for protesting against Biermann's expulsion. In Erfurt, a young stagehand was imprisoned for collecting fifty signatures in support of Biermann.

One year after Biermann's enforced emigration at least twenty people had been put in jail and dozens of others had been forced to leave the country. Some of the emigrants feared, as Manfred Krug, a popular actor and folk singer who also had to leave, put it: 'The last man out will turn off the lights.'[74] However, it would be wrong to assume that this exodus has led to a dull and dreary cultural scene in East Germany. Most important of all, the discussion of the Biermann case has not stopped, despite strenuous efforts by the party to return to a quieter cultural policy. The fate of some of the thirteen initial signatories of the protest letter and to some of Biermann's other supporters since November 1976 illustrates this point.

The well-established East German lyricist and writer, Berd Jentzsch, who happened to be in Switzerland during November 1976, wrote an open letter to Erich Honecker after the Biermann affair in which he describes the atmosphere of growing repression in cultural life in the GDR. Jentzsch wrote why he thought it his duty to publicly demand a reversal of the regime's cultural policies. He referred to searches of writers' flats by the secret police, followed by interrogations lasting for hours. He accused the secret police of confiscating unpublished manuscripts, notes and diaries, letters and books. Jentzsch also complained that more and more good manuscripts were rejected by publishers while the ramblings of party hacks were accepted. These events, he wrote, which had occurred 'frighteningly often' prior to his departure in October 1976, made the party slogan about the 'blossoming of the arts' seem like pure derision.[75] Jentzsch, who was on a working visit to Switzerland, decided to stay there. His writings, however, are not banned in the GDR.

The sculptor Fritz Cremer was put under heavy pressure by the authorities to withdraw his signature. Cremer's son-in-law, Peter Schwarzbach, had been imprisoned for signing the protest letter himself. Cremer was told that Schwarzbach would be freed if Cremer withdrew his signature, which he did. Schwarzbach was released. Cremer's daughter Trini, however, was so disgusted with the whole affair that she has now signed the letter herself.

Volker Braun qualified his signature. A few days after the affair, Braun claimed publicly that the open letter by the GDR artists was used by western commentators to divide artists and the party.[76] However, Rolf Schneider indicates in a short story about the Biermann protest that Braun had been the one who had looked up the address of the news agency in West Berlin to which the protest letter was going to be sent. The authorities, however, apparently knew that Braun changes his mind easily if put under pressure. He was reprimanded by the party for his part in the affair, while others were more severely censured.[77]

The most vulnerable of the remaining eleven writers, the party must have thought, was Sarah Kirsch. She ranks among the best contemporary lyricists in Germany and has won several literary prizes in East and West, among them the Petrarca Prize. She had been treated by hardline functionaries with suspicion for some time. After she had signed the protest letter, her name was struck off the list of party members.

Sarah Kirsch continued to speak her mind. During the summer of 1977 she was subjected to personal abuse and rumours. Threatening slogans were written on the door to her flat in East Berlin, and she was finally told that an application to leave the country would be treated favourably. Sarah Kirsch left the GDR and now lives in West Berlin.[78] Her enforced emigration was seen by one critical artist in the GDR as the result of the politicking of one of the other ten initial signatories of the protest letter.[79]

Guenter Kunert, who is also a fine poet, still lives in East Berlin. In July and August 1977, he was involved in an exchange of open letters with another East German writer, Joachim Seyppel, in which they discussed the pros and cons of the emigration of East German intellectuals. The exchange took place in West German papers, however. The reason, as Kunert pointed out, was that 'our problems cannot be dealt with where we work'. The East Berlin Writers' Union, he complained, was no place for discussion because 'they shut you up before you even open your mouth – as if you were a fool or a mindless child'.[80] This open discussion is not without delicacy as Seyppel moved from West Berlin to East Germany only four years ago and is already encountering serious problems with the authorities, while Kunert is potentially another emigrant should the party so decide.

In some cases the East German authorities pursued a special strategy of preparing the ground before getting rid of an undesired, though famous, artist. Manfred Krug, who counts among the top actors in East Germany, was subjected to such treatment following his support for Biermann. Vicious rumours and lack of work forced him either to give in or to apply for an exit visa. Rather than kissing the rod and maintaining his privileged position, he opted out and went to the West. Krug had played the lead in a film written by Jurek Becker, one of the initial signatories and a prominent East German writer. The film was not shown for two years after Krug had left.

Becker was born in Poland and spent part of his youth in a Jewish ghetto and in Nazi concentration camps. He came to fame after his novel *Jacob the Liar* was published in 1968. This story of how to survive under deadly conditions without losing your sense of humour is partly autobiographic. Until recently, Becker was in a similar position to Manfred Krug before he applied for his exit visa. Becker is a convinced socialist and does not want to leave East Germany, though he does not want to keep quiet either. In an interview with a West German news magazine, he said: 'My identity has changed in some way during the last seven to eight months. Perhaps one of the reasons for this is that I am now 39 and suddenly feel the fear that I will still be behaving tactically when I am 60 – in favour of something which does not even exist then.' Becker therefore believes he must criticise openly now. 'If it is a question of keeping my mouth shut', he said in this interview, 'then I would rather keep my mouth shut in the Bahamas.'[81] Becker and other critical intellectuals in East Germany want to show critical solidarity with the party, not uncritical complicity.

Twelve years ago, Stefan Heym had set the rules of the game – which has been played ever since. In his *The Boredom of Minsk*, a manifesto on cultural freedom published in 1965, he laid down four principles: (1) the party has no monopoly of the truth; (2) there is an imminent conflict between writers and functionaries; (3) taboos have to be disregarded, and (4) hardship has to be accepted while pursuing the first three principles.

Heym himself followed these principles with the result that several of his books were not published in the GDR. However, he is one of the few remaining East German writers who established themselves before the war and thus is less vulnerable to party pressures. Nevertheless, he had to be content with publishing his books in the west. In *Uncertain Friend*[82] and *The King David Report*[83] Heym deals with Stalinism, revealing those aspects of GDR society which are still Stalinist today. In his *Queen against Defoe*,[84] he argues the case of the dissenter's freedom to speak up critically against the authorities. Underlining this last point, Heym spoke in an interview in West Germany in 1972 about criticism and the capability to think in a socialist society. His conclusion was: criticism helps to sharpen a citizen's capability to think, and 'the more that people are made to think the better it is for socialism'.[85]

The thaw beginning with Honecker's takeover from Ulbricht in 1971 led to the publication of Heym's three books just mentioned. His account of the workers' uprising in East Germany in June 1953, however, has only appeared in West Germany.[86]

Three young writers who have had a much greater impact than Heym on the cultural scene in East Germany recently are Ulrich Plenzdorf, Reiner Kunze and Volker Braun. They belong to the new GDR generation of artists who have grown up in East Germany and made their name there.

Ulrich Plenzdorf, a playwright and film-maker, became a national figure almost overnight when he managed to have staged his *The New Sufferings of the Young W.* The *New Sufferings* is the socialist version of Goethe's *The Sufferings of the Young Werther*, published 1774, but in a somewhat satirical form. The patronising approach of party officials and worker activists to youngsters is refreshingly revealed in a language which is that of East German teenagers. Similarly Plenzdorf's film *The Legend of Paul and Paula*, which tackled pious careerism and prim officialdom, also showed, quite convincingly, how far from being emancipated women still are in East Germany, despite the many achievements the party can boast.

Volker Braun's *The Unfinished Story*, which was published in the GDR's leading cultural magazine *Sinn und Form* in 1975, is a savage attack on the cruel and mindless rule of party secretaries in companies and at regional and local level. Based on the party's phobia of anything which smacks of sympathy for the west, East Germans can recognise easily in this story what they have to cope with daily: the entangled bureaucracy of party rule, reminiscent of Kafka's visions.

Reiner Kunze, a writer and lyricist, has won literary prizes in both Germanies and in Austria. His works, however, were not published in East Germany, since he had fallen out with the party over the

Soviet-led invasion of Czechoslovakia in 1968. He gained fame in West Germany for publishing several volumes of poetry in the late 1960s and early 1970s, but without the blessing of the party.[87] Then, in 1973, in a surprise move, he was allowed to publish again in the GDR, and a thin volume, *Book with Blue Seals*, was brought out by Reclam's of Leipzig.

A later anthology, however, was suitable for publication in West Germany only. This book, entitled *The Wonderful Years*, describes the physical and psychological terror used by the East German authorities against youngsters who think critically. Although most of his work was published in the west, Kunze's poems are widely known in the GDR, and as with many other dissident writers, the East German public responded with innumerable letters, giving him support and also asking for advice.[88] Kunze left the GDR in April 1977 and settled in West Germany, not in the wake of Biermann but, as he put it, because of the 'frightening methods of intimidation' used against him.

Several developments, internal and external in nature, have encouraged the strong dissident voices heard in the GDR today. The worldwide recognition of East Germany as a state in its own right, the end of the siege mentality among intellectuals, and the increased consumer orientation of the East German economy have contributed to a climate of critical reflection. Large parts of the population are asking themselves where the East German system of socialism has led them. The economic strain which the GDR has felt more and more since the mid-1970s makes it more difficult for the party leadership to cope with expectations. In order to balance the inner-German repercussions of détente, economic hopes were raised and a rigid demarcation policy was pursued at the beginning of the decade. Neither, however, could stop the ever growing demand for the implementation of basic human rights in East Germany. The Final Act of the Helsinki ECSC brought to the attention of many GDR citizens that the rights granted in East German law, and the obligations towards their citizens embodied in many international agreements, only too often meant nothing to the authorities. The initial good will of the population towards Honecker's new regime thus soon faded, and the years of 1976 and 1977 saw a marked deterioration in the relationship between ordinary citizens and the authorities.

In 1976–7, the party had to make a choice between an internal freeze in the political and cultural sphere, and a more trusting and open policy. Although the Politbureau apparently tried to avoid this choice, the result seems to favour the orthodox and dogmatic approach. In a way this is not surprising. Honecker's record as a hardliner in the mid-1960s and his personal reputation show that his party discipline is virtually unqualified.[89] Thus the conclusion can only be drawn that either Honecker no longer has the support of the majority of the Politbureau, or more likely that the Soviet party demands a more hardline approach.

Three factors will be the main determinants of the future development in the GDR: the economic performance of East Germany, how the population will take to the necessary economies that will have to be made and to the further denial of human rights, and the Soviets' continued backing of Honecker.

The leap in the cost of raw materials and the economic pressures from the Soviet Union on East Germany have made it more difficult for the party leadership to increase the standard of living. Widespread mismanagement and the unwillingness of the labour force to respond enthusiastically to yet another call for rationalisation, economies and voluntary additional shift work are not encouraging. West Germany, on the other hand, is quite willing to help financially, wherever possible, to ease the pressure. Both German governments have a vested interest, though of diverging character, to continue mutual cooperation. While the GDR wants generally more room for manoeuvre by developing good trade relations and obtaining financial subsidies from West Germany, Bonn is mainly interested in promoting contacts between the people in the two states and is willing to pay for this in cash.

Events towards the end of 1977 indicate that the GDR is probably destined for another cold weather period internally and in its relationship to West Germany. Reports in the East German press about the imprisonment of spies from West Germany increased during December 1977 and January 1978. The position of West Berlin, and the four power agreement on Berlin, have been the subject of more frequent propaganda attacks than before. The number of people trying to visit East Berlin who have been sent back grew substantially in 1977. Even the leader of the opposition in the West German Lower House, Helmut Kohl, was refused entry to East Berlin while travelling as a normal tourist.[90] The party leadership wants to prevent too much contact between East and West Germans, and needs a calmer situation at home. It is apparent that the publication of the manifesto of a supposedly inner-party opposition in *Der Spiegel* has shaken the leadership considerably. And it is irrelevant whether the document is authentic or not. The criticisms aired in this manifesto can be regarded as a summary of popular feelings in the country, and their publication has highlighted a dangerous situation for the top ranks of the party elite. Perhaps even more important though is the distrust which the rapprochement between the two Germanies, in the wake of détente and Ostpolitik, must have created in Moscow. The strongly worded attacks on the Soviet Union and the length at which German reunification was dealt with in the manifesto have certainly not improved the relationship between East Berlin and Moscow. As the pursuit of inner-German détente and reforms in East Germany seem to be possible only when the Soviet Union is willing to tolerate them, the immediate future seems to be bleak for any such progress. Experienced party functionaries are realistic enough to acknowledge the weakness of their position in this respect.

NOTES

1. Reiner Kunze, *Die wunderbaren Jahre* (Frankfurt: Fischer Verlag, 1976), p. 54, quotes the late Arnold Zweig, one of the leading figures of East German literature for many years, who said: 'Humanism and strict organisation have always been in contradiction. Even the Jesuits, who left us great spiritual power, were not as strained in their organisation as we are . . .'
2. The term dissenter or dissident is used here to describe anybody who holds a critical or heretical view compared to the official party line.
3. It was made legal in the early 1970s under Honecker, the new party leader.
4. *DDR Handbuch* (Cologne: Verlag Wissenschaft und Politik, 1975) p. 313.
5. Allowances have to be made for normal migration which would occur in any country. Also, not all of the migrants had political motives for leaving.
6. David Childs, *East Germany* (London: Ernest Benn Ltd., 1969) pp. 19–51.
7. *DDR Handbuch*, op. cit., p. 865.
8. For details see my article 'Thinking along Rails', *Index*, Vol. 5, No. 1 (Spring 1976) 27ff.
9. W. Schulz, 'Das Nationenspiel', *Deutschland Archiv* (hereafter *DA*) Vol. 8, No. 3 (March 1975) p. 227.
10. Ibid., p. 229.
11. Ilse Spittmann, 'Honecker und die deutsche Frage', *DA*, Vol. 5, No. 1 (January 1972) p. 2.
12. *Neues Deutschland* (hereafter *ND*) 11.2.1966.
13. Willy Brandt describes the development of the negotiations about the exchange of speakers in this way, *Begegnungen und Einsichten* (Ham-

burg: Hoffmann und Campe Verlag 1976) pp. 127–9. For a different view see D. Childs, op. cit., pp. 51f.

14. Willy Brandt, op. cit., p. 487.
15. For a different view see G. Schweigler, *Nationalbewusstsein in der BRD und der DDR* (Dusseldorf: Bertelsmann Universitaetsverlag, 1973) pp. 82ff.
16. Willy Brandt, op. cit., p. 487.
17. Honecker's speech is reprinted in *DA*, Vol. 8, No. 1 (January 1975) pp. 87ff.
18. *Frankfurter Allgemeine Zeitung* (hereafter *FAZ*) 15.11.1977. The East German news agency ADN denied these reports.
19. *The Times*, 10.10.1977.
20. Dieter Voigt, *Montagearbeiter in der DDR* (Darmstadt/Neuwied: Luchterhand Verlag, 1973) p. 11.
21. H. Taubert, 'Funktion und Aufgaben der soziologischen Forschung', *Berufsbildung*, Vol. 21, Nos. 7–8 (1967) pp. 400 and 405.
22. A review appeared in *DA*, Vol. 4, No. 5 (May 1971) pp. 525–7.
23. B. Hille, 'Interkulturelle Vergleiche', *DA*, Vol. 5, No. 9 (September 1972) pp. 934ff.
24. *DDR Handbuch*, op. cit., p. 864 shows a sudden increase in travel from 3 to 14.5 million visits abroad in 1971 and 1972 respectively. One stimulus was the opening of the Polish/GDR border.
25. F. Graetz, 'Ideelle Stimuli in der DDR-Wirtschaft', *DA*, Vol. 10, No. 10 (October 1977) p. 1073.
26. Dieter Voigt, op. cit., p. 127.
27. F. Graetz, op. cit., p. 1078.
28. 'Die DDR will die Zahl der Exquisit-Laeden erhoehen', *FAZ*, 28.9.1977.
29. Private conversations in East Berlin, 1977.
30. *Der Tagesspiegel*, 13.11.1977.
31. *DDR Handbuch*, op. cit., p. 313.
32. Rainer Hildebrandt, 'Kerkerjahre gegen Warenlieferungen', *Der Tagesspiegel*, 22.6.1976.
33. J. Nawrocki, 'Offener Unmut ueber das SED-Regime', *Die Zeit*, 15.10.1976. D. Schulz, 'Immer mehr Ausreiseantraege', *Der Tagesspiegel*. 27.7.1976. Other estimates mention 200,000 applicants.
34. 'Honecker: Unsere Bilanz ist gut', *FAZ*, 21.2.1977.
35. Angela Nacken, 'Immer mehr wagen den Kampf mit den DDR-Behoerden', *FAZ*, 21.8.1976. Also *FAZ*, 4.10.1977.
36. Hermann Klenner wrote an authoritative article, 'Menschenrechte – Heuchelei und Wahrheit', *Einheit*, Vol. 32, No. 9 (September 1977) pp. 1036–44.
37. Peter Pragal, 'Auf die Hoffnung folgt in Riesa Bitternis', *Sueddeutsche Zeitung* (hereafter *SZ*) 13.11.1977.
38. *FAZ*, 4.10.1977.
39. 'Die DDR auf der Anklagebank', *SZ*, 29.11.1977.
40. Quoted in *IWE*, 1./2.12.1977, 12/1508.
41. *Die Welt*, 25.8.1976.
42. *FAZ*, 31.5.1977. *FAZ*, 7.11.1977.

140 *Opposition in Eastern Europe*

43. *Die wunderbahren Jahre*, op. cit., pp. 38–42.
44. Uwe Siemon Netto, 'Jetzt beten sie wieder', Supplement to *Die Zeit*, 17.9.1976, pp. 19–27.
45. Personal conversation with Biermann, East Berlin, 1976.
46. BBC report by E. Vickers from Berlin, 19.8.1977.
47. 'Die Ausbuergerung der Speerspitze', *Die Zeit*, 20.5.1977, where excerpts of a secret party meeting at the Academy of Sciences in East Berlin are reprinted.
48. G. Bartsch, 'Revolution und Gegenrevolution in Osteuropa seit 1848 (III)', *Aus Politik und Zeitgeschichte*, Beilage zur Wochenzeitung das Parlament, 13.9.1969, p. 43.
49. *Dialektik ohne Dogma* (Reinbek: rororo Verlag, 1964) contains Havemann's speech in Leipzig and fourteen lectures given at the Humboldt Universitaet in East Berlin. *Fragen, Antworten, Fragen* (Munich: Piper Verlag, 1970) is an autobiographical account. *Rueckantworten an die Hauptverwaltung 'Ewige Wahreiten'* (Munich: Piper Verlag, 1971). *Berliner Schriften* (West Berlin: Verlag europaeische ideen, 1976).
50. *Rueckantworten* . . . , op. cit., pp. 73–8.
51. *Sozialismus und Demokratie*, 1968. *Der Sozialismus von morgen*, 1969.
52. *Rueckantworten* . . . , op. cit., p. 127.
53. *Berliner Schriften*, op. cit., pp. 49ff.
54. Ibid., p. 50.
55. Fred Oldenburg, 'Die DDR ein Jahr unter Honecker', *DA*, Vol. 5, No. 5 (May 1972) p. 484.
56. *Protokoll des VII. Parteitags*, 1967, pp. 97ff.
57. *ND*, 13.9.1967.
58. E. Apel/G. Mittag, *Neues Oekonomisches System und Investitionspolitik* (East Berlin: Dietz Verlag, 1965) p. 190.
59. *Einheit*, Vol. 23, No. 12 (December 1978) p. 1465.
60. W. Ulbricht, *Zum oekonomischen System des Sozialismus in der DDR* (East Berlin: Dietz Verlag, 1966) p. 551.
61. W. Harich, *Zur Kritik der revolutionaeren Ungeduld* (Basle: edition etcetera, 1971).
62. W. Harich, *Kommunismus ohne Wachstum?* (Reinbek: Rowohlt Verlag, 1975).
63. *Die Alternative – Zur Kritik des real existierenden Sozialismus* (Cologne/Frankfurt: Europaeische Verlagsanstalt, 1977).
64. *Der Spiegel*, 22.8.1977, p. 31.
65. *ND*, 24.8.1977.
66. *Rudolf Bahro – Eine Dokumentation* (Cologne/Frankfurt: Europaeische Verlagsanstalt, 1977) p. 91.
67. P. Pragal, 'SED antwortet auf Bahros Thesen', *SZ*, 4.12.1977.
68. *Der Spiegel*, 2.1.1978, pp. 19–24 and 9.1.1978, pp. 17–32.
69. *ND*, 16.12.1965. Honecker attacked critical artists virulently.
70. Among them were Juergen Fuchs, Siegmar Faust, Thomas Brasch and the musicians Gerulf Pannach and Christian Kunert.
71. *ND*, 18.12.1971.
72. *FAZ*, 29.11.1977.
73. Sarah Kirsch, Christa Wolf, Volker Braun, Franz Fuehmann, Stephan

Hermlin, Stefan Heym, Guenter Kunert, Heiner Mueller, Rolf Schneider, Gerhard Wolf, Jurek Becker, Erich Arend and Fritz Cremer.
74. *International Herald Tribune*, 18.8.1977.
75. *FAZ*, 24.11.1976.
76. S. Wirsing, 'Die Rueckkehr in den Schoss der Illusionen', *FAZ*, 4.2.1977.
77. Jurek Becker, Sarah Kirsch and Gerhard Wolf were expelled from the party. Stephan Hermlin was severely censured. Expulsion procedures were started against Christa Wolf and Guenter Kunert. Jurek Becker, Volker Braun, Guenter de Bruyn, Sarah Kirsch, Ulrich Plenzdorf and Dieter Schubert lost their seat in the presidium of the Berlin section of the East German Writers' Union. *FAZ*, 22.12.1976.
78. J. Seyppel, 'Nachruf und Gruss nach vorn', *Der Tagesspiegel*, 22.8.1977.
79. Seyppel did not name Stephan Hermlin, but his references are unmistakable. Ibid.
80. Seyppel in *Frankfurter Rundschau*, 26.7.1977, Kunert in *Die Zeit*, 5.8.1977.
81. *Der Spiegel*, 18.7.1977, pp. 128ff.
82. London: Cassel, 1969.
83. London: Hodder & Stoughton, 1973.
84. London: Hodder & Stoughton, 1974.
85. Reprinted in *Queen against Defoe*, op. cit., p. 120.
86. *5 Tage im Juni* (Munich: Bertelsmann Verlag, 1974).
87. *Sensible Wege* (Reinbek: Rowohlt Verlag, 1969). *Der Loewe Leopold* (Frankfurt: Fischer Verlag, 1971). *Zimmerlautstaerke* (Frankfurt: Fischer Verlag, 1972).
88. 'Briefe, die ihn noch erreichten', *Die Zeit*, 22.4.1977.
89. H. Lippmann, *Honecker – Portraet eines Nachfolgers* (Cologne: Verlag Wissenschaft und Politik, 1971) p. 233.
90. *The Times*, 16.1.1978.

5 Opposition and Para-Opposition: Critical Currents in Hungary, 1968–78

by GEORGE SCHÖPFLIN

The definitions of opposition in East European societies have tended to be derived from Polish, Czechoslovak and Soviet experience. They assume the existence of groups of individuals, acting in a more or less organised fashion, who have mounted direct or indirect challenges of their governments by seeking to exert pressure on these governments for specific policy objectives. The aim of constraining these governments to abide by their own legality seems to be one of the characteristic features of opposition in the 1970s. Equally significant is that this opposition prefers generally to act outside the functioning of the system and to bring pressure on the system from outside. The use of western media as a significant lever is, again, one of the striking features of the modus operandi of the opposition. In this context, the free and untrammelled distribution of information has played a central role in the self-generation and self-sustaining aspects of the opposition. Mutual example – encouragement from one opposition group to another – and also imitation are a further feature of opposition. Comparatively little of this is applicable to Hungary.[1] There, the political limits of intellectual activity, of the expression of criticism and thus of exerting some pressure on the functioning of the system from within appear to be sufficiently wide to permit the continued existence and functioning of what may be termed a 'para-opposition'. By this, I mean opposition that does not overtly question the ideological bases of the system, but does accept the leeway for a semi-autonomous political role permitted by that system. In the Hungarian case, the two pillars of orthodoxy which are not open to criticism are the country's alliance with the Soviet Union and the leading role of the party. But given that the Hungarian Socialist Workers' Party (HSWP) interprets its leading role relatively broadly, indirect and implicit criticism of the party has been expressed, and some of this has come close to questioning the

142

leading role itself. But this last has been exceptional and the limits of para-opposition, in all its formal and informal convolutions, have so far been perceived by the authorities as wide enough to permit the larger part of the Hungarian intelligentsia to continue their participation in the politics of the system that has come to be created under the leadership of János Kádár. There has been one exception to this acceptance of the norms of para-opposition: the case of the so-called Budapest School, the new left Marxist sociologists and philosophers who sought to develop the intellectual legacy of György Lukács and to apply their ideas to the practice of Hungarian society. The critique expressed by this group was declared to have crossed the threshold of ideological acceptability and its members were drummed out of public life. At this stage, this group became dissident perforce.

The political background against which both the opposition and the para-opposition evolved can be taken back to the mid-1960s, when the regime embarked on what could have been a genuine experiment in political, economic and social reform. The New Economic Mechanism of 1968 was intended to be accompanied by political reforms. But this process was terminated by the invasion of Czechoslovakia, which signalled the end of possibilities for fundamental change. Thus the reform came to a halt at the very moment when its perspectives began to unfold. This was not, however, visible at the time and for some years the nature of the limits remained unclear. By about 1973, on the other hand, the outlines of the new dispensation were clearer. These consisted of the acceptance of technocratic definitions of reform instead of political goals and the revision of the economic reform with the aim of restricting the possibility for autonomous economic activity at the lowest levels at the Central Committee meeting of November 1972. Second, there were increasing signs of readiness of the regime to use administrative means against the intelligentsia. And third, the neo-Stalinist wing of the party, capitalising on the mounting discontent of the workers, which was focused on wider differentials and the relative prosperity of the countryside, gained sufficiently in strength to remove several of the leading representatives of the reform from the top leadership at the Central Committee plenum of March 1974; this trend was confirmed by the party congress of March 1975. It might have continued in this neo-Stalinist direction, but for the importance of Kádár's personal position in the context of détente and Eurocommunism and the overriding need for stability in Hungary which would have been seriously prejudiced by Kádár's removal.

This process of gradual limitations on the reform was far from evident at the time and this had significant consequences for the intelligentsia. On the one hand, those who sought fundamental changes in society could continue to hope that even after 1968 there remained some chance of this. Those who looked for partial changes or were interested only in pointing to shortcomings in aspects of the system could be more readily co-opted into it, given that the limits of debate remained broad enough to permit a good deal of overt questioning. The technocratisation of the system encouraged co-optation from another angle. It promoted làrge sections of the intelligentsia into the outer fringes – sometimes even closer – of power. The official guidelines on intellectual debate assisted this process: in 1966, the party laid down three categories of publication – supported, tolerated, prohibited – known as the policy of the three Ts from the respective words in Hungarian (*támogatott, tĥrt, tiltott*). The 'tolerated' category could be expanded or contracted as political necessities dictated. At the same time, it permitted the emergence of another significant feature of para-opposition, that of highly critical material 'camouflaged into conformism'.[2] The use of Marxist jargon could on occasion disguise the real nature of a particular contribution and thus be permitted to appear. Beyond this, the regime accepted one further limitation on its capability to deal with dissidents. In a speech to the Central Committee made in December 1972, one which was never published, Kádár stipulated that Hungary had no effective defence against western press campaigns in support of dissidents and must, therefore, give in, in view of its economic dependence on the west.

This investigation of critical currents in Hungary will look at both the oppositional group (the New Left) and the para-opposition. The latter remains surprisingly active, given developments in Poland and Czechoslovakia, and the range of permitted criticism remains broad. It would be entirely misleading to see the para-opposition as in any way homogenous or united; there are widely disparate groups and individuals involved. The one unifying feature of the para-opposition is that its activists are conscious of playing a political role and, indeed, seek to arrogate a political role to themselves. It is this factor that justifies their consideration in an essay of this kind. There are various divisions within the para-opposition and some of the debates within the intelligentsia cannot be defined or understood by reference to any pro- or anti-regime axis. Among the currents to be investigated are the conflict between what might be termed professionalism and ideologisation (marked in the writing of history); the resurfacing of the pre-war urbanist-populist debate, with significant implications for the problem of anti-Semitism in Hungary; the revival of a powerful current of nationalism, with its focus on Transylvania; and the far from clearly understood decline of the critical-oppositional function of the creative (artistic) intelligentsia in favour of the scientific (including social sciences) intelligentsia. These different currents should not be seen as separate and clearly delineated; they obviously overlap in places and their different strands may be intertwined with one another.

THE CIRCUITS OF INFORMATION

Axiomatic to the existence of a para-opposition is that there should be a measure of latitude in what can be published. Since the mid-1960s, this kind of latitude has clearly existed in Hungary and it has done so with a modicum of official encouragement. Public debates have played a significant role in airing political issues and the press has been expected to play a kind of manipulative ombudsman role in taking up single instances of maladministration or abuse of power. Parallel with this, the propagandistic role of the media – most pronouncedly of television – has also continued.

However, in the context of para-oppositional activity, the role of the specialised journals has been the most significant. A distinction should be made here between the large circulation monthlies devoted to a wide range of topics, above all the two Budapest monthlies *Kortárs* and *Új Irás*, and journals which can be regarded as specialist in the strict sense of the word. There is a kind of crude inverse ratio between the obscurity of a journal and the freedom with which it can publish, but over and above that, a great deal can depend on individual editors and their determination. Consequently, some specialist journals have published information and articles in spheres which prima facie appear to be outside their remit. An example of this is an article on the informal networks of authority within an enterprise, but with much broader implications, which appeared in *Ergonómia*, a journal devoted (self-evidently) to ergonomy and industrial psychology.[3]

Particular mention must be made at this point of the monthly journal *Valóság*, which is widely regarded as intellectually the most stimulating journal published in Hungary. A careful assessment of what the journal publishes shows that its editors are highly sensitive to the limits of para-opposition. Politically awkward topics may be given an airing and some highly unorthodox subjects may be given space, together with mainstream restatements of policy or interviews with government ministers. Overall, with one crucial exception, there has been hardly a single critical idea floated in Hungary in the last decade, particularly in the social sciences, that did not involve *Valóság* at some stage of the debate. That exception was the so-called 'social ontology debate', in which the fundamental nature of Marxism in the context of Eastern Europe today was discussed in a highly critical fashion.

The role of the provincial monthlies should also be remarked on in this context. Most of the provincial towns in Hungary support a monthly or quarterly journal. Some of these are of predominantly local significance, being concerned to give space to local writers, poets or the results of local social scientific investigations. A few others – notably *Jelenkor* (published in Pécs), *Tiszatáj* (in Szeged) and *Forrás* (in Kecskemét) – have a role which brings their content to a wider readership. They publish the writings of scholars in Budapest (some of whom are banned from the central journals) or interviews – some of them very outspoken – by national literary figures and *Tiszatáj*, for one, has published material of considerable interest on the Hungarian minorities outside Hungary.

Openly published information can be said to represent the first level of information by which criticism is channelled. Just to demonstrate that these levels are not clear cut, but merge into one another, mention should be made of journals which are not on sale to the public, but which do circulate among those who are concerned. They are also to be found in some libraries, e.g. at the specialised research institutes. I have come across two of these semi-public journals and both contain articles which approach topics with a greater openness than is to be found in the public journals. The two in question are *A Politikai Főiskola Közleményei* ('Announcements of the Political Higher School') and *Rádió és Televizió Szemle* ('Radio and Television Review'). Yearbooks, almanachs, university pamphlets and the like may also fall into this last category.

At the next level of publication are the articles, studies and books which are issued, usually in a cyclostyled format, for 'internal use only'. These are not confidential as such, but they are not sold in the bookshops and their circulation will not exceed a few hundred. On the other hand, they are to be found occasionally in the second-hand bookshops, which suggests that their content is regarded as open. The few such publications that I have come across carry the legend that they may not be cited without the permission of the issuing organisation. Most if not all the research institutes circulate information in this way. It makes the information accessible to members of the institute and to others in similar fields, but the form of publication gives the information a level of de facto confidentiality. The practical result of this is that sensitive subjects can be broached relatively freely and without some of the constraints that would operate with published material.

One of the central aspects of this level of information is that there has been no xerographic or reprographic revolution in Hungary (or anywhere in Eastern Europe, for that matter). Everything that is duplicated or photocopied is strictly controlled and requires permission. Thus there is no automatic access to material, unless one is on the staff of a research institute, in which case access is on a personal basis only. In every institute or equivalent institution, there is invariably a particular person who is officially responsible for duplication and the procedure for duplication ensures that copies can always be traced. The proportion allowed for wastage – a potential source of extra copies – is very small. Hence copies which do circulate do so in a somewhat haphazard fashion and are subject to recall. Thus access to information at this level is a matter of chance depending on personal contacts and involves a fairly limited number of people, not more than a few hundred for any one item.

A variant of this level of information is the material that circulates in manuscript or typescript. This is not samizdat as it is usually understood in the west, in that material of this kind is not intended for wider distribution, but consists of articles or studies which their authors would like a restricted number of colleagues to see. Ostensibly, these studies are written for publication – which guarantees them a certain legal status as draft material (*műhelymunka*) – even though there is little chance that any editor will take the risk and thereby regrade such writings into the widest level of information. Such draft works vary in length; some of them consist of several hundred pages of typescript. The texts of lectures given at research institutes, which may be acceptable in that form, but not in written form whether as officially published or as semi-published, may also circulate in this way. Obviously, given the semi-clandestine nature of this entire enterprise, it would be foolish to attempt to make any estimate of how much material circulates in this way and how much of it does so for reasons of political difficulty and how much is genuinely a first draft which its author passes round his colleagues for comment.

At the highest level of information is the material that is strictly confidential, a category with several subdivisions. It is understood that at the upper levels of the party, a great deal is translated – some of it rather badly, I was told – and is circulated within the Central Committee apparatus only. Précis of the foreign press, notably articles commenting on Hungary, are also treated in this way. The Hungarian newsagency MTI circulates translations from the foreign press twice a week in about 2,200 copies, but as these are available at libraries, the number of those who have access is large – perhaps about 100,000 people. This material has an important role for the intelligentsia.

A number of books are also circulated in this confidential category, perhaps six to seven titles a year are brought out in a few hundred numbered copies by the Kossuth publishing house. These may be translations of books on Eastern Europe by western scholars or, occasionally, sensitive works by Hungarians. A substantial number of these books, which are actually printed, filter out to reach a wider readership through children of the elite. On top of that, another dozen or so copies without numbering are filched by the printers and sold on the black market. Manuscripts of this kind, which have been termed 'official samizdat', carried the legend 'to be used as a manuscript' (*kézirat gyanánt használandó*). József Lengyel's controversial novel *Confrontation* (*Szembesítés*) received this kind of treatment. Another much more confidential category is of material which is printed in cyclostyled form in not more than 100 copies and is intended exclusively for the upper levels of the elite. This material is strictly supervised and much less of it filters out. On occasion, individuals who could not ordinarily expect by virtue of their status to be given access to material in this confidential category are, in fact, allowed to see such publications. The purpose of this may partly be informational; but at the same time such access is an extension of privilege and therefore serves as an instrument of corruption and co-optation.

Entirely outside the officially controlled system of information and launched with the specific objective of breaking through these controls was samizdat proper. This was in its infancy in Hungary by comparison with Poland or Czechoslovakia (at the time of writing, at least) and unlike samizdat elsewhere, it consisted of intellectual reexaminations and reappraisals, rather than accounts of trials or harassments or arbitrary action. This samizdat (discussed in detail below) was thought to circulate among up to about 1,000 people, but could well go on to reach a wider readership among the intelligentsia.[4]

A comment on the network of research institutes is appropriate here. Hungary has followed the Soviet model of organising research, in that research has been hived off to some extent from the universities into autonomous or separate institutes. Whatever the academic effectiveness of this system (my informants accepted that it had its advantages as well as its drawbacks), it has established a series of bodies where discussion and criticism is fairly free. Indeed, one of my contacts described the institutes as 'oases of freedom'. Such institutes may be subordinate organs of the Academy of Sciences or the Central Committee or even the trade unions or the organisation of agricultural collectives. Their significance in assessing levels of information is that they mostly have reasonable libraries, where individual scholars have access to the western press and academic output and where information is exchanged on a personal and informal basis. It is possible that one of the reasons why the creative intelligentsia has declined in influence is that it lacks such institutional underpinning of its activities.[5]

It is very easy to assume that all 'criticism' in Hungary is automatically directed against the regime and that it is perforce hostile to the dominant ideology. This assumption would be misleading. It takes no account of the relatively relaxed application of that ideology in practice and the acceptance of the need for debate by the regime. Consequently, some intellectual currents and debates are by and large 'neutral' in that they do not concern Marxism-Leninism directly. Thus many may be said to be 'hostile' to it only if all expressions of differing opinions are eo ipso interpreted as hostile. The historians' debate is as good an example as any of a debate that was neutral from the standpoint of official ideology, for it turned first and foremost on nationalism and the way in which historians are to interpret the nation's history. Whilst the party has obviously kept an eye on the historians' debate, there have been few signs of direct intervention.

At the same time, there should be no doubt that criticism is made and statements put forward in debate with political objectives in mind. Both the intelligentsia and the political decision makers accept that this is so. The problem lies in the extent and content of the criticism and boundaries set by the party. The political nature of criticism has been stated and reiterated on numerous occasions over the last decade.

The most far-reaching statement of the role of such criticism could in many ways be said to be the work of the philosopher György Márkus.[5] It was the very boundaries of the system that he questioned overtly and directly in the summer of 1968, just before the invasion of Czechoslovakia. In essence, he argued for complete freedom in Marxist philosophy, for all approaches and trends without any kind of administrative interference. Pluralism in Marxism, he argued, was a healthy phenomenon, for Marxist philosophy was still at an early stage of its development, it was still suffering from the legacy of the Stalinist period and it would only achieve the desired synthesis through a confrontation of conflicting views. The problem with 'standard', i.e. official, philosophy was that it had in many ways outlived its usefulness, because Marxist philosophy had to adapt to keep pace with changing circumstances and social realities – it was not something that could have its limits fixed once and for all. Indeed, Márkus went on, constant debate among different trends was especially appropriate for Marxist philosophy, which placed such stress on self-criticism. The avoidance of confronting views with one another would do serious harm – was already doing so – in that by keeping certain questions beyond debate, Marxism was being allowed to ossify and that would lead eventually to ideological disintegration. A living Marxism was more effective than a dead one, Márkus declared, both as the ideology of a political movement and in conflicts with bourgeois philosophy. In effect, Márkus's argument completely undermined the official ideological position and left the regime with no possible response in ideological terms. Márkus was censured for his article and this made it evident that the party would not tolerate pluralism, but it took the party ideologists some time to formulate an answer. When it came, it was in essence a politically grounded rejection of pluralism. Márkus is also the co-author, with György Bence and János Kis, of a work that has acquired an enormous reputation, although it has never been published. This is the study *Is a Critical Political Economy Possible At All?*, sometimes referred to as 'The Anti-Capital'. It has been described as 'basically an attempt to offer a framework to a critical political economy of State socialism, if necessary even reassessing some of the classical concepts and hypotheses [of Marx]'.[6]

Whilst Márkus and the other philosophers involved in the social ontology debate were concerned to safeguard the autonomy of Marxist philosophy and their intellectual right to question the official ideology, a similar claim was put forward by András Hegedüs (and others) for sociology and the social sciences. Hegedüs argued, in effect, in an article published in 1967 that the role of the social sciences in socialist societies was to be that of a surrogate opposition. Whilst a case could be made out for treating the social sciences in general and sociology in particular as a branch of propaganda during the period of consolidating communist rule, once this was accomplished, the time for self-serving apologetics was over. Indeed, such sociology actually did the system a disservice, for it enabled out-dated myths and structures to survive. Hence 'internal analysis – "self-criticism" in Marx's words – had, in historical terms, become not only possible, but also necessary'.[7]

The time had arrived for sociologists to begin stripping away the accumulation of illusions about society, for some of these had rigidified into dogma and were obstacles to change. The particular role of sociology in this context was described by Hegedüs in these terms:

> As the whole previous development of sociology confirms, this science seems to be, on the one hand, the product of self-criticism on the part of socialism, and, on the other hand, that branch of the social sciences which represents society's most direct scientific instrument for acquiring a knowledge of itself and for subjecting social conditions to genuine analysis. [The basic problem of sociology in Eastern Europe:] is it the job of this newly reborn and already fashionable science to provide information and data for the defence of established forms (manipulation) or to help overcome these forms by analysing them critically (the analytic function)?[8]

Hegedüs left little doubt that his conception of the role of sociology was the latter definition.

While the role ascribed to sociology by one of its principal practitioners was intended to bring it into the centre of the political arena, Hegedüs was by no means alone in his claims for the political function of sociology. A very similar claim was put in for sociography by József Darvas, when the Discovery of Hungary movement was launched in the late 1960s. Sociography has been an innovation peculiar to Hungary. It first emerged around the turn of the century and then revived much more significantly in the 1930s, when the Village Explorers' Movement used its method to reveal conditions in rural Hungary. It survived thereafter as a recognised form, with something of a radical pedigree. To someone brought up in the western tradition, sociography can sometimes be a somewhat uneasy mixture. One of its recent practitioners, György Berkovits, defined it in the following, all-embracing terms:

> Sociography, as it has evolved in Hungary, is in no sense a unified form. It is created by using a great variety of methods – reports, case studies, travelogues, autobiographies, interviews, polemics, essays, diaries, portraits, confessions, descriptions, local histories, chronocles, round-ups, reportages. . . . All these may involve elements of history, socio-psychology, economics, ethnography, demography, sociology, literature, statistics, politics and ideology.[9]

Furthermore, sociography in Hungary has always tended to have an oppositional quality, given the varieties of censorship employed by the regime and its predecessors. The principal tension in sociography has been the conflict between the demands of literature and of the social sciences and the emphasis on the former can overstress the role of the individual in the social process. At its best, however, sociographical writing can flesh out the bare bones that is sometimes all that is provided by sociology and to bring the harsh realities of a situation vividly to life. The use made of in-depth interviews by sociographers in recent years has given their output a particular value that has brought some of their writings into the ambit of social anthropology.

Darvas had few illusions about the likely impact of his new series when he launched it in March 1968. It was explicitly intended as a new stock-taking of Hungarian society, which would hark back to the traditions of the Village Explorers of the 1930s. On the other hand, Darvas possibly was a little perturbed by the storm aroused by one of the very first sociographic reports to appear, namely Antal Végh's devastating picture of the Godforsaken village of Penészlek in Szabolcs-Szatmár county. Végh's essay was received with clamorous hostility by the county officials, who regarded his attempt to portray reality as a hostile act. Darvas, who had the backing of the central organs, was quick to defend Végh and noted that 'the better a political leader, the more he is able to draw lessons from literary works like Végh's essay. This is because a politician can discover in such literature something which he frequently cannot discover by any other means'. Two years later Darvas added, 'there are hardly any administrative obstacles today to literary truthfulness, but we can still encounter "atmospheric opposition" (as the reception of a few sociographical works has shown) . . . [the writer] must secure acceptance of the truth that no literature of direct social interest can exist without a critical attitude. Fortunately it is accepted today that this is in the interest not only of literature but also of politics.'[10]

Hungarian sociography of the 1960s and 1970s has some impressive volumes in its canon. Works both in the 'Discovery of Hungary' series and outside it have provided a vivid picture of the daily lives of a fair part of the population, much of it negative. The live of the peasantry has been especially well documented, but the industrial workers have likewise been described in detail. The standard of living of the former has improved greatly when compared with the miseries of the 1930s; the position of the latter has not changed all that much in the circumstances. Clearly, sociography has contributed to the differentiated picture of Hungarian society in the 1970s. On the other hand, there are gaps. A number of important themes have been neglected as being too sensitive. Among these is the situation of the industrial suburb of Budapest, Csepel; the nature of Hungarian national consciousness; the Jewish question; corruption and bureaucracy. In effect, sociography in the 1970s, unlike the 1930s, is governmental rather than oppositional – well within the definition of para-opposition – so that where the interest of the government might be seriously affected, sociographers do not venture. In so far as shortcomings are detailed, these are implicitly attributed to individual problems rather than a derivative of the system as a whole; responsibility is never laid at the door of top level policy makers. In a word, sociography is para-oppositional.[11]

From the standpoint of the party too, it was recognised that the social sciences had something to offer. Whilst policy makers might have been reluctant to go all the way with Hegedüs's formulation, the contention that the social sciences could help the politician was not in question. This continued to be the official standpoint even after the Hegedüs group's exclusion from public life.

By way of illustration, the discussion held under the auspices of *Társadalmi Szemle*, the HSWP's theoretical and political monthly, showed how the relationship was conceived of in official circles.[12] The subject of the discussion was conflicts of interest and interest-relations in a socialist society. Implicit in the published version of the discussion was the overall subordination of the social sciences to the party; on the other hand, it was fairly clear that this subordination would not be interpreted so rigidly as to exclude the scientific value of researches. Thus more than one participant argued that the concept of 'societal interest' (*társadalmi érdek*) was too crude on its own to be much use in analysing conflicts of interest and that a greater differentiation was essential.

There were complaints that a legacy of the past – a politicisation of the social sciences – remained a considerable burden for scholars seeking to understand the precise nature of interest-relations. For example, given the built-in ideological reflexes, it was all too easy for one particular central organ to claim that it and it alone was representing the societal interest, whereas in reality it was no more than one sectional interest among others. The task of social scientists in this kind of a situation was to bring conceptual clarity to the problem and to assist policy makers in determining what the societal interest really consisted of. As Csaba Makó defined it in the discussion, politicians were constantly running up against problems of conflicts of interest and their coordination and, he implied, they needed more refined ways of approaching the concept of societal interest.[13] They expected the social sciences and sociology in particular to provide these conceptual tools. The problem was further complicated by the inclination of leaders at different levels, i.e. middle level officials, to approach the problem of interests purely from the angle of surface phenomena and to attempt to resolve them by the deployment of solutions deriving from such superficial analyses. The results were poor and the short-comings were attributed not to the faulty understanding of the situation, but to subjective errors in management techniques. Makó then provided a concrete instance. It had emerged that workers in the construction industry were primarily looking for easy work and were not interested in raising their productivity. A simple application of management techniques would not have worked in this kind of situation, because the workers in question were essentially using their place of employment to rest after their labours in the far more lucrative private sector.

Another participant, Mihály Bihari, acknowledged the political restrictions and controls over the social sciences. There was strong political predetermination of what could be researched in conflicts of interest, because these were at the centre of what politics were about. It was a key function of the power-political system to shape the hierarchy of interests according to whatever preferences were involved. In this way, the system was given a hierarchy and the highest positions in the hierarchy determined the societal interest. However, the social scientist looked at the problem differently, for he had something to say about the nature of the interest system that had evolved at a certain level of abstraction. By implication, these scientific perceptions would conflict with the political perceptions. But science had to free itself of the restrictions placed on it as to what was a fit subject for research. 'Of course, these factors do more than make research into interest systems difficult. In fact, the nearer the area under research is to political power, the greater the amount of ideological "ballast" encountered.'[14]

The urbanist-populist conflict has been one of the most fundamental cleavages in Hungarian intellectual and political life for at least half a century.[15] The cleavage does not coincide with Marxism and anti-Marxism, but cuts across it. It has repercussions in most areas of life and often remains hidden from sight, operating as a latent *arrière pensée*. The roots of the divide can be traced back to the turn of the century, to the impact of the poet Endre Ady and the repercussions of the emergence of a radicalising bourgeoisie that was beginning to challenge the established gentry middle class. But the locus classicus of the divide was the 1930s, when the populist movement emerged to challenge the established order and launched its sociographical series on conditions in the countryside. The essence of the populist ideology was that the rejuvenation and reform of Hungarian society were to be implemented by drawing exclusively (or predominantly) on the internal resources of Hungarian society itself. As against this, the urbanists argued that Hungarian society should follow the European (West European) road of industrial development and that it should look westwards for its models. (This definition greatly oversimplifies what is an extremely complex debate.) Both sides were thus in opposition to the existing order of the 1930s and both aligned themselves with radical ideologies.

It is self-evident that the solution imposed on Hungarian society by the communists was closer to the urbanist ideology. Nonetheless, this did not automatically mean that the urbanists were absorbed by the communists. Paradoxically, the power of attraction of the communists proved to be rather stronger over the populists, who, especially after 1956, gravitated towards the party that claimed to be ruling in the name of national unity. The protection of the substance of the nation, always a feature of populist thinking, was perceived by the populists as the task of the government and the Kádár regime was accepted as fulfilling that task. Certainly, despite the frequently radical tone that some populists adopted and their vehement rhetoric, they have made less trouble for the regime than the urbanists and the urbanists' heirs.

The problem of the urbanists was that a substantial portion of their ideology became banned from Hungarian politics. Their commitment to liberal democracy and their admiration for western models made their views unacceptable. But by the 1960s, even if urbanism as understood in the 1930s had vanished, new currents arose which consciously or unconsciously owed much to their predecessor and were perceived in these terms by the populists. Among the distinctive features of urbanism in the Kádár period have been its inclination towards professionalism and academic standards, its unwillingness to serve overtly ideological aims, its insistence on investigating history or society free from either nationalist or Marxist romanticism. The different approaches of the urbanists and the populists are in a way encapsulated in the distinction between sociology and sociography, between writing for an influential elite and for a wider public, between scientific precision and rendering the feel of a given social problem.

One of the currents of Hungarian intellectual life that clearly fits into the urbanist category is the Hungarian New Left. Their protagonists, in their search for a genuine Marxist alternative and rejection of official, ritualistic formulae, can be said to be following the urbanist heritage. In this context, urbanism found itself in opposition to the official line. But elsewhere, in the historians' debate for instance, there was no such obvious conflict. Finally, although there is little direct evidence for this, a section of the party apparat sympathises with aspects of populism, notably on the national question and the Jewish question as well. The urbanists are likewise not without influence within the party.

THE NEW LEFT

Of all the various intellectual currents in Hungary, the New Left has attracted the most attention in the west. A fair amount of its output has been made available in western languages and the fate of individual members of what has become known as 'the Budapest school' receives regular coverage in the western press.[16] Furthermore, there has been something of a tendency to regard the various different individuals involved in some kind of difficulty with the Hungarian regime as forming a homogenous group linked by a single ideology. This is certainly not the case, and is rejected by different members of the New Left – if that formulation does not beg too many questions – themselves.

Insofar as the intellectual positions of the Budapest School can be identified, it is probably fair to describe the existence of two separate trends between adherents of different sets of values and assumptions. The differences are firstly generational. The older group are essentially products of the 1950s, of a period when reform of Marxism still seemed feasible and the revitalisation of both Marxian ideas and the building of a society based on these ideas a realistic possibility. The members of this group are rather better known, they had mostly achieved positions of some standing in Hungary and they have almost all left for the west. The younger group, on the other hand, had as their primary political experience the impact of the invasion of Czechoslovakia which they perceived as a defeat and as a consequent shrinking of possibilities. This has made them hostile to the system, which they reject completely, to the extent of rejecting 'compromise' struck by members of the older group in accepting passports. Indeed, for the younger group it is difficult to understand why the regime bothered to take action against the older members of the group at all, for in their view they could readily have been encompassed by the system as it was. They themselves reject all dealings with the regime, which they regard as illegitimate. In practice, the gap between the two groups is not as wide as the younger group would suggest and members of the older group have also spoken out against the regime in uncompromising terms.

A number of political actions can be attributed to the Left in Hungary, which in one case actually predates the invasion of Czechoslovakia. This was the setting up of a non-official Vietnam Solidarity Commission in the mid-1960s; this was the first such non-official body in Hungary since 1956. Although the regime evidently disliked such autonomous activity, it was at a loss for a solution and left it alone. Miklós Haraszti, who was subsequently to be involved in several actions by the Left, was a prominent figure in the Commission. So were a number of other persons who were tried in 1968 on charges of having organised a secret, left-wing anti-government conspiracy, which was liquidated by the secret police; the Commission was eliminated in connection with the conspiracy.

The invasion of Czechoslovakia had an enormous impact on the Left in Hungary. It resulted directly in the Korčula protest letter, which was signed by five Hungarian philosophers attending the Korčula summer school. The five (György Márkus and his wife Mária, Ágnes Heller, Vilmos Sós and Zádor Tordai) were reprimanded. However, the authorities used the protest as a pretext for executing a classic two-front action. They removed both András Hegedüs and József Szigeti from their respective positions in the Sociological Research Group and the Philosophical Institute of the Academy of Sciences. Hegedüs had been in the forefront of criticising the reform in its concrete aspects, whilst Szigeti had been the highly intelligent but strictly orthodox head of the Philosophical Institute. The latter, it appears, miscalculated the likely outcome of the Czechoslovak reforms and expected that 'normalisation' would be introduced in Hungary fairly quickly. He apparently established political contacts with both Soviet and East German sympathisers, with the ultimate aim of removing the leadership. The two-fold removal worked; there was relief over the dismissal of Szigeti and by allowing Hegedüs to continue publishing, the authorities prevented him from becoming a focus of opposition. One of the major consequences of the removal of Szigeti was that for about two or three years the Philosophical Institute was without any effective ideological supervision. This was the high water mark of the social ontology debate, which was carried on in the journal *Filozófiai Szemle*. Márkus's article on trends in Marxism had in any case left the party nonplussed and, although a Resolution on Scientific Policy issued towards the end of 1970 laid down that there could be only one Marxism, this was not actually implemented for another two years or so.

The regime miscalculated the impact of Czechoslovakia on the universities, above all Budapest. In the winter of 1968–9, an activist campaign in support of the official line on Czechoslovakia was launched and this produced a hostile reaction from among the students. The university reform, which had been introduced in January 1969 with the aim of giving students the chance of greater participation in the running of the university, and was certainly intended as a façade, misfired, for students began to play an active role. In this situation the communist youth movement (KISz) leadership was voted out and a new leadership, backed by an alliance of populists and new left-urbanists, took over. The regime, whilst obviously hostile to this development, moved slowly; rather than take direct action, it capitalised on the fragility of the populist-urbanist alliance. In effect, their interests did differ, for while the urbanists sought basic structural changes, the populists were often satisfied with having gained positions of power, at which point – having completed their long march through the institutions – they were prepared to cooperate with the authorities. It took the regime about four years to reconsolidate their control over the universities and many of those who finished after 1969 were on a semi-black list.

The summer of 1973 was in many respects the turning point. In May the Central Committee issued its resolution denouncing the Budapest School. Its ideas were declared to be contrary to Marxism-Leninism and to the policies of the party. Hegedüs, Mihály Vajda and János Kis were expelled from the party; Mária Márkus (who regularly collaborated with Hegedüs), György Márkus, Ágnes Heller and György Bence were likewise deemed to have gone beyond the pale and were excluded from public life. All seven were dismissed from their jobs and, for a while, banned from publishing in Hungary.[17]

On the other hand, none of the group was arrested and they were all given some opportunity of earning a living. Ágnes Heller was able to publish her *Outline Portraits from the History of Ethics* in 1976 in 5000 copies and she also published an article in *Korunk*,[18] the Hungarian language monthly that appears in Transylvania. Hegedüs has given an interview about his life and ideas to *Le Quotidien de Paris*;[19] and reportedly all the members of the group have been quietly encouraged to leave for the west, temporarily at least. It should be noted furthermore that the previously published work of the group has remained within the boundaries of what is tolerated in Hungarian intellectual life. A number of scholarly works published since 1973 refer to books and articles published by members of the group before that date.[20]

At around the same time, using the universities as a base, a group of Left activists organised a petition against the proposed new abortion law, which would have tightened up the conditions under which abortion was made available to pregnant women. The petition, which was handed to the President of the Parliament, Antal Apró, was signed by about 360 people. The protestors were moved by three considerations: the tightening up was seen as hostile to the working class, it was regarded as inherently nationalistic (in that Hungary's falling birthrate had long been a basic complaint of the nationalists) and there was a limited, incipient feminism underlying the motivations of some of the signatories.

The trial of Miklós Haraszti triggered off a much wider action by the Left, which attracted support from beyond the immediate circle of the Budapest School.[21] Haraszti had had a long record of involvement in radical action in Budapest and had run foul of the police. After having been sent down from the university, he took a job as a worker in the 'Red Star' tractor factory in Budapest and subsequently wrote up his experiences as a piece of sociography. This reportage was given the title *Piece-rate*.[22] It contained strong criticism of the activities of the trade unions, as well as of the management, and generally painted a highly depressing picture of conditions in the 'Red Star' factory. The central thesis of the book was that the piece-rate system demoralised and dehumanised the workers by pitting them against the machine in the framework of ever increasing work norms. He attacked the collective contract as a sham, because it was so complex as to be unintelligible. And he found an enormous gap between the shop floor and the management – interestingly, the party and the trade unions were reckoned among the latter.

Haraszti submitted his manuscript to a publishing house and also the journal *Szociológia*, so that copies of it were circulating among groups of intellectuals in Budapest. At that stage, the authorities stepped in and Haraszti was arrested (to be released two weeks later). He was charged with incitement and his trial became a focal point for intellectual opposition. Although comparatively few of the intellectuals who came to give evidence in Haraszti's favour shared his attitudes and values, there was nevertheless some anxiety that the Haraszti trial would be the precursor of a much harder line in the arts. It was the first occasion since 1958 that anyone had been arraigned in court for their opinions. The trial was perceived as having been intended as an act of intimidation against the Left and oppositional intellectuals in general. Several were harassed by the police – Ferenc Fehér, Ágnes Heller's husband, who was arrested briefly on an alleged charge of having tried to smuggle the manuscript abroad, was not alone; others were interrogated.

The trial itself proceeded by fits and starts. It opened and adjourned after one day on the ground that the trial judge was indisposed. It reopened in mid-October and heard a galaxy of Hungarian intellectuals speak in Haraszti's favour, including Hegedüs, the novelist and sociologist György Konrád and the sociologist Iván Szelényi (who had been the editor of *Szociológia* to whom Haraszti had submitted his manuscript). Most of the witnesses praised the literary quality of the book and Haraszti defended himself vigorously against charges against him. After yet another adjournment, the court reconvened in January 1974 and Haraszti was given an 8-month suspended sentence. The trial judge, after rejecting Haraszti's defence, added that she considered that there were two sets of extenuating circumstances in the affair. One was that the people to whom Haraszti had shown the manuscript were close to him politically, which diminished the social harmfulness of his actions. And secondly, that he had tried to have his manuscript published legally. Clearly, the entire affair had been determined politically – this was a political trial – and a compromise of sorts had been struck, not least in the light of the considerable international attention the Haraszti affair had attracted.

On the whole, the Hungarian left was relatively slow in using the western press as an instrument of pressure on the regime. It took the Budapest School some two-and-a-half years to present its case to world opinion through the channel which had been used by Soviet and other East European opposition activists for some years. In February 1976, Ferenc Fehér, who had not personally been criticised in 1973 but was for all practical purposes in the same position as the others, spoke out in an interview with the BBC. He argued that the group as a whole had been isolated and deprived of its civic rights. He reaffirmed the group's adherence to socialism, but insisted on their commitment to socialism with civic rights and democracy.[23]

Another act of political dissent was the letter signed by thirty-four intellectuals in support of Charter 77, on 9 January 1977.[24] The initiative for this letter of solidarity was reported to have come from Prague and the signatures were gathered in the course of one day. Over half of the signatories were associated with the New Left, but several of the others who signed were outside the current. Whilst the international significance of the gesture was considerable – it was the first act of support for the Charter in Eastern Europe outside Czechoslovakia – it played practically no role in Hungary at all. The fact that none of the really major figures of Hungarian life signed – notably Gyula Illyés and Tibor Déry – enabled the authorities to downplay the affair and claim that the signatories were relatively unimportant and uninfluential. This was not entirely accurate. On the other hand, the letter showed that on certain issues a fair number of intellectuals could be mobilised in an act of dissent and that the inclination towards dissent was not confined to the New Left.

It was the Left once more that took the initiative in launching two samizdat publications, in a fashion that had been unprecedented in Hungary. These two volumes – entitled *Marx in the Fourth Decade* and *Profile* – were intended as samizdat in the strict sense of the word, to evade censorship and to reach a wider readership than the informal circulation of manuscripts made possible.[25] *Marx in the Fourth Decade* was a symposium in which 21 younger intellectuals defined their positions on Marxism; there was a marked swing away from the idealistic radicalism of the 1960s – indeed, Haraszti no longer considered himself a Marxist at all – and a determination to look more realistically at existing possibilities for action in society. One of the means of this was seen as being the chance of radicalising the fringes of the intelligentsia and thereby preventing their co-optation. *Profile* was virtually a textbook example of this. It contained the otherwise unpublished writings of thirty-four intellectuals, the majority non-Marxists, from a wide range of intellectual activity. The editor of the volume, János Kenedi, introduced the writings with a penetrating critique of the mechanism of censorship and self-censorship in Hungary, which relied on informal means of control and subtle forms of blackmail.

The intellectual positions associated with the Budapest School, both older and younger groups included, are, of course, complex and varied. Nevertheless, they share some or all of the following propositions. First, they argue that analyses of a society, socialist or otherwise, must proceed from a constant self-criticism, a critical examination of the process of socialist construction. This spirit of criticism, which was located originally in the philosophy of György Lukács, was transposed into sociology and much of the main thrust of its analyses emerged through sociological examinations of Hungarian society. The re-examination of social reality as it actually exists in Hungary, and not as perceived through the distorting mirror of official Marxism, was to be carried out on the principles of Marx and that re-examination, in turn, would provide the foundations for new programmes of social transformation.

The views of András Hegedüs are worth looking at in detail at this point. Hegedüs was in many ways the publicly most vocal member of the School and, at the same time, he was politically active in a more conscious and deliberate fashion than some of the other members. He has, indeed, been criticised for having mistimed his attack on the Reform and to have launched his anti-technocratic campaign even before the technocrats had consolidated their positions.[26] Like the others, Hegedüs began from the proposition that the re-examination of society was essential, given that in Eastern Europe criticism of the party and of its leading organs had come to be interpreted as evidence of counter-revolution. By transforming criticism – an essential instrument of social change – into a branch of propaganda and self-serving apologetics, official Marxism had not only become an empty ritual, but in practice was a burden on the dynamism of socialist development. Hegedüs argued that socialist countries were developing in two ways. They had either opted for 'the state administrative model', where production was determined by a bureaucratic elite in order to satisfy social needs or for a pale imitation of the capitalist model by pursuing market socialism, which suffered from the disadvantage that it was less efficient than capitalism itself.

The alternative road put forward by Hegedüs was that the task of socialism was to 'optimalise and humanise' society. The abolition of the private ownership of the means of production, which should only have been seen as a starting point of the socialist revolution, had become bogged down at that point, with consequent bureaucratisation. This was the core of Hegedüs's thesis. Bureaucratisation derived from a mythicisation of the societal interest, particularly at lower levels of the hierarchy, which led to the rise of conformism, vested interests and deference to the superior levels of the hierarchy. The end result has been in complete contradiction to the demands of democracy. Democracy, in Hegedüs's conception, required that the administration should operate in the interests of the working people and that it should be under effective control from below. Furthermore, only through the exercise of such democratic control would the administration become responsive to the constant changes that were taking place in society. The unit that he suggested should exercise this control was the community, meaning communities both of workers in enterprises and in the population at large. He appeared to have been somewhat sceptical about workers' control, whether on the Yugoslav or the 1968 Czechoslovak model, but he was definite that 'social institutions of the working people' would alone be able to make the administrative machine dependent on society and thus prevent or counteract bureaucratisation.

However, control of the administration was only one side of the picture. The humanisation of socialism had positive aspects as well. What was at stake was the individual in society, his freedom of the widest possible choice. The abolition of private ownership had made little impact on this; individual standards and ideals had not changed very much. The individual remained in the grip of false ideals, in his working life he was subjected to restrictions and his long term aspirations were those of consumerism. This, Hegedüs felt, had little or nothing to do with socialism. His remedies were that education should prepare the individual for a role in life as a person and not as a worker to be integrated into the division of labour; that he should be in a position to be master of his relations in society and to shape his fate. To achieve this, socialism needed a new model of consumption. In the first place, society should provide articles of primary consumption – food, clothing, housing, other basic essentials – free of charge. In the other category, differentiated articles of consumption, everything should be gradually made available to the individual, particularly to youth.[27]

It will be clear from the foregoing that Hegedüs's position and that of the group associated with him had become irreconcilable with the official line. The group had self-evidently overstepped the threshold of what the party permitted in the way of criticism, inasmuch as the Budapest School had embarked on a fundamental and radical critique of the foundations of the regime's legitimacy. If the existing order in Hungary – and elsewhere in Eastern Europe – could no longer be called socialist, then the regime's claim to rule in the name of the proletariat and the socialist revolution was entirely undermined.

As already suggested, it is usual among western observers to regard the Hungarian New Left as a single current; *Les Temps Modernes* did so quite explicitly in its special number. However, the writings that have appeared under the name of Marc Racovski showed that some of the New Left radicals took an even more radical approach to the question of socialism in Eastern Europe than the ideas associated with

Hegedüs.[28] Racovski (a pseudonym) not only rejects that the existing order in Eastern Europe is socialist, but he treats the entire Marxist heritage highly critically. The overt purpose of his study *Towards an East European Marxism* is to recreate the ideological foundations for a Marxism that corresponds to current realities and thereby to reach the ultimate objective 6f socialist democracy. His argument is that the countries of Eastern Europe – Soviet-type societies – are neither socialist nor in transition to socialism nor capitalist, but *sui generis* class-based societies, in which the post-Stalinist order has been consolidated and in which the market socialist model has largely failed in socialist terms. In Soviet-type societies the working class is deprived of all possibilities of autonomous action, with the result that it is repressed to the level of individual response. In a situation of this kind, the growth of personal consumption is the only possible form of autonomy, of extending the area under the personal control of the individual.

As far as the intelligentsia is concerned, the fundamental problem in Racovski's view is to what extent critical intellectuals have succeeded in establishing a counter-ideology, in competition to that propagated by the regime. The intelligentsia is the only stratum in society that is capable – or of which a part is capable – of independent conceptual thought. It does have a group consciousness, within which certain individuals have been prepared to challenge the officially determined limits and to put forward an alternative counter-public opinion. The post-Stalinist system has accepted the existence of conflict in society, but it has retained the power to resolve all conflicts from above. Within this, a small room for autonomous activity has, therefore, been created. Those who seek more than just to take advantage of this have become gradually 'marginalised' vis-à-vis the regime, but they are also to some extent isolated from the main body of the intelligentsia, which has an interest both in preventing the authorities from taking restrictive measures against the marginalised minority and in containing marginal activity, because any increase in non-conformism has tended to increase official pressure on the whole range of intellectual activity. However, Racovski's conception of what this marginalised group can achieve is modest. It cannot establish contact with the working class, given that the workers lack the organisation to make communication possible. But counter-public opinion can radicalise the fringes of the intelligentsia and it can serve something of a role by precept, by being an example in terms of human behaviour. Equally, such marginal activity can mobilise some intellectuals and keep alive alternative concepts in society, insofar as co-optation is prevented.

Separate from the New Left, but not entirely unrelated were the ideas of Iván Szelényi and György Konrád. In a nutshell, they pointed an accusing finger at the continued poverty and backwardness of that particular section of the industrial working class which, while employed in industry, was constrained by' Hungary's underdeveloped infrastructure to live a semi-rural, semi-urban existence, deriving benefit from neither town nor country.

In an outspoken article in *Valóság* Konrád and Szelényi argued that the model of industrialisation adopted in post-war Hungary had created an underprivileged class of peasant-workers and, by implication, that the existing system was doing little or nothing for them.[29] The gist of their argument was that because infrastructural investment had been neglected during the Stalinist period of over-rapid industrial expansion, a belt of satellite settlements had grown up around Budapest, from which a substantial proportion of the capital's labour force was obliged to commute. These satellite settlements – forty-four of them are officially recognised as being within the Budapest agglomeration belt – lack or are gravely short of all the institutions which the state is expected to provide: schools, nurseries, hospitals, theatres, libraries and so on. By contrast, the managerial élite-new middle class has been able to live in Budapest and thus enjoy the benefits of urban existence.

Despite the subsequent departure abroad of both Szelényi and Konrád, their ideas on under-urbanisation continued to influence others. György Berkovits's sociography 'On the boundaries of a world city', which appeared in the Discovery of Hungary series, was explicitly written with the Szelényi-Konrád theses in mind.[30] Berkovits wrote that he used the *Valóság* article virtually as a handbook. He put forward the basic thesis that by shunting its population into the satellite settlements, the capital was exploiting these communes and the individuals who lived there in a colonialist fashion. There is an acute housing shortage in Budapest, so that those who look for work there have to find their housing elsewhere. This is where the agglomeration belt is important, for in this area, sites for building can still be found, where the individual then builds a house for himself. But a large proportion of these estates are without main drainage and running water, because the local authorities lack the financial base to make the investment. Furthermore, those who live in these settlements have to commute, so that a large part of their day is taken up with travelling, often in unpleasant, crowded conditions. In effect, Berkovits hints, there should be no place for this kind of existence in a society that is ostensibly based on the paramountcy of the working class.

However, after 1973, partly as a result of their tangential involvement in the Haraszti affair, Konrád and Szelényi found their positions in Hungary increasingly less tenable by reason of tacit official pressure. This was the background to their brief arrest in autumn 1974, which was followed by a major international outcry and the subsequent decision of the authorities to provide them with means of leaving the country. In fact, the authorities acted because they had discovered the manuscript, entitled 'Towards the class-power of the intelligentsia', on which the two were working.[31]

This is an extremely complex and lengthy study, which attempts to trace the historical antecedents of the existing system in Eastern Europe and to offer a sociological analysis of the nature of power under socialism. It owes something to the ideas of Karl Polányi on archaic economies and is ultimately linked to theories of the Asiatic mode of production. The gist of the argument is that in Eastern Europe, society has been governed on the principle of rational redistribution. This principle has been employed by the intelligentsia for the exercise of its power and this remains the case. Rational redistribution is an independent type of economic development, an autonomous economic and organisational stereotype, which is organically connected with the traditions which have arisen in the social history of the area. It is an autonomous model of social organisation and should not be seen as a haphazard deviation from the western model or as a transitional variant of the bourgeois-liberal model. It is, therefore, connected both with the Asiatic mode of production and, equally, with the self-regulating market of the west.

Under the system of rational redistribution, society is divided into two classes – those who decide on and implement redistribution (the intelligentsia) and those who are deprived of all rights over redistribution (the working class). Redistributive power is legitimised by its rationality and the bureaucracy simultaneously exercises the functions of goal-setting and execution. In this, all institutions are fitted into a single hierarchy at the summit of which a ruling estate, separate from the intelligentsia but dependent on it for its professional competence, has arisen. This body is the party, which is the ultimate guarantor of the redistributive ethos and the final sanctioning authority of all redistributive decisions.

In the Stalinist period, according to Konrád and Szelényi, the party attempted to rule by exercising a monopoly of power. This was eventually recognised to have failed and by the early 1960s, the party –

the ruling estate – struck a compromise with the intelligentsia, the technocratic stratum included, in order to raise the level of rationality in decision and policy making. The working class has been entirely excluded from this compromise and the sole means of mobility out of the working class is by accession to the intelligentsia through higher education. For the intelligentsia, this dispensation is highly favourable, as it ensures them a standard and style of living comparable with that of the party and a share of power. Indeed, in comparison with the pre-1945 period, the power of the technocrat has increased beyond his wildest dreams. The study suggests that eventually the intelligentsia will assimilate the party to its ideology and at that point class rule by the intelligentsia will eventuate. The entire trend of modern East European history has been leading in that direction.

This rough sketch of the Szelényi–Konrád study does not do anything like justice to its highly sophisticated analysis. But it is evident that this sociological approach to the nature of class, power and the state in Eastern Europe has implications that raise a question mark over the legitimacy of the communist party's rule in Hungary and elsewhere. From the party's standpoint it was understandable that a challenge of this kind should have been met with the deployment of administrative and police intervention and the eventual departure abroad of both authors. As they themselves remark in their study they regard the eventuation of class power by the intelligentsia as the moment when the study is published officially in Eastern Europe. One final note: György Konrád's second novel, *The City Founder*, was published in Hungary in the summer of 1977, after it had already appeared in Germany and France. This event was not regarded as in any way significant in Budapest.[32]

LITERATURE AND POLITICS

Literary opposition – the expression of critical or oppositional views through novels, drama or poetry – has an extremely long and honoured tradition in Hungary, as it does elsewhere in Eastern Europe. Indeed, literature, above all poetry, are closely associated with the emergence of modern politics and nationhood and particularly with revolution and revolutionary change. This was as true of 1956 and the role played by Gyula Illyés's 'One Sentence on Tyranny' (*Egy mondat a zsarnokságról*) as it was of 1848 and Sándor Petőfi's 'Arise Hungarian'

(*Talpra Magyar*). The Petőfi Circle of writers played a key role in the build up to 1956 and the expression of political criticism through the somewhat diffuse medium of literature is accepted and expected. Yet paradoxically there have been very few works of literature since 1956 which have played an important political role. That function in the 1960s and 1970s has been taken over by the social sciences. This was predictable, perhaps, or at least it was understandable: it would be very difficult to conceive of a contribution to the debate on the New Economic Mechanism made by a novelist. On the other hand, this does not mean that writers have abandoned their traditional role entirely. They have continued to address themselves to the most elementary aspect of writing, the freedom of speech itself, and one or two have sought to portray in literary terms the impact of the changes undergone by Hungarian society in recent years.

Pride of place among such demands must go to the grand old man of Hungarian literary criticism, Aladár Komlós, who remarked in an interview, 'The writer has less freedom today than he did in other periods, for example at the turn of the century. But compared with yesterday, the recent past that is, it has increased substantially.'[33] An equally outspoken attack on the manipulation of information by the media was made by the late Tibor Déry, who added that he, for his part, preferred gossip because it retained a human dimension.[34] The restrictions on writers are occasionally acknowledged and condemned by the younger generation too. István Csurka insisted very strongly on the political role of the writer in Hungarian society and noted that apart from the prosperity of one particular stratum, people in general lived from hand to mouth.[35] Similarly, Ferenc Karinthy has expressed strong support for freedom of expression in literature, whether it is realistic or absurd or avant-garde. He rejected a black-and-white attitude to writing and called for 'free competition' in order to decide what was best. He added that realism was the approach most likely to create problems, whilst abstractions made life easier. 'An abstract parable about the relationship between power and morality, which is open to various interpretations, and is unintelligible to most, slips through much more easily than, say, if someone writes about what is happening in a co-operative.... How difficult it is for a short story dealing with the real problems of Hungarian life to reach the printed page.'[36]

Karinthy, in fact, subsequently experienced precisely these difficulties. A few months after his interview just quoted, he published an extract from a longer piece of work entitled 'Housewarming'.[37] This extract included a devastating description of the attitudes and morality of the new political élite in a provincial town. It showed the local leaders' behaviour to be very similar to the habits of the pre-war gentry, their corruption, their abuse of power and in one highly significant passage, Karinthy offered a vivid analysis of the ideology of the new élite. The essence of this was the new élite deserved its power, its life-style and its prosperity because it contributed far more to the communal stew-pot than the average man in the street. The anti-egalitarianism of the upper middle strata in Hungary was clearly and explicitly set down. The publication of this extract (parts of the original were cut) created an uproar and a warning was subsequently issued by the party drawing the attention of the literary community to the accepted limits of freedom.

Károly Szakonyi's play 'The Hong Kong Wig' also deals with the attitudes of the new élite.[39] It is a striking presentation of their arrogant attitudes towards the working class, their quest for status symbols, trips to the west, a cottage in the country and so on, as well as their fawning on their superiors in the hierarchy. The play also shows the working class to be unwilling to accept any responsibility, to become involved and their admiration for the status symbols of the managerial élite.

One of the most detailed descriptions of social attitudes is in Ákos Kertész's novel *Makra*, which seeks to portray the problem of being a worker in a rigidly stratified society.[40] The book makes it clear that traditional attitudes towards workers and others of a lower social status remain strong and there is more than a hint that in some respects life is even more difficult for a worker in the Hungary of the 1970s than it was in the 1930s. On the other hand, there is no attempt to criticise the system as such in *Makra*, no hint that any responsibility for this state of affairs might rest with official policy makers. Hence the novel may be regarded as a copy-book illustration of the nature of para-opposition.

At the same time, even though criticism of this kind does appear, a number of authors are prevented from publishing. For example, the critic Imre Kis Pintér, speaking at the Literary Days Conference in Debrecen in 1975, revealed that several younger writers had submitted manuscripts to publishers and were still waiting for the appearance of their works after several years.

He argued that this younger generation concerned itself with the particular problem of the individual in society from the standpoint of the individual rather than that of the collective and added that these younger writers seemed to have given up any attempt to describe social and historical processes on a broader canvas. He suggested that this phenomenon was a reaction against the excessive emphasis on public life in the 1950s.[41]

The main feature of political criticism in literature is that there is a general reluctance to go beyond analysis of partial issues and to leave fundamental questions alone. In addition to the factors mentioned above, the accessibility of fiction by a wider reading public as compared with a sociological treatise is likely to have created stricter criteria of what is tolerated and that, in turn, will have given rise to stricter self-censorship as well. This is all the more easily understood, given the diffuseness of the literary medium, the blurring of dividing lines, plus the memories of the traditional oppositional function of literature. The overall result is not only that Hungarian literature appears to have lost much of its former purposiveness, but also that the contribution made by writers to political change has diminished substantially during the Kádár years.

The problem of Hungary's Jews, the survival of an intense anti-Semitism and the failure of official policies to come to terms with the question of guilt regarding the extermination of a very large part of the Jewish community during the war virtually remain taboo subjects. Indeed, many intellectuals in Hungary regard it as potentially one of the most serious social problems and one where feelings can be very easily manipulated. This perhaps helps to explain why so little sociological work has been published on the subject. It is interesting, too, that it was felt that the problem was easier to tackle through literature. Whilst various Jewish themes had appeared from time to time in works of fiction and very occasionally in sociology and history, Hungarian opinion had paid little attention to this.[42] It was not until the question was broached directly on a popular level in the summer of 1975 in an article by György Száraz that it became a subject of public debate.[43] The way in which the question was raised was in itself interesting. Száraz was an amateur and something of a maverick and his article was unhistorical; it was argued privately that only an essentially isolated non-professional like Száraz could have been allowed to raise the topic, because anything more seriously based and rigorously argued would not have been permitted publication. In this sense, Száraz was regarded as the fool who rushed in where angels had feared to tread. His article, and the expanded version that he published in book form, did, however, burst like a bombshell.

Even before that date, it was true, there had been indications that anti-Semitism among the intelligentsia was gaining increased expres-

sion. The daily *Magyar Nemzet* published a warning that the communist party was neither 'for' nor 'against' Jews because Marxism excluded
the evaluation of individuals from 'a racial, religious or national'
standpoint.[44] Evidently, if a warning of this kind was necessary,
tensions had been rising. However, I was informed early in 1975 that it
was not entirely a matter of anti-Semitism on its own. My informants,
both Jewish and non-Jewish, argued that developments had to be
judged in the context of the renewed urbanist-populist debates. Because the urbanists included a number of Jews, when the subject of
Hungarian nationhood came up for discussion, some of the populists
used anti-Semitism as a lever against them or were thought to have
done so. But the main focus of the debate was not anti-Semitism itself.

It was against this background that Száraz's article appeared. Entitled 'Tracking down a Prejudice', Száraz detailed the long history of
Jews in Hungary, tried to come to grips with the nature of anti-
Semitism, above all with how Hungarian society could stand by and
watch a part of itself be liquidated during the war. Száraz, whose article
subsequently appeared in an expanded version in book form, called for
a debate to clarify the problem, to lay ghosts and to speak openly of
guilt. His contribution was received with very mixed feelings; when he
was subsequently interviewed in *Élet és Irodalom*, the interview was
published under the title 'Why stir up this question?'.[45]

Part of the answer lay in the series of novels, some of them
semi-documentary, which looked at the question of the Hungarian
Jews and the holocaust. György Moldova's 'The Szent Imre March'
was undoubtedly the most influential of these, not least because of
Moldova's status as one of the country's most popular writers. His
novel, which first appeared in *Kortárs*, dealt with the Budapest ghetto
and the appalling conditions in which individuals survived. Moldova's
central theme concerned the nature of the will to survive, but from the
point of view of Hungary of the 1970s, the very fact that he wrote
about the ghetto was of importance. The overwhelming majority of
people under thirty had had little idea that a ghetto had existed at all.
Other works of fiction, notably Mária Ember's 'Hair-pin bend', and
Ervin Gyertyán's 'Spectacles in the dust' also dealt with aspects of the
holocaust, while Ágnes Gergely handled the much more sensitive
subject of the two-fold loyalty of Jews in Hungarian society today.[46]

In the light of the strictly taboo nature of the Jewish question, it
becomes somewhat easier to see why so little has been written about it
by the scientific intelligentsia. The few articles that have appeared
tended to look at anti-Semitism as one aspect of prejudice among

others, notably the extremely powerful hostility towards Gypsies. Thus a school teacher found that the eleven to fourteen-year-olds that she taught showed considerable prejudice against Jews and that they used the word 'Jew' (*zsidó*) as a term of abuse, although without having any clear idea of what it meant; it was even used in this way by a Jewish child.[47] Another article detailed the results of attitude surveys in three north Hungarian villages. This showed that 36.3 per cent of respondents would not take a Jewish spouse and that 13.1 per cent would not welcome Jewish neighbours.[48] Finally, the writer Iván Sándor undertook an investigation into the Tiszaeszlár blood libel case of 1882 (in which members of the local Jewish community were accused of having murdered a young child, Eszter Solymosi). The case may be likened to the notorious Dreyfuss trial, and it was the source of an international scandal in its time. Tiszaeszlár has become synonymous with vicious anti-Semitism and rural bigotry. Sándor found that in the village of Tiszaeszlár, the peasants continued to believe in the validity of the blood libel to this day.[49]

There is also evidence of anti-Semitism within the party machine. In 1973 a relatively senior party official, Ferenc Sütő delivered a strongly anti-Semitic speech, dressed up as anti-Zionism. There is certainly support for this at the middle level of the party organisation, although Sütő himself was reported as having been immediately demoted and transferred to another, less sensitive post,[50] the Hungarian embassy in Ulan Bator.

THE HISTORIANS' DEBATE

There has probably been no other debate that has lasted as long and has involved quite as many people as the historians' debate. Its central subject has been the nature of Hungarian nationhood and how the history of the Hungarian nation was to be treated. Its echoes and reverberations have gone beyond the professional historians and the party itself has felt impelled to intervene. The polarisation in the debate, which at times was conducted with considerable acrimony, tended to move from the axis of party control over the writing of history according to professional standards to a conflict between the neo-populists and the heirs of the urbanists. One of its abiding features has been the insistence of the professional historians on their right to undertake historical analysis without the ballast of either Marxist or nationalist ideology. In the case of nationalist distortions, the arguments have been explicit; the arguments against Marxist distortions have generally been packaged up as attacks on the remnants of Stalinist dogmatism.[51]

The debate originated in 1960, in the post-1956 thaw, when the late Erik Molnár began publishing a series of articles in which he called for the demythicisation of the concepts of nation, people and home-land. Molnár argued that Hungarian historians of the Stalinist period had, in effect, made the same tacit assumption as the nationalist, namely that there had always existed a single unitary Hungarian nation. He rejected this as a nationalist projection of the present on to the past and argued instead that the national ideology cherished by nationalist historians had only been the ideology of the ruling class. He went on to question the view that Hungarian history had consisted of a long struggle for independence over and above class conflict, for this proposition divorced nationhood from both class and contemporaneity.

The nationalist reply, as represented by historians like the late Aladár Mód, paid the due obeisance to fighting nationalism, but then claimed that patriotism in the past should not be written off as an example of false consciousness. Furthermore, and this aspect of the debate continued as a key issue, the historian also had current political responsibilities, in that it was partly his duty to shape the concepts of socialist patriotism in contemporary Hungary. This task was to demonstrate, inter alia, the continuity of popular patriotism and to strengthen socialism by presenting history as a storehouse of examples and precepts. The line of argument represented by the anti-nationalists was unwelcome because it could deprive the Hungarian people of their progressive heritage.

The professional historians' arguments against Marxist distortions likewise have their origins in the work of Molnár. He and his adherents rejected the vulgarisation of the historical process in which 'subjective' and 'objective' factors were confused and which over-stressed the former. History was not shaped by 'revolutionary optimism', but by the 'objective factors' of economic and social life and ignoring these, they contended, led to unhistorical, naïve and unscientific conclusions. A historian who approached his country's history in this fashion, served only to feed his nation's illusions, 'instead of increasing its knowledge about itself'. The price paid for daydreaming in the past had been high. Obviously, on a number of points the Marxist-dogmatist and populist-nationalist lines merged. The historians, in taking the field against this combination, sought to depoliticise their area of research and to introduce professional criteria.[52] To a surprising extent, they have been successful in this, at least insofar as there have been few political obstacles placed in the way of publishing controversial historical works which have had the declared aim of stripping the myths and illusions from Hungarian history.

At a deeper level, the historians' debate centred on the existence and future of the Hungarian nation and, although this seldom emerged into the open, this operated as a tacit centre of gravity in the welter of arguments and counter-arguments. Essentially two conceptions conflicted with one another, whilst a third – that of total subordination to the Soviet Union – was not considered seriously by anyone. The first of these, which had the backing of the professional historians and the urbanists, looked for a solution along the lines of the post-1867 *Ausgleich*. That would involve an acceptance of Soviet overlordship as inevitable for the time being and a quest for establishing a liberal, anti-absolutist consciousness within the confines of what was possible. The other conception was that which underlay the arguments of the neo-populists: a struggle for the independence of the Hungarian nation regardless of the consequences, inasmuch as the nation was a category which transcended all other values and the safeguarding of the 'national essence' was the paramount duty of all members of the nation in general and of the intelligentsia in particular.

Possibly the most significant single work to appear in the debate was Jenő Szűcs's broad-ranging essay on the historical aspect of the nation and its legacy in the modern period.[53] Szűcs's arguments attracted a great deal of hostility and the publication of the work was attended with some difficulty; indeed, it was not finally published in book form until several years after its initial circulation in professional circles. The central theme of the study was the relationship between nationhood and history, particularly the genesis of the relationship between the two, in other words, how the modern nation was linked to its historical antecedents. This was of particular importance in the Hungarian context, Szűcs felt, both because historical antecedents played a greater role in contemporary Hungarian consciousness than, say, in French and because the issue was ineluctably bound up with the imagined and desired content of the new, socialist model of nationhood.

Szűcs's thoroughgoing analysis probed at both the Marxist and nationalist myths of nationhood and showed how they both sought to project existing, contemporary values on to the past. Thus during the

Stalinist period, a stereotyped concept of the class struggle of the proletariat was propagated as the model of the class struggle of the feudal peasantry, in which the oppressed classes were declared to be the true bearers of national progress. This was little different from the nationalist argument that the welfare of the nation had been sustained by the ruling élite of former periods. The pre-communist historians had assumed that history was primarily a process which had the 20th century nation as its immanent objective, so that the category 'national' had been absolutised into an instrument of subjective interpretation. Thus if 'national independence' was 'progressive', any phenomenon which could be classified as a 'national movement' was declared 'progressive'. Thus, in effect, popular was equated with national, even for periods when national in the modern sense did not exist.

These and other unhistorical approaches to history served merely to sustain self-reproducing cycles of errors, in which the nation lived off an unhistorical concept of its own history. The function of history was not to provide a storehouse of exemplars by which the nation should transmit its value system, neither should it be a storehouse of justifications. The relationship between socialism and the nation rested on different conceptual foundations. These recognised the antecedents of the nation but did not confuse them with the phenomenon itself, so that the mediaeval *natio* could in no sense be the same as the 18th century nation. As far as the working class was concerned, this did not deny the concept of nation, but equally it did not regard it as its supreme focus of group loyalty, merely as one of several foci. Consequently Marxist historical writing did not have as its role the recolouring of old, bourgeois nationalist theories or of reversing them mechanistically. Its real function was the critical analysis of history. 'The "aim" of history is not to justify the present, but to gain a better understanding of the present through knowledge of the road to it.'[54]

The conflict between professionalism and politicisation was equally evident in the debate on concepts of history and patriotic education held at Eger in 1971.[55] Thus Péter Hanák, taking up one of the points made by Aladár Mód, flatly rejected the idea that it was possible to pick and choose in history. Mód had argued that historical research should concentrate on the periods and events of Hungarian history to which the present system was the heir and successor, i.e. Rákóczi, Kossuth and Ady. In Hanák's opinion this was false historicism. It might be sympathetic in its components, but there were no organic and linear elements in the process of historical continuity. Another representative of the populist-nationalist line of thinking, Gyula Fekete, attacked the professional historians for their élitism. The discussion in which they were taking part was about public thinking, education and the formation of history teaching; the historians could not, in his view, detach themselves from day-to-day issues for these could not be hived off from their professional concerns.

Some of the issues in the conflict between the professionalism of the historians and the standpoint of their opponents emerged from the reception accorded to István Nemeskürty's popularising history of the period after the defeat of the Hungarian kingdom at the Battle of Mohács in 1526. Nemeskürty's book was extraordinarily popular – its first edition of 6,000 copies in 1966 sold out, it was reprinted three years later in 18,000 copies, which likewise sold out and this was followed by a third edition in 1975 (this time together with two other popular histories by Nemeskürty about the 16th century).[56] There is no doubt whatever that the impact of the book was enormous and that Nemeskürty's popular history reached a far wider readership than that of the professional historians. This undoubtedly contributed to the vehemence with which the latter attacked him.

On its first appearance, Nemeskürty's thesis was criticised for its populist colouring and for its bias against the nobility. Nemeskürty, his critics suggested, had attempted to strip the layers of illusion that still surrounded the defeat at Mohács in the popular mind, to place the blame for the catastrophe fairly and squarely where it belonged – the ruling nobility – and to exonerate the people. As one of his professional critics remarked, in itself demystification was a worthwhile undertaking, but it had to be done with complete professionalism and rigour which were absent from Nemeskürty's methods. What Nemeskürty did instead was to destroy one set of illusions and replace them with another set (to the effect that if matters had been left to the 'people', Hungary might have been saved).[57]

On the third appearance of the book, Nemeskürty was again taken to task for not having paid any attention at all to the professional assessments of the earlier editions.[58] Thus clearly proved errors of fact, dates, places and the like, were repeated, evidently implying that Nemeskürty had not the slightest intention of accepting professional corrections. But as one of the analyses of his book argued, this was not merely a matter of idleness or incompetence. It was directly connected with Nemeskürty's approach to history and the assumptions on which he based his work, namely that the disasters which befell Hungary in the 16th century were the sole responsibility of the ruling class.

Behind these historical academic arguments lay another unspoken question involving significantly more recent periods. Whilst Nemes-kürty was ostensibly and, also, genuinely putting forward a thesis that the ruling class of the 16th century had been responsible for the country's disasters, at the same time his book could also have been interpreted (which it was) as referring to 1944–5. The parallel was clear to anyone versed in the methods of reading historical analogies. In this sense Nemeskürty was also attacking the Horthy regime and contending that the reason why Hungary ended the second world war on the losing side was that the people had been excluded from government. This was precisely the kind of unhistorical conclusion to which the professional historians objected. And that was why Nemes-kürty was accused by one of his critics of having poisoned the historical conception of an entire generation.

The nationalism debate itself was one of the phases of the historians' debate. But in discussing the subject of Hungarian nationalism, a variety of writers succeeded in rehabilitating what had been until then the strictly taboo subject of the Hungarians living outside Hungary. For much of the 1960s, official policy was to ignore the fact that approximately three million Hungarians live in Czechoslovakia (most-ly in Slovakia), Yugoslavia (mostly in Vojvodina), and in Romania (mostly in Transylvania) and that for Hungarian public opinion their fate was a burning issue. But towards the end of that decade, a slow change was observable. The writings of Gyula Illyés, who has long held extremely pessimistic views about the chances of survival of the Hungarians as a nation, were one component in this.[59] He and others gradually succeeded in breaking the taboo. The other component appeared to be a change in official policy – possibly in response to pressure from within the party and from public opinion. This took the form of discussing Hungary's own nationalities – around 5 per cent of the population – describing the various rights they enjoyed and criticising the situation in Transylvania where two million Hungarians live under Romanian rule without the benefit of such rights.[60]

An example of Illyés's approach was his address to the Magyar Nyelvőr Society, where he recounted that nearly a quarter of a group of first year undergraduates were uncertain in their answer to the question what the language spoken by the Szeklers was. The answer, as Illyés pointed out, should have been automatic and the responses showed serious confusion on a key aspect of Hungarian national consciousness.[61]

Illyés, who may be regarded as the leading spokesman for this current of opinion, took the argument one stage farther at the end of

1977, when in a two-part article in the large-circulation daily *Magyar Nemzet*, he not only returned to his theme of the extinction of the Hungarian nation (a proposition which he vigorously rebutted), but he also dealt with the Transylvanian question with unprecedented openness. Although he neither mentioned Romania nor Transylvania by name, it was absolutely clear that this was his topic. He argued that the Hungarians of Transylvania were being deprived of their most elementary human rights, in education, use of language, opportunities for advancement, and he even went as far as to suggest that the minority was the victim of a policy of apartheid.[62]

It can be fairly argued that the intelligentsia, reflecting deeply held views in the population, has achieved something of a success in political terms over the nationalities question. Although public discussion of this problem in all its aspects remains difficult, the limits of what can be published are incomparably broader than when compared with a decade ago.[63] Secondly, official policy makers have responded by taking up the question of the Hungarians outside Hungary in order to promote their interests. This has had a certain amount of success, in that Hungary and its neighbours accept that some cultural connections between Hungary and the minorities should be possible.

Whilst sociology and economics have represented the cutting edge of the social sciences in attacking the limits of criticism, there have been one or two attempts to establish a separate role for political science. On the whole, this has failed and hardly a single study or article has appeared that could be classified as falling into this category. An explicit demand for the legitimacy of a Marxist political science was put forward in 1967 and the theses of this article were approvingly reiterated ten years later. The gist of this article was that Marxism was essentially about politics and its aims could only be implemented by political means, but this did not automatically mean that the political nature of Marxism was the same as the concrete study of political realities. Certain aspects of the political process could only be understood through their autonomous investigation, and not, as so often, through sociology, public administration or law.[64]

Whilst a number of publications in sociology have direct political implications, and were self-evidently written with the aim of influencing the decision makers, overt investigations of political phenomena have been sparse. One rare and interesting example was an article analysing the political responses to the crises of 1919, 1945 and 1956 in the southern Hungarian commune of Mezőhegyes. This showed that the four different social groups identified by the author all approached the different crises with their own autonomous political value systems and that these value systems hardly changed during the century.[65] Political information has received somewhat more attention than attempts at all-embracing analyses. The conference held at Visegrád in 1975 on 'The nature, organisation and role of beliefs in everyday consciousness' turned up a good deal of material with immediate political significance. One of the papers presented at the conference showed that a substantial minority of people regarded Hungary as having been on the victorious side in the second world war and this applied especially to the younger generations who would have had no personal experience of the period, so that their information would have been acquired under the existing system. Interestingly, a small majority of respondents regarded Romania as having been on the victorious side as well. Another conference paper dealt with the level of information among young workers about Rákosi and László Rajk, Rákosi's principal communist victim. The gist of this paper's findings was that the process of association was roughly as follows: Rákosi was vaguely known as 'a Bad Thing' and was therefore associated with 'the fascists' or the 1956 'counter-revolution', whilst Rajk was vaguely known as having been 'a Good Thing' who had suffered in 'the cause' so that it was thought that Rajk had been a victim of fascism or of 1956.[66] Finally, the limited circulation *Rádió es Televizió Szemle*, recently published an article on the emotional significance of political concepts, which asserted that notable gaps existed between the officially desired value system and the actual value system. Thus the answers suggested that the concept of 'people' was felt to be wider and more all-embracing than that of 'state', implying that in the minds of the respondents the two should not be identified absolutely (which is a curious comment on a country that calls itself a People's Democracy); and, further, that the emotional associations with the word 'opposition' were not at all unfavourable, indeed not that different from associations with 'government'.[67]

The striking aspect of these various political type articles is their partial nature. None of them, understandably, attempted to provide a thoroughgoing analysis of the Hungarian political system and its operations. At the same time, given the restrictions, a number of scholars who ought probably to be seen as working in the field of political sociology, have shown themselves interested in discovering and analysing the inner values, processes and interconnections of Hungarian politics.

CONCLUSION

A survey of the Hungarian intellectual scene of the last decade or so shows one dominant feature. This is that the tacit compact on which the Kádár system has been based has changed to a surprisingly limited extent. The essence of this compact, as already suggested, was that there would be no overt questioning of the fundamental legitimacy of the system, and the great majority of the intelligentsia had adhered to this. The groups or individuals who have taken their researches beyond the threshold have been marginalised and effectively placed beyond the confines of the system. The authorities appear to prefer that this is implemented by expatriation rather than censorship. The Budapest School, in particular, overstepped the threshold by questioning the socialist nature of the system directly; there was also some evidence that the Hungarian authorities came under pressure from other East European states to take measures against their New Left critics.

But this did not mean that criticism was ended. Although in private conversation one is regularly told that the atmosphere had deteriorated, a survey of the material which is still being published has tended to suggest that fears on this score have been excessive. There have been two broad approaches to the method of expressing criticism. First, and this is very characteristic of a very large amount of the work done, scholars have preferred to examine limited subjects or undertake what might be termed partial research. Second, where the work might self-evidently suggest the drawing of broad conclusions about the nature of Hungarian politics, this has been studiously avoided. So, for example, there has been any amount of material published to show that political socialisation in Hungary has been at best marginal; but none of the articles or monographs where the evidence for this has been detailed has made this kind of conclusion overtly. The facts are published and are allowed to speak for themselves.

Yet by putting the results of these researches together, a fairly clear in-depth picture of contemporary Hungarian society can be constructed. Its principal features include social inequality exacerbated by an increasingly rigid stratification and low mobility; aspirations which are in no way collectivist; weak institutionalisation; the survival of authoritarian attitudes in human relations and a corresponding weakness of democracy. To what extent criticism on these and other topics influences policy makers is extremely difficult to gauge. Obviously, published work does have some kind of an impact, but as against that, policy makers appear to be reluctant to initiate major changes. Stability shading off into a fairly comfortable stagnation seem to be the main features of the Kádár model in the 1970s.

NOTES

1. The literature on Hungarian politics since 1956 in English is relatively meagre, certainly when compared with what is available as raw material in Hungarian. W. F. Robinson, *The Pattern of Reform in Hungary* (NY: Praeger, 1973) gives a detailed picture of the Kádár model; Peter Toma and Ivan Völgyes, *Politics in Hungary* (San Francisco: Freeman, 1977) is extremely valuable for its range in examining the functioning of the political system; William Shawcross, *Crime and Compromise: János Kádár and the Politics of Hungary since the Revolution* (London: Weidenfeld and Nicolson, 1974) is not without its uses, despite its occasional superficialities. Some of my own ideas are set out in 'Hungary: an Uneasy Stability', in Archie Brown and Jack Gray, eds., *Political Culture and Political Change in Communist States* (London: Macmillan, 1977). Finally it hardly needs to be added that anyone following current developments in Hungary will find the Radio Free Europe research material quite indispensable.
2. Iván Szelényi, 'Notes on the "Budapest School"', *Critique*, no. 8 (Summer 1977) pp. 61–7.
3. Tamás Földvári, 'Informalizmus az ipari szövetkezetek és az állami iparvállalatok külső kapcsolataiban', *Ergonómia*, vol. 10, no. 2 (1977) pp. 77–83.
4. Stefan Mandel, 'Filling a Vacuum', *Index on Censorship*, vol. 7, no. 2 (March 1977) pp. 40–1.
5. György Márkus, 'Viták és irányzatok a marxista filozófiában', *Kortárs*, vol. 12, no. 7 (July 1968) pp. 1109–28.
6. Szelényi, op. cit.
7. András Hegedüs, 'The Self-Criticism of a Socialist Society: a Reality and a Necessity', in *The Humanisation of Socialism: Writings of the Budapest School* (London: Allison and Busby, 1976): originally published in *Kortárs*, vol. 11, no. 7 (July 1967). The quotation is from the English version, p. 162.
8. Ibid., p. 170.
9. György Berkovits, 'Változatok a szociografiára', *Valóság*, vol. 18, no. 5 (May 1975) pp. 46–61 at p. 51.
10. Darvas wrote a number of articles on the Discovery of Hungary series and its problems, notably in *Kortárs*, vol. 12, no. 9 (September 1968) *Valóság*, vol. 13, no. 3 (March 1970) and *Kritika*, September 1970; see also *Izvestiia*, 4 February 1969 and *Magyar Nemzet*, 17 October 1968.
11. Gyula Borbándi, 'Mit fedeznek fel Magyarország felfedezői?', *Új Látóhatár* (Munich) vol. 28, nos. 3–4 (December 1977) pp. 315–36.
12. Vita a *Társadalmi Szemle* szerkesztőségében, 'Társadalmunk érdekviszonyai és a tudományos kutatás', *Társadalmi Szemle*, vol. 31, nos. 8–9

(August–September 1976) pp. 72–97.
13. Ibid., p. 81.
14. Ibid., p. 88.
15. There is no single work dealing with the urbanist-populist debates. Gyula Borbándi, *Der ungarische Populismus* (Munich: Aurora Bucher, 1976) is a useful monograph on the populist movement, which has a brief section on the 1960s, pp. 300–3.
16. There is a great deal of published material on the Budapest School in Western languages. Allison and Busby have published four volumes of their writings in their 'Motive' series. These are (1) András Hegedüs, Ágnes Heller, Mária Márkus, Mihály Vajda, *The Humanisation of Socialism* (London: Allison and Busby, 1976); (2) Hegedüs, *Socialism and Bureaucracy* (London: Allison and Busby, 1976); both these volumes contain essays and studies already published in a variety of journals in Hungary; (3) Mihály Vajda, *Fascism as a Mass Movement* (London: Allison and Busby, 1976); (4) Ágnes Heller, *The Theory of Need in Marx* (London: Allison and Busby, 1976). Hegedüs's *A szocialista társadalom struktúrájáról* (1966) and *Változó Világ* (1970) have been published as a single volume in English, *The Structure of a Socialist Society* (NY: St Martin's Press, 1977). I have not been able to consult the two volumes, *Die Neue Linke in Ungarn*, Internationale Marxistische Diskussion nos. 45 and 53 (West Berlin: Merve Verlag, 1974, 1976). These apparently contain some otherwise unpublished papers. *Les Temps Modernes*, vol. 30, no. 337–8 (August–September 1974) pp. 2736–857 reproduces several of the papers in *Humanisation of Socialism* and also contains an analytical essay by Serge Frankel and Daniel Martin, 'La nouvelle gauche hongroise: sociologie et révolution', pp. 2765–88, a part of which appeared in *Wiener Tagebuch*, June 1973. See also three RFE research papers, dated 16 January, 18 November 1974 and 23 April 1976.
17. William Robinson, 'Who are the real Marxists now?', *Index on Censorship*, vol. 2, no. 3 (1973) pp. 71–7.
18. Ágnes Heller, *Portrévázlatok az etika történetéből* (Budapest, 1976); 'A kötelességen túl', *Korunk*, vol. 33, no. 1, pp. 31–41.
19. *Le Quotidien de Paris* (27, 28 October 1976).
20. For example Ágnes Losonczi, *Az életmód az időben, a tárgyakban és az értékekben* (1977).
21. Details in George Schöpflin, 'The Trial of Miklós Haraszti', *Index on Censorship*, vol. 3, no. 1 (1974) pp. 79–84 and 'Le Procès Haraszti' *Les Temps Modernes*, op. cit., pp. 2834–57.
22. Miklós Haraszti, *The Worker in a Worker's State* (London: Penguin, 1977).
23. Ferenc Fehér's interview appeared under the title 'A Hungarian out in the cold', *The Listener*, 12 February 1976.
24. Text and list of signatories (from which the name of György Márkus is inexplicably omitted) in *Irodalmi Újság* (Paris) vol. 28, no. 1–2 (January–February 1977).
25. A lengthy summary of *Marx in the Fourth Decade* and *Profile* is by Balázs Rab, in samizdat.

26. Szelényi, op. cit.
27. See Serge Frankel and Daniel Martin, op. cit.
28. Marc Racovski, *Towards an East European Marxism*, in Allison and Busby's 'Motive' series in English; I used the Hungarian language manuscript; see also Marc Racovski, 'Le marxisme devant les sociétés soviétiques' *Les Temps Modernes*, vol. 30, no. 341 (December 1974) pp. 553–84. In places, the editors of *Les Temps Modernes* refer to him as 'Racouski'.
29. György Konrád and Iván Szelényi, 'A késleltetett városfejlődés társadalmi konfliktusai', *Valóság*, vol. 15, no. 12 (December 1971) pp. 19–35.
30. György Berkovits, *Világváros Határában* (1976); see p. 341.
31. I relied on the Hungarian manuscript, *Az értelmiség útja az osztályhatalomhoz*: a somewhat revised version is to be published in English by Harcourt, Brace, Jovanovich in 1979.
32. György Konrád, *A városalapító* (1977). In English: *The City Builder* (New York–London: Harcourt, Brace, Jovanovich, 1977).
33. Ferenc Karinthy, 'Irószobám – beszélgetés Komlós Aladárral', *Kortárs*, vol. 21, no. 5 (May 1977) pp. 816–27 at p. 819.
34. *Élet és Irodalom* (22 November 1975).
35. Bulcsu Bertha, 'Interjú Csurka Istvánnal', *Jelenkor*, vol. 20, no. 2 (February 1977) pp. 109–18.
36. *Kritika*, May 1975.
37. Ferenc Karinthy, 'Házszentelő', *Kortárs*, vol. 20, nos. 1 & 2 (January and February 1976) pp. 41–61, pp. 203–36 especially at p. 230.
38. Private information to author.
39. Károly Szakonyi, 'Hongkongi paróka', *Új Irás*, vol. 13, no. 11 (November 1973) pp. 16–58.
40. Ákos Kertész, *Makra* (1972). I am indebted to Peter Toma and Ivan Völgyes, op. cit., where my attention was first drawn to this book; several passages are quoted in extenso, notably in ch. 11.
41. The proceedings of the conference were published in *Alföld*, vol. 27, no. 1 (January 1976) pp. 45–87; Kis Pintér's remarks at p. 75; the introductory paper by Miklós Béládi, 'Merre tart a magyar irodalom', pp. 46–58, is a useful summary of recent Hungarian fiction.
42. For a survey of Jewish themes in post-war Hungarian literature, Iván Sanders, 'Tétova vonzalmak: zsidó témák a kortársi magyar irodalomban', *Új Látóhatár* (Munich) vol. 26, no. 5 (December 1975) pp. 427–43.
43. György Száraz, 'Egy előitelét nyomán', *Valóság*, vol. 18, no. 8 (August 1975) pp. 60–82; the book, with the same title, was published in 1976, in 287 pp.
44. 28 October 1974.
45. 'Minek bolygatni ezt a kérdést?' *Élet és Irodalom*, 11 October 1975.
46. György Moldova, 'A Szent Imre-induló', *Kortárs*, vol. 19, no. 2 (February 1975) pp. 320–1; published in book form, under the same title in the same year; however, some changes were made in the text. Mária Ember, *Hajtűkanyar* (1974); Ervin Gyertyán, *Szemüveg a Porban* (1975); Ágnes Gergely, *A tolmács* (1973). I was not able to consult György Gera, *Terelőút*.

47. Ágnes Havas, 'Nacionalista hatások gyermekeinkre', *Társadalmi Szemle*, vol. 22, no. 3 (March 1967) pp. 97–111 at p. 105.

48. Mária Márkus, 'Büszkeség és előitélet', *Valóság*, vol. 10, no. 4 (April 1967) pp. 63–5.

49. Iván Sándor, *A vizsgálat iratai: tudósítás a tiszaeszlári per körülményeiről* (1976).

50. *Financial Times* (23 January 1973); Toma and Völgyes, op. cit., pp. 157–8.

51. Very little has been published on this subject in English. László Péter's two papers 'A Debate on the History of Hungary between 1790 and 1945', *Slavonic and East European Review*, vol. 50, no. 120 (1972) pp. 442–7 and 'New Approaches to Modern Hungarian History' *Ungarn-Jahrbuch*, vol. 4 (1972) pp. 162–71 are useful accounts of aspects of the debate. By contrast, Hungarian contributions have been legion. A useful bibliography is in the footnotes appended to István Király, 'Hazafiság és internacionalizmus', *Hazafiság és Forradalmiság* (1974) pp. 355–8. An emigré attack on the Molnár school, which by and large follows the populist line, is in Gyula Gombos, *Húsz év után* (Munich: Aurora Bucher, 1970) for example at p. 80.

52. See Zsigmond Pál Pach's defence of Molnár at the debate held at Vácrátót, where he said, 'Molnár did not regard it as his main task merely to show that the dogmatic and sectarian application of Marxism leads to errors, distortions and oversimplifications. He sought essentially to demonstrate that the 'leftist' view of history produced during the personality cult – a peculiar contradiction, it might seem – had conserved and transformed a great deal from bourgeois historiography and views of history. Whereas for Marxists, the nation is a historical and class category, the dogmatist view of history maintained, inter alia, a number of significant aspects of the supra-class conceptions of the bourgeois category of nation. Thus it contributed, willy-nilly, to the obstinate survival of bourgeois ideological relics in consciousness. . . . In that sense, Molnár fought what was basically a two-front struggle against 'leftist' dogmatism and the survival of bourgeois views and the remnants of bourgeois 'nationalism'. A full account of the debate was compiled by Miklós Stier, '"Hazafiság és internacionalizmus", Vitaülés Vácrátóton' *Századok*, Vol. 108, no. 1 (1974), pp. 220–61; Pach at p. 223.

53. Jenő Szűcs, 'A nemzet historikuma és a történetszemlélet nemzeti látószöge', *Nemzet és Történelem* (1975) pp. 13–183. The book was attacked by László Sebestyén, *Vitairat Kézai Simon védelmében* (Budapest 1975, rotaprint); second edition, Garfield, N.J., 1976.

54. Szűcs, op. cit., p. 159.

55. (Compiler) Levente Sipos, 'Vita a történetszemléletről és a hazafias nevelésről', *Párttörténeti Közlemények*, vol. 18, no. 2 (1972) pp. 121–46.

56. István Nemeskürty, *Ez történt Mohács után*, 1966, 1969; subsequently reissued in *Önfia vágta sebét* (1975) which also contains *Krónika Dózsa György tetteiről* and *Elfelejtett évtized*.

57. Ferenc Szakály, 'Egy történelmi bestseller és ami mögötte van', *Valóság*, vol. 12, no. 5 (May 1969) pp. 39–47, and other critiques of Nemeskürty quoted there.

58. Gábor Barta, 'Történelemről írni', *Valóság*, vol. 18, no. 12 (December 1975) pp. 94–107; a reply to Barta, defending Nemeskürty for having made history interesting and accessible to a non-professional readership, is in Kata Beke, 'Ki írjon a történelemről? Barta Gábor Nemeskürty-kritikájáról', ibid., vol. 19, no. 3 (March 1976) pp. 100–3.

59. Gyula Illyés, *Hajszálgyökerek* (1971) and *Itt élned kell*, 2 vols. (1976).

60. For example, László Kővágó, *Kisebbség-nemzetiség* (1977) and Rudolf Joó, *Nemzetiségek és nemsetiségi kérdés Nyugateurópában* (1977).

61. Gyula Illyés, 'A Magyar Nyelvőr ünnepére', *Népszabadság*, 16 January 1972; taking up the point made by Illyés and severely censuring official information policy on Transylvania, Lajos Für, 'Milyen nyelven beszélnek a székelyek?', *Tiszatáj*, vol. 26, no. 8 (August 1972) pp. 57–66.

62. *Magyar Nemzet*, 22 December 1977, 1 January 1978.

63. Examples of this are Csaba Csorba, 'A romániai magyar művelődés és a társadalomtudományi kutatások', *Valóság*, vol. 17, no. 10 (October 1974) pp. 61–78 and László Végh, 'A magyar nemzetiségi kultúra vizsgálata Szlovákiában', *Tiszatáj*, vol. 31, no. 5 (May 1977) pp. 72–6.

64. Csaba Gombár, 'A politikai tudomány kérdéséhez', *Valóság*, vol. 10, no. 10 (November 1967) pp. 85–91 was cited favourably by Mihály Samu, *A Hatalom és az állam* (1977) at p. 428. See also Tamás Szecskő, 'Politika: elmélet és gyakorlat – gondolatok a politikai szociológia műveléséhez', *Valóság*, vol. 10, no. 6 (June 1967) pp. 95–101; and Péter Vas-Zoltán, 'A "politikai tudomány" tartalmának kialakításához', *Magyar Tudomány*, vol. 74, no. 9 (September 1967) pp. 587–601. Gombár returned to his earlier theme in his review of Berkovits's *Világváros Határában*, where he argued that the obvious remedy for resolving the problems of the underprivileged Budapest agglomeration belt was a political one, that of providing it with autonomous political representation, see *Valóság*, vol. 19, no. 8 (August 1976) pp. 106–7. See also Gombár's article on the weakness of democratic traditions, 'Demokratikus politizálás – politikai kultúra', *Társadalmi Szemle*, vol. 33, no. 3 (March 1978).

65. Gábor Vági, 'A közelmúlt és értékelése egy magyar faluban', *Valóság*, vol. 19, no. 2 (February 1976) pp. 70–84. The existence of a strongly authoritarian tradition within institutions emerges from the controversial account of the Szentgotthárd mental hospital, by Péter Hajnóczy, 'Az elkülönítő', ibid., vol. 18, no. 10 (October 1975) pp. 84–100. Something very similar emerges from the spine-chilling description of the disciplinary methods used in private tuition given by a former nun, which have the approval of parents and teachers, Marianna Darányi, 'Julika néni iskolája', *Valóság*, vol. 20, no. 12 (December 1977) pp. 81–92.

66. Some of the papers presented at the Visegrád conference ('A hiedelmek természete, szerveződése és szerepe a mindennapi tudatbal') were published in *Szociológia* no. 2–3, 1976, notably Mária Dankánics, 'Különböző korú munkások tudati képe a második világháborúról', pp. 494–501; another paper, not reproduced in *Szociológia* but available in cyclostyled form, dealt with views of Rákosi and Rajk, Zoltán Jakab, 'Fiatalok vélekedése Rákosiról és Rajkról'. The bulk of the attitude survey work carried out between 1960 and 1970, including otherwise

unpublished material, is reviewed and reproduced in Ferenc Kovács, *A munkásosztály politikai-ideológiai müveltségéröl és aktivitásáról* (1976).
67. Csaba Pléh and István Czigler, 'Politikai foglmak érzelmi jelentése', *Rádió és Televizió Szemle*, vol. 8, no. 3 (1976) pp. 86–98.

6 Socialist Opposition in Eastern Europe: Dilemmas and Prospects

by IVÁN SZELÉNYI

INTRODUCTORY REMARKS ABOUT THE NOTION OF 'SOCIALIST OPPOSITION'

It has been sufficiently documented what a many-coloured phenomenon East European intellectual dissent and political opposition is. Probably the satellite countries could not match the remarkable variety of Soviet dissent, spreading from Orthodox Christians and Baptists to anarcho-syndicalists and the Stalinist old-guard,[1] but one can observe enough political and ideological diversity in the Czechoslovak reform movement[2] or in the Hungarian intellectual opposition in the 1960s and 1970s.[3]

The purpose of this study is to define under what conditions can we meaningfully talk about a 'socialist opposition'. What are the theoretical dilemmas with which socialist oppositional ideologues have been confronted in seeking to develop a critical socialist theory that could meet the needs of the East European working class movements.

The basic theoretical assumption of this paper is that it is not enough to have a handful of people among the dissidents who are committed to socialist values in order to speak about a socialist opposition. The socialist opposition will only emerge when the socialist critics of East European state socialism can come forward with a critical theory that is directly related to the praxis of the workers' opposition and one which can offer direction and programme to the working class movement.

There are quite a few socialists among the dissenting intellectuals, and there is significant resistance among workers against state socialism, but somehow these two necessary components of any meaningfully defined 'socialist opposition', revolutionary theory and revolutionary praxis, have not met as yet.

I have not had a chance to conduct systematic research in samizdat archives, but even without a content analysis of East European samizdat publications one can quite confidently estimate that probably the majority of the dissidents would call themselves socialist. True, many of them do so almost only by 'convention'. Did not heretics in medieval Rome often argue that they were also Catholics, and probably better ones than the Pope himself? In societies which are dominated by holistic ideologies even dissent has to fit into a broadly defined ideological frame, has to operate within the value system and with the conventional terminology of the Doctrine. But the question, who is a 'real' socialist and who only pretends to be one is almost totally irrelevant for the purposes of this paper. I do not want to decide if Sakharov is a socialist or just a bourgeois critic, or who is a better socialist, Jacek Kuroń or Rudi Supek.

Our task is not to classify dissidents into 'socialists' and 'non-socialists', but to define those theoretical issues, irrespective of the ideological beliefs or self-identification of their proponents, that socialists have to deal with if they attempt to understand the new system of political and economic subjugation of the working class, produced by state socialism. One obviously would expect that those dissenting or marginal intellectuals who are sincerely dedicated to socialist values will be more sensitive to these issues, but there is no direct correspondence between the values held by the ideologues and the sociological consequences of their ideologies. Critics and socialist beliefs often oppose East European state socialism on general humanitarian or libertarian grounds. They attack totalitarianism and police oppression; they demand freedom of speech and assembly and the abolition of censorship, and they fight for civil rights. They are socialist in their values, but their critique of Soviet-type societies is not *specifically* socialist and it will be shared by non-socialists, Christians or bourgeois liberals. In this paper I am searching for such a specifically socialist critical theory of East European socialism which does not propose to provide remedies for all human injustice and suffering, but which pursues general libertarian goals by aiming first at the emanci-pation of the working class. The libertarian socialist dissidents will become the ideologues of a 'socialist opposition' only when they develop a specific strategy for the emancipation of the working class, that is, when they become the ideologues of the East European workers' movement.

There is a workers' opposition in Eastern Europe which awaits its ideologies. The East European working class movement is still in its 'Luddite' period. Workers express their discontent and opposition to the regime by withholding production or slowing down the production process, by going on sick-leave even if they are not sick during the harvest season to work on their private plots.[4] This workers' opposition hits the headlines of the western newspapers only on those rare occasions when it unexpectedly erupts into usually poorly organised strikes or violent clashes with the police and the militia on the streets or in the factories. The working class resistance in Eastern Europe is like an iceberg. Western observers and East European politicians can easily underestimate its significance and potential explosiveness, but it is certainly inarticulate, unorganised, and lacks a coherent set of goals.

Thus both components we defined as the necessary preconditions of a 'socialist opposition' are present in contemporary Eastern Europe. There are intellectuals with socialist beliefs who are prepared to 'marginalise' themselves into the existentially insecure position of 'dissidents' and to spend their lives at the borderline of mental asylums, jails, voluntary or enforced exile, and there is a significant spontaneous movement of workers' resistance and discontent. Why do they not meet?

There are obviously social structural factors which have prevented the development of a stratum of 'organic intellectuals' of the working class in Eastern Europe. One of these is increased police control following 1968,[5] not only in Czechoslovakia but everywhere in the eastern bloc. On the other hand, one should not overestimate the extent and vigor of this police oppression, what is labelled by Piccone, with some exaggeration, as 'Gestapo-like management'. The attack which the political police were allowed by the party leadership to launch against dissenting intellectuals was relatively mild and did not measure up in any way to Stalinist or Nazi German oppression, and not even to the repressive measures of the last years of Francoist Spain. Few political trials have been staged against intellectuals and most of them got away with relatively mild, sometimes suspended, sentences. Nowadays the lives of dissenting intellectuals are not threatened any more and the worst that they can expect is a few years in jail or probably just a one-way visa to West Germany or England.

Liehm overestimates the negative consequences of détente. True, the East European regimes have made use of détente by referring to the principle of 'non-interference in internal affairs' when trying to bring intellectual dissent under control. However, in the era of détente the regimes became increasingly sensitive to western criticism and have sought to avoid spectacular international scandals on this score. Détente in general, or more specifically the Helsinki agreements, and the emphasis of the present American administration on human rights have helped the cause of dissent. After all, in the conservative Brezhnev era dissidents have given press conferences in Moscow, have published in the west critical writings under their own name, and sometimes they have been allowed to travel with a national passport in the west, to attend emigré conferences and to give politically sensitive interviews to the world press without any penalty. All these were unimaginable in the liberal Khruschchev era. The penalties the dissidents are faced with are not more serious than before and the risks intellectuals take when they 'marginalise' themselves are less than they were ten or fifteen years ago. In fact, the extent of dissent has not been declining since 1968. On the contrary, there are more dissidents than ever.

Political and police oppression do not explain why the dissidents do not choose to become the 'organic intellectuals' of the working class. Racovski offers another explanation. He maintains that intellectual dissidents cannot establish contacts with the workers since the workers do not have adequate organisations.[6] This is certainly very true, but it still does not explain why ideologies which could orient working class action are not being articulated. In another essay we proposed that the position intellectuals occupy in the East European social structure might be responsible for the inarticulateness of class relations in state socialist societies.[7] We suggested that since under state socialist redistributive economies the 'teleological knowledge' legitimates the right of expropriation of surplus for the first time in history, a dominating class position is offered to intellectuals who, by definition, pretend to have the monopoly of 'teleological knowledge'.

'Positive knowledge', or the articulation of opposing class interest, is only possible when intellectuals do not occupy a major position in the social structure; but when they are defined as a stratum and they can opt to become the 'organic intellectuals' of one of the basic classes. When intellectuals organise themselves into a class this means an end of 'positive knowledge' and of the reign of 'total ideology'. Thus, articulation of working class interest is only possible when intellectuals not only marginalise themselves, but 'betray' their own class, and relinquish their class position. We proposed that this was possible, but only after the intelligentsia consolidates its dominating class position. But this paper is concerned with the nature of theory upon which a socialist opposition can be built rather than with the sociology of the agents who might produce this ideology. Here I merely wish to indicate that there are structural constraints like police oppression, lack of working class organisations and the entrenchment of intellectuals in the dominant power structure, which delay the emergence of working class ideologues and ideologies.

East European socialist dissidents not only have to operate under these structural constraints, but the task they are confronted with in developing the theory of a socialist opposition in a state socialist society is also enormous. East European socialists will have to work out their own critical theory and they cannot borrow it from the western Left. Neither of the two schools of thought of the western Left which were critical of Soviet-type societies – the Maoists and the Trotskyists[8] – had more than a negligible impact on the East European opposition. Perhaps the Trotskyist influence was slightly more significant; Jacek Kuroń's and Modzelewki's 'Open Letter' – which is an important document in the development of an East European socialist opposition[9] – is definitely inspired by the theories of Trotsky, and Djilas. Although far from being Trotskyists, they certainly had been impressed by Leon Trotsky's views on socialist state bureaucracy.

But there are no traces of any systematic Trotskyist influences and there is certainly no Trotskyist movement anywhere in Eastern Europe. Maoism has had even less success. In Hungary, for example, a small group of university students 'played Maoism' during the mid-sixties, but no one took them seriously – except the political police who foolishly staged a trial against them. Following this, the students themselves quickly embraced other 'trendy' ideologies. It is again not our task in this paper to judge whether Charles Bettelheim or Ernest Mandel are right or wrong in their analysis of the Soviet Union, but we have to find an explanation for why socialists in Eastern Europe who are in opposition to their regimes cannot make much use of Maoist and Trotskyist theories, and what are the components of these theories which seem to be irrelevant or insufficient to develop a socialist critique *inside* these countries *on* these societies.

The development of a critical theory by socialists on Eastern Europe is a self-critical exercise. They have to work on a socialist critique of a socialist society which requires the reassessment of certain basic values and a number of dogmas.

It is worth noting how little impact the Maoist and pre-Maoist 'state capitalist' thesis had on East European dissidents. One could expect that for socialists who feel deceived by the oppressive nature of East European societies an easy solution would be to dismiss the socialist character of these societies (which might be the moral motivation of Western 'state capitalism' theorists). True, the Maoists, by flirting with Stalinism as a matter of course, cannot expect much sympathy from East European dissidents. Although one might be impressed by the theoretical sophistication and eloquence of works like 'Economic Calculations and Forms of Property',[10] the explicit or implicit assumption that Stalinism had been real socialism which degenerated under Khruschchev into state capitalism is totally unacceptable for those who have had first hand experience with Stalinism. Indeed, these theorists should keep in mind that they do not have and cannot have any impact whatsoever on any progressive force – dissident or not – in Eastern Europe.

The early pre-Maoist and anti-Stalinist 'state capitalism' theories[11] – which explain the 'restoration of capitalism' with the Stalinist bureaucratisation of the society, rather than with the basically anti-bureaucratic economic reform movements – were also not adopted, as far as I know, by any of the significant East European socialist critics. Although some, such as Marc Racovski, might consider defining Soviet-type societies as neither socialist nor capitalist. But most of those East European socialist critics of Soviet-type societies who are prepared to break all taboos of official Soviet Marxism accept the socialist nature of these societies and tend to regard their task as a self-critical one. This feature of East European ideologues might make a significant contribution to the development of contemporary socialist theory precisely because by being confronted with the inherent conflicts of industrial societies which abolish private ownership they have to reassess critically some of the basic Marxist and Marxist-Leninist doctrines about socialism. This, on the other hand, is not the classical 'revisionist' task. Revisionists aim to transform Marxist socialist theory into an ideology which justifies or accepts, at least in the long run, the existence of private ownership. The socialist theory I expect to emerge from Eastern Europe in the next decade is of a different nature. It will be such an immanent critique of the Marxist-Leninist theory of socialism, probably remaining in the broadly defined value system and scientific methodology of Marxism, which aims to transcend both state socialism and capitalism in order to further advance the cause of the emancipation of the working class.

In the discussion which follows I will address myself to the two 'blocs' of theoretical issues – economic self-management vs. centralised redistributive power and political self-determination vs. the hegemony of the vanguard party – which probably will require such a creative critical reassessment of Marxism-Leninism. I am unable to propose a new theory upon which a socialist opposition, as defined above, can be built. I shall only attempt to identify the issues with which this theory will be predictably concerned. I define these issues and related theoretical problems on the basis of the experiences of the Hungarian Left during the late sixties and early seventies. I have two justifications for limiting my analysis in this way. I have first-hand knowledge of this movement and have an understanding of its internal dynamics. Furthermore, if we are looking for the ideological precursors of an East European socialist opposition, the intellectual development of the Hungarian Left might serve as an instructive example. In Hungary the secret police and the official party ideologues did quite a good job in splitting the left-wing intellectual circle which emerged around the Lukács school. However, despite such party police-induced internal conflicts left-wing critics in Hungary, even when they were forced into marginality, maintained an intellectual interchange among themselves, and displayed a certain degree of theoretical coherence and conscious dedication to socialist values, which is rare among intellectual dissidents in Eastern Europe. I will not review here the intellectual contribution of the Hungarian Left work-by-work, or author-by-author. G. Schöpflin did this remarkably well[12] and those who need more detailed information can rely on other sources.[13] My task here is to sum up those issues, partially by extrapolating from the intellectual discussions of the early seventies the theoretical trends one might expect to emerge, which predictably will become the central ones for a future critical socialist theory.

ECONOMIC SELF-MANAGEMENT *vs.* CENTRALISED REDISTRIBUTIVE POWER

A theory which rejects the economic reform movement cannot serve as the ideology for a genuine socialist opposition in Eastern Europe. But when socialist critics attempt to work out their relationship to economic reforms they are confronted with an extremely complex task. The proponents of economic reforms, 'new economic mechanisms' are usually pragmatist economists, like Evgenii Liberman, János Kornai, Ota Šik or Włodimierz Brus (in the case of these two latter authors I am referring to their work while they still lived in Eastern Europe) who carefully avoided spelling out the ideological and political implications of the proposed economic reforms. They argued against over-centralisation in favour of increased autonomy of the enterprises, of the replacement of allocation of goods in natural forms with commodity exchange, against the administrative control of the movement of labour power etc. They made their case on pragmatic grounds and advanced it in the name of economic efficiency and rationality against economic voluntarism of the 'command economy'.

The reformist economists usually did not use sociological arguments and they tried to avoid debates on the level of political economy. Some, if not most of these reformist economists, had 'grown up' on orthodox Soviet Marxist political economy and gradually became disillusioned with it. They knew that bureaucrats and ideologues responsible for the management of the 'command economy' use the doctrines of the 'political economy of socialism' largely to hide their ignorance of modern economic theories and methods and to cover up for their incompetence in economic decision-making. It must be remembered that reformers were allowed to come forward with their reform proposals only when the wastefulness and inefficiency of the Stalinist command economy became too obvious; when more adequate statistical methods demonstrated that the growth this economic system produced was basically 'pseudo-growth' and when proper statistical measurements did show that economic growth in fact had been quite slow and in certain instances national incomes and living standards substantially declined – as they did most dramatically in Czechoslovakia in the early sixties.

Sitting on the pink clouds of the reform era of the early sixties were philosophers and sociologists who became the would-be left-wing critics and dissidents of the seventies, who had supported the reformist economists but more on political instinct than on the grounds of serious theoretical introspection. In Hungary the idea of a 'New Economic Mechanism' created a whole 'national front' in which technocrats and academic intellectuals joined forces with workers, peasants and peasant-workers against incompetent state and party bureaucrats. Of this alliance the technocrats expected more power, while the working class and peasantry sought to extract higher living standards from the economic reforms. At that time no one with sincere socialist aims could hesitate as to which side of the 'barricade' he belonged.

Because the basic theoretical questions were not clarified at that time it is not surprising that this alliance between the economic reformers and the potential socialist critics was unstable. Long before any reform measure was implemented in Hungary, András Hegedüs, at that time still an official figure, who became the best-known 'dissident' for a few years after 1968, launched an attack against the economic reforms by publishing in 1965 a powerful and extremely influential paper under the title 'Optimalisation and Humanisation'. This paper was a criticism of the reform movement from the point of view of a 'humanistic Marxism' and it expressed the concern that reformers would sacrifice the 'humanistic' goals of socialism on the altar of economic efficiency. This view reflected the general theoretical orientation of those who regarded themselves during the early and mid-sixties as 'creative Marxists' in Eastern Europe. The creative Marxism of the time was a reaction against what one might call 'Stalinist structuralism'. This we may describe as a theoretically naive interpretation of Marxism which, in order to justify enforced 'socialist determinism' and to legitimate the oppressive police state, harked back to the notion of increasing class conflicts and the dictatorship of proletariat.

During the sixties East European critical socialist thinkers were not prepared to launch a frontal attack on these ideologies of orthodox Soviet Marxism, so they just put *Das Kapital* aside and started reading the young Marx. In doing so, they rediscovered Lukács, Gramsci and Korsch, the dialectics of the subject-object, the significance of the 'subjective' and 'consciousness' and suddenly the fight against alienation was found to be more crucial for socialism than class struggle itself. The reformist economists were not ready to conduct their fight against conservative bureaucrats on grounds of 'political economy', but retreated into econometrics and input-output analysis. Like-minded philosophers and sociologists were similarly unprepared as yet to take up the challenge of undertaking a rigorous study of class analysis of East European societies which would have lead them into a too direct confrontation with the dominant official theories.

'Humanistic Marxism' was an arena where future dissidents could find out whether the political police and official ideologists would tolerate the development of a critical theory. The 'humanistic' critique of the regime was not regarded as a major political threat by the Establishment. Thus, critical works by Leszek Kołakowski, Karel Kosik, the Lukács disciples, and the *Praxis* group were published and the authors usually enjoyed the privileges of tenured academic positions. They were criticised and labelled as 'abstract humanists' by orthodox philosophers, but basically the Establishment could cope with this kind of critical analysis. Marxist humanism was a useful preparatory stage for the development of socialist critical thought; but fairly soon it turned out to be a theoretical dead-end street, especially when the analysts were confronted with the complexities of socioeconomic conflicts of the early seventies.

The early humanistic critique of the reform movement turned out to be politically and theoretically untenable. It was not possible to play 'New Left' for very long in Eastern Europe. How could someone keep attacking the economic reform as leading towards an 'acquisitive society', over-emphasising the needs of growth, selling out the humanistic values of socialism to efficiency, etc., when around 1968 the reform movements suffered serious setbacks all over in Eastern Europe. Reform measures were cancelled in Czechoslovakia and seriously curtailed in Hungary and Poland, the only countries where plans for qualitatively new economic mechanisms were considered at all. The mutilation of the reform measures, followed by growing working class dissatisfaction and, from time to time, open resistance, were indicative of severe structural conflicts in the economic realm of East Europe's state socialist societies. Consequently, the more traditional Marxist approach to problems of political economy and class analysis did not seem to be as irrelevant as one might have thought through the prism of humanistic Marxism. The critical philosophical and sociological literature of the early seventies – largely already forced into the 'underground', are unpublished, and circulated in samizdat editions or under pseudonyms in the west – addressed itself increasingly to this new dilemma.[14] I would like to summarise those basic questions which were raised in this context. Although they remain largely unanswered, it should be clear that they present a basic challenge to classical socialist theory.

Contemporary East European societies are based on a 'mixed economy'. The basic redistributive mechanisms are supplemented with self-regulating, market, or market-like mechanisms. Over the last decade self-regulating mechanisms did gain ground and the economic reform movements of the sixties attempted to accelerate this process. How can we interpret these developments in the light of a critical socialist theory? Is it possible to order redistribution vs. self-regulation in the dimensions of socialism vs. capitalism? Can the self-regulating mechanisms accurately be described as market mechanisms? Which mechanism dominates the other in contemporary Eastern Europe? What are the sociological consequences of the development of self-regulating systems and which mechanism is shaping the basic social inequalities in these economies?

Western Maoists and Trotskyists would not hesitate to define self-regulating forces as they operate in contemporary Eastern Europe as market mechanisms and to identify them with capitalism. The 'state capitalism' thesis assumes that in Soviet-type economies today the labour power is exchanged in a market situation and the flow of surplus is regulated by the profit motive, between autonomous enterprises.[15] The Trotskyist 'transitional economy' approach would reject this as an exaggeration. It would warn us that we should not over-estimate the economic autonomy of enterprises and the extent of commodity relationships in these economies.[16] But it would still accept that the existence of commodity production, the fact that production is as yet *not* universal production for use, is the indication of the survival of capitalist elements in this 'transitional economy'.[17]

One important theoretical task for East European critical schools of thought is to further clarify the sociological significance of the commodity form vs. the use value form of products.[18] The concept of use-value is not clearly defined by the classical authors and one might have reasonable doubts whether it is justified to identify the 'commodity form' with market relations and more specifically with capitalist relations of production. It is a historical fact that commodity exchange preceded private ownership and the development of a price regulating market. As long as the prices of the products are not set by the market, the products can take commodity form, and trade and money can exist without the development of capitalist relations of production. Capitalist relations of production can only develop when the labour power is sold on a price-regulating market to private owners of capital who reinvest the expropriated surplus again according to the profit motive, obeying the laws of the price-regulating market. The Soviet-type economies do not meet either of these criteria. Labour power is in fact defined in the commodity form. It is being sold and bought but its price basically is not and cannot be regulated on the market, and the crucial investment decisions usually overrule profit considerations.

The specific nature of the commodity form of labour power requires more theoretical and empirical analysis under the conditions of state socialism. First of all we should not forget that it was the Stalinist collectivisation of agriculture which totalised the commodity form of labour power by transforming in a few years tens of millions of self-employed peasants into wage labourers. Did thus collectivisation restore capitalism in Russia? Of course not, since the price of labour power was not regulated by the market. The owner of labour power is under a statutory obligation to sell his labour for a price which is administratively set and which has in principle nothing to do with the surplus that labour will produce. The owner of labour is not allowed to bargain collectively or individually over the price of his labour power. He cannot decide to withhold his labour and to try to sell the products of his labour rather than his labour power. Under these circumstances we cannot speak meaningfully of a labour market. What we just described is a *socialist non-market trade of labour*. This non-market trade of labour is not socialist because labour power is less of commodity nature than under capitalism. (In fact, state socialism succeeded to define a much larger proportion of labour power as commodity than any capitalist economy. Capitalism always operates with a significant degree of self-employment, which is destroyed by the socialist state.) This is a specifically *socialist* trade of labour since it does not allow private individuals to withhold their labour power from the market and to use their inherited wealth or savings as capital by employing wage labourers and deriving profit from their surplus labour. The party bureaucracy certainly does not fit this description. They also have to sell their labour (including the first secretary of the party) and they are not allowed to accumulate capital or to operate personal inherited or not inherited wealth as capital. It should be clear at this point that our analysis goes beyond the dilemmas of legal or non-legal definition of ownership. The point is not simply that the bureaucrats do not legally own the means of production, but that they also have to sell their labour power and its price is defined by the very same mechanism and on the very same principles as the price of anybody else's labour. Thus, we are talking about the substance rather than the legal form of ownership relations.

The main point I am trying to make here is that the use-value form of a product is not more or less socialist than is the commodity form of the products, and if this is true for the labour power, it should be true for all other products. Let us try to explain this with a hypothetical example. Previously the workers received after working hours each day two oranges free. Reformers decide that from now on, they will not give oranges away free, but they increase the daily wages by 50 kopeks and they set the price of one orange at 25 kopeks. Did the reformers move back one step towards capitalism? Certainly not, all that they did was to increase the autonomy of the consumers. The worker now might decide that he does not like oranges at all, and he would rather buy four apples each day, also worth 50 kopeks. It is just not possible to compare the two systems in terms of socialism vs. capitalism; therefore, the commodity vs. use-value form proves to be irrelevant from this point of view. One important task of an East European critical socialist theory would be precisely to demystify the ideological values attached to the use-value form which has been used extensively under the command economy and is still used in present state socialist societies to hide the actual extent of social inequalities. If the total value of all goods and services to which one is entitled is expressed in monetary form and accumulated in wages, then the unequal access to these goods or services is directly measurable. One can quite easily prove that the allocation of goods in use-value form (or at highly subsidised prices) only made 'social accounting' practically impossible and did not serve 'social justice' at all.

Western critics of state socialism usually assume that economic reforms which replace administrative allocation of goods with a self-regulating commodity exchange will produce more social inequality. This proposition is based on the projection of laws of market capitalism into the qualitatively different economic systems of state socialism. In modern welfare capitalism it is reasonable to assume that the basic inequalities are created on market situations and especially on the labour market and one hopes that by redistributing real income into socially sensitive areas the state will, at least to some extent, modify these inequalities. True, there are good reasons to be sceptical about the extent of the equalising effect of this process of redistribution, but it is still probable that the structure of inequalities is shaped on the market and later modified by redistribution. However, empirical evidence derived from the experience of state socialist societies indicates an opposite pattern. Under state socialism it is the redistribution mechanism that creates the basic inequalities and the self-regulating forces merely modify them in the interest of the otherwise under-privileged groups.[19] The highly skilled, the state and party bureaucrats, the white collar workers and the intellectuals have better access to state-subsidised public housing, superior urban facilities, more modern schools, better equipped and staffed hospitals, more comfortable trade union vacation homes, tax free shops, etc. than have members of the working class. Curiously enough, when we hear that in Hungary or Poland private housing construction is being encouraged, more mortgage funds are made available, etc., these are cited as measures taken in the interest of the working class. But if we learn that private housing construction is cut back and state housing is more heavily subsidised, then we can be sure that the privileges of those who are already privileged are further expanding.

The pattern is somehow the opposite of the western capitalist one. At this point I sincerely agree with Bettelheim that it is not enough to operate in the simple plan vs. market[20]–redistribution vs. self-regulation dichotomy, but one has to try to understand the class consequences of the planning itself; for planning and redistribution can be the mechanisms of a new system of exploitation of the working class. Bettelheim is right. What is needed is a new critical analysis from the view point of class relations: precisely what kinds of institutions

and mechanisms serve the exploitation of the working class and shape
social inequalities and with what kind of mechanism can one fight these
inequalities? To be sure, if one were to follow Bettelheim's own
methodology, empirically one would arrive at very different conclusions than he does. Thus, one will be able to show that the economic
reform measures, the attempts to limit central redistributive power
and the corresponding increase in the autonomy of the consumers,
enterprises, local governments, etc., are basically serving working class
interest and what he believes to be the index of progress along the
capitalist road is, in fact, the indication of the emergence of a new
economic system of socialism and a step towards a self-managing
economic system of socialism as opposed to state socialist redistributive economy.

In other words, one can look at contemporary socialist societies as
composed of two forms of socialism. They are dominated by state
socialism which is based on exploitative centralised redistributive
power; but certain elements of a self-managing socialist economy are
also gradually emerging and are increasingly challenging the monopoly of redistributive power. The East European economic reform
movements certainly do not aim at a revolutionary transformation of
state socialist economic systems. Rather they tend to strengthen the
elements of socialist self-management. Consequently, they should be
judged as progressive measures. This also means that what really
matters in terms of the emancipation of the working class is not the
change in the legal form of ownership, but the nature of institutions
which guarantee the expropriation of surplus and the chances of the
direct producers to challenge powerfully the logic and extent of
expropriation of surplus from them. This is precisely why I believe that
a critical socialist theory upon which a socialist opposition can be based
in Eastern Europe will be pro-reformist, since the economic reforms,
though certainly not in a revolutionary way, challenge the system of
expropriation which dominates the contemporary state socialist
economies.

POLITICAL SELF-DETERMINATION *vs.* THE HEGEMONY
OF THE VANGUARD PARTY. TOWARDS A SOCIALIST
'CIVIL SOCIETY'?

East European socialists working towards a theory of a socialist
opposition must reconsider the Leninist theory of the party and the

state. It seems highly unlikely that any critical theory can reconcile the contradiction between the 'sacrosanct Party' as it is defined in Bolshevik ideology and the empirically observable communist parties, as they have actually functioned in Soviet-type societies in the last sixty years. The personality and teachings of Lenin are still, or probably more than ever, surrounded with an almost religious mythology by the ideological establishment. Intellectuals with socialist beliefs who marginalise themselves usually break away from this mythology and I would propose that one of their most urgent tasks is to systematically analyse how and why Bolshevik ideology is still being used to legitimate a totalitarian, anti-democratic political superstructure.

The issue of human rights, democratic freedoms, freedom of speech, assembly and association, crosscuts ideological divisions among the dissidents and it offers a basis for a broad 'national front' into which all democratic forces of Eastern Europe can be integrated and from which socialists just cannot isolate themselves. The idea of 'democratic socialism' is the most appealing one. This is why Eurocommunism attracts so much attention. This is why the East European Left followed with bated breath the events of the revolution in Chile and Portugal (and earlier in Cuba) hoping to find finally one empirical example which proves socialism is possible without the abolition of basic liberal democratic institutions. But in order to elaborate on a genuinely socialist strategy of democracy one cannot rely any more on the utopia of the 'State and Revolution'. Its phraseology has lost credibility. After sixty years of solid authoritarian record, no one can believe in the democratic nature of 'democratic centralism' which has been habitually misused by the party bureaucracy to legitimate its power monopoly. A new socialist theory of democracy can only be based on the immanent sociological critique of the vanguard party and on a substantive analysis of democratic rights under socialism.

One of the most fascinating, and up to now unresolved, problems is the nature of 'bureaucracy' in the party and in the state apparatus of state socialist societies. Trotsky, who remained faithful to the Leninist principle of the vanguard party, believed that the Soviet bureaucracy he attacked so vehemently was alien from the Bolshevik ideal of the party and that bureaucracy was an aberration which could and should be abolished. But is bureaucratic domination indeed alien from Leninism, and was not the young Trotsky probably right, who together with Plekhanov and Rosa Luxemburg accused Lenin that he intended to replace the dictatorship of the proletariat with the dictatorship of the party bureaucracy? Indeed, the latter proposition seems to describe empirically more accurately of what has happened in Eastern Europe after Bolshevik parties seized power and thus sounds more convincing than any Establishment apology to those who attempt to develop a critical analysis of these parties. Theoretically the crucial question is the meaning of the notion of 'bureaucracy' when applied to state socialist societies. Soviet Marxism, in rebuffing the Trotskyist critique, in fact argued that bureaucracy by definition did not exist under socialism and one should not confuse socialist administration with bureaucracy. Since then Establishment sociologists have carefully avoided the term 'bureaucracy' when discussing public administration in Soviet-type societies.

Without accepting the apologetical conclusions of the Soviet orthodoxy, one has to acknowledge that party and state administration under state socialism are qualitatively different from 'bureaucratic domination' as defined by Max Weber. Bálint Balla in an interesting analysis shows what kind of difficulties one faces in using the Weberian model of ideal-type bureaucracy when attempting to describe the workings of public administration in Soviet-type societies. Balla concluded that the term 'bureaucracy' could not be used and he proposed to replace it with the notion of 'Kaderverwaltung' (administration by cadres).[21] When Weber described the ideal-type of bureaucratic domination he was certainly referring to 'civil societies'. He analysed societies in which goal-setting and execution were separated from each other. He referred to a civilisation which splits the world into 'ends' and 'means', to socioeconomic systems where economy and polity are defined as separate spheres of activities. To use more modern terminology, Weber's theory of bureaucracy applies only to 'non-embedded' societies. Thus, bureaucratic domination represents the domination of the society by experts who monopolise the knowledge and means of efficient implementation of public policies. Under these circumstances goals are being set ideally by a separate political mechanism with democratic procedures while the bureaucracy and its expert knowledge merely facilitate the execution of these goals. Moreover, bureaucracy is based only on 'formal rationality', which only guarantees that experts will choose the most efficient means to reach goals, but it does not guarantee the rationality of the goals themselves which was relegated by Weber into the realm of 'substantive rationality'.

In the light of the above analysis one should be aware that 'socialist bureaucracy' has very little in common with the Weberian ideal-type of bureaucracy. In many ways it is an *alternative form* of domination.

The party bureaucracy does not pretend to be the 'executive branch'. On the contrary, as the 'most conscious and revolutionary force of the proletariat' it precisely claims to have the right to monopolise crucial decision-making and to 'set the course of history'. Certainly no Bolshevik party ever accepted the separation of economics from politics, and party spokesmen have always affirmed the supremacy of political considerations above the economic ones. The vanguard parties of Eastern Europe do not propose to surrender to 'the anarchy of electorism'. They do not legitimate their power with majority vote. They reject free elections as a rational way to make choices between political or economic alternatives. The 'Soviet bureaucrat' does not have to play the game of his western colleagues and to pretend that goals are in fact means in order to increase its own power. The 'Soviet bureaucrat' is supposed to set the goals himself. The East European vanguard parties legitimate their power by 'substantive rationality'. They claim power monopoly by claiming that only the party, armed with the ideology of 'scientific communism', can set goals rationally. Critics of Soviet bureaucratism usually miss this crucial difference between the western capitalist and East European state socialist bureaucracy by failing to realise that state socialist bureaucrats are the negations of the Weberian ideal-type of bureaucrats. They can be more accurately described – to use Davies' terminology – as 'evangelistic bureaucrats' than expert-executives.[22] Probably these critics have been easily misled by internal disputes among different figures of the 'evangelistic bureaucracy'. In power struggles of this kind, more skilled administrators from time to time, challenge their opponents by questioning their competence. This is what happened recently in China in the struggle between Teng and the 'Gang of Four'. But even Teng, who might not care about the colour of the cat which is catching the mouse, does not mean that he wants to leave it up to the cat which mouse it will catch. Teng might be more competent, but there is no indication that he is less 'evangelistic' than his opponents.

But if this is true, then the party administration which legitimates its power monopoly on the grounds of 'substantive rationality' is by no means that alien from the Leninist notion of the vanguard party as Trotsky and his followers have suggested. Leninists confronted with the realities of Eastern Europe find themselves in a 'Catch-22' situation: if one accepts the vanguard party, if one accepts that the consciousness has to be brought into the working class from outside, the working class itself can develop only 'trade union mentality' and will fight only for its immediate economic interests, but is unable to understand its historical mission and thus has to be led, if necessary, against its own will by a revolutionary vanguard, then one cannot develop a structural criticism of the East European societies. The ruling parties and elites in these societies function precisely on these principles and what socialist critics have to do if they want to respond to the needs of working class movements is to challenge these principles. After all of these decades one wonders why are the people not conscious enough to govern themselves; why do these societies still need the tutelage of 'their' parties?

My task here is not to assess Leninism critically. What I am trying to do is to explain why East European critics of state socialism might not find Bolshevism particularly useful to develop their critical theory, and why they might have to move from the ideology of the vanguard party towards the immanent sociological critique of 'vanguardism' as it is actually practised in contemporary Eastern Europe. It is another question whether Leninism was an adequate and perhaps the only adequate theory of revolutionary transformation for early twentieth-century Russia, and whether Lenin himself had a broader understanding of the vanguard party which might not be identical with the actual organisation of the Bolshevik parties after they seized power. Liebman argued with great eloquence that there were a number of 'Leninisms' under Lenin and that following the 1905 revolution, impressed by the experiments of soviets in Petrograd, he moved away from the vision of the party as outlined in the *What is to be Done*.[23] But somehow the harmonious co-existence between the vanguard party and the soviets as institutions of political self-determination (which is what Lenin probably had in his mind – if Liebman is correct – after 1906) did not work out historically and the Leninist notion of the vanguard party turned into an ideology which was used to oppress all genuine attempts at seeking self-determination.

However, if socialist critics start questioning the necessity of the vanguard party (or probably of any *one* party), this might lead them towards an even more general theoretical issue, which might be central for both East European and western socialist theory. And this is the question of 'civil society'. Is 'civil society' identical with capitalism, or is it a broader concept? What is the substance of socialist transformation: is it just a negation of capitalism, or does socialism necessarily also transcend 'civil society'? In other words, is a 'socialist civil society' possible at all?

What quite a few East European critics of state socialism came to believe is that state socialism is not too bureaucratic in the proper

Weberian sense, but that it is not bureaucratic enough. In other words, the politically oppressive nature of this system is due to its 'embeddedness', to the lack of separation of the political sphere from the economic one, of the goal-setting functions from the executive ones. András Hegedüs for example argued at some length,[24] that East European societies need efficiently functioning bureaucracies because no complex industrial society can live without expert administration. In order to avoid bureaucratism, according to Hegedüs, one must establish democratic political control over the administrative bodies. Is then the separation of democratic mechanisms of goal-setting from execution and administration not necessary for any meaningful democracy? Does not the 'embeddedness' of state socialism teach us that without the institutional guarantees of 'civil society' self-management, political self-determination, workers' control, participatory planning and decision-making are turned into empty slogans, caricatures of democracy?

Marx himself on many occasions identified 'civil society' with capitalism. He criticised Hegel for deifying civil society and he proposed that the strength of this theory is that it offers for the first time the tools for a critical analysis *of* civil society. I think if we want to take seriously the lessons we can learn from the experiments with socialism during the last sixty years and if we are actually committed to a meaningful notion of the democracy, self-management and self-determination, we have to reassess critically this proposition. This is a problem which faces the Eurocommunist, as much as the East European socialist critics, and I am persuaded that socialist theorists ought to have at least another look at the meaning of civil society.

In the first instance 'socialist civil society' sounds like a contradiction in itself, but is it? Capitalism, with its system of inherited wealth and privileges by the permanent reproduction of ascribed statuses both for the poor locked up in the vicious circle of poverty and for the rich through inheritance of property, managerial and even political positions are far from being the fulfilment of the ideals of civil society. Historically speaking, capitalism certainly was a step forward to civil society compared with pre-capitalist status societies, but it has produced only a highly deformed version of it. Could not one thus foresee a kind of socialism which, by abolishing privileges based on ownership, might be a further step towards the ideals of civil society? Indeed, what else can be the meaning of 'democratic socialism'?

This second 'bloc' of theoretical issues socialist critics are already confronted with in Eastern Europe is not unrelated to the first one. To put it simply: no significant economic reform is possible in Soviet-type societies without a major political reform, and no real self-management is possible without political self-determination and *vice versa*. Trotsky was not a very good Marxist in believing that distortions in the regime's 'superstructure', which he described and criticised, can occur alongside a sound 'economic base'. Socialists in Eastern Europe have to search for a new form of socialism which transcends state socialism both as an economic and as a political system, and a socialist opposition might emerge as soon as it can come forward with a new theory of socialism which is based on a genuinely self-managed economy and on guarantees for real political self-determination.

The 'ghost' of this alternative socialism has been with us for a long time. Nineteenth and twentieth century socialist theories are pregnant with both visions of socialism, state socialism and self-managing socialism. Marx and Engels in the *Communist Manifesto* saw the essence of socialist transformation in the nationalisation of private ownership; but the Engels defined socialism as the 'free association of the direct producers'. Bakunin rejected the 'elitist' position Marx took in the First International and when Lenin formulated his theory of the vanguard party, Plekhanov, Rosa Luxemburg and Trotsky found him guilty of 'Bonapartism'. Trotsky wanted to nationalise the trade unions but he met resistance from the anarcho-syndicalists, and later it was he who helped crush the Kronstadt rebellion demanding the return of power to the soviets – only to rediscover the soviets' significance for socialism, when it was too late.

Stalin built up in the name of socialism probably the most 'etatist' society history ever produced. He was challenged by Tito and by his notion of self-management. Mao rebuked Tito as revisionist and defended Stalin against Khrushchev; but he still committed himself, at least in theory, to the proposition that workers should be given power to exercise collective control over their own lives. Moreover, he probably allowed a fair degree of autonomy to the communes. Russian tanks smashed attempts towards a more democratic socialism and abolished the workers' councils in Budapest and in Prague. And this is in sharp contrast with the workers of the Upper Clyde shipyards, and elsewhere in England, France and Germany who might occupy their factories but do not request nationalisation and seek to exercise direct workers' control. Though the Chilean communists are still seeking guidance from Moscow, the Chilean workers did not need the tutelage of their vanguard party; they organised their own councils in their slums and distributed milk to their children.

The significance of the East European experience for socialist theory is that now socialist critics have to confront systematically these two alternative visions of socialism. Too much forgiveness during the thirties and forties and too crude a rejection since 1956, and especially since 1968, have prevented the western Left from learning enough from the lessons the Soviet Union offered. First they wanted to explain all crimes from 'historical circumstances'. Later they just labelled them 'state capitalist', and thus they have never found out what went wrong with state socialism, and they were not forced to work systematically on the theory of an alternative socialism. And it is precisely such an alternative theory of socialism that we might expect to come out of Eastern Europe.

NOTES

1. Rudolf L. Tökés, ed., *Dissent in the USSR* (Baltimore, London: Johns Hopkins University Press, 1975).
2. Vladimir Kusin, *Political Grouping in the Czechoslovak reform movement* (London: Macmillan, 1972).
3. See Chapter 5, by George Schöpflin, in this volume.
4. Miklós Haraszti, *A Worker in a Worker's State* (London: Penguin, 1972).
5. Antonin Liehm, 'Intellectuals and the New Social Contract', *TELOS*, no. 23 (Spring 1975) pp. 156–64 and Paul Piccone, 'Czech Marxism', *Critique*, no. 8 (Summer, 1977) pp. 43–52.
6. Marc Racovski, 'Le Marxism devant les societe sovietique', *Les Temps Modernes* (December 1974), pp. 553–84.
7. György Konrád and Iván Szelényi, *Towards the class power of intelligentsia* (New York: Harcourt, Brace, Jovanovich, 1979).
8. David Lane, *The socialist industrial state* (London: Allen and Unwin, 1976) pp. 28–39.
9. Jacek Kuroń and Karol Modzelewski, 'An open letter to the party' (London: International Socialism Publications, 1968).
10. Charles Bettelheim, *Economic calculations and forms of property* (London: Routledge and Kegan Paul, 1976).
11. Bruno Rizzi, *Le bureaucratization du monde* (Published privately, 1939); Anthony Cliff, *State capitalism in Russia* (London: Pluto Press, 1974).
12. See Chapter 5 in this volume pp. 142–86.
13. Serge Frankel and Daniel Martin, 'La nouvelle gauche hongrois: sociologie et revolution', *Les Temps Modernes* (August-September 1974) pp. 2765–88; Iván Szelényi, 'Notes on the Budapest School', *Critique*, no. 8 (Summer, 1977) pp. 61–7; Tibor Hanák, *Die marxistische Philosophie und Soziologie in Ungarn* (Stuttgart: Enke Verlag, 1976). See also William Shawcross, *Crime and Compromise: János Kádár and the politics of Hungary since the revolution* (London: Weidenfeld and Nicolson, 1974).

14. Cf. Miklós Haraszti, op. cit., Marc Racovski, op. cit., G. Konrád and I. Szelényi, op. cit.
15. Paul Sweezy and Charles Bettelheim, *On the transition to socialism* (New York: Monthly Review Press, 1971) pp. 17–18.
16. Hillel Ticktin, 'The contradiction of Soviet society and Professor Bettelheim', *Critique*, no. 6 (1976).
17. Ernest Mandel, *The inconsistencies of State capitalism* (London: International Marxist Group Pamphlet, 1969).
18. The thus far unpublished (either in Hungarian or in a western language) manuscript 'Is a Critical Political Economy Possible at all?' by György Bence, János Kiss and Gyögy Márkus, is an especially significant work from this point of view.
19. Iván Szelényi, 'Social inequalities in State socialist redistributive economies', *International Journal of Comparative Sociology*, vol. 19. no. 1–2 (1978) pp. 63–87.
20. See Paul Sweezy and Charles Bettelheim, op. cit.
21. Balla Bálint, *Kaderverwaltung, Versuch zur Idealtypisierung der 'Bürokratie' sowjetisch-volksdemokratischen Typs* (Stuttgart: Enke Verlag, 1972), especially pp. 9–15.
22. J. Davies, *The evangelistic bureaucrat* (London: Tavistock, 1972).
23. Cf. Marcel Liebman, *Leninism under Lenin* (London: Jonathan Cape, 1975).
24. András Hegedüs, *Socialism and bureaucracy* (London: Allison and Busby, 1976).

7 Industrial Workers: Patterns of Dissent, Opposition and Accommodation

by ALEX PRAVDA

The origins of the term dissent in the religious struggles of sixteenth and seventeenth-century England have given it strong doctrinal connotations. In the context of communist party states such connotations have been reinforced by the long and close association of dissent with the critical intelligentsia. In Eastern Europe dissent has become almost a synonym for protests centring on the freedom of speech and the whole range of civil and human rights. But dissent is not a preserve of the intellectual. Over the past twenty-five years workers' protests and resistance have made a less overt and spectacular, but arguably a more sustained impact on East European development.

In order to analyse workers' dissent the term has to be stripped of its excessively 'intellectual' overtones. We shall use dissent to mean disagreement with official Communist Party values, expectations and policies. Within this broad category a distinction will be drawn between three forms of dissent: the articulation of dissident values, attitudes and beliefs; individual and group nonconformism, i.e. conduct which departs from or is contrary to official norms and requirements; finally, collective protest which both violates official norms and poses a challenge to authority. Where such collective protest assumes large proportions and involves a wide range of issues it becomes opposition.

Because dissent is defined in relation to official norms, expectations and policies, its importance and sometimes even its existence depends as much on official perceptions as on the actors' own intentions. The political environment largely determines the nature and significance of dissent. In Eastern Europe, high levels of ideological and organisational integration have greatly lowered, or in some cases eliminated, the boundaries between economic, social and political spheres. This means that disagreement or nonconformity on what appear to be

209

narrow economic issues often spill over into and are perceived as leading to political questions. It is particularly important to remember in the context of workers' dissent that disputes over specific material issues can thus easily acquire political significance.

How one approaches and assesses workers' dissent and opposition in Eastern Europe largely depends on one's interpretation of workers' general position and role. Such interpretations fall into three broad types: the official party view; the view of workers as an alienated and potentially revolutionary class, and the depiction of them as effectively incorporated into the communist party states.

According to the official line, workers constitute the leading class in socialist society even in its developed or mature stage. Because the communist party proclaims itself to be the party of the working class, it is argued tautologically that the party invariably expresses and serves the workers' interests. Similarly, because workers' 'real interests' (i.e. the interests assigned to them by the party) coincide with party policy, it follows that no true workers' dissent let alone opposition can exist. Any disagreements that arise are largely explained away by references to temporary economic difficulties or to the survival of remnants of capitalist and bourgeois mentality. Even in Hungary, where official recognition has been accorded to the existence and legitimacy of differing interests in socialist society, such differentiation is said to run not along class but only along certain group and territorial lines. Throughout Eastern Europe the traditional identification of working-class interests with the interests of society as a whole (as interpreted by the party) still prevails. Despite the apparent privilege this accords the working class, such an identification effectively precludes the recognition of any particular working-class interests, let alone the legitimation of their articulation.[1]

In direct contrast, many on the radical left, and some academics, maintain that workers in Eastern Europe are an oppressed and exploited class whose interests clash fundamentally with those of the ruling bureaucracy and technocracy. Alienated from the dominant values of these societies, the working class strives not only for material gains but particularly for control of the means of production and for thorough-going transformation of the economic and power structure. Working-class disaffection and dissent are seen as endemic and the emergence of workers' opposition is kept to a minimum only by the use of formidable apparatuses of coercion.[2]

The view most widely favoured in western academic circles has been developed most cogently by David Lane and Zygmunt Bauman.

They argue that workers are a highly differentiated group that is well integrated and incorporated in communist party states. As one of the principal beneficiaries of these societies' development, workers have a strong vested interest in the maintenance of economic and political stability and therefore tend to ally with the bureaucracy against the intellectuals. Outbreaks of workers' dissent are seen not as the expression of any clash between irreconcilable working-class and ruling elite interests, but as the product of exceptional circumstances and bureaucratic mismanagement. Economistic in outlook and action, workers have low expectations and show no desire to assume control of their factories or to bring about radical political change; on the contrary, they are the key to what appears to be the revolutionary-proof nature of communist party states.[3]

Each of these interpretations provides important insights into the problem of workers' dissent yet none of them fully conveys the complexity of the phenomenon. The value of the first two is marred by their dogmatic approach, while the more detached and empirically based incorporation thesis somewhat understates workers' disaffection and expectations and fails to take sufficient account of the impact on workers' of changing economic, social and political conditions. Our objective is not so much to produce any new fourth interpretation as to convey the complexity of the phenomenon of workers' dissent and opposition. We intend to do this by examining the values and attitudes underlying dissent, its forms and content, the economic and institutional factors associated with its incidence and, finally, the ways in which workers' dissent relates to other movements for change.

In order to deal with all these aspects in any depth within the confines of a chapter length study, the following survey focuses on three of the eight East European states. Reference is made, where appropriate, to the German Democratic Republic and Romania; on certain issues use is made of what is often uniquely detailed Yugoslav data, but because of that country's manifold peculiarities, it serves as a valuable source for comparison and contrast rather than as a major constituent throughout the argument. The bulk of the evidence is drawn from Poland, Czechoslovakia and Hungary. These countries were selected for several reasons. First, they provide a wide and representative range of East European economic and social development, political traditions and cultures. Poland could be seen to represent the less economically and socially developed states, Czechoslovakia lies at the other end of the spectrum while Hungary falls somewhere in between. More importantly, between them these three countries have experienced by far the greatest amount and variety of workers' dissent and opposition. By comparing and contrasting these experiences, both between countries and over time, we hope to be able to clarify the relative importance and influence of the national, economic, social, institutional and situational factors which determine the incidence and shape the nature of workers' dissent and opposition.

WORKERS' POSITION IN SOCIETY

A basic problem facing anyone examining workers' dissent and opposition is to define the actors involved, the workers themselves. To do this in quantitative terms seems simple enough. If one takes workers to include all those who perform manual jobs outside agriculture, they constitute the largest social group and the majority, or near majority, of the working population in all East European countries except Yugoslavia. The extent to which blue-collar workers are a cohesive group or a class is far more problematic. At the same time, it has a direct bearing on the nature and potential of workers' dissent. Just as it is central to the 'revolutionary' thesis that workers constitute a class, so the 'incorporation' argument rests on a view of workers as a highly differentiated social group.[4]

Several features of the development of East European societies appear to support the latter concept. The policies of rapid industrialisation and social transformation of the 1950s meant that very large numbers of peasants became unskilled or semi-skilled workers. This made a particularly extensive impact in countries like Poland or Hungary where, in the mid-sixties, one in every two workers was of direct peasant origin and many still worked in agriculture on a part-time basis. By contrast, where, as in the German Democratic Republic or Czechoslovakia, development started from a more advanced level, upward mobility into the working class proceeded on a much smaller scale. As a result the great majority of workers are skilled and from working-class backgrounds. These marked differences in skill and social origin may help to account for the apparent volatility of Hungarian and particularly of Polish workers and the relative sobriety and restraint of their East German and Czechoslovak counterparts.[5]

While social mobility has thus altered the composition of workers as a social group, it seems not to have brought about a radical change in their place in East European societies. With the general elimination of large-scale private ownership and inherited wealth, education and skill have become the major determinants of economic and social position. Yet, not only do those in the professional and higher manual occupations continue to enjoy higher incomes, they also benefit disproportionately from welfare funds. Polish, Czechoslovak and particularly Hungarian studies show clearly that the higher the income group the greater its share of good quality state subsidised housing. The corollary is that manual workers' income inferiority is compounded by their having to spend relatively more on poorer standard accommodation.[6] Social status largely reflects and reinforces such stratification: in all rankings of occupational prestige, blue-collar jobs are placed above manual work in agriculture but below the professions and the higher white-collar categories. While occupation, education, income, material position and life-style do not correspond exactly, all these factors cluster sufficiently to form groups which appear to a majority of at least Poles and Czechoslovaks to possess class qualities. More significant from our standpoint is the relatively high level of blue-collar workers' self-assignment to a working class. A nationwide survey conducted in Czechoslovakia in 1967 suggests that two out of every three workers assigned themselves in this way.[7] Current social trends in Eastern Europe suggest that such levels of working-class assignment may soon be reproduced in countries like Poland and Hungary. As these societies reach advanced stages of economic development so the opportunities for upward social mobility diminish and the channels of social advancement become increasingly clogged. Access to higher education, which provides the key to social advancement, is bound to become ever more difficult for children from manual backgrounds. Unless specific counter-measures are taken, education is therefore likely increasingly to transfer rather than dilute social, economic and cultural privilege. Children from professional and higher white-collar families tend to remain in their parents' acquired social group. There is some evidence that all these factors have combined to bring about a decline in social mobility and a consolidation of class-like divisions.[8]

Workers' systematic inferiority to professional and higher white-collar groups in income, wealth, status and opportunity for social advancement is reinforced by the distribution of power and influence. Representation in party and state bodies, albeit a crude indicator of power and influence, shows a correlation and occupation, education and skill which becomes more pronounced as one moves upwards through these institutional hierarchies. With the exception of Yugoslavia, workers are proportionately under-represented in the memberships of all East European communist parties. But their disadvantage here is marginal when compared with the situation in elected and particularly in executive bodies where workers are heavily outnumbered by the professional and white-collar groups.[9]

What is more important than such inequalities in the distribution of position and office is that most workers also *feel* that they have little influence, let alone power, in society. Evidence from Czechoslovakia, Poland and Hungary suggests that workers see authority and power as being highly concentrated in the hands of already privileged elites within the higher non-manual and professional groups. Even in Yugoslavia, feelings of political powerlessness seem to be far more prevalent among blue-collar workers than within white-collar groups. The Czechoslovak survey already cited found that workers tended more than any other group to view society in terms of a power dichotomy between rulers and ruled, placing themselves in the subordinate category.[10]

Any attempt to assess the overall nature of workers' position in society must give due weight to the effects of mobility and to the considerable differences between skill groups. Yet workers as a whole increasingly exhibit sufficiently distinct economic, social status and power characteristics to warrant the use of the term working class. Because we use this term in its Weberian rather than Marxist sense, the existence of working classes in Eastern Europe does not necessarily entail the existence of any solidary class consciousness. Yet the wide discrepancies between the pattern of distribution prescribed by official norms and that obtaining in Eastern European societies certainly create a climate conducive to the emergence of working-class dissent.[11] Workers' disadvantaged position vis-à-vis the professional and higher white-collar groups provides a source of potential frustration. Whether it generates actual frustration, resentment and dissent depends on the whole complex of values, attitudes and expectations that determine workers' reactions to their social, economic and political situation.

WORKERS' ATTITUDES AND EXPECTATIONS

The ideal worker is usually portrayed as industrious, contented, socially motivated and actively committed to the socialist cause. Not surprisingly, workers depart from this image in many respects. To begin with, there is considerable dissonance between prescribed values and those most widespread within the working class. Despite the continuous emphasis on the social significance of work and on the primacy of moral motivation, workers tend to see their jobs in instrumental and materialistic terms. The great majority are motivated first and foremost by pay and job content; the social significance of labour and contributing to societal progress come very low in workers' priorities. Nor does the Marxist-Leninist Protestant work ethic seem to have been internalised. Although most workers appear to be reasonably contented with their jobs, only a small number seem to believe in making the maximum effort; the 'shockworkers' who live up to official ideals are universally resented and regarded with contempt. And instrumental attitudes towards the job are symptomatic of workers' general alienation from the factory. Most workers, particularly the less skilled, feel very little responsibility for or loyalty to their place of work. Polish and Hungarian evidence suggests that workers see themselves as executors of orders. Control lies with the director, his advisers and top party and sometimes top union officials; together these men are seen as a ruling clique within the enterprise.[12] The fact that most of them are former workers seems to make little difference to the 'them and us' situation which prevails in the factory. Yet the divide between workers and management does not necessarily produce hostility. On the contrary, workers appear to accept it as part of the natural order of things. Management's generally indulgent attitude to indiscipline and work performance, plus the community of interest created by the existence of a powerful central authority, all help to keep antipathy relatively low. Polish and Czechoslovak surveys conducted in the sixties found that only 10–35 per cent of the workers polled felt that relations with management were bad or antagonistic.[13]

One should not infer from the divergence between ideal and real working-class values and attitudes that workers are anti-socialist or anti-regime. What meagre evidence we have suggests that workers generally support socialism and, probably to a greater extent than their non-manual counterparts, accept an authoritarian state. However real the workers' support for the regime may be, it is a conditional support which rests on the regime's provision of what can be called 'cradle to grave' welfare socialism. In specific terms, this workers' concept of socialism centres on full security of employment, a relatively easy day's work for an adequate and steady day's pay, a reasonable and stable standard of living and a relatively low level of pay differentials.[14] All of the above have come to be seen by workers in Eastern Europe as basic socialist rights. The exchange of working-class quiescence and support for the fulfilment of these basic rights can be seen as constituting an unwritten agreement or 'social compact' on which the entire relationship between workers and regime in Eastern Europe depends. By the same token, workers' dissent, protest and opposition largely revolve around policies and measures that have a direct bearing on this 'social compact'.

It might appear from what we have said that the avoidance of workers' dissent is a fairly simple matter: all East European regimes have to do is deliver what amounts to a package of welfare benefits. But the task is far from easy. Part of the difficulty stems from the circumstances in which the compact was formed. Workers' notions of their basic socialist rights and their expectations of the regime still bear the stamp of the conditions of the 1950s in which they took shape. The period of rapid industrialisation and mobilisation, with its low wages and harsh controls, created conditions in which workers' only option was to get by as best they could and to try to attain a relatively low level of security and stability. With the passing of the worst excesses of mobilisation in the late fifties, workers' maximum expectations came to be taken for granted as socialist rights. And as living and working conditions have steadily improved, so new expectations have emerged of higher pay, more interesting work and a rising as well as steady standard of living.[15]

WORKERS AND ECONOMIC REFORM

The problems created by this accumulation of expectations are compounded by the increasing economic difficulties involved in their fulfilment. The economic conditions of the last fifteen years have made low labour productivity, full job security and price stability – all closely associated with the social compact – increasingly costly. Efforts to make the economy more efficient, exemplified by the Czechoslovak New Economic System and the Hungarian New Economic Mechanism (NEM), have generated considerable working-class criticism and dissent. Workers tend to react to the idea of economic reform with a wariness rooted in natural conservatism and reinforced by a lack of information. Not surprisingly, they are reluctant to jeopardise security and stability for the sake of greater but also riskier material gains. As one Czech worker put it in 1968, only fools would exchange security for the unknown.[16]

The most obvious threat to workers' security is presented by reformers' attempts to reduce over-staffing and eliminate unprofitable sectors. Both the Czechoslovak and the Hungarian reforms included the closure of several hundred small plants and the transfer of a very small percentage of the total workforce. Despite the small numbers involved and the repeated assurances that all would be given alternative employment, workers still reacted with alarm to the idea of anyone being made even temporarily redundant. Although the growing labour shortage in Eastern Europe has probably reduced workers' initial apprehensions, the caution with which all closures and workforce reduction schemes continue to be handled testifies to workers' persistent sensitivity on the whole issue.[17]

A more substantial threat to the 'social compact' comes in the area of consumer prices. The high inflation rates and cuts in living standards of the early fifties, followed by long periods of virtual price immobility, have made East European workers hyper-sensitive to even small price rises. Workers have become used to regarding price stability as the only real safeguard of their standard of living. Given such attitudes, it is not surprising that economic reformers' talk about the need to reduce price subsidies and controls has been sufficient to set off widespread fears of inflation. Modest price increases of the order of three per cent are greeted with alarm and attempts to decentralise price formation can lead, as they have done in Hungary, to charges of profiteering and calls for the reimposition of central control.[18]

The basic problem facing the proponents of price rationalisation is the workers' tendency to conceive the relationship between prices and the standard of living in zero-sum terms. In an attempt to change this *idée fixe*, party and government spokesmen have repeatedly argued that any price increases produced by economic reform will be more than offset by wage rises based on higher productivity. From the workers' point of view this argument's main difficulty lies in the key role assigned to productivity. As labour productivity increases have become almost the sole source of economic growth, politicians have gone out of their way to impress upon workers that all wage increases have to be earned by more effective work as measured by technically based norms. Such talk, however, arouses rather than allays workers' suspicions. The majority associate productivity increases and norm rationalisation with the time-honoured upward 'readjustment' of norms on a kind of ratchet principle which meant that workers had to work harder to earn the same wages.[19]

Workers also tend to react with hostility to a closely related element of economic reform, the tying of wages to enterprise performance and profitability. In Hungary this policy encountered strong objections from workers in the largest and often least profitable factories. They argued that the policy meant undermining workers' security and exposing them to the unsocialist mercies of the market and managerial parsimony. In the event, these fears were confirmed by the low level of wage awards offered by management in the first years of the NEM. The low awards brought more vehement protests from workers and trade union officials who called, with some effect, for an end to the profit-wage nexus and for a restitution of central controls.[20]

This particular episode serves to illustrate a more general point relating to the problems involved in decentralising decision-making to enterprise management. Notionally such decentralisation, and the increased mutual dependence it creates between management and workers, should encourage greater collaboration. In practice, however, increasing management's say on conditions and wages tends to weaken the old community of interest based on subordination to central authority, and to shift the focus of workers' dissent to management policies and move the locus of conflict into the enterprise.[21]

The last major area of economic reform policy which has generated working-class criticism and dissent concerns the distribution of pay. Economic reform is generally associated with attacks on so-called 'levelling' tendencies and with a concerted drive to widen differentials in favour of technical and managerial groups. The mechanisms most widely employed to effect such changes usually involve weighted distribution of bonuses. The profit-sharing scheme introduced as part of the NEM in 1968, for instance, was quite blatant in this respect, giving managers 10-20 times greater bonuses than those which were to be received by workers. Workers' hostile response to this and similar attempts to combat 'levelling' stems from what appear to be strong egalitarian tendencies. Evidence from Czechoslovakia, Poland and Yugoslavia suggests that most workers, particularly the lower skilled, think that existing differentials are too high and want to see maximum incomes kept to three or four times the lowest wage. This indicates that workers' resentment is directed not so much against technical personnel, whose pay is often only fifty per cent greater than that of the average worker, as against the far higher incomes and material benefits enjoyed by top managers and administrators.[22] In this sense, workers' opposition to a more economically 'rational' differentiation of pay should be seen as part of their objection to the existence of conspicuous privilege in socialist society. Such wider dimensions of the workers' case have emerged particularly strongly in Hungary where criticism of higher differentials have been accom-

panied by attacks on 'moneygrubbing' and bourgeois life-styles. Fuel-
led by what can be seen as an amalgam of self-interest and righteous
indignation, working-class pressure has proved sufficiently strong to
scotch the most inegalitarian distributional schemes and to keep
differentials relatively low.[23]

Indeed, over the whole range of reform policies which workers have
perceived as threatening the 'social compact', their dissent and protest
has effectively toned down or eliminated what have appeared to them
as the worst excesses of rationalisation. To be sure this success must be
attributed in part to the fact that workers' hostility to reform has been
used by its opponents to strengthen a wider case for central control of
the economy.[24]

NONCONFORMIST ACTION

Various forms of activity – spontaneous job changing, absenteeism,
pilfering – can all be subsumed under the heading of individual
nonconformity. In western capitalist societies such diffuse spontaneity
would be labelled deviant rather dissident. Given the emphasis placed
in communist party states on compliance and on the unity of all kinds
and levels of conduct, acts of individual nonconformity easily acquire
dissident connotations, they become acts of proto-dissent. Not only
the authorities, but the workers themselves tend to see nonconformity
in this light. A recent survey of working-class communists in Poland
found that one in five thought that indiscipline was the best way to
express dissent.[25]

Changing jobs spontaneously is the most widespread and overt type
of nonconformity: between a third and a half of all labour mobility is
caused by workers leaving jobs of their own accord. The numbers
involved in what is categorised as labour turnover vary between
countries and over time, but for the last twenty years they have
fluctuated at between 25 and 35 per cent of the workforce. While this is
not high by western standards, it causes concern in Eastern Europe on
at least two counts. Firstly, turnover is economically costly as workers
spend a month or more between jobs and work less efficiently both
before leaving and on taking up their new post. The spontaneity of
workers' action not only disrupts economic calculations but also can be
seen as an assertion of the individual's independence of central
control.[26] Although job changing is the most marginal kind of nonconformity in dissent terms, a few workers do defy legal regulations, and

for the majority it is the only way they can effectively protest against poor conditions and pay.

Most of the workers involved in turnover are young, low skilled and low paid; a disproportionate number come from sectors like construction where conditions are bad and prospects uncertain. Unsatisfactory living and working conditions still play a major part in prompting these workers to take action, although Hungarian, Czechoslovak and Romanian evidence shows that pay is becoming an increasingly predominant motivating force[27]. This confirms the general trend we noted earlier towards higher and more positive material expectations.

Economic reform has had a mixed effect on turnover. On the one hand, its relaxation of administrative controls has opened up greater possibilities for this kind of nonconformity. The emphasis on rationalisation, however, has resulted in sustained efforts to reduce turnover levels. Both these aspects are reflected in Hungarian experience. The decentralisation of economic controls, coupled with a growing labour shortage, resulted in a sharp rise in the number of workers changing in the first years of the NEM. The authorities responded with stronger administrative controls and better incentives for long service. In Eastern Europe generally, this stick-and-carrot approach has had some effect on turnover. At the same time, such moves tend to produce protests, as they did in Hungary, against the infringement of workers' freedom of movement and choice.[28]

Indiscipline, the violation of factory and legal regulations, can be seen as a more explicitly dissenting kind of nonconformity. Ideally, socialist workers should be self-disciplining and not require controls reminiscent of the capitalist system. But, as we noted earlier, workers' commitment is not sufficiently developed to allow for such auto-regulation. Official statistics on absenteeism, which is the most visible form of indiscipline, indicate very low levels. In Poland and Czechoslovakia unexcused absence from work in industry comes to less than a man-day per annum, and even in traditionally high absenteeism sectors like construction the figure is only two to three man-days. But such statistics grossly underrepresent the scale of this type of nonconformity. To begin with, a great deal of absenteeism and indiscipline generally is tolerated and goes unreported by managers anxious to keep relations harmonious both with workforce and higher authorities. Furthermore, judging by continual complaints of malingering, a substantial amount of absenteeism goes under the heading of sick leave. In Poland and Hungary improvements in sickness benefits in the early seventies were followed by such sharp rises in sickness absence that both regimes have recently reintroduced more stringent controls and higher fines for malingering.[29]

Several aspects of absenteeism make it a cause for official concern. Unlike job changing, absenteeism and general indiscipline are spread throughout the workforce, affecting young and old alike. Moreover, one form of indiscipline leads to another. Many workers do not only absent themselves without leave but do private work in factory time. Pilfering is notoriously widespread and regarded by most workers as a natural perk. One Polish survey found that whereas a majority of the population were prepared to condone thefts of factory property, hardly any were willing to apply the same standards even to damaging property borrowed from workmates. In Czechoslovakia, workers' general disaffection from the Husák regime has found expression, or arguably sublimation, in widespread indiscipline of all kinds. Popular attitudes are summed up by the saying 'If you don't steal from the state you rob your own family'.[30]

From the regime's point of view all these acts of proto-dissent, though objectionable, are by no means totally negative. Moonlighting has long taken pressure off wages, and general indulgence towards misconduct has helped reduce tensions in the factory. An ability to get away with breaking some of the rules can give workers a certain feeling of freedom and help to divert their nonconformity and dissent from other more dangerous channels. But with the growing importance of labour productivity, such diversion has become increasingly costly. Economic considerations account in large part for the tougher line taken on indiscipline in recent years. Administrative sanctions have been prominent in the attempts of both the Czechoslovak and Polish authorities to stem absenteeism and pilfering. As in the case of turnover these measures have had some effect but they have also produced objections to the infringement of the right to an easy work climate which many workers see as part of the 'social compact'.[31]

COLLECTIVE PROTEST ACTION

There are three forms of workers' collective protest action. In descending order of frequency and ascending order of political significance these are the go-slow, the strike and the strike-cum-riot.

Slowing down the rate and intensity of their work is probably the most widespread form of workers' collective protest; yet, by virtue of its covert nature, it is also the most elusive. Some idea of what is involved in an Eastern European slow-down can be gathered from a detailed account by two Hungarian sociologists of one such action taken in the metal sheet working shop of a rail coach building plant in Budapest in 1968.[32] Early in 1968 the management tightened piece-rates, reduced overtime and withdrew bonuses. As a result, the men's earnings dropped. There was no immediate reaction from the workers, but when the situation somewhat improved they became uncoopera-tive. Turnover and absenteeism increased. More importantly, the older workers refused overtime and reduced their output by half. In the knowledge that they were indispensable to the whole plant's production line, these workers were prepared to take a temporary drop in their earnings for the sake of higher returns in the long term. Their calculations proved correct and the management was forced to bring back the higher piece-rates and introduce special bonuses. The workers responded promptly to these concessions by taking on over-time and trebling output.

Several interesting points emerge from this case and might be said to have some general bearing on slow-downs. First, the action was taken as a protest against measures which brought about a deterioration in the workers' earning power and thus threatened the stability central to the 'social compact'. Workers' objectives were to restore and only slightly to improve on their old position. Secondly, it was a highly circumscribed action in which not even all the workers in the shop were involved; the younger workers could not afford to take the temporary cut in pay involved. Nonetheless, it is significant that the whole strategy of the slow-down was planned and coordinated by a small core of opinion-leaders whose authority was sufficient to get the older workers to bring about a halving and then a tripling of output. Finally, although the entire action by-passed official channels, it was not considered to be exceptional, it even seemed to be tacitly accepted as a way in which workers used their collective industrial muscle to resolve disagreements with management.

Strike action meets with no such acceptance. In communist party states strikes are generally considered to be illicit and unacceptable. Open approval of the workers' right to strike given at times of political turmoil, as in Czechoslovakia in 1969, merely underlines the illegiti-macy of strikes in conditions of normalcy. Only in Yugoslavia have strikes long enjoyed a curious quasi-legitimacy; they are tolerated as a last resort against bureaucratic injustice but not recognised as a regular instrument of workers' protest. In the rest of Eastern Europe strikes are not proscribed as illegal acts but rather seen as anachronisms in a socialist system that amply safeguards workers' rights and interests.[33] It is not difficult to explain official reluctance to sanction strike action. Just as it is the covert nature of slowdowns that makes them tolerable forms of dissent, so it is the visibility rather than the substance of strikes that damns them in states where public compliance is far more important than conformity of belief and private action. Furthermore, because the party assumes special responsibility for all that concerns the working class, overt conflict between workers and their superiors reflects badly on party performance and weakens party legitimacy which still derives much of its strength from representing working-class interests.

The status of strikes imposes severe restraints on their use by workers to voice protests. Management, party and trade unions as well as security forces do all in their power to prevent strikes from breaking out; nearly all stoppages are therefore wildcat actions. The only reliable strike statistics we have are for Yugoslavia which, between 1958 and 1969, experienced an average of 145 strikes per year.[34] On the basis of scattered reports, it seems reasonable to estimate a much lower level of strike activity for the rest of Eastern Europe, with a few dozen strikes a year being the overall maximum per country. There are obviously departures from any such average: the German Democratic Republic and in recent years Hungary seem to have had very few if any strikes while Polish workers have regularly exceeded the norm. The rest of Eastern Europe may have far fewer strikes than Yugoslavia, but those that do occur tend to involve much larger numbers of workers. Although, as in Yugoslavia, most East European strikes are restricted to one enterprise, enterprises are bigger and on occasion strike actions embrace a group of factories and even a whole city or area. Organised multi-enterprise strikes are still very much the exception, yet some coordination and sympathy action emerged during the Polish events of 1970–1971 and 1976 and in the course of the Romanian coal miners' strike in 1977.[35] On very rare occasions such large-scale strike actions, themselves involving perhaps tens of thousands of workers, spill over into city and region-wide demonstrations and rioting. This happened in the GDR and Czechoslovakia in 1953, in Hungary in 1956 and in Poland in 1956, 1970 and 1976. In as much as these strikes-cum-riots involve very large numbers of workers and their families, and tend to spark off sympathy actions in other areas, they are the nearest one comes in Eastern Europe to *working-class* protest action.

The inadequacies of available evidence rule out anything but impressionistic generalisations about the strike-proneness of sectors or areas. It is notable, however, that the more serious strike actions are often undertaken by workers who live in tight-knit communities and particularly by those who have a tradition of militancy. Strike traditions seem to build up quickly and greatly to increase workers' readiness to resort to this form of protest; strikes tend to recur in the same factories and cities. Strikes-cum-riots are more liable to break out in peripheral areas where strikes in a few key enterprises are sufficient to disrupt the entire local economy and thus directly affect the whole population.[36]

While such large-scale disturbances can last for up to five days or more, the overwhelming majority of workers' protest actions are very short, ranging from a few hours to one or two days. Brevity is largely inherent in the nature of strikes in Eastern Europe. Most of them are spontaneous protests, walk-outs rather than well conceived and planned campaigns of action. Organisation and strategy often seem to develop in an *ad hoc* fashion in the course of conflict. Workers' spokesmen are elected, or as often merely emerge, at hurriedly conferred mass meetings which are usually characterised by confusion rather than purposive activity. Only where conflict becomes longer drawn out, or some experience has been accumulated in past actions, do workers seem to be able to organise more effectively. The Adolf Warski shipyard in Szczecin, which went on strike in December 1970 and again in January 1971 is a case in point. During the first strike organisation was haphazard; the second time around a structure of elected delegates was created, demands were systematically processed and cogently formulated and workers' commissions were established to supervise their eventual implementation.[37]

Even where organisation is relatively good, other more fundamental factors weaken and foreshorten strike action. The generally large size of the enterprises in which these strikes take place facilitates short sharp protests but makes longer action difficult to sustain. More importantly, the militancy of many of the workers, particularly the lower skilled of peasant origin, thrives initially on conflict but is ill-suited to prolonged campaigns. A combination of no strike funds, external pressure and initial concessions can easily lead to a differentiation of sectional interests which makes it difficult to continue the action.[38]

Precisely in order to prevent any consolidation of workers' protests, East European authorities tend to respond very swiftly to strikes. Local officials descend on the factory, berate management and promise workers the speedy investigation and resolution of their main

grievances. Yugoslav evidence shows that strikes are a highly successful and effective form of protest, and this is born out generally by East
European experience.[39] When strikes are large, and particularly when
they lead to violent demonstrations, initial official reaction is often one
of disbelief and indignation. However, the high-ranking party and
government leaders, who are invariably sent to deal with such outbreaks of working-class protest, soon become conciliatory. It is not the
workers but local officials who are usually blamed for the conflict; the
dismissal of the most unpopular of them serves both to punish 'incompetence' and to provide convenient scapegoats. Workers' grievances
are sympathetically heard and often very frankly discussed in long and
heated debates between party representatives and strikers. As a rule
the workers' most urgent demands are conceded even when this
involves substantial economic costs.[40]

The speed of regime response and the high success-rate of strike
action underscores the power exercised in these states by workers'
collective protests. No communist party leadership can afford to
ignore or whole-heartedly to condemn action taken by large sections
of the working-class. But neither can it publicly condone strikes and
violent demonstration. So that while most workers' grievances are
acknowledged as being well-founded, the actions to which they give
rise are almost invariably condemned. The various 'excesses' are
conveniently attributed to 'hooligans' and to anti-socialist influences,
thus absolving the working class as such of any blame and at the same
time justifying the extensive mopping-up operations which follow all
strikes and demonstrations.[41] In a combined punitive and prophylactic
action, the security forces arrest putative leaders and organisers and
very large numbers of participants are harassed and dismissed from
their jobs.

When compared with the *furore* their collective protests arouse,
strikers' demands appear relatively modest. Only in certain circumstances do workers press first and foremost for an improvement in
their material situation. Such 'ameliorative' demands for better conditions and higher pay take priority where wages are low and traditions
of militancy are strong, or when the economic climate and structure
makes this kind of claim seem realisable. The preponderance of
'ameliorative' demands in Yugoslav strikes is closely linked with the
highly decentralised nature of economic decision-making in that country. The fact that questions relating to pay and working conditions and
organisation can be determined at enterprise level explains why most
Yugoslav strikes are targeted at local management. By the same token,

the generally centralised conditions prevailing in the rest of Eastern Europe discourage strike action against local management and lead workers to undertake collective protest action to demonstrate to the all-powerful centre their discontent, either with the local situation or directly with national policy. It is remarkable to what extent the larger strikes, and particularly the strikes-cum-riots, are essentially protests designed not so much to improve conditions as to reverse specific party and government measures which workers see as threatening their standard of living.[42] The priority accorded by strikers to the restoration of the *status quo ante*, to what may be called restitution demands, stems logically from workers' overriding concern with safeguarding the welfare rights embodied in the 'social compact'.

Within the category of second rank demands one can distinguish between the straightforward calls for better conditions and those which have wider implications. Under the latter heading one can include criticism of managerial inefficiency and demands for the dismissal of incompetent managers and administrators not only at local but also at national level. As one Polish striker forcefully declared in 1971, if the economists in Warsaw were found to have squandered workers' hard earned resources they had to be sacked. Closely allied to this kind of criticism are the objections voiced by striking workers to what they see as excessive numbers of overpaid administrators. Working-class egalitarianism generally tends to come through strongly in the form of demands for greater equalisation of bonuses and for the reduction of top salaries. At Szczecin in 1971 a proposal was even made, in true Communard tradition, to bring all party and government salaries closer into line with the average industrial wage.[43]

While many of the above complaints have obvious political overtones and implications, demands of an openly political nature do not figure prominently in workers' protests. By far the most strongly voiced of these are what could be called self-regarding demands arising directly from the course of collective action: calls for strike pay, for the release of arrested workers, for future security from prosecution and for the punishment of those responsible for abusive behaviour against the working class.[44] Broader political demands appear rarely and then only in the form of slogans which arise spontaneously in the heat of confrontation during strike-cum-riot situations. Such slogans occasionally denounce party rule in general, but they are mainly directed against local officials and especially against local security forces. As the products of anger at the treatment accorded to workers' substantive economic demands, these political slogans are far too ephemeral and inchoate to be taken as evidence of any programmatic political content to workers' actions. Of greater significance in this context are the more specific and purposive demands for institutional reform, participation and consultation which appeared in the last two strike waves in Poland. In 1970–1 Polish workers called not only for free elections to party and trade union factory committees, but also for a general rejuvenation of both these organisations. While economic demands remain uppermost in strikers' minds, the emergence of such calls indicates that Polish workers at least have begun to realise that the best way to secure their social compact rights is to ensure that party and unions defend working-class interests. In a sense, the explicit demands of 1971 and 1976 represent the maturation of a long-standing concern with improving communications which has traditionally found expression in strikers' insistence on publishing their grievances and speaking directly with party leaders.[45]

WHAT MAKES WORKERS PROTEST: ECONOMIC CONDITIONS AND FACTORS

Identifying the immediate precipitants of collective protest actions appears to be relatively straightforward. As a rule, the smaller strikes are set off by changes in norms, wage allocation or wage payment which adversely affect workers' earning power or at least are thought to do so. While such factors also play a part in bringing about larger strikes, these seem to be triggered primarily by central policy measures which reduce or threaten workers' purchasing power. Such measures can vary in form – workers' protests in Czechoslovakia in 1953 were a direct response to a currency reform which effectively decimated their savings – but large increases in the price of foodstuffs stand out as precipitants. And given the general sensitivity of East European workers, and particularly of the large number of women among them, to any movement in the consumer price index, it is not surprising that rises of 15–30 per cent in Poland in 1970, and of more than double that amount in 1976, provoked widespread strikes and working-class demonstrations. Yet food prices were raised by 25 per cent in Poland in 1960 and by a third in Hungary in 1976 without any large-scale workers' protests.[46] Evidently, in order to explain the phenomenon satisfactorily one has to go beyond price increases.

The extent to which price increases operate as a trigger to working-class protest is conditioned by the context in which they are introduced. If we look at the factors leading up to the strike wave of December 1970 some obvious secondary precipitants emerge. The announcement of redundancy plans and of a new wage system which tied all future rises to productivity must have appeared to workers as a concerted attack on their social compact rights. Coming on top of these longer term threats to earning power, the decision to increase food prices made the situation intolerable. The importance of the combination of price increases with other factors is confirmed negatively by Hungarian experience. The food price increases of 1976 came after a series of concessions had been made to workers' criticism of economic reform policies. In 1970 an inegalitarian and unpopular profit-sharing scheme had been replaced by one which did not discriminate as much against workers; at the Central Committee plenum of November 1972 a decision had been taken to loosen the links between wages and productivity and to boost the wages of lower paid workers.[47] All this did not prevent complaints about inflationary trends in 1976, but it did apparently have sufficient compensating effects to avoid any outbreak of working-class protest.

Marked differences between protest and non-protest situations also emerge if we turn from precipitants to economic background factors. As can be seen from the figures set out in table 7.1, the period immediately preceding the price increase of 1960 in Poland was one of rising real wages, whereas the years leading up to the increases and protests of 1970 witnessed the slowest rate of wage growth since the early 1950s. Between 1966 and 1970 real wages in Poland grew by just over 2 per cent per annum. Hungarians, on the other hand, enjoyed a fairly steady annual growth in real wages of 3.5 per cent from the mid-1960s, rising to over 4.5 per cent in the years immediately preceding the 1976 price increases.

In view of these figures it is not surprising that Polish workers saw the attempts to tighten wages and increase prices as a two-pronged attack on what was already a bare material minimum. In terms of relative deprivation, the outbreak of working-class protest in December 1970 can be seen as the product of what Gurr has called a pattern of 'decremental deprivation', i.e. where expectations stay relatively constant but capabilities are seen to stagnate or fall. The same kind of pattern appears to hold for the upsurge in Yugoslav strikes between 1958 and 1962 and for the burgeoning of strike activity in Czechoslovakia in 1968–9.[48]

Feelings of relative deprivation stemming from workers comparing their lot with that of reference groups, can be seen as contributing to

Table 7.1
Real Wages in Poland and Hungary 1956–76 (annual percentage change)

Year	Poland	Hungary
1956	11.6	11.4
1957	8.3	17.9
1958	3.3	4.3
1959	5.1	4.9
1960	-1.5	1.9
1961	2.6	0.0
1962	0.4	1.9
1963	2.4	4.5
1964	2.1	2.4
1965	0.0	0.0
1966	3.3	2.2
1967	2.5	3.7
1968	1.3	2.3
1969	1.6	4.5
1970	3.1	4.7
1971	5.5	2.3
1972	6.4	2.2
1973	11.5	2.8
1974	13.8	5.6
1975	11.8	3.9
1976	3.8	0.5

Sources: Poland: 1956–66, *Rocznik Statystyczny 1967* (Warsaw 1967), p. 522
1967–9, *Rocznik Statystyczny 1970* (Warsaw 1970), p. 497
1970–5, *Rocznik Statystyczny 1976* (Warsaw 1976), p. 80
1976, *Trybuna Ludu*, 27 January 1977
Hungary: 1956–65, *Statistical Yearbook 1965* (Budapest 1965), p. 252
1966–75, *Statistical Yearbook 1975* (Budapest 1975), p. 351
1976, *Népszava*, 13 February 1977

the incidence of strikes in certain enterprises and working-class action in certain areas. One can trace the discontent of East Berlin building workers in 1953, or that of Poznań metal workers in 1956, at least in part to their awareness of gains made by other groups. The role played by such comparisons helps to explain the prominence in strikes and general protests of workers from the higher, though not the highest paid industrial groups. Similar factors help to account for the outbreak of working-class protest in peripheral areas, where workers' dissatisfaction with their standard of living is compounded by the whole local population's shared feelings of neglect by the centre. In the case of the Baltic ports, such feelings of area deprivation were heightened by comparisons with international standards.[49]

However important stagnation of living standards may be in creating the pre-conditions for working-class protest, material improvement in itself is no guarantee of workers' quiescence. While the East German strikes of 1953 and the Poznań protest of 1956 appear to confirm the importance of decremental deprivation, they also indicate the role played by fluctuating living standards and, above all, by rising expectations. In each case the measures which triggered workers' actions came at a time of improving conditions or at least at one of promised improvement. The best example of working-class protest following a period of rising living standards is provided by the Polish events of 1976. Precisely in order to avoid a repetition of 1970, food prices were frozen, wages were raised and greater welfare benefits made available; as a result real incomes in Poland rose by 40 per cent between 1971 and 1975. More importantly, workers themselves felt that their material position was improving – while in 1972 only one in four thought that their earnings had improved, a 1975 survey found this opinion to be universal.[50] Nevertheless, the price rise announced in June 1976 still set off working-class protests all over the country.

There are several possible strands to an explanation. The first is that the material improvements of 1971–5 were spectacular but superficial and uneven. Housing is a case in point. After 1971 more housing units were built than in the previous quinquennium but this seems to have had relatively little impact on many workers' actual position. One survey of workers in 154 of Poland's largest industrial enterprises found that housing lists had lengthened and that only a third of respondents were satisfied with the situation. Moreover, many Poles did not enjoy the full benefits of the rapid rise in income because the supply of quality goods failed to keep pace with purchasing power.[51] In addition to such deficiencies, mounting pressure was being exerted on the 'social compact' by the regime's efforts to increase economic efficiency. From 1974 Gierek and others began to talk in terms ominously reminiscent of the Gomułka period: work discipline had to improve and all future wage increases had to be fully justified by productivity. These points were driven home by the fall in the rate of wage growth and the far lower rates projected in the 1976–80 plan (see table 7.2).

Table 7.2
Percentage Increases in Aggregate Real Income in Eastern Europe

	Bulgaria	Czechoslovakia	GDR	Hungary	Poland	Romania
1966–70	30	19	25	19	10	31
1971–75	16	18	27	18	40	46
1976–80 Plan	17	14	21	15	18	30

Source: K. Bush, 'Indicators of Living Standards in the USSR and Eastern Europe' in *Comecon: Progress and Prospects* (NATO, Brussels 1977) p. 204 Table 4 (sources given).

The economic conditions and factors associated with the incidence of workers' actions thus present a complex picture. One cannot simply reduce acts of collective dissent to protests against higher work norms or even against higher prices. Such measures do precipitate most large-scale strikes, but only if they are accompanied by pressure on other social compact rights and are set against a background of one of two types of economic development. The first type of background is characterised by stagnating living standards which produce a pattern of 'decremental' relative deprivation. More commonly, however, the background is one of improving conditions which raise expectations that cannot be satisfied without violating some of the compact rights which workers seem unwilling to surrender. The more rapid and discontinuous the improvement, the more disruptive its effects are likely to be.

WHAT MAKES WORKERS PROTEST: INSTITUTIONAL ASPECTS

The various combinations of background, contextual and precipitating economic factors appear to account in large part for the outbreak of workers' protests, yet they by no means provide a full explanation of the phenomenon of collective dissent. To begin with, two major non-economic factors figure prominently in the origin and development of workers' actions. Firstly, the way in which sensitive economic measures are handled, particularly at national level, is often as important as their substance in determining working-class reaction. Hungarian policy in 1975–6 shows how careful handling can help to minimise workers' dissident response to unpopular measures. The 1976 price increases were announced well in advance, publicly discussed and their introduction was phased over a seven-month period.

Poland, on the other hand, exemplifies how such measures should not be introduced. The 1970 price rise was not only timed to coincide with Christmas but it and the 1976 increase were sprung on an unprepared public, presumably in the hope that suddenness and surprise would disarm the workers. Yet it was just this lack of warning and the arrogance it implied that provoked such an angry working-class reaction.[52]

Secondly, the way in which the authorities deal with outbreaks of workers' protest often plays a major part in determining their development. Before concessions are offered, attempts are frequently made to extinguish collective dissent by force. Ceausescu, for instance, started off by telling a mass meeting of 35,000 striking coal miners in 1977 that they would be 'crushed' if they did not return to work. But the use of force is almost invariably counter-productive. Attempts to pre-empt full blown strikes by arresting workers' leaders tends rather to strengthen workers' resolve and can even lead to street demonstrations protesting as much against the authorities treatment of demands as against the measures that prompted them in the first place. And it is the sending in of militia, troops and police at this juncture that transforms orderly demonstrations into violent confrontation and rioting in which a whole array of latent discontents is expressed in hostile slogans and in attacks on buildings symbolising authority and power. Finally, reprisals and prophylactic coercion in the aftermath of protest can, as happened in Poland in 1976, generate further workers' dissent.[53]

The mishandling of both policy changes and protest action is symptomatic of a deeper lack of understanding between workers and decision-makers that lies at the root of much working-class dissent. This lack of understanding can in turn be traced to deficiencies in the institutions which link the two groups. The party, the trade unions and the various bodies for participation in production are all supposed not only to maintain close contact between the shop-floor and higher levels, but also to explain central policy measures and facilitate the articulation and resolution of workers' grievances. Where these functions are fulfilled, the risk of price increases or stagnating living standards bringing about collective protest is greatly reduced. On the other hand, where these organisations perform ineffectively, workers are very likely to resort to dissident methods to press their demands.

The clearest indication of the close connection between institutional performance and collective dissent is provided by Polish developments. Strikers' demands in 1971 for institutional reform demonstrated workers' concern in this area but little was done to improve the situation. A poll of workers in the largest factories in 1975 showed that a majority thought party, trade union and workers' councils had shown no signs of becoming more effective. Arguably, such lack of institutional improvement contributed in large part to perpetuating conditions conducive to collective dissent. According to a survey of 2,800 worker communists conducted after June 1976, an overwhelming majority not only expressed no confidence in the main institutions but 40 per cent went so far as to select strike action as the best way of resolving conflicts.[54]

While Poland may be an extreme case in this respect, institutional performance presents serious problems throughout Eastern Europe. Institutions generally seem to suffer from two deficiencies. The first is an inability to adapt and respond to changing conditions and demands, an inflexibility which Zvi Gitelman has called 'overinstitutionalisation'.[55] Secondly, they appear not to command sufficient working-class confidence to enable them to fulfil their functions of articulation and mediation. By focusing on these aspects of Party, trade union and workers' participation, we hope to be able to assess their respective capacity and potential to pre-empt collective dissent.

In theory the party organisation in the factory is supposed to articulate workers' grievances and demands, mediate and resolve conflicts and, above all, ensure smooth and efficient production. The overriding importance of this last function tends to lead in practice to a preoccupation with production and a close involvement with management. This bias is reflected by the composition of the party's executive bodies. Although skilled workers are present on such bodies in large numbers, they are relatively less active and influential than their technical and managerial counterparts who tend to dominate proceedings and to create a climate inimical to criticism of management policy. The proximity of outlook and the overlap in personnel between management and party often creates the impression among workers that the two are in partnership, and that the party cannot effectively represent working-class interests. One recent Slovenian survey found that a majority of workers thought that party officials' interests differed from, or even opposed, their own. This is borne out by Polish evidence which suggests that one in two workers prefer to take their complaints directly to management and that only one in four have any confidence in the party as a workers' organisation.[56]

The party is also supposed to act as a link between the factory and higher party bodies, to explain and mobilise support for central policies and keep decision-makers informed of the climate of workers' opinion. It is here that malfunctioning has contributed most directly to the outbreak of workers' protest action. For instance, the post-mortems of the events of December 1970 in Poland made it clear that party activists in the factories were given hardly any warning of the impending price increases and therefore had no chance to prepare workers for the shock. Furthermore, their reports on likely shop-floor response were ignored by regional and central party authorities. This helps to explain why many party activists decided to breach Party discipline and take a leading part in many of the strike actions. Even if these activists toned down some of the workers' most radical demands, their presence on the other side of the barricades was enough to prompt considerable efforts to improve communications within the party. Direct links and special information services were established between the party organisations of 164 of the largest industrial enter-prises and the Central Committee apparatus. And in order to demon-strate the party's intention to keep in touch with opinion at the grass-roots, Gierek paid visits to over 200 factories in the four years following 1971. Yet the persistent levels of dissatisfaction with party performance, plus the apparent ignorance of workers' attitudes exem-plified by the decision to increase prices in 1976, show that these problems cannot be solved by streamlining and public relations exercises.[57]

In order to communicate effectively correspondents have at least to understand and be willing to be receptive to each other's standpoints. Many Polish party officials have demonstrated their apparent inability to do either – hence strikers' calls for a rejuvenation and regular rotation of party cadres. But the problem of contact between workers and party is not peculiar to Poland. In Hungary similar concerns about the gap between party officials and the working class appeared, if in far more moderate and generalised form, in the early 1970s; recently, echoes of such complaints have been heard in Yugoslavia. Official response in the Polish and Hungarian cases has been to intensify working-class recruitment and increase workers' representation in party bodies, but so far the results have been marginal.[58] In any event, increasing the number of workers in the membership and in elected bodies can have little real impact on parties that are strongly hierarchi-cal and elitist and bound by their functions to place the interests of the economy as a whole above those of the working class.

In this respect the trade unions might appear to have greater potential to articulate workers' grievances and thus pre-empt collective dissent action. For although the trade unions are consistently urged to mobilise workers to fulfil production plans, they do have a special responsibility for protecting their members' material interests. In theory, these two aspects of trade union work should be complementary; in practice, production interests seem to take priority. Even if trade union committees have a stronger worker contingent than their party equivalents, their composition is still frequently determined by executive selection rather than election and their proceedings tend to be heavily influenced by the non-manual members. What is more important is that trade union officials as a body see their role more in terms of helping production than defending workers' interests.[59] As a result, while trade unions perform a whole range of useful tasks, from administering social welfare to negotiating collective agreements, their overall approach is one of labour management. This is reflected by and compounds unions' weak position in the factory power structure and their timidity in supporting workers in conflict situations. Union backing for strikes is wholly exceptional in most of Eastern Europe; even in Yugoslavia trade unions supported only one in eleven of the stoppages between 1958 and 1969. In view of all this, it is not surprising that Czechoslovak, Polish and Yugoslav evidence shows that a majority of workers are highly critical of trade union performance and do not turn to them with their grievances. The gap between workers and union officials widens as one moves up the trade union hierarchy; it stems from a difference between officials' and workers' perceptions of union priorities. Whereas, as we have noted, officials stress production promotion workers give preference to defence of members' interests.[60]

Despite the manifold problems that beset the unions' performance as workers' organisations, several factors point to their being potentially the most effective channel of communication and mediation between workers, management and higher authorities. First, the care they do take of working conditions gives them wider support than that commanded by the more influential but also more authority oriented party organisations. Second, the strength of workers' expressed preferences for unions as defence organisations means that they have a ready-made constituency and role. Indeed, Polish and Yugoslav evidence shows that, of all the institutions in the enterprise, it is the unions that workers would like to see gain most in stature and power. And the existence of a popular preference for unions as an interest organisation has come through in the movements for trade union reform that have accompanied all the major political upheavals in Eastern Europe.[61] Finally, the importance of the unions in relation to workers' dissent is negatively confirmed by the coincidence in Poland of consistently poor trade union performance with recurrent complaint and dissent action. The lack of response to the 1970–71 calls for trade union reform, coupled with the subsequent deterioration in union performance, must be held to have contributed to the misunderstanding and accumulation of tension that led up to the events of June 1976.[62]

In a more positive vein, there is some evidence to suggest that more effective unions can help prevent workers' collective protests. The absence of large-scale workers' dissent in the GDR since 1953 might in part be attributed to what a recent study of East German trade unions describes as their 'active promotion' of members' interests.[63] The connection emerges far more clearly in the case of Hungary where the introduction of the NEM was accompanied by a more forceful emphasis on the unions as organisations representing and defending workers' interests. The Labour Code of 1967 granted trade unions new powers, the most important of which is the factory committee's right to veto any management move that violates legal regulations or infringes what is vaguely termed 'socialist morality'. The veto has the effect of suspending the measure in dispute pending the decision of higher union and administrative authorities. In the event, despite union leaders' exhortations, factory committees seem to have made use of the veto on only 150 occasions. This could in part be put down to timidity and a slowness to adjust to new powers. However, the mere existence of the veto has apparently often been sufficient to deter management from trying to push through unpopular measures and unions have tended to use their new power only as a last resort. While it is difficult to gauge the extent to which the strengthening of the factory committee has enhanced its popularity, it does seem to have helped to pre-empt collective protest. Only one strike has been reported in Hungary since 1968 and it is reasonable to assume that without the veto there might have been at least another 150.[64]

Trade union performance at national level has also contributed in several ways to the lowering of tension and the avoidance of open conflict. First, union leaders have played an active part in the debate on economic reforms, presenting these to the workers in modified and often more palatable form. Second, they have aggregated and articulated – if sometimes in more moderate terms – demands from the shop-floor. Finally, they have been able to do all this more effectively because of the standing they have achieved by successfully amending and even eliminating some of the most unpopular aspects of the NEM. The trade unions have made use of their right to be consulted on all policies affecting workers' interests to lobby against schemes such as the tying of wages to productivity or to enterprise profitability. That the party leadership decided in 1972 to stem the more technocratic elements of the NEM and to boost the wages of the lower paid can be attributed in large part to consistent union pressure.[65] In this way changes have been brought about without any resort to extra-institutional, illegitimate methods. Hungarian developments show that by moving some way in the direction of interest representation and defence, trade unions can establish themselves as workers' spokesmen and thus divert dissenting opinions into more controllable institutionalised channels.

The third and final institution, participation in management, should ideally pre-empt not just collective dissent action but all forms of dissent within the factory. In theory, by giving workers a direct say in decision-making participative bodies should fully integrate their interests with those of the enterprise. With the exception of Yugoslavia, however, anything approaching genuine workers' participation and self-management has been achieved in Eastern Europe only for short periods: Hungary 1956, Poland 1956–7 and Czechoslovakia 1968–9. What passes for participation and self-management in most of Eastern Europe are processes that involve workers in policy discussion and in enterprise affairs in a very superficial way. Meetings of the production conferences and committees, which operate in Czechoslovakia, Hungary and the GDR, all tend to be occasions for the presentation of reports and the putting of formal questions. Neither is scrutiny over management performance exercised nor is there any lively debate. And it is not surprising that the majority of workers derive no sense of involvement or participation in decision-making from such meetings; they look on them as a tiresome and rather pointless exercise.[66]

Even where considerable legal powers are assigned to workers' councils the results seem little better. In Poland, for instance, elected workers' councils, together with the union and party committees, constitute conferences of self-management. These conferences are endowed with an impressive array of powers which mean that no major management decision can be taken and implemented without the approval either of the full conference or of the workers' council. Yet two sets of problems severely handicap the functioning of these bodies as effective channels of participation and involvement. First, the narrow limits set by central planning and control on the scope of decision-making at enterprise level restrict the conferences to the distribution of incentive funds and to details of production.[67] Second, although workers are strongly represented on the full workers' councils and conferences, only a small number of them take an active part in the proceedings. Moreover, workers are heavily outnumbered on the workers' councils' Presidia, as we have noted they are on the party and union executives, by the non-manual groups. And it is these executive bodies, rather than the full councils and conferences, which seem to take all major decisions. According to research done in the 1960s, workers themselves were under no illusions on these scores. Not only did they rate the workers' council, which is the participative body *par excellence*, as being the least influential in the enterprise, but they saw it as representing management and not workers' interests.[68] Little has happened in the last decade to change Polish workers' disillusionment with participation and self-management. Calls voiced during the 1970–1 protests for a reform of the whole self-management structure resulted in vague promises of improvement. Although such possibilities have again been aired recently in press discussion, nothing tangible has emerged so far.[69]

Elsewhere in Eastern Europe more has been done to improve participation. Since the establishment of working people's councils in Romania in 1968, increasing stress has been laid on the need to expand factory democracy. Yet the authorities' apparent unwillingness to give these councils anything more than virtual consultative powers augurs badly for their effective operation.[70] Concern about the ineffectual nature of production conferences led Hungarian unions in the early seventies to press for an expansion of factory democracy. And after experimenting with various schemes, the decision was taken in 1977 to opt for participation through trade union bodies rather than via a structure of elected worker delegates. The new body, which came into operation at the beginning of 1978, comprises a joint meeting of the union committee and council plus the shop stewards. This meeting possesses somewhat less extensive powers than the Polish self-management conference, but given the Hungarian trade unions' track record there is every likelihood that these will be exercised more effectively and will exert considerable influence and control over management.[71] Nonetheless, all this constitutes an expansion of trade union power rather than one of workers' participation in a strict sense. As the situation currently stands in Eastern Europe, with the exception of Yugoslavia, production committees, workers' councils and their equivalents fail to give workers a feeling of involvement; they neither command popular support nor are they viewed as workers' bodies. It follows from this that such workers' participation cannot function effectively as a channel for grievances and demands and can do little or nothing to alleviate the problem of workers' dissent.

Can one therefore conclude that workers' participation has little to contribute to resolving the whole problem of dissent? It would be unjust to base an assessment of the potential of workers' participation in this area on the performance of the quasi-participation operating in nearly all of Eastern Europe. In order to gauge the capacity of workers' participation we should look at the authentic forms of participation and self-management which have emerged for short periods in Poland, Hungary and Czechoslovakia and have been at the heart of the Yugoslav system for almost thirty years.

The first question, and in fact the first difficulty, relates to the viability of authentic participation in the economic and political environment of Eastern Europe. An obvious yet nonetheless important point is that genuine workers' councils cannot function without considerable economic decentralisation. Polish, Hungarian and Czechoslovak experience clearly showed that such workers' councils are incompatible with a semi-command let alone a command economy. If established within such a structure they tend to operate as a major centrifugal force and therefore to encounter staunch opposition from the economic bureaucracy. Moreover, as economic controls are so closely intertwined with political ones, workers' councils accretion of power within the enterprise tends to affect not just the influence of management but also that of the party. In Poland, Hungary and Czechoslovakia the councils' insistence on pursuing an independent policy, and their attempts to establish national organisational networks, were perceived as a threat to party control and democratic centralism. And because the very existence of powerful and popular workers' councils undermines the role of trade union organisations, unions have always had an ambivalent, if not hostile, attitude towards authentic participation. This has led them to help emasculate workers' councils, as happened in Poland, or to monopolise participation as in the Hungarian case.[72] The short life of genuine workers' councils and their general coincidence with periods of political turmoil reinforces the conclusion that they are not viable in the economic and political conditions normally prevailing in Eastern Europe.

Even where authentic participation is able to operate it does not seem to provide a satisfactory solution to the problem of workers' dissent. Contrary to the role assigned to them by proponents of the revolutionary class thesis, workers do not respond enthusiastically to the idea of participation. The initiative in establishing Polish and Czechoslovak councils was taken not by the workers but by factory party and union officials. Furthermore, in both instances workers supported the councils not so much as participative bodies as interest organisations which would help obtain improved material benefits. But, even in Yugoslavia, where widespread support based on concepts of control and co-management has developed over the last twenty years, workers' perceptions of the councils' achievement still tend to focus on material benefits and not on involvement in the factory.[73] This can perhaps be accounted for by the relative lack of impact the councils have had on the power structure. Yugoslav research shows that while workers would like to see the council wielding the greatest influence in the enterprise, they perceive the reality of the situation in terms of continuing management predominance. Similarly, workers may constitute a majority on the councils, but this majority is diminishing, and on the more influential management boards they are becoming increasingly outnumbered by the white-collar groups. If one examines workers' own ranking of the relative influence of occupational groups within the factory, it seems as if self-management has had a nugatory impact. A hierarchy based on education and skill still prevails, leaving the manual workers at the bottom of the ladder. All this might help to explain the uneven nature of workers' support for the councils as well as the widespread feeling that they do not maintain sufficiently close contact with the shop-floor. When combined with the councils' inherent tendency to a production and management standpoint, such shortcomings help to account for the persistence of collective dissent and for the direction of a significant proportion of that dissent action against the councils themslves.[74]

In the context of reducing the feelings of powerlessness and alienation which Yugoslav research has found to be associated with dissent, workers' councils have had surprisingly little effect. Participation does not seem to have become an important source of satisfaction and while council membership does appear to reduce feelings of powerlessness within the factory among the less skilled groups, it also brings about a marked increase in their work alienation.[75]

In view of the popular support enjoyed by Yugoslav workers' councils one should be wary of exaggerating the above weaknesses. Yet, together with the problems of economic and political viability we noted earlier, they seriously reduce the potential of workers' participation as an institutional solution to the problem of dissent.

The evidence relating to the party, the unions and workers' participation suggests several conclusions. Overinstitutionalisation constitutes the most pressing problem in the context of the immediate
outbreak of protest action. But increased flexibility alone cannot solve
the more fundamental deficiencies of which it is itself a symptom. All
the institutions, in varying degree, appear to suffer from an inadequate
rapport with the workers and from a consequent lack of shop-floor
confidence. This in turn stems largely from a strong functional inclination to production concerns and a management orientation. Workers,
however, want organisations that will first and foremost represent and
promote their interests rather than those of production. In view of this
strong popular preference, the trade unions seem to have the greatest
potential for pre-empting collective dissent and Hungarian developments demonstrate what can be achieved by relatively modest change.

WORKERS' DISSENT, OPPOSITION AND POLITICAL REFORM

While strikes and protest actions show that many workers' demands
have political overtones and wide-reaching political implications, they
do not give a clear indication of workers' political intent. And even if
large-scale working-class protests may catalyse, and may be used by
politicians to accelerate, leadership changes, as happened in Poland in
1970, there is no evidence that workers actually take action primarily
to bring about such transfers of power. In order to explore the problem
of what, if any, political intent can be said to characterise workers'
dissent we must examine their behaviour in conditions which almost
compel the adoption of a political standpoint. Just such a setting is
provided by the three major political upheavals which have taken
place in Eastern Europe since Stalin's death: the Polish and Hungarian
crises of 1956 and the Czechoslovak reform movement of 1968–9. We
are concerned here not with any detailed delineation of the workers'
role in these developments but only with trying to discern the broad
patterns of working-class response.

Workers tend to react to the first signs of political ferment with
scepticism and economic rather than political action. Indeed, workers'
first response has usually been to take advantage of the relaxation of
central controls by pressing for material improvements. Even if such
strikes have been used by reformers to speed the process of change, as
was the case with Poznań in 1956, from the workers' standpoint they

are protests against material conditions and not against the slowness of political change.[76]

The slowness of workers' reaction to political change and their general reluctance to promote reform stems not so much from any inherent working-class authoritarianism as from a widespread indifference to politics. Eastern Europe is no exception to universal trends and only a small minority of workers, predominantly those in the skilled groups, seem to take any real interest in political affairs.[77] Moreover, most workers tend to be wary of political change because instability often brings economic disruption and reform programmes usually include proposals for economic rationalisation which threaten workers' social compact rights. It is not surprising, therefore, that it takes a good deal of time and pressure to induce workers to come out in favour of political reform. By the time workers take action of this kind, old policies have generally been discredited and reform popularly acclaimed. In this sense workers' pro-reform stance in all three major crises should be seen as an endorsement and a strengthening of a popular consensus for democratisation.

The same could be said, if to a lesser extent, of workers' far more energetic efforts to defend reform policies once these have come under external pressure. The remarkable mobilisation of Polish, Hungarian and Czechoslovak workers behind reform once it came under Soviet attack can be attributed to several factors. First, pressure and intervention crystallise the political issues at stake. Whereas in the early stages workers were either unable or unwilling to understand the oft confused and confusing political situation, intervention clearly identified political reform with the national cause and thus created a black-and-white situation. Second, workers' emotional attachment to the national cause was far more widely and intensely felt than any intellectually-based attachment to democratic values. Lastly, outside intervention posed a direct threat to existing policies and developments. We have already noted the tendency of East European workers to take militant action in protest against threats to their material status quo; the same effect is produced by what are seen as threats to national achievements and national sovereignty.

The actual form and intensity of working-class pro-reform mobilisation has varied considerably. In Poland in 1956 workers demonstrated their readiness to fight in support of Gomułka, and their armed stance helped to defeat the planned conservative coup and to deter the Soviet Union from intervening physically in the crisis. In Czechoslovakia in 1968 the workers openly declared their support for Dubček as outside pressure increased; their response to the invasion was a show of solidarity with action confined to short protest strikes carefully timed not to cause excessive disruption of production. Only in Hungary in 1956 did workers reply in kind to the use of force; they not only staged prolonged general strikes but were at the centre of armed resistance.[78] These variations in working-class reaction can be related directly to the strength of nationalist and anti-Russian feeling and to the propensity of the working class in each of these countries to take militant action. The high ranking of Polish and Hungarian workers on all these counts is explicable in terms of deep-rooted nationalist and anti-Russian traditions and perhaps in terms of the high proportion of volatile workers of peasant stock. By the same token, Czechoslovak workers' relatively low level of militancy can be traced to the absence of any strong nationalist and anti-Russian traditions and to a largely hereditary working class with an inclination towards caution and non-violence.[79]

Even after the crisis of intervention or threatened intervention has passed, the extent to which workers dissent from or oppose the reversal of reform policies seems to depend largely on how reform relates to the national cause. Hungarian workers actively defended political reforms precisely because for some time after intervention these continued to symbolise national independence; they opposed the Kádár regime because it was closely associated with national betrayal. Gomułka, on the other hand, managed to emasculate the reform programme after 1956 without any marked opposition from the workers because he continued to personify Polish sovereignty and was thus able to justify his new line in terms of the national interest. Both effects emerged in the course of working-class reaction to post-invasion events in Czechoslovakia. On the one hand, the Soviet occupation ensured the continued identification of the reform programme with national self-determination and helped to sustain workers' opposition to 'normalisation'. At the same time, workers were partly constrained in their resistance by leadership appeals that compromise and restraint was necessary for the national good.[80]

While the nationalist nexus helps to explain the overall pattern of working-class response, the strength and endurance of workers' opposition to the reversal of reforms also depends on the extent to which workers' organisations take up the reform cause. It can be argued that workers' minimal resistance to political retrenchment in Poland after 1956 can be traced to their lack of any strong institutional base. Trade union reform remained largely on paper and the workers' councils were already weakened by internal differences before they were emasculated in 1958 by regime action. In the revolutionary Hungarian situation, workers' councils, organised on a district and regional as well as on a factory basis, gave a much stronger lead to working-class resistance and were only suppressed by the extensive use of force. That Czech workers' defence of the reform programme persisted for so long after August 1968 is largely to be attributed to the popularly-based workers' councils and, above all, to the activity of the rejuvenated trade union movement. It was trade union officials who played the most important part in organising and coordinating working-class resistance to normalisation; that is why nearly 50 per cent of all union officials were purged in the years following 1969.[81]

In view of the solid institutional and organisational base for workers' resistance and opposition that existed in Hungary and Czechoslovakia, the question arises, why was such resistance not more effective? Part of the answer lies in the vicissitudes of the nationalist connection and in the array of coercive and administrative weapons used by the regime to stem workers' dissent and opposition. Nevertheless, some weight must be assigned to the weaknesses of workers' political resolve and commitment. Workers' councils in Czechoslovakia, for instance, concentrated on economic issues and tended to shy away from direct political involvement. Their greater political commitment notwithstanding, the trade unions in 1968–9 were concerned first and foremost with their own position and tended to react to regime policy rather than take any political lead. Even in Hungary, workers' political involvement was in large part one of anti-intervention struggle. And even the Greater Budapest Workers' Council, which did take a political lead and for a time established a position comparable with that of the Petrograd Soviet, found it difficult to reconcile the politically militant district councils with their more economically oriented factory counterparts.[82]

In the final analysis, the political action of workers' organisations can only be as strong as the political resolve of their membership. Without doubt, the heat of conflict politicised a great many workers in these countries, but with the passing of immediate crisis, political commitment seems to wane and the primacy of material concerns is quite rapidly reasserted. Much of the bitterness and disappointment of post-crisis retrenchment seems to have been assuaged by relatively steady economic progress and rising living standards. But even so, such material compensations, while mollifying workers' actions, often divert open opposition into widespread and diffuse forms of dissent such as absenteeism, poor work performance and abandonment of party ranks.[83]

WORKERS AND INTELLECTUAL DISSENT

Perhaps the clearest indication of the connection between workers' dissent and the wider cause of political reform is provided by the relationship between workers' dissidence and that of the critical intellectuals. A coincidence of the two, let alone an alliance between them, would constitute a formidable force for change which party leaders would find it extremely difficult to resist. But any such collaboration has long been dogged by two closely related factors: a lack of understanding and a dearth of common interests and values.

The widespread lack of understanding between the two groups can be traced to the social and cultural distance that separates workers from the intelligentsia as a whole. This in turn is nurtured by a lack of contact and communication – deliberately made difficult by political authorities – which has bred mutual suspicion and the formation of stereotype images on both sides. Workers tend to regard the critical intellectuals as part of a privileged intelligentsia; many intellectuals think of workers as being materialistic, conservative and even authoritarian in inclination. Polish developments have shown most starkly what the indifference and even antipathy that results from such lack of understanding can produce. In 1968 the workers did little or nothing while students and intellectuals were persecuted; in 1970–1 the intellectuals stood by as workers fought police and troops. Ironically, students were even singled out for praise by conservative politicians for their sober and responsible behaviour during the disturbances.[84]

Such blatant non-cooperation is neither universal nor immutable. Where political circumstances have brought about a relaxation of bureaucratic controls over communication and contacts, intellectuals have attempted to establish links with the working class and correct popular misconceptions. All three major political crises in Eastern Europe have seen writers, philosophers and journalists visiting factories and informing workers about the political situation as well as trying to convince them of the mutual benefits of collaboration. Though some of these visits were successful in alleviating suspicion, their overall impact on worker-intellectual relations has been small-scale and short-lived.[85] Students have made a more sustained effort to break down the barriers separating them from the working class. In 1956 Polish students contacted workers in the largest factories while in Hungary some of the workers' councils combined with local students' revolutionary committees to form People's Revolutionary Committees at the height of the intervention crisis. Czech students in 1968–9 not only established regular contact with workers in many of the largest factories, but also managed to reach agreements with some of the most politically active trade unions. According to these agreements, the most important of which was signed with the metal workers' union, both sides were to exchange information and generally to collaborate to preserve what remained of the reform programme from further debilitation. While such pacts marked a significant advance in worker-student relations and formed the basis for an alliance, they failed to hold up under sustained pressure. When in June 1969 the Husák regime banned the students' union, there was only minimal protest from the factories.[86] Although this lack of response can in part be explained by the immense pressure under which the trade unions and workers' councils were labouring at the time, it also underscores the limitations of collaboration between the two groups.

The second problem that besets relations between intellectuals and workers is an inadequate fund of common interests and values. As we have noted workers are primarily concerned with material security and stability and an equitable distribution of financial rewards. They appear to set less store by the civil liberties and democratic rights which constitute the critical intellectuals' central concerns. Similarly, intellectuals are not particularly interested in welfare questions and in egalitarianism; indeed, many of them seem to favour a highly differentiated society. Some, like Bauman, have gone so far as to state that there is a clear dichotomy of working-class and intellectuals' interests stemming from a fundamental contradition between democratic freedoms and welfare socialism.[87] In reality the situation is less clear-cut.

Workers may well be generally wary of change and instability but their attitude to democratising reform is not invariably and unconditionally hostile. Much hinges whether the political and economic status quo that is being challenged is providing the socialist welfare rights they so prize and on the extent to which proposals for democratic reform are linked with measures that threaten those rights. Furthermore, even if workers appear to be more prepared than intellectuals to accept an authoritarian political regime, they still seem to place a high value on individual freedom and many, particularly the higher skilled, are receptive to arguments for greater democracy and participation. Equally, by no means all intellectuals can be identified with the anti-egalitarianism of the technical intelligentsia. Polish and Yugoslav evidence suggests that some professional groups, like teachers, are as egalitarian-minded as the workers themselves.[88] The main problem seems to be not so much a dichotomy of irreconcilable interests and

values as a lack of common concerns and principles for which both groups are prepared to fight and to risk sacrifice. Intellectuals might well sympathise with workers' material grievances and with demands for the extension of union rights but they do not tend to promote them in the same way that they sometimes champion human rights and democratisation. Many workers doubtlessly subscribe to the principle of free speech but they are not generally prepared to take up the cudgels on its behalf. And even when such action has been taken, as was the case in Czechoslovakia in 1968, it has often lacked vigour. The unique Workers' Committees for the Defence of the Freedom of the Press were remarkable but short-lived and declined after the invasion when other workers' organisations flourished.[89]

It seems to require the exertion of some kind of pressure which impinges on workers and intellectuals alike to induce collaboration. The joint action of Hungarian workers and students in 1956 was made possible only by the climate of national unity created by Soviet intervention. Similarly, resistance to externally imposed policies was the basis on which the Czech worker-student agreements rested. The experience of national unity in the face of external pressure can even have a fundamental effect on relations between the working class and the intelligentsia as a whole. Separate surveys conducted in Czechoslovakia before and after the invasion showed a significant shift towards social harmony and understanding. Whereas before August only 45 per cent of the communist worker respondents thought that there were no antagonistic classes in Czechoslovak society, after the invasion this view was taken by two in three workers.[90]

It is largely the continuing existence in Czechoslovakia of a regime associated with national capitulation that has sustained workers' sympathy for intellectual dissidence and has made possible workers' involvement in Charter 77. The Charter itself was a straightforward protest against the violation of human and civil rights under the Husák regime and was organised by intellectual dissidents. Yet it has been supported by Czech workers in two ways. Tacit support was evidenced by workers' universal refusal to comply with official requests to condemn the Charter; the party had to make do with denunciations signed by factory directors instead of the workforce. Far more positive and direct support has been given by the large number of workers who have appended their names to the document at considerable risk to themselves and their families. While only 17 of the original 242 signatories were workers, the proportion grew rapidly in the course of the year: one in two of the group of signatories whose names were made public in December were workers and in overall terms workers constitute approximately a third of the 828 dissidents who have signed the Charter to date. Even if some of these 'workers' may be intellectuals who now hold factory jobs, this still leaves a large and growing number of blue-collar workers who are prepared openly to protest against the violation of civil and human rights.[91]

To be sure, this degree of commitment to human rights is unusual for East European workers. The developments surrounding the Charter should be viewed within the context of national unity and against the background of the relatively high level of political awareness and interest of the Czech working class. Nevertheless collaboration between workers and intellectual dissidents cannot be seen as a uniquely Czech phenomenon. Recent developments in Poland show that cooperation can take place in different circumstances. Instead of workers participating in an intellectual-led protest against a universally unpopular regime, in Poland it has been a case of intellectuals coming out in opposition to regime suppression of working class dissent.

In September 1976 a small group of intellectual dissidents established the Committee for the Defence of the Workers (KOR) whose objectives were to secure the release and reinstatement of all workers who had been arrested or sacked for participating in the wave of strikes and riots which had taken place in June. Together with the Catholic Church and a wide cross-section of intellectual dissidents KOR also pressed for an independent enquiry into the handling of the strikes and for punishment of all officials found guilty of violating workers' legal rights. On a more practical level, the Committee, alongside the Catholic Church, organised a large-scale collection of funds to support families of men who had been arrested or dismissed from their jobs. By mid-1977, partly as a result of the combined pressure from KOR and the church, all sentences had been suspended, all those arrested in the aftermath of the June events had been released and many of them reinstated in their jobs.[92]

Although the Committee failed to attain all its objectives the campaign marked a significant advance in relations between workers and intellectuals. For the first time in Eastern Europe intellectuals had not merely protested but, at considerable personal cost, had fought against the suppression of workers' rights. Even if their actions can be seen as partly motivated by fear for their own position in a climate of generally tightening controls, they still represented a conscious effort to make up for the inaction of 1970–1 which had produced a nadir in worker-intellectual relations. According to a survey of young workers in Szczecin in 1975 only a tiny minority supported the idea of collaboration between workers and intellectuals, the great majority were totally indifferent to the idea.[93] It is difficult to assess the extent to which the KOR campaign has changed such attitudes. It is reasonable to assume that a measure of trust was established between intellectuals and the several hundred working-class families who received financial aid from KOR. Knowledge of the Committee's activities is probably widespread in the areas directly affected by the post-June repressions yet it is doubtful whether KOR made a national impact. Whereas in Czechoslovakia the official campaign to elicit public condemnation of the Charter ensured that the entire population knew of its existence, the Polish media remained largely silent on KOR activities. According to some reports, many worker activists have not heard of the Committee's campaign and even KOR's organisers acknowledge that they have only a limited number of worker collaborators.[94] And in a sense the events of 1976–7 can be seen in terms of a unilateral intellectual initiative rather than in ones of equal partnership. Even in Czechoslovakia, where a significant number of workers spontaneously supported intellectual protest action, the great majority have given only passive encouragement.

Nonetheless, in both cases there is some evidence of a rapprochement of outlook. Just as suppression of national self-determination has strengthened Czech workers' support for democratic liberties, so the repeated use of coercion against the working class has apparently sensitised Polish workers to issues of human rights. The party commissioned poll conducted after June 1976, which has already been cited, found that freedom of speech came at the top of workers' priorities for reform.[95] Moreover, intellectual dissidents themselves have made a deliberate attempt to create a common pool of concerns which could serve as the basis for solidarity with the working class. Both the Chartist intellectuals and those involved in KOR and its successor, the Committee of Social Self-Defence, have broadened the traditional focus on civil liberties to take in economic rights that are central to workers' concerns. They have put forward demands for improvements in working and living conditions, for modifications in labour law and even for reform of the trade union movement. And while such a shift in emphasis is most evident in Czechoslovakia, where economic issues have been discussed in Charter documents and in Poland, where these points have been raised in joint worker-intellectual publications like *Robotnik*, similar trends have appeared elsewhere in Eastern Europe. In the GDR, for instance, Havemann has recently criticised low wage rates and has expressed sympathy for workers who have resorted to strike action to improve their material situation.[96] Furthermore, there seems to be a growing realisation, especially among younger intellectual dissidents, that traditional attempts to convert reformist-minded politicians to the cause of democratisation must be replaced by a strategy of pressing for the implementation of human rights in the broadest sense, embracing economic as well as political liberties, in alliance with the working class.[97]

To be sure, it is far too early to assess the importance or the impact of such developments. Despite the significance of the advances made in Czechoslovakia and Poland, collaboration between workers and intellectuals remains highly dependent on the catalyst of regime repression. Nonetheless, the increasing willingness of intellectuals to promote economic rights augurs well for future cooperation between the two groups.

CONCLUSIONS

What light does the development of workers' dissent and opposition shed on their general position in East European states? In particular, does the evidence help to assess the validity of the three interpretations to which we referred at the outset?

Workers' instrumental attitude towards their role in the factory and in society indicates widespread alienation which belies the official image of a contented, industrious and committed working class. It might be argued that such alienation is a universal feature of industrial society, and proponents of the incorporation thesis could claim that the individual nonconformity it produces is perfectly acceptable to East European rulers as it keeps dissent diffuse and thus helps to stablise the political system. While nonconformity, which we have called proto-dissent, does have a functional dimension, it not only increases the dissonance between official norms and workers' real values and behaviour but also imposes an increasingly heavy burden on the economy. Similarly, workers' extractive attitude to the state could be seen as facilitating their quiescence, and indeed East European workers seem generally to support the regime and the socialist system. Yet the conditional nature of this support – dependent on the maintenance of the 'social compact' – makes it vulnerable to changing economic conditions. As we have seen, economic rationalisation has placed considerable strains on the 'social compact' and has generated a good deal of working-class dissent.

Just how formidable such dissent becomes depends on the extent to which workers act together in an organised fashion. Opportunities for social mobility and material acquisition, so the incorporated worker argument runs, produce a privatised worker absorbed with his own welfare and dissenting, if at all, in isolation from his colleagues with whom he has little fellow feeling. Class consciousness, let alone class action, is virtually non-existent. It is true that the class action posited in the 'revolutionary class' thesis is not generally to be found in Eastern Europe; only on very rare occasions do large-scale protests assume anything resembling working-class proportions. Nonetheless, there does appear to be some movement towards the beginnings of working-class solidarity. To be sure, workers' views continue to differ according to skill and sector, but there seems to be a growing fund of shared values and interests and an increasing awareness of a common economic, social and even political position. The hardening of social boundaries coupled with the pressure on social compact rights serves to strengthen workers' awareness of a shared class predicament. While such an awareness does not constitute a sufficient condition for the existence of conscious class action, it creates a favourable climate for its development.

Although the overwhelming majority of workers' dissident actions are spontaneous protests, levels of organisation are rising. There are indications that workers' opinion leaders who have been 'siphoned off' into the party or trade union structure are not always effectively neutralised as organisers of workers' dissent actions. Yugoslav, Hungarian, Czech and Polish evidence suggests that members of the factory level organisation *aktiv* are often highly frustrated because of feelings of powerlessness and take a leading role in workers' protests. While workers' collective action is still relatively rare, short-lived and small-scale, attempts to close existing outlets for individual nonconformity and attacks on social compact rights increase the likelihood of resort being made to such forms of dissent. The recent Romanian miners' strike and, more notably, the two waves of stoppages and rioting in Poland show that very large numbers of workers can be prompted to take protest action by measures which they see threatening their material welfare. Moreover, successful protests – and, as we have noted, most of them are successful – tend to reinforce workers' self-confidence and build up class consciousness. A survey of young workers in Szczecin in 1975 showed that their pride in being members of the working class and their high estimation of workers' power stemmed from the events of 1970–1.[98]

One of the major points at issue between the 'incorporation' and the 'revolutionary class' interpretations is whether workers' actions are economistic or political in nature. We have seen that workers almost invariably protest against attacks on their achieved levels of material welfare and that their demands tend to be modest economic ones. However, there are signs that as educational levels and expectations rise, so these demands are becoming more positive and more ambitious. Many economic demands have strong social and ideological overtones and implications: criticism of national economic policy and the repeated calls for a more egalitarian distribution of pay, let alone the frequent attacks on social privilege, cannot be confined by any economic straitjacket. To be sure, economic concerns still come at the top of the workers' list of priorities, yet the institutional roots of much protest action and, more specifically, the demands put forward by Polish workers for free elections to unions and party at factory level and for more meaningful participation, make their protests highly political. And such concerns are not restricted to Poland; anxiety about the performance of the party and the unions is widespread among East European workers.

Even if this wide array of concerns and demands is uncharacteristic of economistic and incorporated workers, it does not necessarily signify the existence of any revolutionary class. In terms of the development of the political system workers are still conservative by inclination. They do not rapidly and spontaneously join movements for political reform nor do they show any ready enthusiasm for taking over control of the means of production. Only under certain conditions do workers become involved directly in political action. National crises prompt them to defend political reforms against external threat. And recent developments in Czechoslovakia and Poland suggest that large-scale repression coupled with intellectual dissidents' espousal of workers' economic demands can also lead to the politicisation of workers' protests. Such worker-intellectual collaboration, albeit highly significant, lacks organisational resources and its prospects still hinge to a large extent on official policy providing sufficient ground for collective protest.

Even without political objectives, workers' dissent still presents East European leaders with considerable problems. In order to avoid workers' protests it is advisable to eschew not only sudden and sharp food price increases but also stagnating living standards and discontinuous economic development. Workers' sensitivity to any infringement of the 'social compact' means that politicians have to tread very cautiously in any attempts to reduce overmanning, to tighten labour discipline and to tie wages to productivity or widen differentials. While Poland is an extreme example of an East European state where maladroit handling of economic changes and workers' protests has created a situation in which policy-makers are severely constrained by working-class pressure, most East European leaders have found their economic options limited by workers' demands. In varying degree they are all caught up in a vicious circle of economic improvement fuelling workers' rising expectations which can only be satisfied by improvements in economic efficiency. Such improvements are impossible, however, without economic rationalisation which meets with resistance from many workers. The current decline in economic growth rates and the sharp fall in projected rates of growth in living standards in part reflect the general problem of sustaining economic progress under these conditions which make an increase in workers' dissent more rather than less likely in future.

There seem to be three ways in which to minimise such dissent. The first involves the radical devolution of decision-making to the enterprises. The partial decentralisation of decision-making, such as has taken place in most East European economies, can often compound rather than alleviate the problem. The considerable power retained by the centre means that workers' protests continue to be directed against national policies and thus can be easily take on political connotations while greater management powers multiply the points of conflict at enterprise level. Only radical devolution along Yugoslav lines can effectively divert strikes and other workers' protests away from national targets. Strikes may become more frequent but they tend to be smaller and targeted against local management and thus largely devoid of political content.

The other two options are more politically feasible for East European leaders inasmuch as they do not involve such drastic and large-scale restructuring. The first involves creating effective institutional channels to articulate workers' grievances and mediate their demands, perhaps along the lines indicated by trade union reform in Hungary. More effective unions would undoubtedly help to prevent the accumulation of discontents and their translation into protest action. Yet there are also certain risks inherent in such a course. As Hungarian experience has shown, more effective union defence of workers' interests limits economic policy choices and can slow down growth. Moreover, powerful trade unions might lead to a weakening of party control and, in view of workers' strong preference for unions as defence organisations, union reform could stimulate a general growth of interest group activity. The last option is a much longer-term solution: a re-education of the workers that would loosen their attachment to security and stability and induce them to accept stricter discipline and greater risk for higher if less certain rewards. In effect, this would involve replacing the existing 'social compact', which is labouring under increasing strains, with a new one, more dynamic and flexible and also, ironically, more capitalist in nature.

NOTES

1. See A. Hegedüs, 'The Relevance of the Trade Union Debate', in Hegedüs, *Socialism and Bureaucracy* (London: Allison and Busby, 1976), p. 90; Kádár, cited in W. F. Robinson, 'The Pattern of Reform in Hungary Part I', Radio Free Europe (RFE) *Hungarian Background Report*, no. 17, 1970, p. 85; P. A. Toma and I. Volgyes, *Politics in Hungary* (San Francisco: W. H. Freeman and Co., 1977), pp. 62–3. Cf. S. Widerszpil, *Skład polskiej klasy robotniczej. Tendencje zmian w okresie industrializacji socjalisticznej* (Warsaw: PWN, 1965), pp. 92–6.
2. See, for instance, J. Kuroń and K. Modzelewski, 'An Open Letter', in G. L. Weissman, ed., *Revolutionary Marxist Students Speak* (New York: Pathfinder Press, 1972), pp. 58–75; C. Harman, *Bureaucracy and Revolution in Eastern Europe* (London: Pluto Press, 1974). A. Giddens gives a far more moderate and reasoned version of the thesis in *The Class Structure of the Advanced Societies* (London: Hutchinson, 1973), pp. 251, 268–9.
3. See Z. Bauman, 'Social Dissent in the East European Political System', *European Journal of Sociology* XII (1971), pp. 30–31 and 'Officialdom and Class', in F. Parkin ed., *The Social Analysis of Class Structure* (London: Tavistock, 1974), p. 146; D. Lane, 'Dissent and Consent under Socialism', *European Journal of Sociology*, XIII (1972), p. 44 and *The Socialist Industrial State* (London: Allen and Unwin, 1976), pp. 91, 98–100.
4. See Kuroń and Modzelewski; and Lane, *The Socialist Industrial State*, pp. 99–100.
5. For discussion of the relationship between volatility, militancy and peasant origins, see R. F. Hamilton, *Affluence and the French Worker in the Fourth Republic* (Princeton: Princeton University Press, 1970), pp. 121–9. For composition of the working class in Eastern Europe see Bauman, 'Social Dissent', pp. 34–5; W. D. Connor, 'Social Change and Stability in Eastern Europe', *Problems of Communism*, XXVI, no. 6 (November-December, 1977), pp. 20–1; Toma and Volgyes, p. 44; Widerszpil, p. 259; and V. Rollová, 'Sociální diferenciace podle ekonomického postavení a problém spolenčenských tříd', in P. Machonin *et al.*, *Československá společnost* (Bratislava: Epocha, 1969), p. 330.
6. See I. Szelényi, 'Housing System and Social Structure', in P. Halmos ed., *Hungarian Society, Sociological Review Monograph* no. 17 (Keele: Keele

University Press, 1972), pp. 270, 282, and *Social Inequalities in State Socialist Redistributive Economies – Dilemma for Contemporary Socialist Societies of Eastern Europe* (Flinders University of South Australia, School of Social Sciences paper, 1977), pp. 4, 21.

7. B. Jungmann, 'Sebehodnocení a sebeidentifikace', in Machonin *et al.*, pp. 365, 376; cf. the lower but considerable self-assignment found in one Polish sample, see J. Malanowski, *Stosunki klasowe i różnice społeczne w mieśce* (Warsaw, 1967), p. 344.

8. See Connor, p. 26; Bauman, 'Social Dissent', p. 44; and S. Ferge, 'Social Stratification in Hungary', *Valóság*, October 1966, translated in RFE *Hungarian Press Survey* 1850 (29 July 1967), pp. 17–22.

9. See C. Gati, ed., *The Politics of Modernization in Eastern Europe* (New York: Praeger, 1974), pp. 234, 236; *Rocznik Statystyczny*, 1976 (Warsaw: GUS, 1976), p. 291; and B. Denitch, *The Legitimation of a Revolution. The Yugoslav Case* (New Haven and London: Yale University Press, 1976), p. 91.

10. See Jungmann, pp. 367, 373; L. Brokl, 'Moc a sociální rozvrstvení' in Machonin *et al.*, pp. 244–50; Malanowski, p. 345; H. Kovács, *A munkásosztály politikai-ideológiai műveltségéről és aktivitásáról* (Budapest: Kossuth, 1976), table 4; and V. Arzenšek, 'Alienation and Self-Management' (paper presented at the Second International Conference on Participation, Workers' Control and Self-Management, Paris, 7–10 September, 1977), p. 6.

11. See H. H. Gerth and C. Wright Mills, eds., *From Max Weber* (London: Routledge and Kegan Paul, 1948), pp. 181, 184; and A. Etzioni, *The Active Society* (New York: Free Press, 1968), pp. 329.

12. See R. Dyoniziak, *Społeczne uwarunkowanie wydajności pracy* (Warsaw, 1967), pp. 73–4, 136–7, 146–9; A. Matejko, 'Some Sociological Problems of Socialist Factories', *Social Research 36*, no. 3 (Autumn 1969), p. 463; K. Doktor, *Przedsiębiorstwo przemyslowe* (Warsaw: Książka i Wiedza, 1964), p. 223; *Odborář*, no. 4, 1968, p. 11; M. Haraszti, *A Worker in a Worker's State* (London: Penguin, 1977), pp. 71–2, 154; and A. Hegedüs and Rozgonyi, 'Social Conflicts in Industrial Plants', *Valóság*, December 1967, translated in RFE *Hungarian Background Report* no. 3, 1968, p. 11.

13. See Z. Sufin, 'Wspolzależności medzy technicznymi organizacejnymi i spolecznie warunkowanie pracy', *Studia Socjologiczno-Politiczne*, 15 (1963), p. 32; L. Kazmyrczuk, cited in D. Pirages, *Modernization and Political Tension Management: a Socialist Society in Perspective* (New York: Praeger, 1972), p. 128; Matejko, 'Some Problems', p. 452; *Hospodařské noviny*, 7 July 1967; and *Odborář*, no. 10, 1969, p. 9. Levels of antagonism in Western European countries, notably France, appear to be much higher, see M. Mann, *Consciousness and Action among the Western Working Class* (London: Macmillan, 1973), p. 35.

14. For instance see A. Matejko, *Social Change and Stratification in Eastern Europe* (New York: Praeger, 1974), p. 108; W. F. Robinson, *The Pattern of Reform in Hungary: a Political, Economic and Cultural Analysis* (New York: Praeger, 1973), p. 344; and Doktor, p. 195. For support for 'cradle to grave' welfare in the Soviet Union, see A. Inkeles and R.

256   *Opposition in Eastern Europe*

Bauer, *The Soviet Citizen. Daily Life in a Totalitarian Society* (Cambridge, Mass.: Harvard University Press, 1959), pp. 233–8.

15. Matejko, *Social Change*, pp. 109–110; *Népszabadság* 5 October 1969 (survey of 5000 Győr workers); A. Sarapata, 'Plynnośc w przedsiębiorstwe przemysłowym', in G. W. Osipow and J. Szczepanski eds., *Społeczne problemy pracy i produkcji* (Warsaw: Książka i Wiedza, 1970), p. 298; and J. Kulpińska, *Spoleczna aktywność pracowników przedsiębiorstwa przemysłowego* (Wroclaw, 1970), p. 74.

16. Vörös, *Literárni listy*, 30 May 1968; *Zemedelské noviny*, 17 February 1968. Cf. Hungarian workers' wariness, G. P. Lautner, *The Manager and Economic Reform in Hungary* (New York: Praeger, 1972), pp. 83, 86–7.

17. See J. Rézler, 'Recent Developments in the Hungarian Labor Market', *East European Quarterly*, X, no. 2 (1976), pp. 255–64; V. Holešovský, 'Czechoslovak Economy in the Seventies', in *East European Economies Post-Helsinki* (Washington D.C.: US Government Printing Office, 1977), p. 706; H. Shaefer, 'The State of Economic Reform in Hungary', *RFE Hungarian Background Report*, no. 4, 1973; K. Macsári, *Népszava* 30 July 1967, translated in RFE *Hungarian Press Survey*, no. 1839 (30 July 1967), pp. 9–11; and A. Pravda, 'Some Aspects of the Czechoslovak Economic Reform and the Working Class in 1968', *Soviet Studies*, XXV, no. 1 (July 1973), pp. 109–10. For an account of one case of redundancy in Yugoslavia, see G. Hunnius, 'Workers' Self-Management in Yugoslavia', in G. Hunnius, G. D. Galson and J. Case, eds., *Workers' Control* (New York: Random House, 1973), pp. 308–9.

18. Robinson, p. 327; 'Internal Party Problems and the NEM', RFE *Hungarian Background Report*, no. 6, 1973, p. 21; R. Portes, 'The Strategy and Tactics of Economic Decentralisation', *Soviet Studies*, XXIII, no. 4 (April 1972), p. 642; and cf. Hunnius, 'Yugoslavia', p. 307.

19. Dyoniziak, p. 187; Doktor, pp. 225, 228–30; *Odborář*, no. 10, 1969. For the official line here, see Gierek, *Trybuna Ludu*, 9 December 1975, and Strougal, *Rudé právo*, 14 April 1976.

20. *Népszava*, 11 April 1971 cited in W. F. Robinson, 'What is a Socialist Society', RFE *Hungarian Background Report*, no. 13, 1971, p. 26; *Népszava*, 11 October 1973, cited in RFE *Hungarian Situation Report*, no. 37, p. 3; and R. Portes, 'Hungary: Economic Performance, Policy and Prospects', in *East European Economies Post-Helsinki*, p. 786.

21. Hegedüs and Rozgonyi, p. 10; and L. Gilejko, 'Formirowanie się i rola samorządu robotniczego', in W. Wesołowski, ed., *25 lat Polskiej Ludowej: struktura i dynamiku spoleczeństwa polskiego* (Warsaw 1970), pp. 188–90.

22. See A. Malewski, 'Attitudes of the Employees from Warsaw Enterprises toward the Differentiation of Wages and the Social System in May 1958', *Polish Sociological Bulletin*, no. 2, 1971, p. 29; Małanowski, pp. 19–22; *Hospodařské noviny*, no. 12, 1972, p. 6; Hegedüs and Rozgonyi, p. 11; Denitch, pp. 172–4; and A. Whitehorn, 'Alienation and Industrial Society' (paper presented at the Second International Conference on Participation, Workers' Control and Self-Management, Paris, 7–10 September 1977), p. 6. For the 1968 scheme in Hungary, see Portes, 'Hungary', p. 785.

23. Toma and Volgyes, p. 34; *Népszava*, 10 and 31 December 1972, cited in W. F. Robinson, 'Hungary's Industrial Workers: increasing success as a pressure group', RFE *Background Report*, no. 2, 1973, pp. 5–6; and cf. *Tvorba*, 4 January 1976.

24. Hungary provides by far the best example of this; see Robinson, *The Pattern of Reform*, pp. 359–60, 332–3; and Portes, 'Hungary', pp. 785–95.

25. See the report of a survey of a national sample of 2800 worker communists conducted after the events of June 1976, O. MacDonald, 'Poland: Party, Workers and Opposition', *Labour Focus on Eastern Europe*, I, no. 2 (May–June 1977), p. 3.

26. Sarapata, pp. 284–8; Rézler, p. 258; Portes, 'Hungary', p. 782; *Tribuna*, 2 March 1973 and *Svět Práce*, 28 October 1973.

27. J. Venyige in *Közgazdasági. Szemle*, no. 9, 1973, pp. 1022–36, abstracted in *Referativny sbornik: Ekonomika promyshlennosti*, no. 4, 1974, pp. 22–23; M. Komarek in *Odbory a společnost*, no. 3, 1975, pp. 96–102; and M. Cernea, 'Individual Motivation and Labor Turnover under Socialism', *Studies in Comparative International Development* (Fall 1973), pp. 305, 314–15.

28. RFE *Hungarian Background Report*, no. 8, 1977, p. 5; Rézler, pp. 258, 266; Portes, 'Hungary', p. 782; and, for the GDR, see B. Mieczkowski, *Personal and Social Consumption in Eastern Europe* (New York: Praeger, 1975), p. 254.

29. *Trybuna Ludu*, 21–22 September and 24–26 October 1975; *Népszabadság*, 12 March 1976, cited in RFE *Hungarian Situation Report*, no. 11, 1976, pp. 6–7. For official figures, see *Statistická ročenka 1970* (Prague: SNTL, 1970), pp. 238, 273; *Rocznik Statystyczny 1976*, pp. 163, 217; and M. J. Ziomek, *Absencija w Pracy* (Warsaw: PWE, 1964), pp. 17, 62.

30. See Karel Honza, 'Co si myslí dělníci', *Listy* v, no. 4 (1975), pp. 1–4; Dyoniziak, p. 107; *Odbory a společnost*, no. 4, 1973, pp. 83–89; and *Élet és Irodalom*, 20 June 1970, cited in RFE *Situation Report*, no. 25, 1970, p. 2. A summary of the results of the survey, conducted in 1961, is to be found in Pirages, pp. 119–22.

31. *Trybuna Ludu*, 24–26 October 1975; *Rocznik Statystyczny 1976*, p. 163; *Práce*, 3 July 1970; M. Šarišsky, 'Problematika pracovnich absencií v podnikovej praxi', *Odbory a společnost*, no. 2, 1975, pp. 98–102; and H. Szostkiewicz, 'Niektóre czinniki zakłocające funkcjonowanie zakładu pracy', in S. Widerszpil, ed., *Socjologia w zakładzie pracy* (Warsaw: CRZZ, 1973), pp. 259, 264.

32. L. Héthy and C. Makó, 'Work Performance, Interests, Powers and Environment (The case of cyclical slowdowns in a Hungarian factory)' in P. Halmos, pp. 125–49.

33. M. Gamarnikow, *Economic Reforms in Eastern Europe* (Detroit: Wayne State University Press, 1968), p. 155; *Práce*, 13 March 1969; and *Odborář*, no. 7, 1968, p. 10.

34. N. Jovanov, 'O Štrajkovima u Socialističkoj Federativnoj Republici Jugoslaviji', *Proceedings* of the Annual Conference of the Yugoslav Sociological Association at Portorož, 10–13 February 1972, vol. 3,

pp. 111, 122, cited in P. Jambrek, *Development and Social Change in Yugoslavia* (London: Saxon House, 1975), pp. 193-4.

35. P. Barton, *Misère et révolte de l'ouvrier polonais* (Paris: Les Editions Ouvrieres, 1971), pp. 62, 126-34; and A. Mihailescu, 'Miners Strike Jolts Ceausescu', *Labour Focus on Eastern Europe*, I, no. 5 (November-December 1977), pp. 8-10.

36. Łódź is a case in point; see Barton, pp. 148-9; cf. the occurrence of strikes in 1953 in the GDR in areas with strike traditions, see A. Baring, *Uprising in East Germany 17 June 1953* (London: Cornell UP, 1972), pp. 155, 164.

37. E. Baluka and E. Barker, 'Workers' Struggle in Poland', *International Socialism*, June 1977; E. Wacowska, *Poznań 1956-Grudzien 1970* (Paris: Kultura, 1971), p. 170; and Mihailescu, p. 12. The only accurate figures for the duration of strikes are for Yugoslavia between 1958 and 1969 when 78 per cent of strikes lasted less than a day; see Jovanov, p. 122, cited in Jambrek, p. 194.

38. Baluka and Barker, p. 25; and E. Wacowska, *Rewolta Szczecińska i jej znaczenie* (Paris: Kultura, 1971), p. 104. East European experience seems to confirm generalisations based on French evidence, see A. Shorter and C. Tilly, *Strikes in France* (London: Cambridge U.P., 1974), pp. 13, 227, and Hamilton, pp. 121-129.

39. According to Jovanov's study of Yugoslav strikes between 1958 and 1969 only 23 per cent were unproductive from the workers' standpoint; see Jambrek, p. 197, Cf. strike results in Czechoslovakia in 1968; see *Radio Prague* 12 April 1968 and *Železničář*, 12 June 1968.

40. M. Gamarnikow, 'A New Economic Approach', *Problems of Communism*, XXI, no. 5 (September-October 1972), pp. 20-1; and Mihailescu, p. 10.

41. For instance, see the East German party Central Committee resolution on the events of 1953, Baring, pp. 167-8 and that of the Polish Party in February 1971, *Nowe Drogi* (special number, no date) translated in RFE *Polish Press Survey* no. 2313 (14 July 1971), pp. 2-10.

42. Baring, pp. 72-3; Wacowska, *Poznań*, pp. 170-1; Baluka and Barker, pp. 21-22; Pravda, pp. 111-112; and S. Stankovic, 'Workers' Strikes not permitted but tolerated in Yugoslavia', RFE *Background Report*, no. 247, 1977, pp. 5-6.

43. *Glos Szczeciński*, 14 January 1971, translated in RFE *Polish Press Survey*, no. 2282 (9 March 1971), p. 4; *Glos Koszalinski*, 15 February 1971, translated in RFE *Polish Press Survey*, no. 2287 (23 March 1971), pp. 2-3; and Mihailescu, p. 12.

44. Baring, pp. 32-3; Wacowska, *Rewolta*, pp. 26-7; and 'Polish Workers and Party Leaders', *New Left Review*, no. 72 (March-April 1972), pp. 36-7.

45. Barton, p. 134; *Glos Szczeciński*, 9-10, 11 and 16-17 January 1971, translated in RFE *Polish Press Survey*, no. 2282 (9 March 1971), pp. 6, 15, 18; and Baring, pp. 72-5.

46. R. Hiscocks, *Poland: Bridge for the Abyss?* (London: Oxford University Press, 1963), p. 288; *Népszabadság*, 4 July 1976, cited in RFE *Hungarian Situation Report*, no. 24, 1976, p. 4; A. R. Johnson, 'Polish

Perspectives, Past and Present', *Problems of Communism*, xx, no. 4 (July–August 1971), p. 59; and *Dissent in Poland 1976–1977* (London, 1977), pp. 50–1. Prices were also raised in Hungary in 1966; see Portes, 'The Strategy and Tactics', p. 647.

47. *Népszabadság*, 17 and 24 November 1972, cited in Robinson, 'Hungary's Industrial Workers'; Portes, 'Hungary', pp. 785–7. For Polish experience here, see Gamarnikow, 'A New Economic Approach', p. 21.

48. Jovanov, p. 111, cited in Jambrek, p. 193 (for income levels in Yugoslavia, see p. 261); and *Statistická ročenka*, 1970, p. 23. For a discussion of patterns of relative deprivation, see T. R. Gurr, *Why Men Rebel* (Princeton: Princeton University Press, 1970), p. 46.

49. B. Seidler, *Życie Literackie*, 21 February 1971; D. Lane, 'Social Groups in Polish Society', in Lane and G. Kolankiewicz, eds., *Social Groups in Polish Society* (London: Macmillan, 1973), pp. 314–15. Cf. Wacowska, *Poznań*, pp. 161–2; and Baring, p. 31.

50. For the 1972 poll, see *Życie Partii*, April 1973, and for that of 1975, see A. Wajda, 'Jedność społecznych i ekonomicznych celów polityki partii w wielkich zakladow pracy', in A. Łopatka, J. Błuszkowski and K. Konstanski, eds., *Organizacje partyjne wielkich zakładow pracy* (Warsaw: Książka i Wiedza, 1976), p. 66. For the other instances of rising expectations, see Baring, pp. 3–20, and Wacowska, *Poznań*, p. 158.

51. Wajda, p. 69; and *Polityka*, 15 March and 13 December 1975.

52. Barton, pp. 113–14; Karkoszka, *Nowe Drogi* (special number, 1971), translated in RFE *Polish Press Survey*, no. 2318 (13 August 1971), p. 4; and *Trybuna Ludu*, 3 August 1976. For Hungary, see *Radio Budapest 28* and 30 November 1975, cited in RFE *Hungarian Situation Report*, no. 50, 1975.

53. See Seidler; Komitet Obrony Robotników, *Zeszyt I* (London, 1976); and *Dissent in Poland*, parts 4–6.

54. Wajda, p. 75; and MacDonald, p. 3.

55. See 'Development, Institutionalization and Elite-Mass Relations in Poland', in J. F. Triska and P. M. Cocks, eds., *Political Development in Eastern Europe* (New York: Praeger, 1977), pp. 124ff.

56. Arzenšek, p. 29; A. Owieczko, 'Samorząd robotniczy w przedsiębiorstwe przemysłowym a zaloga', *Studia Socjologiczno-Politiczne*, 22 (1967), p. 79; also cited in Gitelman, p. 133. Cf. M. Hirszowicz and W. Morawski, *Z badań społecznym uczestnictwem w organizacji przemysłowej* (Warsaw 1967), p. 228. For workers' representation in the Polish party, see A. Stasiuk, 'Czynni i bierni członkowe partii w zakładzie przemysłowym', *Studia Socjologiczno-Politiczne*, 16 (1964), pp. 80–90; and Héthy and Makó, p. 139.

57. *Polityka*, 13 December 1975; J. Kubaszewicz *et al.*, 'Rola organizaceji partynych w wielkich zakładach pracy', *Nowe Drogi*, no. 4, 1976, pp. 64–71; and Wajda, p. 75. For criticism of communication in 1970, see Karkoszka at the February 1971 meeting of the Central Committee, *Nowe Drogi* (special number, 1971) translated in RFE *Polish Press Survey* no. 2318 (13 August 1971), pp. 4–5, 14.

58. See J. B. Weydenthal, 'Party Development in Contemporary Poland', *East European Quarterly*, xi, no. 3 (Fall 1977), pp. 344–7; Robinson,

The Pattern of Reform, pp. 337–40; Zupanov, *NIN*, 26 September 1976.

59. Robinson, *The Pattern of Reform*, p. 329; K. Ostrowski, *Rola związków zawodowych w polskim systemie politicznym* (Warsaw: PAN, 1970), pp. 75–6; Hirszowicz and Morawski, pp. 267, 325; and Arzenšek, p. 14.

60. Hirszowicz and Morawski, p. 332. Arzenšek found in an eleven-enterprise survey in Slovenia in 1973–4 that only one in four workers thought that the unions represented their interests, pp. 21, 29.

61. Owieczko, pp. 79, 82, cited in Gitelman, p. 133; Hirszowicz and Morawski, p. 238; cf. V. Rus, 'Influence Structure in Yugoslav Enterprises', *Industrial Relations*, 9, no. 2 (February 1970), pp. 151, 154. For union reform movements, see T. Lowit, *Le syndicalisme de type soviétique* (Paris: Armand Colin, 1971), pp. 270–1, 279–81.

62. L. Gilejko, *Związki zawodowe w procesie przemian społeczne w PRL* (Warsaw, 1972), pp. 123–5; and Wajda, p. 75.

63. C. B. Scharf, *Labor Organizations in East German Society* (Stanford: unpublished PhD Thesis, 1972), pp. 313ff.

64. Robinson, pp. 238–40; Gamarnikow, 'Economic Reforms', p. 147; 'Hungary: one year after Part I, the Political Scene', RFE *Hungarian Background Report*, no. 17, 1973, p. 12; and *Népszava* 11 August 1970, cited in RFE *Hungarian Situation Report*, no. 32, 1970, p. 7.

65. Robinson, 331–5; *Népszava*, 27 September 1969, cited in 'Hungarian Trade Unions to assume a more active and critical role', RFE *Hungarian Background Report*, no. 48, 1969, pp. 2–3; and *Népszava*, 11 August 1970, cited in RFE *Hungarian Situation Report*, no. 32, 1970, p. 7.

66. Héthy and Makó, p. 146; Haraszti, pp. 135–6; Scharf, pp. 238–52; *Scienteia*, 10 July 1977, cited in RFE *Romanian Situation Report*, no. 24, 1977; and A. Pravda, 'Workers' Participation in Czechoslovakia, 1968–1969', *Canadian Slavonic Papers*, XIX, no. 3 (September 1977), p. 314.

67. Gilejko, 'Formowanie', pp. 188–92; and G. Kolankiewicz, 'The Working Class', in Lane and Kolankiewicz, pp. 139–40.

68. Hirszowicz and Morawski, pp. 60–1, 78, 97, 107; Gilejko, 'Formowanie', pp. 202, 205; and cf. Owieczko, p. 79, cited in Gitelman, p. 133.

69. See R. Stefanowski, 'Workers' Councils 1956–1977', RFE *RAD Background Report*, no. 160 (Poland), 1977, pp. 19–20.

70. See *Scienteia*, 12–15 July 1977, cited in RFE *Romanian Situation Report*, no. 24, 1977, pp. 10–12.

71. *Népszava*, 1 May 1977, cited in RFE *Hungarian Situation Report*, no. 17, 1977.

72. See A. Babeau, *Les conseils ouvriers en Pologne* (Paris: Armand Colin, 1960), pp. 193–4, 251–69; Pravda, 'Workers' Participation', pp. 328–32; B. Lomax, *Hungary 1956* (London: Allison and Busby, 1976), p. 85; and J. Kolaja, *A Polish Factory* (Lexington: University of Kentucky Press, 1960), pp. 27–34.

73. P. Blumberg, *Industrial Democracy* (London: Constable, 1971), p. 229; Babeau, pp. 56–7; M. Jarosz, J. Kulpińska and H. Szostkiewicz, *Samorząd w opiniach załog fabrycznych* (Łódź, 1962), pp. 101, 106; and Pravda, 'Workers' Participation', pp. 321–5.

74. One in five of the strikes between 1958 and 1969 were directed against workers' councils; see Jovanov cited in Jambrek, p. 197. On workers' attitudes, see V. Rus, pp. 150–5; L. Benson, 'Market Socialism and Class Structure: the Workers and Managerial Power in the Yugoslav enterprise', in F. Parkin, ed., pp. 255, 263–4; and R. Supek, cited in Denitch, p. 165.

75. J. Obradović, 'Participation and Work Attitudes in Yugoslavia', *Industrial Relations*, IX no. 2 (February 1970), p. 169; and Arzensek, p. 11.

76. Kolankiewicz, pp. 98–100; Wacowska, *Poznań*, p. 115; Lomax, pp. 19, 22; and Pravda, 'Some Aspects', pp. 114, 121–2.

77. One survey of 608 Polish workers in 1970 found that 18.3 per cent of the unskilled and 25 per cent of the skilled respondents were interested in politics; see T. Gospodarek, 'Z badań nad kulturą polityczną w zakładach wielkoprzemysłowych', *Studie Socjologiczne*, no. 41 (1971), p. 287. For Hungarian workers' attitudes, see L. Molnár, N. Ferenc and B. Szalai, *Ipari munkások politikai aktivitása* (Budapest: Kossuth, 1970), p. 109 which shows very low levels of interest, while Kovács, table 1, indicates higher interest than in Poland.

78. See K. Syrop, *Spring in October* (London: Weidenfeld and Nicolson, 1957), pp. 135–43; R. Littell, ed., *The Czech Black Book* (London: Pall Mall, 1969); Lomax, pp. 84, 111; and P. Kecskemeti, *The Unexpected Revolution* (Stanford: Stanford U.P., 1961), pp. 109, 115.

79. The best analysis of the various traditions is to be found in A. H. Brown and J. Gray eds., *Political Culture and Political Change in Communist States* (London: Macmillan, 1977). For the radicalising effect of rural origins, see Hamilton, pp. 121–9.

80. Kuroń and Modzelewski, p. 60; Lomax, pp. 94–5; and Kecskemeti, pp. 146–7.

81. *Práce*, 3 and 10 January 1969, and *Rudé právo*, 1 February 1972. For Poland see Babeau, pp. 220–6, and for Hungary Lomax, ch. 5.

82. Ibid., pp. 158–60; J. J. Marie and B. Nagy eds., *Pologne-Hongrie* (Paris: 1966), pp. 297–304; and Pravda, 'Workers' Participation', pp. 333–4.

83. For rises in the standard of living in post-crisis years, see *Rocznik Statystyczny*, 1967, p. 522 and *Práce a mzda*, no. 7, 1971, p. 387. For changes in absenteeism in Poland see Ziomek, pp. 17, 62, and for fluctuations in party membership in Czechoslovakia, G. Wightman and A. H. Brown, 'Changes in the Levels of Membership and Social Composition of the Communist Party of Czechoslovakia 1945–1973', *Soviet Studies*, XXVII, no. 3 (July 1975), pp. 414–17.

84. Moczar at the Polish Party Central Committee meeting in February 1971, *Nowe Drogi* (special number 1971), translated in RFE *Polish Press Survey*, no. 2314 (15 July 1971), p. 8; and Barton, pp. 186–7. For general relations, see Malanowski, pp. 274, 298; K. Wąsiak, 'Views of Szczecin Working Youth concerning the Role of Social Classes in Poland', *Kultura i Społeczenstwo*, no. 2, 1976 translated in Joint Publications Research Services, *East European Political, Sociological and Military Affairs*, no. 1307 (1961), p. 61; and L. Vaculik, *Literární listy*, 21 April 1968.

85. See Lomax, p. 48; and A. Oxley, A. Pravda, A. Ritchie eds., *Czecho-*

slovakia: the Party and the People (London: Allen Lane, 1973), pp. 177–90.

86. P. Tomalek, *Czechoslovakia 1968–1969: the Worker-Student Alliance* (Cambridge, Mass.: MIT paper, 1971), pp. 18–37; Lomax, pp. 81, 95, 98, 110; and Kolaja, p. 41.

87. Bauman, 'Social Dissent', pp. 49, 50 and 'Twenty Years After: the Crisis of Soviet-Type Systems', *Problems of Communism*, XX, no. 6 (November–December 1971). Hungarian survey evidence indicates a high level of worker support for the regime despite awareness of the lack of democratic rights; see Kovács, tables 4 and 14.

88. Malewski, pp. 19–22; Denitch, pp. 173–4; Piekalkiewicz, pp. 212, 223; and G. Kolankiewicz and R. Taras, 'Poland: Socialism for Everyman?', in Brown and Gray, pp. 108–9.

89. See V. V. Kusin, *Political Grouping in the Czechoslovak Reform Movement* (London: Macmillan, 1972), pp. 34–6.

90. Kroubek, *Nová mysl*, no. 1, 1969, pp. 78–87.

91. See J. Kavan, 'One Year of Charter 77', *Labour Focus on Eastern Europe*, I no. 6 (January–February 1978), p. 2; *Palach Press Bulletin*, nos. 5–6 (March 1977), pp. 17, 27–8.

92. Komitet Obrony Robotników, *Zeszyt I*; and *Wypadki czercowe i działalność Komitetu Obrony Robotników* (London, 1977); and *Dissent in Poland*, pp. 79–151.

93. Wasiak, p. 62.

94. See MacDonald, p. 4.

95. Ibid., p. 3.

96. Havemann interview in *Le Monde*, 21 February 1978; Charter Document no. 7, *Labour Focus on Eastern Europe*, I, no. 2 (1977), pp. 11–13; and *Robotnik* nos. 1–3, abstracted in RFE *RAD Background Report* (Poland), no. 255 (1977), pp. 14–15.

97. See for instance, A. Michnik, 'The New Evolutionism', *Survey*, 22, nos. 3–4 (Summer–Autumn 1976), pp. 267–77.

98. Wasiak, pp. 45, 52.

8 Potential Sources of Opposition in the East European Peasantry

by PAUL G. LEWIS

The resistance that the peasants of Eastern Europe offered to the establishment of communist power was centred on the conflict stemming from the peasants' desire to retain an independent form of agriculture in contrast to the communist leaders' determination (more pronounced in some cases than in others) to achieve the social transformation of the countryside in a collectivist direction. It is now a decade and a half since this collectivisation process was largely brought to a close. This transformation of the social features of the East European countryside, commencing in 1949, lasted some thirteen years and turned out to be a smoother and more thoroughgoing process in some countries than in others. The pace of collectivisation slowed markedly following Stalin's death and in some countries a number of collective farms were dissolved. A second phase of collectivisation was launched between 1957 and 1959 and the establishment of collective agriculture in most countries of Eastern Europe was more or less complete by 1962. In Yugoslavia and Poland a second phase of collectivisation never was launched and agriculture there has largely remained in the hands of independent farmers since the fifties. The trauma of collectivisation thus lies even further back in those countries.

Concurrent with and following collectivisation the East European regimes have placed a major emphasis on a policy of planned industrialisation. As a result of this the contribution of agriculture to national income and the proportion of the population engaged in farming has dropped sharply since the establishment of communist power in Eastern Europe (see Table 8.1). But despite this decline in the relative weight of the agricultural population in East European societies the number of those who might be encompassed by the term 'agricultural' still reached nearly 47 million in 1970. The peasantry and the agricultural population therefore still occupy an extremely important place in East European society. There can, too, be little doubt that

Table 8.1
Proportion of the Economically Active Population in Agriculture[1]

	1960	1970	Total agricultural population (1970)
E. Germany	18%	13%	2.216 million
Czechoslovakia	26%	17%	2.424 million
Hungary	38%	25%	2.486 million
Poland	48%	39%	12.669 million
Bulgaria	57%	47%	3.958 million
Yugoslavia	64%	50%	10.143 million
Romania	65%	56%	11.336 million
Albania	71%	66%	1.437 million
			46.769 million

collectivisation had an extremely important effect on the social consciousness of the peasant population. It was one of the most unpopular processes set under way by communist leaders and was one of the most potent sources of conflict during the early years of communist power. It put in reverse the process of recovery that was taking place in agriculture following the end of the war, bringing about a fall in farm output and cutting living standards in the countryside; it was responsible for forging an unprecedented degree of solidarity between diverse groups in opposition to national policy; and, in Poland and Hungary, it provided a good deal of the force behind the movements that pressed for changes in the leadership of those countries in 1956.

But with the passage of years it might now be usefully asked how far collective agriculture remains an issue of prime importance in determining the nature of the relationship that pertains between the East European peasantry and the communist regimes. It may well now be the case that the issue of private or collective ownership and production no longer plays such an important part in forming peasant social and political attitudes. If this is the case then a closer examination of subsequent development in the agricultural sector of East European society is called for. If change in the peasants' social consciousness has occurred and new values have been accepted then new issues of conflict may have arisen in relations between peasant farmers and the communist authorities. After an examination of the present status of the issues that were central to the conflicts of the collectivisation period I shall continue with a discussion of the contemporary social position of the peasantry and of more recent topics of possible disagreement that may have emerged as alternative sources of peasant opposition to the prevailing system in Eastern Europe.

CONFLICT ISSUES OF THE EARLY COMMUNIST PERIOD

The conflict that characterised the collectivisation period, particularly during its first phase in the early fifties, was, of course, not just limited in its scope to the ownership of land and to the control of the resources employed on it. The economic, social and political battles that were fought at this time were also bound in with the communist regimes' efforts to defeat all opposition to their assumption of power, to establish their claim to authority on a firmer base and to assert their legitimacy as inheritors of the communist revolutionary tradition. It was for a combination of reasons associated with these factors that the peasantry provided a focus for the social transformation that was envisaged by the communist leaders. In a number of countries, particularly in Hungary, Poland and Bulgaria, peasant parties had provided the basis for political opposition to the communists' seizure of power and the peasants, somewhat paradoxically, appeared as the group most attached to the principles of parliamentary democracy. Apart from the peasant parties, another major focus of opposition to the communist parties were the churches. This was particularly true of the Catholic Church, in whose international organisation the communists saw a direct ideological and political competitor. It was, moreover, precisely in the countryside and amongst the peasants that the traditional churches found their most fervent and unquestioning supporters. The two major institutional opponents of East European communism, therefore, both looked to the peasantry as their primary social constituency.

There were also pressing socioeconomic reasons for the young communist regimes to turn their attention to the countryside at an early stage. Industrialisation was a high priority – both on ideological grounds, with the commitment to the construction of the workers' state, and for socioeconomic reasons, to put right the problem of economic backwardness which had contributed to the political weakness of the East European states between the wars. The countryside was seen as a reservoir of manpower for newly built industries and as a source of the capital that had to be found if those industries were to come into existence. It hardly needs to be said, of course, that virtually all were in agreement that some radical measures needed to be taken to cope with the problems of East European agriculture and the population it was barely able to maintain. In general it was a backward agriculture (certain areas, such as Bohemia and Western Poland were exceptions in this respect): inadequately equipped, conducted within an inappropriate structure of land holdings, and insufficiently productive to sustain or occupy the many millions who had to depend on it for their livelihood. There were, then, ample reasons for launching a programme of radical change in the countryside, although not for the policy of collectivisation which actually lowered production levels, starved agriculture of much needed resources, disrupted the economic infrastructure of the countryside and stiffened the resistance of its inhabitants.

Developments during the first stage of the collectivisation process, therefore, provided the peasants with firmly based grounds for resentment towards and suspicion of the communist regime. Feelings of rural solidarity were greatly strengthened by state intervention and the attack launched on the villages by regimes whose authority was not generally accepted. With the death of Stalin and the adoption of a New Course in the Soviet Union the pressure eased also in the East European countryside. Collectivisation virtually came to a halt in Romania and Poland. Seizing the opportunity provided, a number of peasants in Czechoslovakia and Hungary dissolved the production co-operatives they had unwillingly been led to set up. In Yugoslavia the collective sector was even more severely diminished following the chaos and economic decline that ensued with Tito's attempt to prove himself holier than the Pope of Stalinist communism with Yugoslavia's departure from the Soviet bloc in 1948. Deleterious though the economic effects of collectivisation throughout Eastern Europe were, it seems likely that the halt to the process was occasioned as much by the general opposition of the peasantry to the nature and activity of the communist regimes (in a situation where virtually no other channels for articulating opposition were available) as by opposition to the policy on economic grounds. There is certainly some evidence that the collective farms were received even with some favour by small peasants whose resources were too slender for successful farming on an individual basis. Whilst it is difficult to decide on the relative weight of the factors involved in peasant-state relations during the early fifties, however, there can be little doubt that together they evoked strong opposition from the peasant population of Eastern Europe.

There was a delay of some years in most countries before the collectivisation drive was resumed. In Yugoslavia, now outside the immediate orbit of Soviet influence, the drive never was resumed and peasant agriculture was left more or less to its own devices, with the state concentrating its attention on the location and operation of key industrial enterprises in the countryside as a means of furthering economic growth in the underdeveloped regions. In Poland, too, the pressure to collectivise was not reapplied with the strength it was elsewhere. For a more complex set of reasons the vast majority of farm land (over 80 per cent until 1974, a similar proportion to that in Yugoslavia) remained in private ownership. In other countries, however, the collectivisation process was resumed following the period of stocktaking that occurred after the death of Stalin and with the passing of the crisis that occurred in 1956 with developments in Hungary and Poland. The process recommenced in Bulgaria in 1957 whilst in Hungary Kádár cautiously waited until 1959 before reapplying the pressure. The process was largely complete by 1962 and, in 1965, no East European country (with the exception of Poland and Yugoslavia) had less than 89 per cent of its farm land in social ownership – that is, comprising production cooperatives or state farms.[2]

Whilst there is little evidence of any marked enthusiasm for the formation of collective farms on the part of the peasantry there is also little to suggest that the communist authorities are now faced with any significant opposition from the peasants to the institutions that comprise collectivised agriculture. In most countries, it appears, the peasants have largely accepted collectivisation as a fait accompli and it is unlikely that where collectives have been established their members harbour any real hope of returning to private ownership or would contemplate opposition to the regime on this score. It is, for example, significant that in Czechoslovakia, which presented the most sympathetic field for the exercise of social initiative in Eastern Europe during the sixties, no serious demands for decollectivisation were apparently made by the peasants. Czechoslovakian agriculture is, of course, among the more advanced in Eastern Europe, which might have tended to make the Czech or Slovak agriculturalist more amenable to collective productive. Nevertheless, the absence of any move to decollectivise, wrote Kusin, 'must count as one of the most surprising phenomena of the Prague Spring'.[3]

This, of course, is not to suggest that all, or even the majority of peasants have successfully adapted to the new social organisation or feel at home in the collective institution. Fischer-Galati's attempt to chart the sentiments of the Romanian peasant probably represents the feelings of many. The socioeconomic changes promoted by the communists have probably not, he writes, been successful in securing the positive support of the Romanian peasantry for the regime. There is probably still a widespread desire for a return to some kind of (non-communist) 'normalcy'.[4] Yet, whilst the communist regimes remain sensitive to the pressing problems of the agricultural sector (as they have over recent years), permit improvements to be made within the cumbersome collective institutions they have imposed on the countryside and make sure that some measure of social and material improvement is achieved in the countryside, it is unlikely that this desire for a return to a 'non-communist normalcy' will be translated into a definite political aspiration, let alone any kind of determined action. Opinion polls carried out in 1968 in Czechoslovakia suggested that 80 per cent of farmers felt that their wages were lower than those of industrial workers and that half believed that the countryside subsidised the cities.[5] But this was not associated with feelings of dissatisfaction with the system of collective farming: 67 per cent of farmers were in favour of collective agriculture and 75 per cent thought that work in the collective sector was easier than on individual farms. The exceptions to the above generalisation, of course, are Yugoslavia and Poland where attempts at large-scale collectivisation have not recurred since the early fifties. In Yugoslavia there are no signs that the regime is eager to risk the economic and political dislocation that further collectivisation would entail and to this extent here also collective production and land ownership are unlikely to emerge as political issues. In Poland, however, the situation is somewhat different. The regime has never disavowed its intention to create a socialist countryside based on collective agriculture (although frequently, one suspects, this objective has been voiced more for the benefit of Soviet ears than for inclusion in a serious programme of social change). The ownership of land has, therefore, remained more of a live political issue in Poland than in the other countries of Eastern Europe. Reports still circulate that such proposals as that to give the state powers to take over badly farmed land in the interests of agricultural improvement had to be dropped to forestall peasant fears of collectivisation.[6] Yet, even in Poland it appears, some shift in peasant views on collective agricultural production is taking place, at least amongst the younger generation. One survey on young people's views of how the countryside should be organised in the future indicated a surprising degree of acceptance for state farms, which now occupy only some 16 per cent of the farm area.[7]

It is surely no coincidence that it is also in Poland that another of the focal points of the conflict that characterised the early years of communist power still retains much of its earlier importance. The Catholic Church remains a factor of outstanding importance in Polish national life and it is with particular reference to the religious aspect that one attempt to explain the differing fate of collectivisation in Poland and Czechoslovakia has been made. Adams and Adams thus point to the crucial role of Catholicism as a symbol and fortifier of national identity during the partitioned Poland of the nineteenth century and in subsequent years.[8] It played an important national and political role, one that was generally distinct from and in opposition to the structure of the state. Unlike churchmen in Czechoslovakia and Yugoslavia, too, those in Poland were not tainted with charges of collaboration with the Nazis during the occupation.[9]

It is, then, not difficult to see that the Polish Church was able to perpetuate this important role when what many saw as a further period of alien domination began with the establishment of communist power in the late forties. The strength and relative success both of the peasantry and of the Church in resisting communist policy during the early years seem to have encouraged relations of mutual support between the two groups. Recent developments also suggest that the Church views the retention of a private peasantry as a major objective, whilst the adherence of the mass of the Polish peasantry to the Catholic faith remains a means for them to preserve their distinctive way of life and to demonstrate their continuing separation from the communist state and its organisation.[10] There still exists, writes one informed scholar, a form of 'automatic faith' amongst the rural population and whilst certain changes in rural Catholicism can be detected they should by no means be identified with the abandonment of the Catholic faith.[11]

It is unlikely that religious faith plays such an important part in the social life of the peasantry in other parts of Eastern Europe. Apart from the fact that nowhere else is the Church (of the Catholic or any other denomination) so strongly associated with a largely independent peasantry (generally the bastion of traditional faith) it is only in Poland that the population is so overwhelmingly subject to the authority of one Church and one, moreover, which has proved its strength as a national institution on so many occasions. Thus in Poland, it may be concluded, the Church continues to serve as a factor in the peasants' resistance to the imposition of collective agriculture, resistance which could well develop into opposition if the regime chose to impose collectivisation more forcefully. In other countries the few available studies indicate that religious practice is freer and in some cases more prevalent than during the early fifties, when collectivisation was accompanied by an overt general attempt to curb the power of all religious institutions and to undermine their support among the peasant population. On the other hand, the relaxation of the pressure exerted on the churches and the greater freedom of religious obser-vance now permitted means that the religious sphere is one less likely to serve as a channel for discontent.

In a Czech village some increase in religious practice had taken place with the loosening of restrictions on the church in the late fifties, but it did not appear to be regarded as a development of great significance in the social life of the peasant farmers.[12] Religious observance in a Calvinist Hungarian village was also found to be in a process of decline, with church life in the mid-sixties being largely restricted to special holidays and the weekly services barely attracting any attendance at all.[13] Nevertheless, it would be unwise to overestimate the degree of secularisation among the peasants of Eastern Europe or to minimise the role of the churches, either actual or potential. A wider survey amongst the Moravian farming population discovered that 73 per cent of respondents were full believers, that is believing in the existence of God and either praying in private or attending church.[14] The conclu-sion of the Czech author was that 'religion has retained relatively wide-spread support among the masses and . . . it remains an ideology whose influence must not be ignored'. Toma and Volgyes also report a Hungarian finding that 43 per cent of women in one village usually attended church once a day and state that 'village priests are very powerful in shaping the values of young and old alike'.[15] A further study of a Slovenian village established that Catholicism retained its moral significance in peasant social life although peasants were still loath to ally themselves openly with the church for fear of discrimination.[16] To the extent, then, that such attitudes and beliefs are relevant to political behaviour the influence of religion may still prove to be of considerable importance.

The third factor associated with the conflicts of the early fifties and the determination of the newly founded communist regimes to trans-form rural society was the part played by some peasant political parties in opposing the takeover of the state system by the communist groups. As was the case with non-communist socialist and workers' parties the communist forces attempted to neutralise peasant parties by a combi-nation of suppression, subdivision and incorporation ('bourgeois' parties were generally deemed unsuitable participants in the political system of the new people's states and were unable to re-emerge as political forces). Thus the rump of the former Polish Peasant Party was incorporated within a United Peasant Party in 1949 and a similar course of fragmentation occurred within the Bulgarian Agrarian

Union, permitting the survival of a subdued fraction within the communist-dominated Fatherland Front. The Czech Agrarian Party, a leading organisation before the war, was, however, not allowed to re-establish itself, whilst in East Germany a Democratic Farmers' Party was founded in 1948 precisely to neutralise potential right-wing forces within the agricultural population. In cases where peasant parties were permitted to survive they were almost totally deprived of political power, although the Polish party has on occasions showed signs of acting as an autonomous political force. Despite this subordination the ruling communist parties have remained continually vigilant to the possibility of these skeletal parties showing signs of political life and threatening to articulate demands relevant to their formal constituency – the peasantry. On several occasions, for example, the communist leadership has pointed to the possible danger of a resurgence of 'agrarianism' in Poland and of the possibility of peasants pursuing political interests at variance to those of the regime. The likelihood of these front organisations representing a genuine political threat to communist domination and developing as an authentic political organ of peasant' interests is, however, a remote one. It is evident to all, including the peasants, that these organisations have no capacity to develop as competitors to the ruling communist parties. It is precisely because of this fact that recent signs of agrarianism and peasant political opposition to the regime have been detected not in the organisations which claim to be the inheritors of the independent peasant political movements but in formally non-political bodies. Thus following the Soviet invasion charges were made that the Czech Collective Farmers' Union represented a revival of the pre-war Agrarian Party. Similar charges of illegitimate political activity have been laid at the door of Yugoslav agricultural cooperative organisations.[17]

On the face of it, it seems unlikely that direct political opposition might spring from the peasantry. From the evidence available it seems rather as if the peasants have accepted the consequences of the establishment of communist power, which spell the impossibility of formal political opposition to the regime and, in all but two cases, the reduction of private property in land to minor proportions. Recent political opposition, indeed, has emanated not from the peasantry but from intellectual groups (Czechoslovakia, Poland, Yugoslavia, East Germany) and in one case (Poland) from the working class. No peasants have shown signs of repeating their anti-regime activities of the 1953–6 period. The rise of new kinds of cooperative organisations and the desire to express interests within them seems rather to reflect

the peasants' awareness that the early stages of communist development are now past and its results largely accepted. Their demands and
aspirations now relate to their position within socialist society and to
their situation in an economic system whose structure is clearly determined by the communist authorities. Such interests are rarely to be
pursued in political organisations. The Yugoslavian peasantry is thus
described by Denitch as being 'by and large outside of the political
system today, neither hostile nor particularly supportive . . . the peasants at this point are politically and socially neutralised and do not
form a potential base for an opposition movement'.[18] Peasants, for
example, form only 7 per cent of the League of Communists of
Yugoslavia and a similarly low proportion of the Hungarian Socialist
Workers' Party. Peasant apathy and the weakness of the party in the
countryside was equally a major target of the Albanian Cultural
Revolution in the Sixties.[19] The acceptance by the peasants of the new
political and economic order has not been such as to bring about a
radical transformation in political attitudes. The consequences of
communist rule have therefore been to deflect peasant interest from
the political sphere, which might carry certain advantages in terms of
the avoidance of political opposition but which also threatens to limit
the legitimacy of the regime in the countryside and to restrict the
breadth of its political support.

THE POSITION OF THE PEASANTRY IN
CONTEMPORARY EAST EUROPEAN SOCIETY

The most striking indication that the peasantry and the agricultural
population of Eastern Europe have changed significantly since the
collectivisation period and have largely passed beyond the issues that
were then the source of conflict is the similarity in the problems
surrounding the farming population both in countries with collectivised agriculture and in those where individual land tenure persists. It
should not, of course, be forgotten that the structure of farm holdings
and agricultural activity varies considerably between countries that
can generally be described as having a largely 'collective' form of
agriculture. Under this heading are grouped both state farms, in which
employees are paid for their work along similar lines to those in any
other state enterprise, and collective farms proper or production
cooperatives (see Table 8.2). The latter are formally associations of
peasants who have pooled their land and resources for purposes of

Table 8.2
Proportion of Farm Area under Different Forms of Ownership, 1975[20]

	cooperative	state	private
Bulgaria	—	90%	10%
Czechoslovakia	61%	30%	9%
East Germany	82%	8%	10%
Poland	2%	16%	82%
Hungary	70%	15%	15%
Romania	54%	30%	16%
Yugoslavia (1974) – socialist sector:	15%	—	85%

joint cultivation and whose income therefore depends on the success of their joint endeavour. In most cases, however, steps have been taken to ensure that collective farmers receive a guaranteed minimum wage and their situation in this respect has been brought closer to that of the state farm worker.

There is, too, considerable diversity in the way that production activity is organised on the collective farms, or production cooperatives, in the East European countries. In Hungary, for example, a variant of share-cropping emerged at an early stage on one collective with a single family retaining responsibility for production on one particular plot (the Nádudvar system). The material interest of the family in the profitability of production on that portion of the farm proved highly conducive to high output levels and the innovation has been widely emulated. In general the Hungarian interpretation of the collective principle has proved to be highly flexible, which has been reflected in the relative success of Hungarian agriculture. In Bulgaria, on the other hand, there has developed a tendency to establish larger and more complex agricultural and, since 1970, agro-industrial units (the Agro-Industrial Complexes). Centralised control of farmers and direction of their activities has thereby been enhanced (the incorporation of formerly collective farms within the Complexes has meant that these are all now categorised under the 'state' heading in Table 8.2). A further difference in the organisation of production by collective and state farmers concerns their retention of small plots of land for personal cultivation. Whilst collective farms in Bulgaria have thus come under more direct state control the farmers themselves have retained larger than average private plots. In 1969, for example, the private plots of state and collective farmers accounted for 10.7 per cent of the farm area whilst only 0.4 per cent was farmed by independent agriculturalists working on their own account. It appears that such state and collective farm plots have been combined with the area

274 Opposition in Eastern Europe

farmed by independent peasants in the totals reproduced in Table 8.2. It is, however, only in Yugoslavia and Poland that privately farmed land accounts for the great majority of the agricultural area. Even in these two cases, though, the predominance of the private producers is somewhat less pronounced if the production levels of the private and collective sectors is compared. Despite their considerably smaller area the socialist holdings in Yugoslavia, for example, made up 46 per cent of market deliveries in 1974.[21] In countries such as Hungary, where cooperative cultivation predominates, on the other hand, production on private plots is responsible for a surprisingly high proportion of gross agricultural output (25 per cent in the Hungarian case). The simple distinction that can be drawn between countries with largely collective agriculture and those in which private farming predominates, i.e. Poland and Yugoslavia compared with the other East European states, therefore fails to take account of the diversity within the two groups of countries and fails to indicate the similarities that can be detected within the peasantries of Eastern Europe.

Of these similarities one of the most important concerns the increasingly critical view taken by the peasant of his traditional social position and of the inadequacies of the rural social environment.

Peasants' consciousness of their frequently miserable condition has, of course, been a source of dissatisfaction and a spur to peasant movements throughout history. Developments since the establishment of communist power in Eastern Europe have, however, brought this awareness out with a renewed sharpness precisely because of the heightened rate of change during this period and even of the undoubted improvements in the peasant condition that have been secured. Whatever the disruption and antagonism that the collectivisation drive provoked it has begun a process of radical change in the nature of agricultural production and has raised the question of the survival of the peasantry in a particularly acute form. Whatever the nature of the political regimes that have been instituted and the attitude of the peasantry to the political authority they embody their promise of a new kind of society, one geared to the needs and aspirations of all working people, provides the agriculturalist with an undoubted right to demand an unprecedented degree of change in his social condition. Whilst the peasantry is almost universally endowed with traditional values by the social theorist it should not be forgotten that these values have led peasants to aspire to a particular kind of change, not generally a denial of the necessity or desirability of change in general. Frequently these values have led peasants to fight for the restoration of ancient rights which have somehow been eroded in the course of social development; increasingly in modern times these values have prompted peasant participation in revolutionary movements and the downfall of a number of *ancien régimes*. It is certainly the case that developments in Eastern Europe since the Second World War have involved the peasantry in an accelerated process of change. The expectations aroused by the peasant movements of the inter-war years also undoubtedly contributed to the response of peasants to this process.[22]

But while the initial establishment of communist power and early attempts at collectivisation evoked peasant opposition it does now seem that the resulting balance of social forces has been accepted, however grudgingly, as the new social reality. Yet this does not necessarily mean that the peasant is content with his new social position. Indeed, acceptance of the new social parameters seems rather to be associated with further expectations of and demands for change and it is on the degree to which they are satisfied that the future attitudes of the peasants to the communist regimes will depend.

The basic feature of East European social change in this respect relates to the rapid growth of the industrial sector of the economy and to associated changes that are generally covered by the term modernisation. This points to the growth of non-agricultural employment and to the growing number of town-dwellers, to the provision of social facilities, medical care and education, and to the rise of an urban-industrial value structure and to greatly enhanced geographical and social mobility. One immediate consequence of this is the passing of the expectation that a child born into a peasant or agricultural family will adopt an agricultural occupation in adult life. Thus, writes Halpern:

> The peasant has stubbornly resisted collectivisation, but it seems he is even more determined to gain access to the seeming attractiveness of urban life. His attachment to his land appears to vary inversely with the degree to which other opportunities become available.[23]

For the engineers of social change this success in weaning the peasant away from his stubborn attachment to the land and, thus, from private ownership has created a new situation in the countryside. The most visible result of this is the outflow of young people from agriculture and the ageing of the agricultural work force. In some areas this has been so pronounced as to threaten the capacity of the agricultural population to reproduce itself and also raises doubts concerning the effectiveness of production activity on the farm. In the countries where small farms have persisted this has raised particularly acute problems for the process of farm inheritance. In Poland, for example, the proportion of farm owners aged 60 or over rose from 31 to 35.5 per cent between 1970 and 1974. On farms of between two and five hectares, which are frequently too small to attract the young farmer but which occupy 20 per cent of the farm area, 40.7 per cent of the owners were sixty or over in 1974.[24]

In Yugoslavia a survey of young people in rural Croatia found that only 24 per cent showed a desire to remain living in the countryside. Their outlook was highly similar to that of urban youth and attitudes to such matters as self-management and the necessity of religion differed little from those of young town-dwellers, 43 and 40 per cent respectively thought that religion was 'necessary' to man.[25] Neither are such problems restricted to areas where private farms predominate. They have arisen also to a significant extent in East Germany and Hungary and the scale of movement out of agriculture was an important factor behind the Bulgarian decision to proceed with the establishment of the Agro-Industrial Complexes.[26] By making the facilities offered by industrial employment more accessible to the agricultural population it was hoped to secure a greater degree of stability in the rural work force.

One striking index of the pull that urban-industrial facilities have exerted on the agricultural population is the development in several countries of a large group which combines agricultural work with industrial employment. The importance of this group of peasant workers is such that in Hungary, Yugoslavia and Poland about 50 per cent of agricultural families derive some of their income from non-agricultural employment. This phenomenon is open to varying interpretations with respect to its social implications. The peasant-worker category may be seen as a transitional group, marking the partial dissociation of a family from reliance on agriculture until family circumstances or urban opportunities permit a complete transfer to the urban-industrial environment. Alternatively, it may be viewed as the response to a temporary phase either in industrial development (whilst a temporary shortage of labour exists) or in the labour requirements of agriculture (a temporary surfeit of labour in the co-operative or private farm due to demographic, generational or technical processes of change). Again, it can be seen as a specific factor in the particular form taken by East European economic development. This could be interpreted either in the sense that off-farm employment acts as a form of support for peasant farming or socialist agriculture at its particular stage of development and with the specific limitations placed on it, or that industry needs to draw on rural, and otherwise agricultural, labour in a situation where the authorities are unwilling or unable to provide the urban infrastructure that would permit the permanent transfer of the needed labour force to the towns. Finally, it could also represent the development of a suburban life-style in a situation where ties with the village community are still strong for a substantial proportion of the rural population whilst urban or industrial employment is preferable for financial or other reasons. In view of the diverse social and economic conditions that pertain throughout the regions (not only the countries) of Eastern Europe there can be little doubt that no single interpretation of combined agricultural and off-farm employment will cover all cases. Certain aspects of the situation, however, do point to factors in an explanation.

Firstly, from what has been noted previously concerning the rapid development of urban-industrial aspirations amongst the agricultural population there is a strong desire for movement out of agricultural work into industrial or non-agricultural employment. But whatever the strength of this desire it does not appear likely, given the prevalence of the peasant-worker phenomenon and in view of the economic situation in the communist states, that those combining two occupations are likely to be fully assimilated by towns and industry in the short to medium term (say, up to thirty years). In several countries peasant-workers constitute a major part of the national work force. By 1971 almost half of Yugoslavian agricultural households had at least one member in non-agricultural employment and non-agricultural income had exceeded that drawn from farming in rural households already by 1965.[27] In 1972 in Poland 54 per cent of families with farm holdings exceeding 0.1 hectares had at least one member in off-farm employment and in 31 per cent of the families this involved the head of the household. In 1974 in Hungary 20 per cent of the national work force combined two occupations, a proportion only slightly lower than that whose income was drawn solely from agriculture.[28] Amongst heads of rural households in Hungary 64 per cent found their main employment outside agriculture.[29]

Peasant-worker employment is generally concentrated in the less skilled sections of industry and, given the limited capacity for labour intensive industrial development, it is impossible to foresee the absorption of the dual-occupation group in fully non-agricultural employment. Peasant-workers have in the past (in earlier centuries as well as the twentieth) found employment in spheres where manual labour rather than industrial skill was required. East European industry has already in earlier stages of industrialisation absorbed considerable numbers of unskilled workers from the countryside and the level of development which it has now reached indicates that higher productivity and technological development is needed rather than more rural emigrants. The Polish sociologist Galeski, commenting on the technical underemployment of the rural labour force (indicating the number of workers who could be released from agriculture if the structure of land holdings were transformed and if a higher level of provision of technical resources were possible), suggests a figure of two million 'surplus' agriculturalists.[30] Such a number is clearly far beyond the present requirements of Polish industry. It is not, therefore, likely that all peasant-workers represent a group who are transitional in any immediate sense to the industrial environment.

From a rather different viewpoint Konrád and Szelényi have argued that peasant-workers already form a permanent part of the industrial labour force but are unable to make a full transition to the urban industrial environment. The crucial transition in this view is the one from rural to urban residence and they suggest that, in Hungary at least, the peasant-worker phenomenon is a manifestation of under-urbanisation – a situation in which industrial growth has occurred but where the accompanying urban infrastructure of dwellings and other goods and services has not been provided. The division between town and country, therefore, increasingly becomes a form of stratification, with only supervisory and skilled employees being afforded the luxury of urban residence and non-skilled workers having to make do with inferior rural living conditions. It is unclear as yet how far this generalisation provides an adequate explanation for the expansion of the peasant-worker group. Whilst Hungary suffers from a certain shortage of labour, for example, the Polish economy tends to have an over-abundant labour supply and industrial employment seems to be highly prized by the peasants. Matejko thus suggests that the Polish peasant-worker is not so well off as the urban employees but has a higher income and a 'more attractive daily experience' than the mass of the peasantry.[31] Recent statistics, however, cast some doubt on the accuracy of this judgment. In 1975 the per capita income of an agricultural peasant family was indeed only 82.5 per cent of that in a worker's family, but peasant-worker income was even lower at 80.4 per cent.[32] Moreover, in Hungary in 1973 those with dual agricultural occupation had a higher per capita income than both blue-collar and cooperative peasant families, although peasant-workers had a lower income than cooperative peasants in 1968.[33] Such figures do raise questions as to whether peasant-workers are so disadvantaged in Hungary, especially in comparison with a country like Poland.

In some cases, particularly in Yugoslavia and Poland, there can be little doubt that industrial employment provides an essential supplementary income for peasant families whose holding is not sufficient to maintain the family but who are nonetheless loath to cut off all ties with the land. In this sense industrial employment contributes to the maintenance of a structurally weak agriculture but may accord with the interests of peasant families. For many young Polish people from peasant families, it appears, farming still exerts a strong attraction, albeit one which is increasingly tempered by an awareness that more dependable and more easily earned income is to be gained from non-agricultural employment and that a more attractive social environment is to be found in the towns. Volgyes has estimated that the traditional attachment to the land retains most of its strength in Yugoslavia, Poland, Romania and Slovakia.[34] For independent farmers especially the ownership of land still represents a form of security, particularly for older generations.[35] In other cases the agricultural livelihood can provide for the education of family members and enable them to gain white-collar jobs, returning to assist at the harvest when their help is required.[36] In villages close to industrial centres a satisfying combination of urban and rural values can be achieved, enabling use to be made of urban employment and other facilities without the loss of the advantages to be gained from participating in a still thriving village community.[37]

But in general, and certainly in a significant proportion of cases, the large group of peasant workers in contemporary Eastern Europe does reflect an important shift in peasant attitudes away from the traditional acceptance of the peasant's lot towards more ambitious expectations of social and material improvement. It seems highly unlikely that economic and social development will occur at a pace in the East European states sufficient to enable these expectations to be met in full. To what extent, then, is this shortfall likely to give rise to frustration or even opposition to the regimes whose actions can be held responsible for this state of affairs? The answer to this question is likely to depend as much on the possibilities of agricultural and rural social development as on the development of the urban-industrial sector of the economy. The enhanced expectations of the peasant population have risen in association with the undoubted progress that has been

made in the rural sector over the past few decades and to the extent
that future improvement is possible the frustration of peasant farmers
may be kept within tolerable levels. So long as this occurs and if a
certain level of social and occupational mobility is maintained the new
outlook of the peasantry need not necessarily lead to disruptive social
change. Despite their views on the proletarianisation of the countryside Konrád and Szelényi note that:

> people at a social disadvantage realistically estimate the low likeli-
> hood of being able to change their situation; hence, they see it in a
> favourable light and show even less desire for change than their
> actual dissatisfaction would indicate[38]

This is likely to be particularly true in Hungary where the material
advantages gained from peasant-worker status are quite considerable.

The benefits of industrialisation and economic development have
certainly not been unappreciated by the inhabitants of the East
European countryside. In comparison with the onerous material conditions of the peasantry before the war living standards are undoubtedly far higher (probably of the order of 250 per cent). The fact of this
material advance has been recognised and welcomed by the agricultural population.[39]

Continuing disparities, however, in income between industrial and
agricultural groups have existed and provided a basis for criticism and
resentment, as well as acting as a further incentive to rural emigration.
In the early sixties, for example, the net annual income of the collective
farmer in Czechoslovakia averaged 85.5 per cent of that of a worker in
the rest of the socialised economy, although he worked 14 per cent
longer.[40] In the Slovenian countryside, too, factory work was seen as
the only way of making ends meet for the peasant family.[41] Despite
certain improvements in the years immediately following the abandonment of the collectivisation drive the gap between rural and urban
incomes in Poland failed to show any sign of closing during the sixties.
There are, however, indications that the situation has now improved as
governments have recognised the pernicious effects that peasant disadvantage has on agricultural productivity and rural migration. Prices
paid for agricultural produce were raised significantly in 1971 in
Poland and some years earlier in Hungary, Romania, Czechoslovakia
and Yugoslavia (although, in the latter case, the private peasant
suffered considerably from the effects of inflation). According to
Wädekin the disparity between the income of collective farmers and

that in the rest of the economy has now been largely overcome, with the exception of Romania where problems of labour productivity remain acute.[72]

The Hungarian experience, however, indicates other problems this situation might create in East European society. The rising income of farmers to levels higher than those of the average worker provoked further criticism and,

> in turn, caused resentment in the industrial workers, who have frequently felt that they are the stepchildren of the system because persons in management, the party, and the government bureaucracy, and now many peasants are in a much more favourable situation.[43]

While peasants may feel they have the right to expect an income no lower than the national average the workers feel themselves equally entitled to an income certainly no lower than and, in many cases, somewhat above the average. There can be no doubt that the industrial working class occupies a special place in the ideology espoused by the regimes and has particular importance in party activities. It is equally significant that in many East European families expenditure on food accounts for nearly half of the family income. Higher incomes for the agricultural population therefore have an important bearing on the position of urban workers. But these factors carry more weight for the regimes' leaders than for peasant farmers, who will continue to feel disadvantaged as long as any disparity persists in living standards and they may well express this dissatisfaction through the quantity and quality of the produce that emerges from their farms, if not in more direct fashion.

It is, of course, not simply monetary income which is involved in a comparison of rural and urban living standards. Access to general social, welfare and cultural facilities is also involved in such a comparison, particularly for peasants who are subject to much information from the mass media on the degree of progress that has been achieved under communist regimes. It is, however, far more costly to provide such facilities for the rural population. It has been estimated that provision of such social goods was only at one fifth of the level made in the towns in Poland in the mid-sixties.[44] Efforts to improve welfare provision for the farming population did, however, begin at an early stage. State insurance for agricultural workers was introduced in 1957 in Bulgaria and in 1958 in Hungary. It is evident that governments have recognised the need to provide a comprehensive welfare service if conditions in the countryside are to bear comparison with those of industrial workers and not to provide a disincentive for the rural young to stay in agriculture. Yet provision for private and cooperative farmers has continued to lag behind that for industrial employees. The state health scheme was extended to cover private farmers in Poland only in 1970 while the commutation of land for retirement pensions was introduced in 1974. The terms in which one peasant couched his response to the latter measure are indicative of its importance for some sections of the rural population:

> This fact should be entered into history following the hard and, for the peasant, sorrowful times of aristocratic and *sanacja* rule, when peasants were treated as blacks now are in Rhodesia.[45]

In countries, however, where the agricultural population is considerably smaller it has been possible to introduce a far more satisfactory range of social provision. In East Germany, for example, the urban-rural disparity in terms of education, health, welfare and holidays has been largely overcome and the living standards of rural workers are in many ways rather better than those in the towns.[46] But the process of providing similar levels of equality throughout Eastern Europe is far from complete and it is difficult to see how comparable levels of educational and medical facilities could be provided, not to speak of the general cultural and social opportunities available in the urban environment. Yet it is in such terms that the social transformation has evidently been understood by much of the peasant population, particularly its younger members. If greater comparability of provision cannot be achieved and if agriculture is not permitted to generate its own specific system of rewards (as it has to some extent in Hungary and amongst the wealthier farming groups in such countries as Poland) then it is possible to foresee increasing frustration and resentment amongst the farming population.

Nevertheless, it is not just in terms of income or even of general living standards that all peasant farmers evaluate their occupation or way of life, either in present or future terms. Their capacity to conduct agriculture as they think appropriate, their sense of its value both in personal and social terms and their view of its possibilities of future development are also important. It should not be assumed that such factors no longer play a part in the peasant's assessment of his condition. To some extent feelings of genuine collective ownership have emerged amongst East European farmers. The high level of production on some farms in Czechoslovakia has been attributed to their members' identification with the cooperative institution and their capacity to participate in its management.[47] Farmers in one Czech village were reported to have adapted quite successfully to the collective system (although the retention of private farming would have been preferred) but the process of merging farms to create larger and more impersonal units was raising more serious doubts.[48]

Insofar as governments continue to recognise the importance of this personal involvement with the fate of the farm unit (as they have increasingly done since the disastrous effects of collectivisation during the early fifties) the satisfaction of at least some farmers in their work should continue and the effectiveness of production thus rise. This awareness may be seen in Bulgaria, where the promotion of the mammoth Agro-Industrial Complexes is accompanied by the provision of an above-average proportion of land for use as private plots and considerable encouragements being offered to peasants to develop production on them.

A similar approach appears to exist also in Hungary. Discussing the development of cooperative farming in that country Donáth writes that:

> (the) new type of worker will not only possess the ability to grasp the more important interconnections of production and management, but his demand will also become stronger that he should participate – in different ways – in the management of a production section or of the whole farm. . . . The maintenance of the cooperative form of ownership is (also) justified by the fact that it offers greater and more direct opportunities for incentives – that is why the cooperatives are more efficient than the state farms in several areas of production – and this will for a long time remain the most important stimulant of production.[49]

This view, however, carries implications which other East European regimes may find less acceptable. The growth of incentives of the agricultural sector has also been associated with demands for more control over the supply of resources for farm production, the marketing of produce and over mechanisms for determining the price paid for farm output. This has found greater acceptance in Hungary where supply and marketing cooperatives are sufficiently strong to compete with state agencies and where producers' cooperatives have won the right to band together to protect their members' interests. In 1975 it was decided that unions could be established to protect the interests of all collective employees and workers, regardless of whether they were constituent members of the cooperative.[50]

Thus despite the differences in agricultural structure it appears that the Hungarian state is less able to dictate to peasant farmers than the Polish. As Adams points out 'Having acknowledged peasant self-interest to be the legitimate driving force in socialist agriculture, Hungary's policy-makers are compelled to meet many of the peasant's demands.[51] In other countries the political implications of similar developments have met with less acceptance. The Farmers' Union established in Czechoslovakia in 1968 (designed to perform functions similar to those of the Union of Farmers abolished in 1948) apparently found enthusiastic support in the countryside but was subsequently charged with displaying right-wing tendencies and articulating an agrarianist ideology. Agricultural cooperatives in Yugoslavia also appear to have shown signs of evolving into political organisations and of becoming critical of state policy.[52] Not all East European regimes, therefore, are as tolerant as the Hungarian with regard to such interest groups and to the expression of criticism by the farming population. Agricultural development and the social advance of the agriculturalist, though, are likely to be associated with pressure for greater freedom in this sphere.

A factor that might provide a focus for peasant discontent and thus provide a platform for opposition is regional identity and the association of diverse forms of social inequality with identifiable ethnic, cultural or national groups. It is difficult to establish whether peasants, tending to represent traditionalism within national societies, are inclined to hold views more strongly coloured by nationalist or ethnic feelings and to act primarily on the basic of such sentiments. In Yugoslavia, the East European country where such divisions appear currently to have most importance, there are some indications that the virulent expression of Croat nationalism in the early seventies evoked a positive response amongst the peasantry.[53] Yet there is little reason to suppose that nationalism is a stronger determinant of peasant actions than it is of other groups. Indeed, it is generally members of the intelligentsia who appear to have attached more importance to its values. It is, however, undoubtedly true that the peasants of such countries as Poland and Hungary shared the desire for greater national independence that was demonstrated by the actions of the vast mass of the population of those countries in 1956.

Nationalism and similar aspects of social differentiation are more likely to play a role in social development in combination with other kinds of social differences. These, indeed are often associated with ethnic or national considerations. In the more isolated mountainous areas of Slovakia, for example, private farms are more frequently found than elsewhere, as it is not generally practicable to organise cooperative production under these conditions. Such farmers are generally poorer than the average, largely because of restrictions placed by the state on private agriculture, but also because of the difficult conditions under which agriculture has to be practised.[54] It would, then, not be difficult to understand if such peasants had proved to be strong supporters of demands for the improvements in the position of Slovakia that were made in the early and mid-sixties. Yet it would be difficult to ascribe such developments to nationalism per se. Such an association of ethnic differences with socioeconomic inequality is also clearly visible in Yugoslavia. Whilst Slovenia shows a degree of economic development not far below that of Western Europe some southern regions are at a level more similar to the Middle East. Thus, in the mid-sixties, Slovenia's per capita product was nearly six times greater than for Kosovo.[55] Whilst the poorer and more backward parts of the country are more agricultural in nature it would, again, be surprising if some association of socioeconomic disparities were not identified with ethnic and regional factors. This appears to have been the case with the criticism launched by the Albanians in the underdeveloped Yugoslav region of Kosovo.[56] Lang also suggests that the gap between the rich and poor regions of Yugoslavia may pose a serious threat to its political stability.[57] It is notable in this connection that the less developed regions suffer from serious rural overpopulation, and hence from disguised unemployment. As with all the factors discussed in the preceding pages, peasant grievances arising in connection with them are likely to emerge in acute form when two or more factors interact and when peasant feelings of disadvantage thus multiply.

NEW SOURCES OF STABILITY AND DISCONTENT IN THE COUNTRYSIDE

From the preceding discussion it would appear that significant problems do persist in the agricultural sector of the East European economies and that sources for the development of social and political dissatisfaction on the part of the peasantries of those societies which could, under certain conditions, develop into outright opposition can still be identified. It is, however, important to point out that the foci of discontent, existing or potential, are generally different in kind from those which were evident during the early years of communist authority in Eastern Europe. The issue of cooperative production in contrast to individual peasant farming has now been largely superseded. Collective production is now firmly established as the dominant institutional form in most countries of Eastern Europe and it appears that the peasants have largely accepted it as such, albeit with no great enthusiasm. However, the fact that most regimes are now more disposed to recognise the importance of material incentives and private initiative (in the form of private plots and the internal organisation of production cooperatives) within this dominant institutional form makes it more acceptable to the peasant and demonstrates a greater sensitivity to the needs of agricultural production on the part of the authorities. Similarly, the attacks on the various religious institutions and the ruthless suppression of non-communist political bodies and their participants, past, present or potential, that accompanied the early collectivisation drive no longer appear as such significant factors under the conditions of the seventies. A modus vivendi has now been reached with most of the religious institutions of Eastern Europe and, whilst organised political opposition is certainly not tolerated, a greater sensitivity to political attitudes and a willingness to tolerate certain forms of criticism is now more apparent. Finally the political, economic and social conditions of Eastern Europe are now also considerably different. The presence of communist leadership in Eastern Europe is now firmly established and its authority is generally accepted if not positively supported by the peasantry, as it is by other major social groups and the international community in general. Industrial development has been greatly advanced throughout Eastern Europe – agriculture is no longer seen as a primary fund of resources for the development of the national economy and the necessity for balanced industrial-agricultural development is increasingly recognised. In proportionate terms the salience of the peasant farming group has been considerably reduced.

This, however, does not mean that grounds for discontent on the part of the agricultural population no longer exist or that the factors implicit in the long-standing 'peasant problem' have all disappeared. The differences between material and social conditions in the urban and rural sectors retain their importance, the demand for occupational and social advancement remains strong, and changes in the condition of the worker in agricultural production are still sought. Particularly important is the intensity of the peasants' desire for change and the radical nature of the expectations that they now hold of society. Tepicht's statement that 'peasants have entered a new stage of development: they are no longer willing to be the outcasts of society'[58] is linked, moreover, with a suggestion that the changes that have taken place in the name of socialist revolution are best understood in terms of their underlying peasant character. The particular form taken by socialist industrialisation is thus seen as most suitable for the peasantry of all social groups, both as agricultural producer and as source of potential occupants of new industrial and administrative roles. The great majority of East European peasant families will now have links with members who have benefitted from this kind of social advance. Further:

> The mixed families in question, while appreciating the material rewards currently accruing to them from their farms and from the non-agricultural jobs of their children, place the highest value on the advantages and prestige which they expect from the eventual rise in the new social order of their 'family delegates'. It is because of this expectation that the peasantry constitutes today the most solid base of support for the existing government.[59]

In many respects this view of the primacy of the peasantry in relation to the development of socialism in Eastern Europe is a persuasive one. In the analysis of a concrete social situation, however, the factors making for peasant support of the regime and specific grievances making for opposition to a given policy or situation are difficult to weigh up.

Also difficult to decide is how far the changes that have taken place in Eastern Europe accord with peasant interests. It is difficult, at first glance, to accept the idea that collectivisation was in the interests of the peasantry. Yet, as Tepicht points out, 'The conflict between personal and collective interests, between immediate and longer-term interests of a class, a social group or a nation, can well oppose a class, a social group, or a nation to its own representatives'.[60]

It is, moreover, difficult to see how the problems of the East European agricultural sector could have been ameliorated without the rapid growth of industry, and this in turn implied the need for a transfer of labour and resources out of agriculture into industry and a restructuring of the farm economy. The very size of the contemporary peasant-worker group can perhaps serve to indicate the extent to which East European industrial development has accorded with the interests of the peasantry. Yet this does not mean that all grounds for dissatisfaction have been removed.

Whilst the direction of change may be in accordance with peasant interests the pace of this change may still be too slow to satisfy the demands that previous developments have evoked amongst the peasants. This conclusion emerges quite clearly from the material already discussed in this essay. The scope, too, of the transformation desired by the peasants may be so broad as to imply the virtual disappearance of the peasantry as a social group. Such a process has taken place in a number of advanced western countries, resulting in the development of a market-oriented agriculture and the emergence of a numerically small but productive group of farmers, but rarely in the absence of social conflict and frequently with considerable violence. The seemingly intractable problems encountered by communist regimes in developing an advanced farm sector suggests that the obstacles which this line of development is likely to encounter are well-nigh insurmountable, at least in the foreseeable future. If this analysis is accurate a large part of the peasantry is likely to suffer a certain degree of frustration for some time, although, as suggested earlier, it may be possible to contain this frustration within acceptable limits. A final problem relevant to potential opposition emerges from another aspect of Tepicht's view of the place occupied by the peasantry in East European social development. The integration of the peasantry within socialist society to a degree not previously reached in Eastern Europe exposes it to influences and pressures not previously known in the countryside. It follows that the satisfaction of peasant desires and expectations is now dependent not just on agricultural and rural conditions but also on those experienced by other groups in society with which peasant families now have close ties and with whose situation they are significantly involved through their 'family delegates'. Thus, whilst many of the earlier problems associated with the peasant situation have found solutions or some degree of ease in the post-war development of Eastern Europe, those who remain in the countryside and have inherited the activity of peasant farming may increasingly be affected by developments in other sectors of society and by the discontent of other groups. In this way new forms of social linkage have emerged which point to the possibility of novel forms of opposition. It is just possible in this connection that the notion of the worker-peasant alliance may gain a significance quite unintended and certainly unhoped for by the communist leaders who first employed it.

NOTES

1. FAO *Production Yearbook* (Rome: Food & Agriculture Organisation of the UN, 1975), pp. 37–8.
2. R. C. Gripp; *The Political System of Communism* (London: Nelson, 1973), p. 88.
3. V. V. Kusin, *Political Grouping in the Czechoslovak Reform Movement* (London: Macmillan, 1972), p. 54.
4. S. Fischer-Galati, *Twentieth Century Rumania* (New York: Columbia University Press, 1970), p. 213.
5. H. G. Skilling, *Czechoslovakia's Interrupted Revolution* (Princeton, N.J.: Princeton University Press, 1976), p. 586.
6. *Financial Times* (London), 3 March 1977.
7. *Polityka* (Warsaw), 3 July 1976.
8. A. E. Adams and J. S. Adams, *Men versus Systems: Agriculture in the USSR, Poland and Czechoslovakia* (New York: Free Press, 1971), pp. 189–91.
9. Cf B. D. Denitch, *The Legitimation of a Revolution: the Yugoslav Case* (New Haven: Yale University Press, 1976), pp. 68–9.
10. P. Green 'The third round in Poland', *New Left Review*, no. 101–2 (April, 1977), pp. 78, 96.
11. E. Ciupak 'The changing face of rural Catholicism', *Polish Perspectives*, vol. XIII (March 1975), p. 31.
12. Z. Salzmann and V. Scheufler, *Komarov: a Czech Farming Village* (New York: Holt, Rinehart & Winston, 1974), p. 120.
13. E. Fel and R. Hofer, *Proper Peasants* (Chicago: Aldine, 1969), p. 384.
14. Adams and Adams, p. 224.
15. Ibid., p. 99.
16. I. Winner, *A Slovenian Village: Zerovnica* (Providence, R.I.: Brown University Press, 1971), p. 197.
17. S. K. Pavlowitch, *Yugoslavia* (London: Ernest Benn, 1971), p. 348.
18. Denitch, pp. 4–5.
19. N. Pano, 'The Albanian cultural revolution', *Problems of Communism*, vol. XXIII, no. 4 (July–August 1974), p. 49.
20. *Wies Wspołczesna* (Warsaw), October 1977, p. 159, and *Yugoslav Survey*, February 1976, p. 56.
21. *Yugoslav Survey*, May 1976, p. 163.
22. G. Jackson, 'Peasant political movements in Eastern Europe', in H. Landsberger, ed., *Rural Protest: Peasant Movements and Social Change* (London: Macmillan, 1974), p. 315.
23. J. Halpern, 'Farming as a way of life: Yugoslav peasant attitudes', in J. Karcz, ed., *Soviet and East European Agriculture* (Berkeley, Calif.: University of California Press, 1967), p. 381.
24. A. Wyderko, 'Demographic and occupational transformations in the Polish rural areas', in *Zagadnienia ekonomiki rolnej: Socio-economic problems of the Development of the Polish Agriculture* (sic) (Warsaw: Państwowe Wydawn. Rolnicze, 1976), p. 165.
25. Denitch, pp. 64–5.

26. See Karcz, p. 219 and N. Oren, *Revolution Administered: Agrarianism and Communism in Bulgaria* (Baltimore: The Johns Hopkins University Press, 1973), p. 168.

27. W. G. Lockwood, 'The peasant-worker in Yugoslavia', in B. L. Faber, ed., *The Social Structure of Eastern Europe* (New York: Praeger, 1976), p. 284.

28. P. Toma and I. Volgyes, *Politics in Hungary* (San Francisco, Calif.: W. H. Freeman, 1977), p. 131.

29. G. Konrád and I. Szelényi, 'Social conflicts of underurbanization: the Hungarian case', in M. Field, ed., *Social Consequences of Modernization in Communist Societies* (Baltimore, Maryland: The Johns Hopkins University Press, 1976), p. 166.

30. *Polityka*, 4 September 1976.

31. A. Matejko, *Social Change and Stratification in Eastern Europe* (New York: Praeger, 1974), p. 75.

32. *Wies Wspotczesna*, August 1977, p. 60.

33. Toma and Volgyes, p. 131.

34. I. Völgyes, 'Attitudinal and behavioral changes among the peasantry of Eastern Europe', Paper presented to the annual meeting of the AAASS held on October 13–16, 1977, in Washington, D.C.

35. See, for example, the interviews with Yugoslav peasants which appeared in *Polityka*, 27 March 1976.

36. See, J. Held, 'Continuity and change in Hungary in historical perspective', in J. Shapiro and P. J. Potichnyi, eds., *Change and Adaption in Soviet and East European Politics* (New York: Praeger, 1976), p. 97.

37. A. Olszewska, *Wies uprzemysłowiona* (Warsaw, 1969), pp. 142–3.

38. Konrád and Szelényi, p. 177.

39. Cf Fischer-Galati, p. 213 and Salzmann and Scheufler, p. 121.

40. G. Lazarcik, 'The performance of Czechoslovak agriculture since World War II', in Adams and Adams, p. 403.

41. Winner, p. 161.

42. K-E Wädekin, 'The place of agriculture in the European communist economies: a statistical essay', *Soviet Studies*, vol. XXIX (August, 1977), p. 249.

43. B. Racz, 'Political changes in Hungary after the Soviet invasion of Czechoslovakia', *Slavic Review*, vol. XXIX, (December, 1970), p. 645.

44. B. Mieczkowski, *Personal and Social Consumption in Eastern Europe* (New York: Praeger, 1975), p. 41.

45. *Wies Wspotczesna*, August 1977, pp. 56–7. *Sanacja* was the authoritarian regime introduced in Poland by Piłsudski between the wars.

46. K. Sontheimer and W. Bleek, *The Government and Politics of East Germany* (London: Hutchinson, 1975), p. 162.

47. T. Bergmann, *Farm Policies in Socialist Countries* (Westmead: Saxon House, 1975), p. 97.

48. Salzmann and Scheufler, p. 60.

49. F. Donáth, 'Economic growth and socialist agriculture', *New Hungarian Quarterly* 66 (Summer 1977), pp. 121–2.

50. Toma and Völgyes, pp. 43–4.

51. Adams, p. 468.

52. Pavlowitch, p. 348.
53. F. Singleton, *Twentieth Century Yugoslavia* (London: Macmillan, 1976), p. 224.
54. See Adams and Adams, pp. 243–4.
55. D. Dyker, 'Yugoslavia: unity of diversity?', in A. Brown and J. Gray, eds., *Political Culture and Political Change in Communist States* (London: Macmillan, 1977), p. 68.
56. P. Shoup, 'The national question in Yugoslavia', *Problems of Communism*, vol. XXI (January–February, 1972), p. 24.
57. N. Lang, 'The dialectics of decentralisation: economic reform and regional inequality in Yugoslavia', *World Politics*, vol. XXVIII (April 1975), p. 328.
58. J. Tepicht, 'A project for research on the peasant revolution of our time', *Journal of Peasant Studies*, vol. II, (April 1975), p. 263.
59. Ibid.
60. Tepicht, p. 260.

Index

absenteeism, 219, 221–2, 244
Adams, A. E. and J. S., 269, 289 n8 n14, 290 n40 n51, 291 n54
Ady, E., 155
'agrarianism', 271
agriculture, 263, 266, 286–7
  Bulgaria, 273–4
  Czechoslovakia, 266, 267
  Hungary, 273
  population, 263–4, 276–7
  prices, 281
  production cooperatives, 273
  supply and marketing cooperatives, 284
Agro-Industrial Complexes (Bulgaria), 273, 276, 283
Albrecht, J., 99
alienation, 61, 210, 215, 240, 250
Amalrik, A., 3
Albanian cultural revolution, 272
Amnesty International, viii, 122
Andrzejewski, J., 108 n75
anti-Semitism, 10, 21, 67–8, 105 n18, 145, 170–2
Apel, E., 140 n58
Arend, E., 140 n73
Arzenšek, V., 255 n10, 259 n56, 260 n59 n60, 261 n75
Asiatic mode of production, 166

Babeau, A., 260 n72 n73, 261 n81
Bahro, R., xxi, 128–31, 140 n66
Bakunin, M., 207
Balla, B., 202
Baltic coast riots, 70–2, 74, 83, 87, 230
Baluka, E., 258 n37 n38 n42
Baranczyk, S., 95
Barghoorn, F. C., vii, 56, 59 n31
Baring, A., 258 n36 n41 n42 n44 n45, 259 n49 n50
Barker, E., 258 n37 n38 n42
Barta, G., 185 n58
Barton, P., 106 n30, 258 n35 n36 n45, 259, 261 n84

Bartsch, G., 140 n48
Battěk, M., 43
Bauer, R., 256 n14
Bauman, Z., 210, 246, 254 n3 n5, 255 n8, 262 n87
Becker, J., 134, 140 n73, 141 n77
Beke, K., 185 n58
Béládi, M., 183 n41
Belgium, 50
Belgrade conference, 18
'Belgrade Eight', xviii
Bence, G., 150, 158
Benson, L., 261 n74
Berend, I. T., 24 n12
Bergmann, T., 290 n47
Berkovits, G., 151, 165, 181 n9, 183 n30, 185 n64
Berlin Wall, 113, 114, 121, 124
Berlinguer, E., 50, 51, 108 n75, 111 n132
Berlinguer, G., 43
Bettelheim, C., 191, 199–200, 207 n10
Bieńkowski, W., 64, 94, 99, 111 n133
Biermann, W., 124, 131–4, 140 n45
Bihari, M., 154
Bil'ak, V., 29, 35, 43
Bleek, W., 290 n46
Blit, L., 109 n90 n99
Blumsztajn, 67
Błuszowski, J., 259 n50
Böll, H., 47
Bolshevism, 201, 204
Borbándi, G., 181 n11, 182 n15
Brandt, W., 115, 116, 138 n13, 139 n14 n16
Brasch, T., 140 n70
Bratislava, 43
Braun, V., 129, 133, 135, 140 n73, 141 n77
Brecht, B., 126
Brezhnev, L. I., 30, 45, 50, 56, 189–90
  constitution (1977), 80
  doctrine, xxi, 15, 78
Brno, 30
Brokl, L., 255 n10

Bromke, A., 106 n40
Brown, A. H., vii, 11, 24 n3 n19, 105 n23, 181 n1, 261 n79 n84, 262 n88, 291 n55
Bruesewitz, Pastor, 123, 124
Brus, W., vii, 65, 107 n68, 193
Bruyn, G. de, 141 n77
Budapest School, 17, 19, 143, 156–7, 158–9, 182 n16
  and civil rights, 160, 161
  intellectual positions, 161–3
  see also New Left
Bulgaria, xxiii, 271, 273–4
bureaucracy, 21, 135, 153, 162, 166, 191, 198, 201–5

capitalism, 19, 125, 126, 196–7, 198, 199, 205–6
Carillo, S., 50, 51
Case, J., 256 n17)
Catholic Church, 37, 123, 265, 269
  see also Polish Catholic Church
Ceausescu, N., 232
censorship
  Hungary, 147, 152, 161
  Poland, 79, 94, 95–6
Cernea, M., 257 n27
Chafee, Z., 24 n9
Charter 77, xiv, xxii, 17–18, 25 n23, 29, 52–6, 59 n25, 107 n60
  Hungary, 161
  Poland, 79
  workers, 247–8, 249
Childs, D., 138 n6 n13
Chile, 201, 207
China, 41, 51, 131, 203
Chojecki, M., 111 n123
Císař, C., 44
Ciupak, E., 289 n11
civil society, 60, 205–6
class, xx, 164, 167, 190, 200
  conflict, 195
  Czechoslovakia, 247
  intelligentsia, 190–1
  workers, 212–14, 251
Cliff, A., 207 n11
Cocks, P. M., 259 n55
Codreanu, C., 9–11
Cohn, L., 99
collective farms, 273, 283

collectivisation, xvii, 197, 163–8, 287–8
  Bulgaria, 267
  Czechoslovakia, 267–8
  Hungary, 264, 267
  New Course, 266
  peasant attitudes, 267, 268, 274–5, 286
  Poland, 63, 264, 266, 267, 268
  and religion, 270
COMECON, 15
command economy, 194, 199
commodity forms and relations, 197, 198
communism, xix, 12, 27, 46, 125, 128
communist party
  and culture, 65–6
  and economy, 127
  and intelligentsia, 166–7
  leadership, xiii
  and peasantry, 272
  and redistribution, 166
  vanguard role, 192, 201, 204
  and workers, 159, 232, 233–4
  see also under Country headings
Connor, W. D., 254 n5, 255 n8
consultation (Poland), 82, 109 n70, 227, 234
consumerism, xv, xviii, 164, 198
  Czechoslovakia, 44
  and depoliticisation, 15–16
  East Germany, 114, 119, 125, 126, 136
  and stability, 14, 16
Cremer, F., 133, 140 n73
Croatia, 7, 284–5
Crooked Circle Club, 64
Csorba, C., 185 n63
Csurka, I., 168
Cuba, 201
Cyrnakiewicz, J., 62, 71
Czechoslovak Communist Party, xviii
  Central Committee plenum (Sept. 1969), 28, 33, 37
  ex-members, 36, 37–42
  Fourteenth (clandestine) Congress, 30
  leadership, 27, 32, 35
  membership, 35–6, 57
  socialist opposition in, 18–19

Czechoslovak Communist Party—*cont.*
    Thirteenth Congress, 36
Czechoslovakia, xiii, xiv, xxiii, 8, 9,
    19, 25 n23, 26–58, 144, 211
    Agrarian party, 271
    federation, 29, 31, 34
    and Hungary, 177
    invasion of, xiii, 9, 26, 27, 48, 68,
        105 n20, 114, 122, 129, 136,
        143, 156, 157, 158, 243
    KAN, 29
    K231, 29
    personnel changes, 29, 32–3
    Prague Spring, 18, 26, 28, 47, 50,
        54, 55, 68, 105 n19, 125, 157,
        158, 187, 241–4 *passim*, 267
    Slovakia, 53, 58 n1
    Social Democrats, 29
    Socialist Movement of Czecho-
        slovak Citizens, 18, 39–43, 54
    Ten Points Manifesto, 33–4, 39
    traditions, 27
    Twenty-eighth of October Mani-
        festo, 39
    and USSR, 29–30, 34, 37, 38,
        45–6, 50
Częstochowa, 89, 90
Czigler, I., 186 n67
Czuma, A., 101
Czywinski, B., 94

Dacjgewand, 67
Dankánics, M., 185 n66
Darányi, M., 185 n65
Darvas, J., 151, 152, 181 n10
Davies, J., 203
democracy, xviii
    Fascist concept of, 8
    Hungary, 155, 162–3, 180, 205
    liberal concepts of, 4–6, 18, 24
    see also socialism, socialist demo-
        cracy
democratic centralism, 130, 201
Denitch, B. D., 255 n9, 256 n22,
    261 n74, 262 n88, 272, 289 n9
    n18 n25
Déry, T., 161, 168
de-Stalinisation, 56, 68–9
détente, xiv, xxii, 55, 77–8, 189–90
    Czechoslovakia, 45, 47–9, 56

East Germany, 115, 126, 127
    Hungary, 143
    Poland, 80, 101
dictatorship of the proletariat, 128,
    195, 202
dissent, xxiii, 17, 61, 209
    and USSR, xxiv, 187
    and workers, 209–10, 221, 252–3
dissidents, xxiv, 16–22, 188, 190
    ideas, 17–19, 20–2, 27
    and masses, 20–2, 27
Djilas, M., xviii, 191
Dobrosielski, M., 107 n64
Doktor, K., 255 n12 n14, 256 n19
Donáth, F., 283, 290 n49
Dubček, A., 28, 29, 30, 31, 32, 33,
    35, 44, 69, 242
Ducke, K., 118
Dyker, D., 291 n55
Dyoniziak, R., 255 n12, 256 n19,
    257 n30
Dziewanowski, M. K., 104 n7, 106
    n42

East Berlin, 116, 119, 125, 133, 137
Eastern Europe, xiii, xiv, 7–9
East Germany, xiii, xv, xviii, xix, xxiii,
    113–38
    constitution (1968), 122–3
    demarcation policy, 114–16, 120
    Democratic Farmers' Party, 271
    Federation of Democratic Com-
        munists, 130
    migration from, 113–14, 120–2
    special shops, 118–19
    and USSR, 116, 126–7, 137–8
    and West Germany, 113, 115,
        120–1, 127–8, 137–8
    see also Socialist Unity Party of
        Germany
economic performance, 194
    East Germany, 136, 137
    Poland, 76, 81–2, 83
    and workers, 252–3
economic reform, 16, 194–6
    Czechoslovakia, 39
    East Germany, 126–7
    Hungary, 17, 143, 217–18, 236,
        237
    Poland, 64, 72, 77, 97, 206

proponents of, 193–5
socialist critics of, 194–5, 197
and workers, 72, 77, 216–19, 250
economics and politics, 16, 203,
205–6, 209–10
education, 51, 70, 79, 94–5, 158,
213
egalitarianism, xx
Hungary, 169
Poland, 69–70, 76–7, 246
social attitudes, 246
and workers, 218–19, 226, 252
Yugoslavia, 246
Eger, 175
Elblag, 84
elections, 34, 42, 89, 203, 227
Ember, M., 171, 183 n46
émigrés, 41, 43
Engels, F., 206
Erfurt, 115, 132
Eurocommunism, xiv, xxii–xxiii,
1–2, 98, 201
and Czechoslovakia, 18, 28, 30,
41, 43, 45, 49–51, 54
and East Germany, 131
and Hungary, 143
and Poland, 101, 111 n131
and socialism, 205
and USSR, xxiii, 51

Faber, B. L., 290 n27
Faust, S., 122, 140 n70
Ferge, S., 255 n8
Fehér, F., 20, 160, 182 n23
Fekete, G., 175–6
Fel, E., 289 n13
Ferenc, N., 261 n77
Field, M. G., 59 n33, 290 n29
Fischer-Galati, S., 24 n13, 289 n4,
290 n39
Flying University (Poland), 94–5
Földvári, T., 181 n3
France, xxii, 4–5, 7, 8, 50, 128, 172,
207
Frankel, S., 182 n16, 183 n27
freedom, xix, 125–6, 130, 163
cultural, 134
of movement, 117–18, 120–2
of speech, 77, 79, 168, 247
Fuchs, J., 140 n70

Fuehmann, F., 140 n73
Für, L., 185 n61

Gajewski, W., 94
Gałęski, B., 278
Galson, G. D., 256 n17
Gamarnikow, M., 257 n33, 258 n40,
259 n47, 260 n64
'Gang of Four', 203
Gati, C., 255 n9
Gdańsk, 17, 70, 71, 84
Gdynia, 71
Gehlen, A., 130
Gellhorn, W., 24 n10
Gera, G., 183 n46
Gergely, A., 171, 183 n46
German Democratic Republic, *see*
East Germany
Gerth, H. H., 255 n11
Giddens, A., 254 n2
Gierek, E., xv, xix, 17, 68, 111 n126,
256 n19
and church, 89, 92
and events of June 1976, 81, 82,
83, 103
and intellectuals, 96, 99
and party apparatus, 75
reform policy, 74–7
and workers, 71–3, 83, 86, 230,
234
Gilejko, L., 256 n21, 260 n62 n67
n68
Gitelman, Z., 233, 259 n56, 260
n61 n68
Gombár, C., 185 n64
Gombos, G., 184 n51
Gömöri, G., 104 n2
Gomułka, W., xix, 63, 64, 67–8, 71,
74–5, 111 n133, 230, 242, 243
Gospodarek, T., 261 n77
Graetz, F., 118, 139 n25 n27
Gramsci, A., 195
Grass, G., 47
Gray, J., 11, 24 n19, 105 n23, 181 n1,
261 n79, 262 n88, 291 n55
Great Britain, xxiii, 4–5, 50, 189,
207, 209
Green, P., 289 n10
Griffiths, W. E., 104 n4
Gripp, R. C., 289 n2

Gurr, T. R., 228, 259 n48
Gyertyán, E., 171, 183 n46
gypsies, 172

Hájek, J., 29, 47, 48–9, 52–3, 58 n15 n19
Hajnóczy, P., 185 n65
Halmos, P., 257 n32
Halpern, J., 275, 289 n23
Hamilton, R. F., 254 n5, 258 n38, 261 n79
Hanák, P., 175
Haraszti, M., 157, 159–60, 161, 166, 182 n21 n22, 207 n4, 255 n12, 260 n66
Harich, W., 127–8, 130, 140 n61 n62
Harman, C., 254 n2
Hartz, L., 4, 24 n4
Havas, A., 184 n47
Havel, V., 15, 25 n21, 53, 59 n32
Havemann, R., 124–6, 131, 140 n49, 249–50, 262 n96
Hegedüs, A., 20, 25 n27, 150–1, 153, 157–8, 160, 162–3, 181 n7, 182 n16, 194–5, 204, 254 n1, 255 n12, 256 n21 n22
Hegel, G. W. F., 126, 205
Hejzlar, Z., 29
Held, J., 290 n36
Heller, Á., 20, 25 n27 n28, 157, 160, 182 n16 n17
Heller, C. S., 106 n27
Helsinki, European conference on security and cooperation, xxi, xxii, 1, 14–15, 18, 24 n1, 101, 189–90
    and Czechoslovakia, 47, 48–50
    and East Germany, 121, 123, 136
    and Poland, 78–9
Herling-Grudziński, G., 111 n131
Hermlin, S., 140 n73, 141 n77 n79
Héthy, L., 257 n32, 259 n56, 260 n66
Heym, S., 134–5, 140 n73
Hildebrandt, R., 139 n32
Hille, B., 139 n23
Hirszowicz, M., 105 n23, 259 n56, 260 n59 n60 n61 n68
Hiscocks, R., 258 n46

history, 144, 149, 172–8
Hochman, J., 43
Hofer, R., 289 n13
Holešovský, V., 256 n17
Honecker, E., xxii, 115, 116, 118, 126, 131, 135, 136–7, 138 n3, 139 n17 n34, 140 n69
Honza, K., 257 n30
Horthy, Admiral M., 13, 177
housing, xx, 165, 199, 213, 230
Hübl, M., 43, 44
human rights, viii, xiv, xviii, 1–24, 201
    Czechoslovakia, 34, 51–2, 54–6
    Eastern Europe, 2, 6–11
    East Germany, 114, 120–3, 136
    international covenants on, 34, 52
    liberal-democratic concepts, xiv, 3–6
    Poland, 78, 80, 93, 98
    and political change, 2–4
    potentials of movement, 23–4
    Society of (Czechoslovakia), 29
    Universal Declaration of, 18, 79, 123
    and USSR, 1
Hungarian Socialist Workers' party
    Central Committee, 149
    Central Committee plenum (Nov. 1972), 143, 144
    Central Committee plenum (Mar. 1974), 149
    Congress (Mar. 1975), 143
    and workers, 234
Hungary, xiii, xv–xvi, xviii, xix, xxi, 7–8, 20–1, 142–81, 180, 211
    abortion law, 159
    Academy of Sciences, 149, 157–8
    Discovery of Hungary movement, 151, 152
    invasion of, 68, 243
    Magyar Nyelvör Society, 177
    policy on criticism, 149
    reforms, 143–4
    Revolution of 1956, xvii, 241–5 *passim*
    under-urbanisation, 165
    urbanist-populist debate, 154–6, 158

Village Explorers' movement, 151, 152
and USSR, 142, 174
and West, 144
Hunnius, G., 256n17n18
Husák, G., xiv, 14, 19, 25n21, 28, 30, 32, 34, 35, 42, 43, 45, 59n32, 247

Illyés, G., 161, 177–8, 185n59n61
income, 77, 231, 279–81
see also wages
individual rights, *see* human rights
Indra, A., 29
industrialisation, *see* modernisation
information
Hungary, 145–9
see also mass media
Inkeles, A., 255n14
intellectuals, xvi, 190
and church, 91–2
coopted, 22
Czechoslovakia, 17, 53
East Germany, 124–31
Hungary, 144
marginal, 21, 164, 188–9, 190
'organic', 189
Poland, 60–1, 62–4, 77–9
and technocrats, 22
intellectual–worker linkage, xvi, 20–2, 187–90, 245–50, 252
Czechoslovakia, 38, 245–6, 247–8
East Germany, 249–50
Hungary, 164–5
Poland, 69–70, 74, 83–6 *passim*, 102, 245, 248–9
intelligentsia, 164, 166–7
and Communist Party, 166–7
Czechoslovakia, 37
East Germany, 114, 128, 131–6
Hungary, xvi, 143–4, 145, 149
Poland, 63, 79
interests, 153–4, 210
Intershops, *see* East Germany, special shops
Italy, 50
Communist Party, xxii, 1–2, 43

Jackson, G., 289n22
Jakab, R. Z., 185n66
Jakeš, M., 29
Jambrek, P., 258n34n39, 259n48, 261n74
Jarosz, M., 260n73
Jaroszewicz, P., 71, 80, 81, 87–8, 89
Jelen, C., 104n10n11
Jena, 132
Jentzsch, B., 132
Jewish question, 153, 156, 171–2
see also anti-Semitism
Johnson, R. A., 104n6, 105n18, 258n46
Joó, R., 185n60
Jovanov, N., 257n34, 258n39, 259n48, 260n74
Jungmann, B., 255n7n10

Kafka, F., 135
Kaminski, F., 109n84
Kapek, J., 29
Karcz, J., 289n23, 290n26
Karinthy, F., 168–9, 183n33n37
Karkoszka, L., 259n57
Karl-Marx Stadt, 119–20, 123
Kaser, M. C., vii
Kaplan, K., 59n19
Kavan, J., 262n91
Kazmyrczuk, L., 255n13
Kecskemeti, P., 261n78n80
Kende, P., 104n3, 105n21
Kenedi, J., 161
Kertész, Á., 169, 183n40
Khrushchev, N. S., 50, 190, 192, 206
Kielanowski, J., 94
Kindersley, R., vii
Király, I., 184n51
Kirsch, S., 133, 140n73, 141n77
Kis, J., 150, 158
Kisielewski, S., 66
Klenner, H., 139n36
Kliszko, Z., 65, 105n11
Koch, H., 130
Kohl, H., 137
Kolaja, J., 262n86
Kołakowski, L., 63, 65–6, 91, 104n5, 195

Kolankiewicz, G., 104 n2, 105 n23 n24, 106 n26 n29, 107 n51 n61, 259 n49, 260 n67, 261 n76, 262 n88
Kolder, D., 29
Komarek, M., 257 n27
Komlós, A., 168
Konrád, G., 20–1, 22, 25 n29, 165–7, 183 n29 n32, 207 n7, 278, 280, 290 n29 n32
Konstanski, K., 259 n50
KOR (Workers' Defence Committee), 20, 84–6, 92, 96, 248–9
  and church, 89–90
  and trade unions, 85
  see also KSS-KOR
Korčula letter, 157
Kornai, J., 193
Korsch, 195
Kosík, K., 110 n104, 195
Kovács, F., 186 n66
Kovács, H., 255 n10, 261 n77, 262 n87
Kövágó, L., 185 n60
Kowalik, T., 94
Kraków, 66, 93
Kriegel, F., 29, 30, 59 n19
Kronstadt revolt, 206
Kroubek, M., 262 n90
Krug, M., 132, 134
Krushe, W., 124
KSS-KOR (Social Self-Defence Committee–KOR), 93–4, 102–3, 249
Kubaszewicz, J., 259 n57
Kulpińska, J., 256 n15, 260 n73
Kunert, C., 140 n70
Kunert, G., 133–4, 140 n73, 141 n77
Kunze, R., 123, 135–6, 138 n1
Kuroń, J., 64–5, 84, 85, 92, 98, 99, 104 n9, 105 n19, 107 n62, 108 n74 n75 n80, 110 n105, 111 n130 n132 n137, 188, 191, 207 n90, 254 n2 n4, 261 n80
Kusin, V. V., vii, ix, xiv, 207 n2, 262 n89, 267, 289 n3

Labedz, L., 104 n4, 111 n124
Labour
  power, 197–8

  supply, 114, 278
  turnover, 118, 219–20, 221, 222
Landsberger, H., 289 n22
Lane, D., 104 n2, 105 n23, 207 n8, 210, 254 n3 n4, 259 n49, 260 n67
Lang, N., 285, 291 n57
Lange, O., 64
Lautner, G. P., 256 n16
law, 9, 44, 55, 79
Lazarcik, G., 290 n40
Lederer, I. J., 24 n11
Lederer, J., 43
legitimacy
  bases of, 3, 15–16
  building of, 23, 265
  Czechoslovakia, 12, 57
  Hungary, 163, 167, 180
  lack of, xiii
  and peasantry, 272
  perception of, xviii–xix, 12–13, 15
  Poland, 74
Lehmann, T., pastor, 123
Leipzig, 119, 124
Lengyel, J., 148
Lenin, V. I., 50, 201–2
Leninism, 40, 201–2, 204
  see also Marxism-Leninism
Lewis, P. G., ix, xvii
liberalisation, xviii, 1
Liberman, E., 127, 193
Ličko, P., 43
Liebman, M., 204
Liehm, A. J., 107 n69, 189, 207 n5
Lipiński, E., 84, 94, 97–8, 108 n74, 111 n126
Lippmann, H., 141 n89
Lipski, J., 96
Litera, J., 43
literature, *see* writers
Littell, R., 261 n78
Lockwood, W. G., 290 n27
Łódź, 73, 84
Lomax, B., 260 n72, 261 n76 n78 n80 n81 n85, 262 n86
Łopatka, A., 259 n50
Losonczi, Á., 182 n20
Lowenthal, R., 57, 59 n33
Lowit, T., 260 n61

Lubienski, 88, 109 n93
Lukács, G., xv, 19, 143, 193, 195
Lukasczewicz, J., 77
Luxemburg, R., 201, 206

MacDonald, O., 257 n25, 259 n54, 262 n94
Machonin, P., 254 n5, 255 n7 n10
Machovec, J., 110 n113
Macierewicz, A., 99
Macsári, K., 256 n17
Maimski, P., 99
Makó, C., 153 – 4, 257 n32, 259 n56, 260 n66
Malanowski, J., 255 n7 n10, 256 n22, 261 n84
Malewski, A., 256 n22, 262 n88
Mandel, E., 191
Mandel, S., 181 n4
Mann, M., 255 n13
Maoism, 191, 192, 196 – 7
Mao Tse-tung, 206
Marchais, G., 51
Marie, J. J., 105 n21, 261 n82
market mechanisms, 166, 196 – 8
Márkus, G., 149 – 50, 157 – 8, 181 n5, 182 n24
Márkus, M., 20, 25 n27, 157, 158, 182 n16, 184 n48
Martin, A., 107 n54, 109 n95
Martin, D., 182 n16, 183 n27
Marx, K., 50, 128, 129, 150, 162, 195, 205, 206
Marxism
  East Germany, 114, 116 – 17
  Hungary, 149 – 50, 156, 164, 178, 192
  Poland, 63 – 4, 66, 91
Marxism-Leninism, xx – xxi, 63, 149, 192
Marxist critique
  East Germany, 124 – 31
  and humanism, 195 – 6
  Hungary, 20, 146, 149 – 50, 157 – 8, 161, 195
  Poland, 64 – 5
Masaryk, T. G., 9, 12, 13
mass media, xxii, 90, 145 – 6, 281 – 2
  see also Western media
Matejko, A., 104 n2, 106 n26,

255 n12 n13 n14, 256 n15, 278, 290 n31
Matwin, W., 99
Mende, E., 121
Michnik, A., 19, 25 n26, 65, 66, 67, 91 – 2, 93, 94, 95, 98, 99 – 100, 104 n10, 110 n103 n105, 111 n129 n131 n135 n138, 262 n97
Mickiewicz, A., 65
Mieczkowski, B., 257 n28, 290 n44
Mihailescu, A., 258 n35 n40 n43
Mihajlov, M., xviii
Mikolajska, H., 84
Miller, A., 47
Mills, C. Wright, 255 n11
Mink, G., 107 n50
Mittag, G., 140 n58
Mlynář, Z., 47, 48 – 50, 58 n15
Moczar, M., 64, 67 – 8, 74 – 5, 261 n84
Moczulski, L., 101
Mód, A., 173, 175
modernisation, xiv, xx – xxi, 9, 21
  agriculture, 265 – 6
  Czechoslovakia, 26, 57
  Hungary, 165, 278
  and peasants, 275 – 7
  Poland, 4, 77, 103
Modzelewski, K., 64 – 5, 104 n9, 105 n19, 108 n74, 191, 207 n9, 254 n2 n4, 261 n80
Moldova, G., 171, 183 n46
Molnár, E., 173, 184 n51 n52
Molnár, L., 261 n77
Mond, G., 104 n8
'moonlighting', 221
Morawski, J., 64, 99
Morawski, W., 105 n23, 259 n56, 260 n59 n60 n61 n68
Mortimer, E., 24 n3
Moscow Protocol, 30
Mueller, H., 140 n73
Müller, J., 43

Nacken, A., 139 n35
Nagy, B., 105, 210 n22, 261 n82
national identity, xviii
  East Germany, 113, 114 – 16
  Hungary, 153, 179

nationalism, xvii, xviii, 5
Croatia, 284-5
Hungary, 7, 173-8 passim
Czechoslovakia, 37
peasants, 284-5
Poland, 67
workers, 242-4 passim, 252
national minorities, 177-8
Nawrocki, J., 139 n33
Nazi Germany, 12, 189
Nemchinov, V. S., 127
Nemeskürty, I., 176-7, 184 n56 n57, 185 n58
Netto, U. S., 140 n44
New Economic Mechanism, see economic reform, Hungary
new evolutionism, 98, 100-1
new left
Czechoslovakia, 32, 38
France, 128
Hungary, xv, 143-4, 156-67, 193
Western, 191, 207
see also Budapest School
Nitsche, H., 122
Nitschke, K-H., 122
'normalisation', 26-7, 33, 56, 157
Nováková, V. (pseud.), 58 n16
Novotný, A., xviii, 17, 27
Nowak, S., 70, 106 n27
Nowy Targ, 84

Obradović, J., 261 n75
Obzina, J., 52
Ochab, E., 99
oil and energy crisis, 16, 77, 81, 137
Oldenburg, F., 140 n55
Ollyés, G., 167
Olszewska, A., 290 n37
opposition, xvii-xviii, xix-xx, xxiii, 61, 142, 209
see also para-opposition, socialist opposition
Oren, N., 290 n26
Osipow, G. W., 256 n15
Ostoja-Ostaszewski, A., 107 n56
overinstitutionalisation, 233, 241
Owieczko, A., 259 n56, 260 n61 n68
Oxley, A., 261 n85
Ozdowski, J., 88

Pach, Z. P., 184 n52
Pachman, L., 43
Pajdak, A., 99
Pannach, G., 140 n70
Pano, N., 289 n19
Panslavism, 8
para-opposition, xv, xxi, 142-3, 144-5, 169
Paris Commune, 130, 226
Parkin, F., 254 n3, 261 n74
Patočka, J., 53
Pavel, J., 29
Pavlowitch, S. K., 289 n17, 291 n52
peasants and farmers, 263-89
condition of, 274, 283
cooperative organisations, 271-2, 284
Czechoslovakia, 38-9, 283
Hungary, 152, 284
and land, 279, 283
and opposition, 271-2
outlook, xvii, 272, 275, 279-80, 283-4, 287-8
and parties, 265, 270-1
Poland, 102, 269
and regime, 264, 268, 272, 286-7
Romania, 267-8
social transformation, 265, 275, 289
sources of discontent, 280, 285-8
and welfare, 281-2
Yugoslavia, 272
see also private farming
peasant-workers, xx, 165, 276-9
Pelikán, J., 18, 19, 25 n24, 39, 43, 58 n207
Péter, L., 184 n51
Petöfi, S., 167
Petöfi Circle, 168
Pfahlberg, B., 4-5, 24 n5
philosophers, 77, 143, 157, 194, 195
Piasecki, B., 62, 67
Piccone, P., 189, 207 n5
Piekalkiewicz, J., 262 n88
pilfering, 219, 221
Piłsudski, J., 12
Pintér, I. K., 169-70, 183 n41
Pirages, D., 257 n30
Pléh, C., 186 n67

Plekhanov, G. V., 201, 206
Plenzdorf, U., 135, 141 n77
Plogstedt, S., 32
pluralism, 22, 61, 63, 103, 149–50
Polányi, K., 166
Poland, xiii–xv, xviii, xxiii, 17, 19, 60–104, 144, 211
  Academy of Sciences, 94
  centre right opposition, 101
  Committee for Student Solidarity (SKS), 93–4
  Constitution of 3 May 1791, 7, 80
  constitutional amendments (1975–6), 78–81, 89, 96
  December 1970–January 1971 events, 70–4, 234, 251
  June 1976 events, 80–4, 103, 230, 236
  Letter of the Fifteen, 78
  Letter of the Fifty-Nine, 79, 84
  Letter of the Fourteen, 79
  Letter of the Hundred-and-One, 79
  March 1968 events, 65–8
  National Democratic Party, 101
  national sovereignty, 80, 97–8
  October 1956, xvii, 63, 69, 241–4 *passim*, 245
  parliament (Sejm), 63, 80, 85, 87–8, 90–1, 93
  Socialist Students Union (SZSP), 93–4
  and USSR, 78–9, 97–8, 103–4
  and West Germany, 97
police, *see* repressive action
Polish Catholic Church, xiv, 60–1, 63, 86–7, 269
  Clubs of Catholic Intellectuals (KIK), 87
  and constitutional amendments, 88
  episcopate, 88–90
  and human rights, 78, 90–1
  and intellectuals' opposition, 91–2, 101–2
  neopositivists, 63, 87, 89, 100
  and opposition, 86–92
  Pax, 67
  and events of June 1976, 89–90
  and state, 77–8, 87–8, 90, 92

  writers, 66
  Znak, 79, 87–8
Polish League for Independence, 17, 25 n22, 97–8
Polish P.E.N. Club, 96
Polish United Workers' Party (PUWP)
  administrative reforms, 76
  cultural policy, 78
  ex-leaders' letter, 99
  factions in, 64, 67–8, 74–5, 103
  and ideology, 77–8
  leading role of, 78–9
  membership, 75
  Seventh Congress, 78
  and workers, 71, 75, 227, 233–4, 252
Polish Writers' Union, 96
political change, xiv, xvi, 2–3, 7–10, 241–4
political culture, xiv, 2, 11
  Czechoslovakia, 34
  Eastern Europe, 11–13, 23
  Poland, xiv–xv, 61, 80, 98, 101, 103
political instability, 14–15
political participation, 23
political socialisation, 180
political stability, xix, 13–14, 103, 181
political trials, *see* repressive action
political values, xiii, 178–9, 215–16, 264, 275
Pomian, K., 104 n3, 105 n21, 106 n45
populism, 154–6, 158, 174, 176
Portes, R., 256 n18 n20 n22, 257 n24 n26 n28, 259 n46 n47
Portugal, 201
Potichnyi, P. J., 290 n36
Poznań, 83, 229, 230, 241–2
Pragal, P., 139 n37, 140 n67
Pravda, A., ix, x, xvi, xix, 105 n26, 256 n17, 258 n42, 260 n66 n72 n73, 261 n76 n82 n85
Praxis group, 195
Prchlík, V., 43
Prenziau, 124
prices, xxiv

prices—*cont.*
Hungary, 227–8, 231
Poland, 70, 73, 81–2, 227–8, 230, 232, 234
and workers, 81–2, 227–8, 231
private farming, 263, 273, 281, 286
Bulgaria, 274, 283
Hungary, 189, 274
Poland, 274
Slovakia, 285
Yugoslavia, 274
Protestant Church, 37, 123–4
Pruszcz, 84
public opinion, *see* survey data
purges, 21, 35–6, 44, 75, 106 n42
Pyjas, S., 92, 93, 110 n108

Rab, B., 182 n25
Racz, B., 290 n43
Racovski, M. (pseud.), 163–4, 183 n28, 190, 192, 207 n6
Radom riots, 80, 84
Rajk, L., 179
Rákosi, M., 179, 186 n66
Rakowski, M., 108 n70 n73
Ranki, G., 24 n12
redistributive power, 166, 190, 196, 199–200
reformism, *see* revisionism
regime response, xiii–xiv, 12–13, 23, 103–4
relative deprivation, 228–9, 231
religion, xvii, 15, 53, 79, 92, 270, 286
East Germany, 122–3
and peasants, 269–70, 276
see also Catholic Church, Polish Catholic Church, Protestant Church
repressive action, xiv, xvii, xxii, 68, 128, 189, 190
Czechoslovakia, 28, 31–3, 42–3, 51, 53–4
East Germany, 120, 122, 129, 132–4, 136
Hungary, 157, 158–60, 166
Poland, 60, 66, 83–6 *passim*, 93
and workers, 83–6 *passim*, 225, 232, 244, 245
revisionism, 19, 68–9, 192
Czechoslovakia, 37–8, 57–8

Poland, 63–4, 68–9, 98–9, 100
see also Marxist critique
Revolutionary Socialist Party, 31–2
Rezler, J., 256 n17 n19, 257 n26 n28
Ritchie, A., 261 n85
Rizzi, B., 207 n11
Robinson, W. F., 181 n1, 182 n17, 254 n1, 255 n14, 256 n18, 257 n23 n24, 259 n47 n58, 260 n59 n64 n65
Rollová, V., 254 n5
Romania, xviii, xxiii, 7, 10, 50, 177, 179, 223
ROPCIO (Movement for the Defence of Human and Civil Rights), 20, 91, 94, 99, 101, 102
Rostock, 119
Rozgonyi, 255 n12, 256 n21 n22
Rupnik, J., x, xiv, xv
Rus, V., 260 n61, 261 n74
Russian Revolution (1917), 9, 65, 125
Russo-Turkish War, 7

Šabata, J., 30, 43, 44
Sakharov, A., 188
Second International Hearing, 122
Šalgovič, V., 29
Salzmann, Z., 289 n12, 290 n39 n48
samizdat, xxi, 187–8, 196
Czechoslovakia, 28, 41, 45
East Germany, 129
Hungary, 148, 161
Poland, 85, 95–6, 103
Samu, M., 185 n64
Sanders, I., 183 n42
Sándor, I., 172, 184 n49
Sarapata, A., 256 n15, 257 n26
Šarišsky, M., 257 n31
Sartre, J.-P., 47
Scandinavian Communist parties, xxii
Schaff, A., 63
Schapiro, L., 55, 59 n30, 104 n1
Scharf, C. B., 260 n63
Scheufler, V., 289 n12, 290 n39 n48
Schneider, R., 133, 140 n73
Schöpflin, G., vii, x, xv, xvi, xix, 24 n3, 182 n21, 193, 207 n3
Schreiber, T., 107 n67

Schubert, D., 141 n77
Schultz, D., 139 n33
Schulz, W., 138 n9
Schwarzenbach, P., 133
Schweigler, G., 139 n15
scientific intelligentsia, 77, 127, 145
Sebestyán, L., 184 n53
SED (Socialist Unity Party of Germany)
Central Committee plenum Dec. 1971, 131
Central Committee plenum, Dec. 1974, 116
cultural policy, 131–2, 135, 136
democratisation proposals, 113, 127, 130
Eleventh Central Committee plenum 1965, 131
opposition within, 137–8
Seidler, B., 259 n49 n53
Sekaninová, G., 59 n19
self-management, 192–3, 200, 205, 206
see also workers' councils
Seyppel, J., 133, 141 n78 n79 n80
Shaffer, H., 256 n17
Shapiro, J., 290 n36
Shawcross, W., 181 n1
Shorter, A., 258 n38
Shoup, P., 291 n56
Sik, O., 29, 193
Sipos, L., 184 n55
Šilhan, M., 43
Singleton, F., 291 n53
Skilling, H. G., 18, 289 n5
Škutina, V., 43
Słonimski, A., 66
Slowacki, R., 109 n91
Smolar, A., 110 n117
Smrkovský, J., 31, 44, 45, 49
social and economic rights, xii, xiv, xix, 5–6, 17, 19, 84–5, 215–16
'social compact', xvi–xvii, xx, xxiii, 4
Poland, 82–3, 102, 230
and prices, 217
and workers, 216, 219, 221, 226–7, 228, 231, 242, 250–2, 254
social contract, see 'social compact'
social inequality, 120, 199–200, 213

social mobility, xiii, xx, 70, 167, 180, 212–14, 251
social sciences, 22, 144, 145, 150–6, 178–9
socialism, xx, 18–19, 125, 135, 188
and democracy, 92, 99–100, 201, 206
East Germany, 126–7, 136
and humanism, 195–6
Hungary, 162–3
and workers, 215
socialist democracy, 34, 46, 164
socialist opposition, 187–207
theory of, 188, 191–3, 206–7
sociography
Hungary, 151–3, 159
sociology, 117, 143, 150–1, 162, 194–5, 202
Sonnenfeldt doctrine, 98
Sontheimer, K., 290 n46
Sós, V., 157
Soviet-type economies, 196–9
Soviet-type societies, 164, 192
Spain, 50, 189
Communist party, xxii, 1–2
SPD (Socialist Party of Germany), 115
Spittman, I., 138 n11
Stalin, J. V., 206
Stalinism, xvii, 128, 130, 149–50
Czechoslovakia, 27
East Germany, 135
Hungary, 165, 175
Poland, 63, 77, 91
standard of living, xvii
Czechoslovakia, 194
East Germany, 118, 137
peasants, xvii, 280–1
Poland, 69–70, 81–2, 230
rural–urban levels, 281–2, 287
Stange, J., 121, 122
Stankovic, S., 258 n42
Starachawice, 84
Stárek, J., 57, 58 n13, 59 n34
Stasiuk, A., 259 n56
state capitalism, 191–2, 197
state, concepts of, 128, 130
state farms, 268, 272
state socialism, 187, 198, 199, 200, 205

Stefanowski, R., 260 n69
Steinsbergova, A., 99
Stier, M., 184 n52
Stomma, S., 79, 87, 88-9
Stoph, W., 115
Story, J., 24 n3
strikes, xvii, 222-7, 253
  Czechoslovakia, 31, 222, 227-8
  East Germany, 114, 119-20, 223, 229, 231
  Hungary, 223
  Poland, 70-4, 79, 80-4, 224, 226-8, 232-3
  regime response, 71-3, 81-3, 224-5
  Romania, 223, 232, 251
  slowdowns, 221-2
  Yugoslavia, xxiii, 222-3, 225, 228, 253, 261 n74
Strong, J. W., 106 n40
Strougal, L., 256 n19
Strzelecki, J., 94
students, xx
  Czechoslovakia, 30-2, 245-6
  East Germany, 115-16
  Hungary, 158, 247
  Poland, 60, 65-7, 70, 92-4
  and workers, 70, 106 n31, 245-7
Sufin, Z., 255 n13
Sugar, P. F., 24 n11
Sulik, B., 106 n37
Supek, R., 188, 261 n74
surplus value, 190, 197, 200
survey data, xv, xvi, xxiv
  Czechoslovakia, 27, 48, 213-14, 247, 268, 270
  East Germany, 114-15, 117-18, 136
  Hungary, 172, 270
  Poland, 76, 219, 221, 230, 233, 248-9, 268
  Yugoslavia, 240, 276
Süto, F., 172
Sweden, 50
Switzerland, 132
Syrop, K., 261 n78
Szakály, F., 184 n57
Szakonyi, K., 169, 183 n39
Szala, S., 261 n77

Száraz, G., 170-1, 183 n43
Szczecin, 71-3, 84, 224, 226-7, 251
Szczepański, J., 256 n15
Szecskö, T., 185 n64
Szeklers, the, of Transylvania, 177
Szelényi, I., x-xi, xvi, xxi, 20-2, 25 n29, 160, 165-7, 181 n2 n6, 183 n26 n29, 207 n7, 254 n6, 278, 280, 290 n29 n38
Szigeti, J., 157
Szlajfer, H., 66, 67
Szostkiewicz, H., 257 n31, 260 n73
Szücs, J., 174-5, 184 n53 n54
Szydlak, J., 77, 88

Taras, R., 105 n23, 262 n88
Taubert, H., 117, 139 n21
technocracy and technocrats, xvi, xxi, 22-3, 39, 75, 77, 143, 144, 167, 194
Tejchma, J., 78
Teng Hsia-p'ing, 203
Tepicht, J., 287-8, 291 n58 n60
Tesař, J., 43, 44
Thiery, M., 111 n123, 112 n140
Tigrid, P., 57
Tilly, C., 258 n38
Tito, J. B., 206, 266
Tőkés, R. L., xi, 24 n2, 58 n1, 107 n62, 207 n1
Toma, P., 181 n1, 183 n40, 184 n50, 254 n1 n5, 257 n23, 290 n28 n33 n50
Tomalek, P. (pseud.), 262 n86
Tordai, Z., 157
Torre, P. F. del la, 24 n3
trade unions, xvii, 232, 234-6, 241, 253-4
  Czechoslovakia, 30-2 passim, 36, 244
  East Germany, 236
  Hungary, 149, 159, 236-8
  Poland, 70-2, 74-6 passim, 79, 84, 99, 227, 233, 236, 243, 252
  and strikes, 235
  and workers' councils, 239-40
  Yugoslavia, 235
Transylvania, 145, 158, 177, 178

travel, xxii, 114, 117–19, 120–2
  see also freedom of movement
Triska, J. F., 259 n55
Trotsky, L., 191, 201, 206
Trotskyism, 191, 196–7, 201–2, 204

Ulbricht, W., 140 n60
UNESCO, 18
Unger, L., 110 n108, 111 n134
United Nations, 6, 91
United Peasants' Party (Poland), 270
Ursus tractor factory, 80, 84, 85, 86
USA, 1, 4–5, 51, 190
USSR, 1, 7
  and Eastern Europe, xxi, xxiii, 14–16, 98
  and normalisation, 26
  and political stability, 13–17
  and USA, xxiii
  and Western left, xxiii, 207
  and workers, 243
  see also under Country headings
use value, 197, 198–9

Vácrátóton, V., 184 n52
Vaculík, L., 261 n84
Vági, G., 185 n65
Vajda, M., 20, 25 n27, 158, 182 n16
Vas-Zoltán, P., 185 n64
Vatican, the, 92
Végh, A., 152
Végh, L., 185 n63
Venyige, J., 257 n27
Vickers, E., 140 n46
Vietnam Solidarity Commission (Hungary), 157
Vodsloň, F., 59 n19
Vogel, W., 121, 122
Voigt, D., 117, 118, 139 n20 n26
Völgyes, I., 181 n1, 183 n40, 184 n50, 254 n1 n5, 257 n23, 270, 279, 290 n28 n33 n34 n50
Volkmer, W., xi, xv, xix, xxi
Vörös, M., 256 n16

Wacowska, E., 258 n37 n38 n42 n43, 259 n49 n50, 261 n76
Wädekin, K-E., 280–1, 290 n42
wages

Hungary, 231
peasants, 268, 273
Poland, 81, 106 n26, 231
  workers, 215–16, 220, 225, 228–9
Wajda, A., 259 n50 n51 n54 n57, 260 n62
Walter, F., 117
Warsaw, 64, 66, 84
Warsaw Treaty Organisation, 15, 26, 27
Wasiak, K., 261 n84, 262 n93
Weber, M., 202–3
Weissman, G. L., 254 n2
Werblan, A., 105 n18
Werfel, 67
Wesołowski, W., 256 n21
West, the, xxii, 47, 101, 119, 144, 190
West Berlin, 133, 137
Western mass media, 1
  and Czechoslovakia, 47
  and East Germany, xxii, 113, 114, 122, 133, 156
  and Hungary, 148–9, 160
West Germany, xv, 67, 97, 189, 207
Weydenthal, J. B., 259 n58
Whitehorn, A., 256 n22
Widerszpil, S., 254 n1 n5, 257 n31
Wightman, G., 261 n83
Wilson, W., 9
Winner, I., 289 n16, 290 n41
Wirsing, S., 141 n76
Wojtyła, Cardinal, 89
Wolf, C., 140 n73, 141 n77
Wolf, G., 140 n73, 141 n77
women, 135, 159
workers, xvii, 100, 188–9, 209–54
  and class, 190, 212–14, 251
  Czechoslovakia, 30–1, 42, 52, 248
  demands, 71–4, 225–7, 232, 252
  expectations, 215–16, 220, 230, 253
  Hungary, 143, 152–4, 159, 165, 169, 175, 179, 217–18, 222, 241–4 *passim*
  and ideology, 190–1
  and management, 118, 215, 218, 225–6

workers—*cont.*
nonconformity of, 209–10, 219–21, 250
outlook, 196, 211, 214–16, 242, 250
and peasants, 289
Poland, 60–1, 69, 74, 85–6, 252
and political change, 241–4
political representation, xvii, 213–14, 232–3
position of, 164, 167, 188–9, 210–11, 250–2, 281
productivity, 217–18, 221, 228
protest action, 80–4, 85–6, 103, 135, 223–4, 227, 228–9
Workers' Committees for the Defence of the Freedom of the Press, 247
workers' councils, 163, 207, 237–40
Czechoslovakia, 31, 206, 240, 244
Hungary, 206, 238, 244
Poland, 64, 69, 71, 72, 233, 237–8, 240, 243–4
Romania, 238
Yugoslavia, xviii, 237, 240

writers
East Germany, 131–6
Hungary, 167–72 *passim*
Poland, 64, 77, 96–7
Wrocław, 67
Wyderko, A., 289 n24
Wyszyński, Cardinal, 87–90 *passim*, 92, 109 n87

youth, xx, 38, 65, 116, 117, 123, 158
Yugoslav Communist League, xxii, 50, 234, 272
Yugoslavia, xvi, xvii, 177, 211, 285

Zablodski, J., 88
Zambrowski, A., 64, 67, 104 n9
Zara, N., 105 n14
Zapotocký, A., 27
Zieja, J., 90
Ziomek, M. J., 257 n29, 261 n83
Zionism, 67–8
Zupanov, J., 260 n58
Zweig, A., 138 n1
Zygier, J., 105 n14